REAL TIME
VISUAL EFFECTS
FOR THE
TECHNICAL ARTIST

REAL TIME VISUAL EFFECTS FOR THE TECHNICAL ARTIST

Chris Roda

CRC Press
Taylor & Francis Group
Boca Raton London New York

CRC Press is an imprint of the
Taylor & Francis Group, an **informa** business

First edition published 2022
by CRC Press
6000 Broken Sound Parkway NW, Suite 300, Boca Raton, FL 33487-2742

and by CRC Press
2 Park Square, Milton Park, Abingdon, Oxon, OX14 4RN

CRC Press is an imprint of Taylor & Francis Group, LLC

Library of Congress Cataloging-in-Publication Data
Names: Roda, Chris, author.
Title: Real time visual effects for the technical artist / Chris Roda.
Description: First edition. | Boca Raton, FL : CRC Press, 2022. | Includes
bibliographical references and index.
Identifiers: LCCN 2021047643 | ISBN 9780367860127 (hbk) | ISBN
9780367444488 (pbk) | ISBN 9781003009795 (ebk)
Subjects: LCSH: Digital cinematography—Technique. | Digital
video—Technique. | Computer animation—Technique. |
Cinematography—Special effects—Technique. |
Photography--Retouching--Data processing.
Classification: LCC TR860 .R63 2022 | DDC 777—dc23/eng/20211122
LC record available at https://lccn.loc.gov/2021047643

ISBN: 978-0-367-86012-7 (hbk)
ISBN: 978-0-367-44448-8 (pbk)
ISBN: 978-1-003-00979-5 (ebk)

DOI: 10.1201/9781003009795

Typeset in Futura
by codeMantra

From a new teacher to my original teacher/mentors:

To Jeffery Light who lit the fire and encouraged me to start this VFX journey.

To James Abello who enabled me to continue this journey.

The idea behind this book could not have been conceived if it were not for your initial patience and encouragement.

Contents

Chapter 2: Visual Effects Rules   21

Chapter 3: Color Theory   37

Chapter 5: Material Effects

Contents

Chapter 6: Simulations

Chapter 7: Particles   325

Chapter 8: Conclusion   373

Index   379

Acknowledgments

I would like to thank the following people and organizations whose contributions enabled the creation of this book.

I knew this project would be challenging and turned out to be more demanding than ever thought possible. The following contributors ensured the message remained readable and understandable: Yunhao Huo, Katerina Voziyanova, Bryan Venzen, and Brian Salisbury.

I would like to thank Epic Games for providing the real-time engine used for creating this book's images and Side FX Software for providing the three-dimensional asset, procedural simulation and texture authoring software. Other images were contributed by Epic games, Riot Games, the Smithsonian Institute, Imirza, and Spire Animation Studios.

The creation of visual effects often requires the efforts of a small army of digital artists. My dedicated artists consisted of Clem White, Yolanda Patino, Rene Bencik, Emma Condie, Ally Rybinski, Rong Zhuang, Ian Rich, Joris Putteneers, Jose Robles, Ha Roda, Nicholas Zuccarello, Jinguang Huang, Joe Bonura, and Katerina Voziyonova.

Last, but not least, I would like to thank my wife, Ha, and my two children, Zephyr and Thaleia, for providing me with the love and support needed to deliver this project.

Author

Chris Roda is a Technical Art instructor at the Florida Interactive Entertainment Academy (FIEA), a graduate degree program in interactive, real-time application development at the University of Central Florida. Early in his career, Chris was a visual effects artist in the film and television industries where he contributed visual effects for films such as *Spider-Man, Titanic, and The Fifth Element.* Before coming to FIEA, Chris was a CG Supervisor at Electronic Arts, where he worked on video game titles such as *NCAA Football* and *Madden NFL Football.* In addition to teaching, Chris works on generating tools and pipelines for the creation of immersive experiences: the amalgamation of the narrative of films, the interactivity of video games, and the immersion of theme parks.

Introduction

Visual effects have been my passion for over 30 years. It has been my gateway for using computer graphics to generate alternative realities. Visual effects make the unbelievable real. They make miracles and the impossible happen. They create worlds, both in fantasy and in real life, that could not possibly exist. They also take what is very real but is imperceptible and make them visible. Visual effects invent fantastic and unbelievable elements that look and feel at home in whatever environments they are placed in. Most importantly, visual effects create story world credibility. They help cement participant presence in whatever game, film, or experience they collaborate with. When done correctly, visual effects provide the vehicle which gently immerses participants, without question, into game worlds or narrative experiences.

WHY THIS BOOK?

Visual effects are an enormously vast and possibly complex realm of study. In the early days of off-line, film production, visual effects were often unexpected phenomena generated during the three-dimensional rendering process. Visual effects artists were often the best digital artists who understood the ins and outs of the entire rendering pipeline and were able to exploit its eccentricities to generate fantastic yet desirable results. They were able to extract components from each stage of computer graphics production, reconfigure, and re-combine them to create imagery that was never before possible.

As hardware and software improved over time, so did the visual effects. New and friendly interfaces make the progression for generating visual effects easier, more predictable, and more efficient. A visual effects artist no longer needs to understand the intricate details of the rendering process. Armed with traditional art training, a solid understanding of visual design and the right tools, an artist can create almost anything. Many artists pride themselves in not being technical as they surrender themselves to the purest creative expression.

Ironically, as the interfaces have improved and become friendlier, the underlying technology has continued to expand geometrically. In order to be made user friendly, the technology must be tamed, limited and bound sufficiently to be manipulated by the exposure of a minimal set of dialable parameters. The unlimited technological potential is still there, it is just hidden beneath amiable interface layers. A visual effects artist can be only as good as the exposed tools. All that is required to tap into that potential is a bit of understanding of the underlying systems and the willingness to crawl under the hood and get dirty with some oily math.

Metaphorically, this book is an introduction to hot-rodding real-time rendering engines. When a sports car is purchased from the dealer, the buyer possesses a very highly crafted piece of hi-tech machinery. Without any understanding of auto-mechanics, with only the control of the accelerator, brake, and steering wheel, the driver has a commanding presence on the road. However, when the driver wishes to tap into the true potential of the

DOI: 10.1201/9781003009795-1

vehicle, a small amount of mechanical familiarity is required along with the willingness to make a few small modifications to the engine, exhaust, and suspension. Only then will the real potential of the vehicle be exposed. Real-time rendering engines are the same in spirit. With a little bit of understanding of the underlying technology and a rudimentary set of math skills, the visual effects artist can put the real-time engine into overdrive.

The contents of this book re-introduce real-time engine fundamentals in a language that is comprehensible by any willing artist. Only the basic concepts are discussed. All the gory details are left in the technological conference journals. However, when the artist wishes to further explore any of the topics presented in this book, sufficient nomenclature provides suitable signposts and directions for deeper exploration. This book is written from an artist's and a teacher's perspective in such a way that it will inform and educate but not drown the reader in mathematical complexity.

The world of visual effects is immeasurably vast. There are an infinite number of good solutions for any type of problem. The question is not so much how to solve the problem but what solution solves the problem best considering the context of the situation. With a subject area that is so broad, how can a single book be written about it? There may be no way to cover every specific topic in essential depth within one text. The best visual effects artists realize this early in their career and don't try to master everything. They reinvent prior solutions to fit in the context of new situations.

Realistically, visual effects cannot be mastered in one semester. They are a lifelong learning pursuit. This book does not try to be a definitive guide but attempts to introduce the broad topic areas that contribute to the realm of visual effects and demonstrates simple and common solutions addressing each topic area. Rough coverage of the fundamentals is provided so that any artist can modify any strategy to address any situation. This is not a book of tutorials. This book provides essential coverage of the fundamental tools visual effects artists should have in their tool kit so they can address any situation with courage as well as creativity.

INTENDED AUDIENCE

This book is intended for artists wishing to understand visual effects topic areas and their fundamental solution strategies. It is written from an artist's perspective but is in no means dumbed down. There is math in this text. However, math does not venture beyond basic algebra and geometry levels. There is no specific code included. There are, however, strategies and algorithms provided that can easily be implemented within the context of any modern game engine using common and widely used tools and functions.

This text was originally written to supplement courses created for undergraduate and graduate-level game developers. It does not assume prior technical or coding experience. The techniques in this book can be implemented by experienced artists wishing to expand their existing palette of tools or for the programmer seeking an introduction to the impact visual effects has on the rendering pipeline. Producers and designers may also be interested in this book as an introduction to the language and terminology employed by all visual effects artists.

This is a book written for artists and technical artists. High technical, white-paper information will not be found here. The information is kept simple and abstract to be implemented in any real-time rendering engine or any digital content creation (DCC) software. This text is intended to be software agnostic. Visual effects can be juggled in just about any modeling/rendering/game engine software. Part of what makes visual effects artists' valuable is their ability to adapt and improvise based on their available resources.

There are no tutorials in this book. The information is presented theoretically but is absolutely implementable in any package. Tutorials tend to focus on implementing a single type of effect on one type of software. From this book's perspective, when the fundamental concepts are understood they can be integrated into any pipeline. When the core ideals are understood, they can be bent, warped, and melded with other ideals without being concerned with the interface idiosyncrasies of a particular software.

Visual Effects Artists versus Technical Artists

There is an ongoing discussion concerning if visual effects artists are to be classified as their own independent tribe or as technical artists. This classification varies greatly between industries and production companies. This book attempts to treat both equally and interchangeably. Visual effects artists may identify themselves as digital artists who are focused exclusively on the art and design of the phenomena they are producing, using only the tools they are provided. Technical artists derive from a similar perspective but employ additional math and create new tools to complement the creative workflow. This book treats both as artists first. There is a considerable amount of technology introduced in this book but presented at a level non-technical artists can easily understand and discuss with technical artists the necessary strategies for future tool fabrication.

HOW THIS BOOK IS ORGANIZED

This book is broken into seven chapters. The first three chapters introduce visual effects and establish fundamental topics all artists should be aware of. The last four chapters are devoted to visual effects categories and strategies used to implement them.

- **Chapter 1: What are Visual Effects?** explains the distinctions between special effects and visual effects and explores all possible realms which may be considered visual effects.

- **Chapter 2: Visual Effects Rules,** provides a collection of the best and most effective mental strategies a visual effects artist can adopt to ensure a rewarding and long-lasting career.

- **Chapter 3: Color Theory,** explains the usage of color from the perspective of a digital artist. Working with pixels instead of pigments has dramatic consequences that all digital artists need to be aware of in order to master the medium.

- **Chapter 4: In-Camera Effects,** explains the importance of lighting as the most profound and fundamental of all visual effects. A quick introduction to the tools and art of lighting is provided. This chapter also introduces the fundamental concepts of principle in-camera, otherwise known as post-process effects.

- **Chapter 5: Material Effects,** introduces the incredibly vast and powerful techniques of creating visual effects within objects' materials.

- **Chapter 6: Simulations,** covers the benefits and drawbacks of using simulation effects and introduces the foundational tools for creating and deploying simulations without destroying application framerate.

- **Chapter 7: Particles,** introduces particle effects as the amalgamation of lighting and in-camera, in-material and simulation effects. The chapter covers the composition of particles, how they are integrated with the other types of effects and general strategies for their rendering.

- **Chapter 8: Conclusion,** concludes this book with the classifications of visual effects which do not necessarily fit within the designations of earlier effects, where the visual effects industry is headed in the near future, and a basic strategy for starting a career in visual effects.

CONVENTIONS

Many of the terms and applications mentioned throughout this book may seem to go in multiple directions and even be contradictory. To avoid confusion, the conventions used throughout this book are listed below.

Experiences

Without getting too philosophical, real-time visual effects have more applications than just video games. All of the effects presented in this book may have originated from games but are now usable in any real-time application spanning from games to simulation and education, architecture, medicine, marketing, industrial and any form of virtual, augmented, or mixed reality experiences. These are momentous times as even traditional narrative media such as film, television and live events are transitioning toward real time. Instead of listing all possible avenues upon which visual effects can be applied, this book simply refers to all possible applications as, "real-time experiences," or simply, "experiences."

Story Worlds

Just as all real-time experiences are no longer the domain of just video games, the thematic environments which visual effects are surrounded by and attempt to integrate with must be re-labeled. The convention employed by this book is "story worlds." The use of this terminology is not intended as a slight against games which may be more focused on gameplay over story. The term story world describes the thematic environment which surrounds the real-time application. Even gameplay driven games such as Tetris and Pacman take place within some type of story world pretense, even as simple as, "An electronic maze filled with hovering pellets which are consumed by a munching disk while being pursued by ghosts in the machine."

Art Directable

Throughout this book, there is continuous reference to an adverb, "art directable." Art directable refers to the ease at which the visual content of the visual effect is changed or updated, based on recommended feedback. For example, when observing a visual effect, an art director may advise the effects artist to increase the fire intensity of an explosion, reduce the smoke, increase the sparks and make the upper surface of the exploded object dissolve more rapidly than the lower portions. Increasing the number of sparks may be very art directable and simple to implement. Depending how the effects artists implemented the effect, changing the distribution of the dissolving object may not be art directable and could require an entirely different design to the effect.

Users

From this book's perspective, there are no differences between Visual Effects Artists and Technical Artists. They both produce real-time visual effects. Visual Effects artists may focus more on the art and design aspects of the phenomena they are producing. Technical Artists deliver the same results but may employ more mathematics or invent their own tools to aid in delivery. Regardless of the tools they employ for creation, both produce similar results and therefore their labels are interchangeable.

SOFTWARE DISCLAIMER

This book attempts to be software agnostic. All presented strategies are universal and should be applicable to any real-time rendering engine. All digital content creation tools (DCCs) used for generating the assets populating these engines are intended to be universal as well. Great effort was made to avoid reference to any software specific applications or features. For consistency, all of the images generated for this book were produced using Epic Unreal Engine, SideFX Houdini, and Adobe Photoshop. This book is not an endorsement for any of these products. They just happen to be the author's favorite tools of choice. Any real-time engine should be able to reproduce these results. Any DCC should be able to generate assets to use in these engines.

PREREQUISITES

This probably comes across as cliché as all texts request this of their readers. Not much is needed in order to explore this book's contents other than a willingness to learn. Many artists, even self-proclaimed technical artists, declare they don't do math. Maybe they had a bad math-related experience in middle school or had never been presented with a useful application for the math they were learning. Others proclaim they don't deal with technology as it interrupts the creative process. This is always surprising since they are practicing digital art in a technical medium.

Regardless of the barriers, the greatest artists have always been masters of their media. Great painters understand enough chemistry and physics to mix their own pigments, fashion their own brushes, and stretch their canvases. Sculptors blend their own substances and fabricate their own tools. Luckily, visual effects only require a small amount of physics. With a small amount of math and technical understanding, visual effects artists can increase their potential for artistic expression exponentially.

This book requires basic addition and subtraction complemented with some multiplication and division. Technical artists traditionally only use multiplication. They use numbers larger than one to increase a product, smaller than one to make it smaller and negative numbers to represent the opposite or flip directions. Small amounts of algebra and basic geometry are useful for solving formulas. Calculus and linear algebra are great disciplines and will significantly help visual effects artists in the long run. However, they are not essential for this book nor are they requirements for entrance into the field.

A real-time visual effects artist must have a real-time rendering engine to practice her skills. Unreal Engine and Unity, at the time of this book's writing, are very popular engines. Their basic functionalities are free to use and don't require payment until certain monetary thresholds are achieved using those engines. Aside from Unreal Engine and Unity, there are many other engines which are free to use, such as Lumberyard from Amazon. Many engines, such as Godot, are open-source. While most larger studios use customized engines, the availability of free-to-use engines should not slow the visual effects artist.

The choices for DCC software used for generating in-engine content are as diverse as real-time engines. While there are expensive three-dimensional creative suites available, such as Side Effects Houdini, Autodesk Maya, and 3DS Max, each should provide a free trial period or free learner's version in order to fine tune one's skill. Blender is an upcoming open-source, three-dimensional package. Two-dimensional image manipulation software is also required. Commercial packages such Adobe Photoshop and Illustrator are industry stands. Open-source and free-to-use tools such as Gimp and Krita are also excellent packages.

There has never been a better time to start one's journey into real-time visual effects. The availability of outstanding real-time rendering engines and DCCs has removed most barriers from entering the field. There is a plethora of excellent material on-line to demonstrate almost any technique expected from a starting visual effects artist. A visual effects artist should have no limitations for exploring this diverse field.

INTRODUCTION

When considering the components that make up the real-time production process, visual effects are the most difficult to define. For brevity, instead of defining all that visual effects are, it may be easier to identify what visual effects are not. Within any computer-generated scene, the participant will find multiple familiar items: environments, animated characters, and props. Artificial environments define the story world's settings, bounding what is conventional. They introduce the participant to what is typically expected or what is plausible for the scene. Characters are animated from keyframes or from motion capture. They interact with the environment and other characters. Props are passive objects with which both characters and environments act upon. Visual effects are everything else found in that story world. When a component is not considered an environment piece, an animated character, or prop, it is a visual effect (Figure 1.1).

Visual effects are the lighting that make a forest look foreboding in the middle of the night and enthusiastic in the morning. They provide the camera flares in the early sun and make the world appear blurry in times of obscurity and confusion. Visual effects are what make static objects appear as if they are moving, such as barber poles or wind-blown foliage, and make water appear to be flowing and rippling. They generate dramatic destruction such as collapsing buildings and the subtle bounce of a princess's hair as she rides her horse. When not captured as on-set special effects, visual effects provide rain, snow, smoke, fire, and rainbow-colored pixie dust from magical wands.

Generating emotional impact is a primary objective of the computer-generated pipeline. Skillful writing and compelling performances drive computer-generated imagery (CGI) characters to interact with their environments and props to create memorable visual experiences. Visual effects complement these fundamental components and influence emotional mood and tone. They make dire situations feel more dreadful and happy situations more

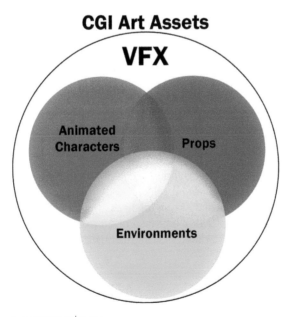

FIGURE 1.1 Visual effects in the computer-generated scene.

DOI: 10.1201/9781003009795-2

festive and alive. They make mundane events feel like epic, destiny threatening circumstances. Visual effects complement and supercharge scene components to create emotionally driven adventure.

Real-time environments can be anything from the mundane to the outrageously unbelievable. They may represent any moment in time from the present to the ancient past and to the unforeseeable future. Environments may take place underwater, within outer space, or in alien worlds. Visual effects make these settings feel real, natural, and believable. They add credibility to their surroundings making them feel as if they have always existed.

Story world credibility is threatened when alien beings or fantastic creatures are introduced. Foreign characters are thematically integrated with familiar settings through the exchange of visual effects techniques. For example, consider a frog demon summoned by an evil wizard to wreak havoc on a medieval hamlet. Simply introducing the character into the environment without the aid of visual effects feels artificial and cheap. Adding visual effects makes the demon creature, although very alien, feel natural within the experience. The lights of the village illuminate the demon while the fire in its eyes illuminates itself as well as its immediate surroundings. The lighting in the town casts shadows onto the demon and conversely, the demon casts shadows back onto the environment. When the demon collides with scene objects, they are damaged or destroyed. When the demon lumbers by, it leaves footprints kicking up dirt and sand. The creature spits slime and soaks the surroundings and all who come within immediate contact. The exchange of visual effects integrates alien components within familiar environments.

Visual effects take an ordinary experience and make it larger than life. They push the experience from the real to the hyper-real. Very rarely do the events of real-life match the emotional impact generated by the same situations. Instead of displaying what is real, visual effects create the story world constructed by our emotions. Visual effects push the impact of natural phenomena to the catastrophic. They add vibrant colors and brilliant lighting to otherwise mundane situations. Visual effects make reality conform to the emotional stories created with our imaginations.

From a pure commercial perspective, visual effects are the components added to an experience to cue the audience something special or wonderful is occurring. This is the extra icing on the cake, the extra polish to the scene, or the extra glitter to the gold. Visual effects appeal to the curiosity and invite outsiders to participate within the offered story world.

Visual effects are diverse. They can be anything from the lighting that controls the scene's emotional mood and tone to the shapes a frog morphs while transforming to a prince. They can be the dark clouds that roll on to a field of battle to the armies that lob projectiles at each other. Visual effects can be the blood and destruction spilt on the battlefield as well as the foliage that grows and replaces them. Instead of replacing characters, props, environments, and their animations, visual effects complement these components within their thematic story worlds.

VISUAL EFFECTS ARE ANIMATIONS

All visual effects are animations. The visual effects industry evolved from animation. All original visual effects artists were former animators or had mastery of the 12 principles of animation. Visual effect images need to move and change over time; otherwise they are simply pretty pictures. This condition even covers lighting and post-processing which may not appear to change. Over the course of an experience, they can and often do change. The contrast of the same scene between two different contexts has a dramatic impact on the experience's emotional mood and tone.

SPECIAL EFFECTS

There is an important distinction to be made between visual effects and special effects. While visual effects are important components of the CGI production pipeline, "Special Effects" is a live-action production term reserved for phenomena requiring unique attention. Usually mechanical in nature, these phenomena may include mechanized props and scenery, scale models, animatronics, pyrotechnics, and atmospheric simulations such as physical wind, rain, and snow. Examples of mechanized props are exploding toilets, collapsing stages, and imploding buildings.

Special effects also include prosthetic makeup that makes actors look non-human. These include any mask or prosthetic that moves or behaves in an unnatural way.

Before the evolution of computer visual effects, all optical effects were considered as special effects. These phenomena were manipulated after primary image capture and were considered as part of the "in-camera" process. Source images were transferred from source film to destination film using optical printers, mattes, and other multiple exposure techniques.

Computer-generated imagery originated as a subsection within special effects and evolved into its own area of specialization. Now, any imagery created or manipulated in post-process using a computer is considered as a visual effect while any phenomena captured concurrently with live footage is considered a special effect.

OFF-LINE VISUAL EFFECTS

Any special effect captured or manipulated after primary exposure and before final coloration was considered as part of the "in-camera" process. These were also called "off-line" effects because the techniques were performed away from the expensive on-set production process. These effects included optical effects, models, and miniatures which were filmed and optically integrated with source footage. Being off-line meant extra time and attention could be devoted to the special effects without impacting or delaying primary production.

Computers were originally used to assist with the off-line filming of models and miniatures. Computer motion-controlled camera rigs generated impossibly complex camera movements and multiple camera passes which duplicated camera movements with every iteration. Different camera passes were filmed under different lighting conditions to generate mattes and isolate diffuse, shadow, and highlight information layers. Computers were also used for assembling these layers during optical printing.

Three-dimensional CGI was first used in the 1976 film, *Futureworld*. Used sparingly afterward, the use of CGI gained significant attention in the 1982 films *Tron* and *Star Trek II: The Wrath of Khan*. Other landmark films such as *The Last Starfighter*, *Young Sherlock Holmes*, *The Abyss*, *Terminator 2: Judgment Day*, and *Jurassic Park* contributed CGI to evolving into a significant special effect technique. CGI continued to replace optical special effects until evolving its own *visual effects* category.

The 1995 film *Toy Story* became the first full CGI film. Instead of providing only special effects components, computers were used for generating all visual production content. This landmark event initiated a transition of many animated films from hand-drawn to computer generated. While computers are still used for generating CGI films, the process is still relatively slow. This limitation is changing radically.

In this book, the term *off-line* refers to all CGI production performed after original source exposure and before final coloration. While this term applies to all live-action visual effects, it also describes the production process for CGI-animated films. Being off-line frees artists from generating frame-rate dependent images, allowing focus on quality over performance (Figure 1.2).

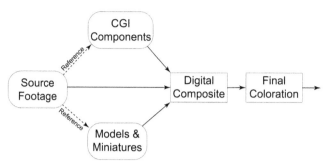

FIGURE 1.2 Off-line production process.

REAL-TIME VISUAL EFFECTS

Real-time visual effects are components of larger computer applications running fast enough to display fully rendered images at frame rates between 30 and 90 frames per second. Compromises to the visual effects must be made to prevent them from being computationally intensive enough to impact the framerates of their larger programs. Off-line visual effects are not impacted by this condition.

Although considered a relatively modern technological development, real-time computer graphics are almost as old as off-line. In the mid-1980s, the rise of Silicon Graphics and their three-dimensional computer graphics workstations empowered the first commercially available, real-time, three-dimensional simulations. The image quality was limited and primitive but did not prevent Silicon Graphics from generating a presence in the simulation and visualization industries. During the mid to late 2000s, high-end graphics workstations became obsolete as three-dimensional graphics cards became available. Graphics cards or Graphics Processing Units (GPUs) have continued to become faster and more powerful. As of the time of this book's writing, GPUs are now capable of real-time, ray-traced rendering; something that was considered pure science fiction in the 1980s. GPUs render the same three-dimensional worlds in real-time that once took weeks of off-line processing time in the 1990s. The distinction in quality between off-line and real-time rendering is now blurring.

In many considerations, real-time visual effects are more difficult to create than off-line. While their level of visual quality may not always be as sophisticated (although that line is blurring), the real-time condition introduces added complexities. The relatively free-roaming, real-time camera prevents hiding information from pre-established camera views. Because the content creator cannot control the direction of participant focus, all scene elements must appear consistent from all camera angles. Thematically, off-line production can manipulate audience attention to maximize narrative impact. This ability is greatly reduced in real-time and disappears entirely with augmented and virtual reality applications. What was once occluded in off-line scene composition is now exposed in real-time. This exposure requires greater project pre-planning and resources to ensure visual consistency from all camera perspectives. Effective real-time visual effects, now more than ever, must be sensitive to thematic narrative.

DRAWBACKS OF REAL-TIME VISUAL EFFECTS

Although the quality lines separating off-line from real-time visual effects are indistinguishable, real-time visual effects have a significant drawback. All visual effects must be authored within the real-time rendering engine. This phenomenon is explained more thoroughly later in this book. No two rendering engines are the same and therefore cannot produce the exact same visual results given the same input. There are many outstanding, off-line DCC packages that are effective for generating off-line visual effects. The output from these packages do not translate directly into mass-market real-time rendering engines. The data must be conditioned and re-configured to be input into real-time engines. When rendered, the differences between the off-line and real-time renderers prevent the two from maintaining visual parity.

Just because off-line and real-time packages cannot duplicate each other's appearance, does not mean that they cannot support each other. Off-line packages provide outstanding pre-visualization and prototyping services which the real-time packages use as visual targets. Techniques such as "Vertex Caching" enable off-line software to pre-generate sophisticated simulations that can be imported into real-time. These "pre-baked" simulations, when played back in real-time, are exponentially more sophisticated and more efficient than any simulation generated in real-time.

REAL-TIME USES

What started with Silicon Graphics in the mid-1980s with simulation and scientific visualization has snowballed into a diverse range of applications. Real-time applications now reach into every aspect of multimedia. Visual effects complement every application.

Video Games

Video games are the first applications that come to mind when considering real-time visual effects. From atmospherics such as rain and snow, to simulations depicting epic destruction and to the visualizations of the unbelievably fantastic, visual effects are essential components for generating immersive and captivating gaming experiences (Figure 1.3).

Live-Action Production

Live-action production, which was once strictly off-line, is now transitioning to embrace real-time production methods. Pre-visualization empowers directors to observe and interactively compose thematic scenes before sets are built and performances are captured, saving productions phenomenal cost, and guaranteeing effective narrative intent. Set design and lighting are pre-modeled to provide virtual blackboards to work out lighting and other production challenges before live-action capture. Integrated with traditional green-screen techniques and virtual environments, real-time composting provides acting talent holistic environments to interact with and avoids further post-production visual effects (Figure 1.4).

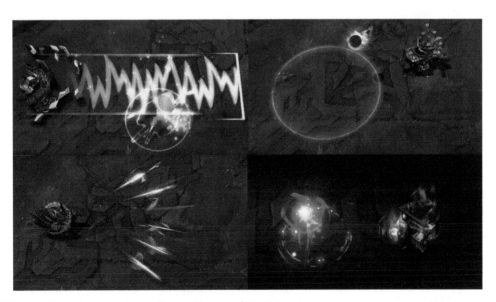

FIGURE 1.3 League of legends magic. (Image Sources Courtesy of Riot Games.)

FIGURE 1.4 UE4 virtual production. (Image Courtesy of Epic Games © 2021, Epic Games, Inc.)

FIGURE 1.5 Live-action sets and visual effects. (Image Courtesy of Epic Games © 2021, Epic Games, Inc.)

Live entertainment production has also integrated with real-time. Concerts, competitions, sporting events, and other live-action events are pre-visualized and pre-lit in real-time. Set extensions and environmental control are pre-choreographed with stylish motion graphics to produce impactful and memorable live experiences (Figure 1.5).

Cinematics

Cinematics are real-time short movies. Performers and their environments are generated and played back entirely within real-time. Cinematics are common narrative components found in video games. They are now found in marketing and episodic venues. Full-length cinematic productions are not far into the future (Figure 1.6).

FIGURE 1.6 Full-length cinematic venture. (Image Courtesy of Spire Animation Studios.)

Simulation

Simulation continues to grow as a significant real-time application. Visualization, training, and modeling industries are dependent on real-time content for aiding doctors, soldiers, healthcare providers, and first responders by providing safe and consequent-free environments to develop and fine-tune lifesaving skills. Visual effects are crucial components for establishing realistic training scenarios.

Augmented Reality (AR), Virtual Reality (VR), Mixed Reality (MR), and Cross Reality (XR)

While immersive virtual reality has been around almost as long as real-time CGI, the development of free-to-use real-time engines and consumer-focused head-mounted displays has made these elements to of our everyday lives. Augmented and virtual reality applications are dependent on real-time display. Visual effects are essential components for integrating and establishing alternative reality integrity.

Architecture

Architects have been using three-dimensional computer graphics since the mid-1980s. Real-time environments empower architects and designers to rapidly iterate and produce the most effective versions of their creative visions and communicate their intent to stakeholders. They also help identify and navigate around costly design errors. Architects employ walk-though, immersive VR, and AR experiences to holistically juxtapose the past, present, and future (Figure 1.7).

Automotive/Transportation

Real-time visualization has become a significant tool in the automotive and transportation industries. Like architecture, real-time solutions provide designers an environment to prototype and refine concepts and then interact with their results without having to build expensive physical models. While visual effects do not significantly contribute to this area, they are used extensively in the visualization and marketing departments. Visual effects bring products to life and guide audience attention.

Inside the driver's seat (or in the cockpit), the driving experience is pre-visualized in real-time so designers may understand the impact of the interior design for safe and effective navigation. Visual effects are crucial for

FIGURE 1.7 Architectural visualization. (Image Courtesy of Imerza.)

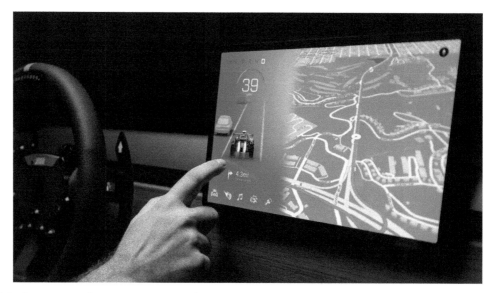

FIGURE 1.8 Real-time user interfaces. (Image Courtesy of Epic Games © 2021, Epic Games, Inc.)

prototyping realistic driving experiences. They are even used to create user interfaces which are easy to read and interact with (Figure 1.8).

Visual effects also aid in teaching vehicles how to drive by themselves. Games and simulations are created to teach autonomous vehicles how to safely operate without human interaction. Visual effects are integral components of these simulations.

Scientific Visualization

An interactive, scientific visualization is almost always generated as a real-time visual effect. Visual effects techniques are essential for displaying natural phenomena from the microscopic worlds of viruses to the movement

FIGURE 1.9 Interactive cultural experiences. (Image Courtesy of the Smithsonian Institution.)

and behavior of galaxies. What were once exclusively computed off-line, real-time visual effects are core components for interactive scientific visualization.

Location-Based Experiences

Real-time technologies dramatically impact museums, art galleries, and other location-based experiences. Interactive historical and cultural exhibits educate and inform while integrating the past, present, and future into singular contexts. Visual effects play an important role collaborating in real-time to emphasize content and generate larger-than-life experiences (Figure 1.9).

REAL-TIME VISUAL EFFECT TYPES

Real-time demands make visual effects one of the most challenging of all technical art disciplines. They are the juxtaposition of the most complicated technical and the most creative design components. The first visual effects artists were the best of all digital artists. They possessed a solid foundation in art and design all the while manipulating and exploiting every aspect of the rendering pipeline. They needed to be proficient with the 12 principles of animation and write code to duplicate each. They were required to model, draw, and paint sufficiently to create magical characters and bring them to life. Due to the primitive hardware of the time, visual effects artists also understood system IT in order to drive the best computational performances. Visual effects artists were the first CGI Jacks of the trade.

With a seemingly endless variety of real-time applications, it is easy to conclude there is an infinite number of types of visual effects. To help wrangle this endless herd of kittens, this book breaks real-time visual effects into four categories based on implementation: in-camera, in-material, simulation, and particles. Of course, other categories might be considered as visual effects such as procedural modeling and procedural animation. However, examples such as these may be considered as technical extensions of traditional artists' roles and not typical visual effects situations. In this book, coverage for each visual effect type is limited to introducing each's fundamental processes and ideologies. The entire book could be devoted to each category implementation. Most modern visual effects are complex aggregates of simpler instances from each category. These categories are adequate to help any artist handle any visual effects demand.

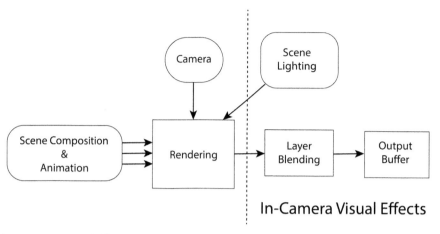

In-Camera Visual Effects

FIGURE 1.10 Real-time in-camera visual effects.

In-Camera Effects

In-camera visual effects are the closest in spirit to the original special effects employed in live-action production. While traditional off-line visual effects are everything done to captured images after initial exposure and before final coloration, real-time in-camera visual effects are all effects performed during or after initial scene rendering and before the final output-merger stage of the rendering pipeline. No additional visual effects actors or components are introduced to the pipeline (Figure 1.10).

These visual effects are broken into two sub-categories: lighting and post-processing. While not traditionally viewed as a visual effect, lighting, in the author's perspective, is the most important of all visual effects. Nothing in the art production pipeline has a greater impact on the emotional mood and feeling of the real-time experience than lighting (Figure 1.11).

Post-processing is all additional operations done to rendered image layers before the final merge. Since these manipulations are performed after initial rendering, post-processing significantly impacts overall experiential mood and atmosphere with the least amount of effort (Figure 1.12).

Material Effects

Beyond in-camera effects, in-material effects are the most widely implemented type of visual effect. In-material effects are processes performed inside scene object materials which manipulate the stages of the rendering pipeline. Objects and characters with visual effect materials are rendered in separate layers from other scene components. All object materials are potential visual effect generators. Significant advantages of these types of visual effects are that they are relatively simple to implement, they are extraordinarily art directable, and when performed consciously, they do not draw heavily on computational resources. While this technique offers the greatest potential for variation, there are two primary strategies: animated texture maps and vertex manipulation (Figure 1.13).

Simulations

While in-material effects are relatively computationally inexpensive, simulations are the most expensive. Simulations are movements and deformations computed in real-time to mimic natural physical phenomena. Because they duplicate the physics of experience's theme world, simulated objects integrate with their environments seamlessly. Simulations help establish the integrity and realism of the experiential universe. Instead of manipulating visual effects objects from within their materials, simulations animate and deform in world-space,

FIGURE 1.11 Same scene lit in two different ways (bright and creepy).

from the context of the entire rendering engine, not the individual object. Simulations provide the most natural looking animations but are expensive and difficult to art direct (Figure 1.14).

Particles

When most people think of visual effects, they think about particles, procedural simulations of tiny, abstract objects. Particles are the aggregate of all the other types of visual effects. They can manipulate lighting and provide layers of post-processing. They must be rendered and can take advantage of all the techniques available from the in-material rendering pipeline. They are also primitive simulations which reflect the physics of the story world's universe. From a pure programming perspective, they are difficult to implement, requiring specialized tools to create and edit. Ironically, because the tools and interfaces have evolved since the late 1980s, they can be implemented easily. They can take moments to learn yet require a lifetime to master. Their ease of entry makes them the most design intensive and art directable aspect of visual effects. As the aggregate of all other visual effect types, they are also the most complicated and technically demanding. All visual effects artists sit somewhere between these two radical extremes (Figure 1.15).

FIGURE 1.12 Same scene with two different post-processes.

FIGURE 1.13 In-material visual effects.

FIGURE 1.14 Simulations.

FIGURE 1.15 Particle visual effects.

CONCLUSIONS

Real-time visual effects are the evolution of live-action special effects applied within real-time rendering engines. Special effects manipulate scene objects during live-action capture. Off-line visual effects manipulate exposed footage after initial capture and before final coloration. The off-line visual effects process is independent of frame rate and can be performed very quickly or very slowly. Real-time visual effects are framerate dependent and must not negatively impact the performance of the real-time rendering engine. Within the real-time art production pipeline, visual effects are all components which are not key-frame animated environments, articulated characters, or props.

Real-time visual effects complement and manipulate the mood and emotion of their story worlds, yet they are bound directly to their rendering engine. They must be visually mastered within the context of their rendering engine, making them difficult to implement and refine.

Despite their limitations, real-time visual effects are found in all real-time applications including video games, live-action production, cinematics, simulations, all forms of mixed reality, architecture, automotive and transportation, scientific visualization, and location-based experiences.

While infinite in possibilities, this book breaks real-time visual effects into four categories: in-camera, in-material, simulations, and particles.

INTRODUCTION

Visual effects are the most creative aspect of being a Technical Artist. They provide an opportunity to focus on creating "fine art" and design. Creatively, the artist does not need to be technically savvy to create beautiful content. Ironically, visual effects are also technical enough such that the artist may focus purely on their science and engineering. Visual effects are a perfect juxtaposition of the artistic skills and the technical elements. Each artist controls the ratio of the two. This chapter focuses on the rules for creating and designing visual effects regardless of their technical or creative requirements.

Many of these rules are subjective. They may not be so much as rules as they are guidelines for creating pleasing visual effects. Some are based on technical conditions which carry subconscious impact, such as white and black points. These rules are ordered to provide logical flow that is easy to remember. Some may seem contradictory. These are situationally conditional rules that require the creative eye of the artist whose job is to balance the artistic skills and the technical elements.

This list of rules is not complete. It is continuously growing and expanding. The list refines itself as time and technology progress. The opportunity for integrating other artists' rules is exciting. The path for technical artist growth is not paved with ability but growth and learning. Any offered critique from this chapter is not intended to establish superiority but to provide opportunity to learn and understand from an alternative perspective. Analyzing any visual effect provides opportunity for growth.

Many of the concepts regarding artistic principles, narrative support, composition, and interpretation are derived from working in film and television production. These concepts are integrated with the constraints and technological demands of the real-time realm. Up and coming media formats such as virtual reality, augmented reality and mixed reality, integrate narrative and technical elements. Regardless of their medium, these rules guide the visual effects artist to creating more impactful and aesthetically pleasing visual effects.

VISUAL EFFECTS ARE NOT THE STORY

Visual effects are fun. They are showy and spectacular. They draw attention to themselves. They are also subtle and may never be noticed. Regardless of their intention, visual effects are not story or the gameplay, they complement both. Unless the story is about the visual effects, they must support the story, not compete with it. When visual effects and story exchange priority, the experience feels artificial.

Visual Effects Add Credibility

Visual effects make the unbelievable visible. They make impossible story worlds real. None of the magical game universes of *Skyrim* and *Azeroth*, the alien landscapes of *Star Wars*, or the dinosaurs of *Jurassic Park* would be possible without visual effects. Even when impossible in our own mundane reality, visual effects provide what is expected to be seen in the context of their story worlds. They provide what is necessary for the audience to believe the world has always existed. They provide credibility to the justification of alternative realities.

Visual Effects Are the Glue

In a story world or gameplay universe, there are characters and environments which must be implemented as visual effects. Many characters are pure digital effects such as Thanos from the *Avengers* or a young Benjamin Button. The environments of *Rapture* and *Night City* are entire worlds composed of dizzying layers of visual

DOI: 10.1201/9781003009795-3

effects. Visual effects glue characters to their environments, integrating them seamlessly. They cast shadows on each other. When they generate light, adjacent surfaces are illuminated. One of the most memorable visual effects integrations is Gandalf's showdown with the Balrog on the *Bridge of Khazad Dum*. The Balrog is a mythical creature bathed in fire. Gandalf is a vagabond wizard wielding a shining staff. They meet on a fictional bridge spanning a cavernous Dwarven mine. The Balrog's fire illuminates the world and Gandalf. Gandalf's staff projects white lighting into the scene and onto the Balrog. Both characters cast shadows onto the bridge. The exchange of light, fire, and shadow cements the characters and environment to a single holistic scene.

Visual Effects Help Story Flow

The greatest visual effects are not observed. Of course, they are visibly seen but flow so well within their story worlds, they are never noticed as visual effects but as crucial components of the story. Audience presence is always maintained. Excellent visual effects make extraordinary phenomena seem normal to the story world and yet are not so dramatic that they draw attention away from the story. The Rihanna dance scene in *Valerian and the City of a Thousand Planets* is an outstanding example. The character is an alien performer whose role is to shapeshift continuously during her performance. The exhibition is exotic and fascinating but never draws attention to itself as a visual effect. Further reflection after the scene reveals that not only were visual effects carefully sprinkled to embellish the act but also were so holistically integrated, the entire performance could have only been generated as one, encompassing visual effect.

NEVER SHOW VFX OUT OF CONTEXT

Ironically, while their purpose is to support the story and integrate with the scene, visual effects cannot exist outside context. Without proper context, visual effects are only pretty moving pictures. When a visual effect is displayed by itself, none of its subtle components making it an effective storyteller (its scale, lighting, motion, weight, and integration), are evident. Only the base visual qualities of the effect are observable. Without the scene, it feels naked and incomplete (Figure 2.1).

Visual effects displayed in a portfolio or in a demo reel should always be shown in context of the scenes they were originally intended for. Within the story context, the artist demonstrates her ability to make an effect that is visually pleasing and complements its intended scenario. When displayed out of context, there are no environments for them to support. The effects are only half complete. Once exhibited within the context of their original

FIGURE 2.1 Visual effect out of context.

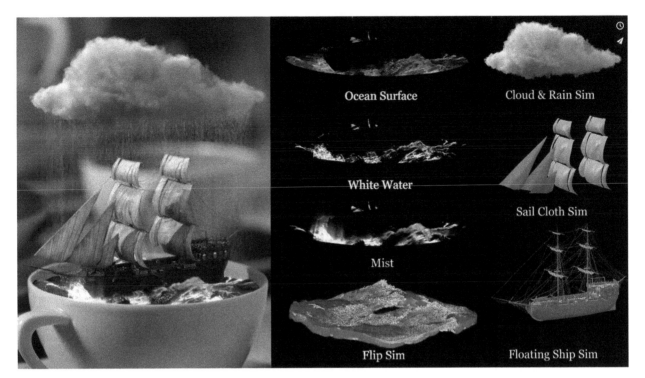

FIGURE 2.2 Excellent visual effects display. (Image Courtesy of Jinguang Huang, https://www.jinguanghuang.com/.)

intention, effects should be broken down into their individual layers and displayed to demonstrate each layer's visual qualities. Exhibiting visual effects with this strategy demonstrates the artist as being aesthetically skillful and technically savvy (Figure 2.2).

SCALE IS KING!

Visual effects are all about motion. Without motion, a visual effect is just an interesting picture. (The curse of writing a visual effects book!) Mastering scale and mass are two of the most important skills an animator must master to create the illusion of life. Without effective manipulation of these two parameters, the effect is foreign and out of place. Large simulations need to move slowly to demonstrate their scale and mass. Smaller objects must be lively and accelerate quickly. When visual effects move too quickly or too slowly with respect to their scale and mass, they lose credibility.

VISUAL EFFECTS DON'T SCALE

This rule complements the prior rule. (It is a friendly warning to designers and compositors who like to repurpose assets.) While visual effects are digital objects that can be duplicated and translated effectively within a single scene, they hold up poorly when transported to a different scene with a different scale. Visual effects artists spend hours manipulating effects' size, weight, speed, maneuverability, and acceleration in order to integrate them within their environments. When transplanted to alternative destinations that don't share the same scale from which the effect was initially authored, they fail. The velocities are not re-scaled properly and are inappropriate for the current scene. Particles may spawn from incorrect locations. Effects appear as if too heavy or not heavy enough like giant toys or toy giants (Figure 2.3).

Details and shapes are sensitive to scaling. Certain objects and other phenomena appear and behave differently at different scales. For example, a candle flame appears proper when an inch or two high. When scaled to fit a burning house or car, the effect loses credibility.

FIGURE 2.3 Toy-sized giant.

Effects components and shapes do not scale proportionately. Each must be adjusted to compensate for the changes in scale. Whenever a visual effect is scaled to fit within a new environment, it needs to be re-created or re-adjusted. Wise artists configure their effects to change disproportionately to compensate for scale. Regretfully, such configuration requires significant investment of time. This is an additional reason why they should never be shown out of context. Audiences can never appreciate the time and attention required to generate and integrate the effects. When displayed out of context, they are only half complete.

LIGHTING INTEGRATION IS QUEEN

Once effects' scales and animations have been configured to complement their immediate surroundings, lighting integration is the next important factor for marrying effects with their scenes. There are three components contributing to effects integrating with their surroundings: the incoming light, their shadows, and their projected lights. In real-time, the default interaction with the native lighting should be sufficient to light effects properly. The effects artist must ensure they are renderable (Figure 2.4).

Shadows play a significant role in integrating effects with their environments. For effects to appear "natural" in their word they must cast and receive shadows with their environments. Casting shadows informs the audience the effects have substance and can interact with lighting similarly to all the other objects in the scene. Receiving shadows reinforces effects' physical ability to interact with scene lighting the same as all other objects (Figure 2.5).

Just as effects need to correctly receive light, they must project light back onto their environments. Their impact on their surroundings is achieved by either placing light emitters within particles or parenting interactive lights to the effects. These subtle components pay large dividends reinforcing effects' credibility (Figure 2.6).

WHITES AND BLACKS

A real-time rendering engine is a predictable machine. Whatever input it receives, it will output pixel values ranging from the darkest black, (0.0, 0.0, 0.0), and the brightest white, (1.0, 1.0, 1.0), and all of the millions of colors between. When the engine receives input beyond these two-extreme values, the output is clamped. When the resulting pixel has a channel value greater than 1.0 the result is clamped to 1.0. When the value has a

FIGURE 2.4 Correct and incorrect lighting.

FIGURE 2.5 Casting and receiving shadows.

channel value less than 0.0, the result is clamped to 0.0. No object in the scene can be rendered brighter than pure white or darker than pure black. Evidence of clamping is observed when a pixel in the frame has a channel value equal to 1.0 or 0.0. When there are pixels with these values, it is a guarantee that there are other pixels which are clamped similarly. When a portion of the object is clamped, not all of the object information is displayed. Some portions are within acceptable rendering range while others are not (Figure 2.7).

Artists and development teams spend many hours creating objects intended to be displayed in their entirety. The only technique to guarantee all objects are rendered to their full potential is for the visual effects artist, lighter, renderer, or compositor to verify nothing in the scene is rendered as pure white, or pure black. When this requirement is met, the scene is *"White or Black Balanced."*

FIGURE 2.6 Projecting light on the environment.

FIGURE 2.7 Render clamping an object.

A simple demonstration of the need for this rule is to take any outer-space frame from a *Star Wars* scene created from the 1970s through the early 1990s. When the frame's gamma is pushed to an extreme value, large chunks of pure whites and blacks become visible. These large, clamped chunks are areas of screen space which could have been used to display important information. Consciously, these clamped chunks may not be noticeable. Subconsciously, they are noticed and produce feelings of lost or withheld information.

The following is a strategy for preventing any information loss due to clamping. Examine an average frame from a dark or bright scene using a pixel color sampling tool. Identify the brightest and darkest pixels in the scene, the *white* and *black* pixels. Compare all of the other frames against these white and black pixels. When no pixel in

FIGURE 2.8 Mismatch of effect and story world.

the scene is darker than the *black* pixel or brighter than the *white* pixel, no information is being lost due to clamping.

STYLE CONSISTENCY

Most visual effects are not generated from scratch. Instead, their concepts are borrowed from previously generated effects and repurposed to suit the thematic needs of the current story world. The risk of this strategy is creating a mismatch of fundamental styles. This style mismatch is often observed in cartoony, stylized effects in photo-realistic story worlds or two-dimensional effects in three-dimensional settings (Figure 2.8).

Visual effects must match the visual style of their story worlds less the audience challenges their integrity, believing something in the scene is not quite correct. Subconsciously, the discrepancy creates an agitation in the observer's eyes as they attempt to balance the contrasting styles. To demonstrate this phenomenon, consider frames from *Who Framed Roger Rabbit* and Ralph Bakshi's *Cool World*. Both films deal with two-dimensional characters interacting within three-dimensional, photo-realistic worlds. The character of Roger Rabbit is lit to match his scenes and casts and receives shadows with the three-dimension set. While the character is unusual (an animated cartoon rabbit), he is easy to watch and his visual presence does not distract from the story. In the film *Cool World*, the two-dimensional characters are not lit to complement their environments and no shadows are exchanged. As perversely delightful the movie is, it is hard to watch.

There are many sources for these contrasting styles. The first may be the limited skills of the visual effects artist. The effect technique may have been borrowed from a different styled source without awareness of discrepancy in styles. Multiple individuals may have contributed to the scene with inadequate reference images to assist with their unification. Or, very simply, the effect was created at a different time frame from the scene and the contrast in styles was never noticed. Regardless of their reasons, visual effects must match the styles of their intended story worlds.

VISUAL REFERENCES

It is not uncommon to work with young artists who refuse to work with reference images. Sometimes they claim to possess great imaginations and the visions in their heads are crystal clear. Other times they have preconceived definitions of what great artists are and feel they should simply create. They don't need references. Other times, they are simply lazy. Artists MUST work from visual references when creating visual effects.

There is a saying, "A visual effect is never done until they pry it from my cold, dead fingers." In many perspectives, this is true. No epic visual effect is totally complete. More can always be added or removed. Development resources are limited. There is rarely enough time to finish any effect. Effects are rarely solo and travel in herds. Only so much time is allocated to complete the entire herd of effects, let alone a single one. Often the visual effect is more complicated than what was anticipated and requires more time to flesh out. When the production pipeline is slow or expensive, limited iterations prevent effects from improving to desired quality. Occasionally the creativity or experience levels of the burgeoning artist require more time to achieve the desired state of quality. A reference image behaves as a visual target establishing what "done" means. Surpassing the reference target in quality is always a reason for celebration as there are typically just enough resources to drive the herd of effects to match their visual targets.

Occasionally the requested visual effects sound too simple or are communicated from a state of verbal understanding of finality. "I have a good image in my head," "My designer requested I implement …," or "I will know it when I see it," are common statements justifying no references. As visual effects manifest, mental images change and evolve. *Feature Creep* sneaks its way into the process as the implemented visions solidify. (*Feature Creep* is a term used when a producer, director, or executive requests the inclusion of a new element very late in the development cycle.) Imaginations are wonderful things that are always changing. Implemented visions rarely surpass imaginary images. The imagination strives to improve upon the current perspective. Visual references anchor imaginations and prevent the development process from drifting.

Reference images should capture the essence of the *Minimal Viable Product* (MVP) of every visual effect. They need to be mutually understood representations of the desired target state. Reference images may be anything. They can be quick thumbnail drawings or elaborate concept art. They can be derived from an established style guide or they can come from other games or films. If need be, they can even be doodles on napkins. Any images establish lines of communication, which encourage idea sharing and collaboration. Use visual references as compasses to validate progress and keep the development process on course.

MISSING VFX

This rule is sad and disappointing but is regretfully true more often than not. No one will ever miss a visual effect that is not there. Unless the visual effect disappears over the course of the game or the narrative, very few audience members will ever notice when a visual effect has been cut or marginalized. Working from a visual target or MVP creates a minimal expectation. As long as that expectation is met, anything extra will never be missed. There may be other astute artists who take notice and suggest the effect could have been improved with additional components. However, average audiences will never notice.

NEVER DUPLICATE VFX

Never re-use pre-generated effects taken from older projects. Audiences remember and are quick to comment when noticing repurposed assets. They feel developers are lazy or perhaps do not care about them. Similarly, never use canned effects directly from development software. A canned effect is a pre-generated macro intended to get an effect to the 80% completion point in an exceptionally short period of time. No client ever wants canned or duplicated effects. They expect all effects to be custom-made to match the uniqueness of their projects. This is a reasonable request as all visual effects should match their story worlds. When the same story worlds are revisited in sequels or off-shoots, the visual effects should evolve and grow. Audiences are disappointed and letdown when they see the same visual effects from prior installments. Re-using and repurposing visual effects provides opportunities to improve older effects and push them to the next level. When prior MVPs retard or limit old effects, new incarnations stand on the pre-created foundations and grow forward.

NEVER TAKE FROM TUTORIALS

This next rule is a painful warning to all inspiring visual effects artists. Never use visual effects in your portfolio or demo-reel taken from tutorials. This is the kiss of death that is only slightly less bad than plagiarizing someone else's work. The computer graphics industry is tiny. The chances of a reviewer being the author of the tutorial, or knowing the author, are simply too great. Knowledgeable reviewers recognize tutorials a mile away. Using tutorials destroys all artist credibility. Just because a tutorial was visually duplicated does not imply understanding of the visual effect. All it demonstrates is the artist's ability to duplicate the observed video.

When starting in the industry, tutorials are great references! They remove ambiguity with the concept or software. However, the end result is just the beginning. Visual effects artists must learn the techniques, know them, make them their own and then use them in unique and original applications. Modifying tutorials to make them work with radically new situations, changing their weights, scales and overall visual appearances demonstrate effect competency.

NEVER START FROM SCRATCH

Contradicting the prior rule, unless the resources are available and the situation demands pure originality, never start visual effects from scratch. Time and other valuable resources are rarely present for this luxury. Of course, there are situations requiring visual effects to be re-invented but they are few and far between. Instead of starting over with each effect, start with existing effects as place holders. When the situations are applicable, use tutorials for the initial versions. When borrowing visual effects from other artists, reverse engineer them and understand how every component contributes to the final results. Make the old visual effects your own. Deviate from them. Customize and repurpose them. Make them unrecognizable! Working from this perspective is incredibly beneficial. Artists learn and reinforce old effect comprehension while becoming more dynamic and pliable. Clients are made ecstatic with the delivery of shiny new effects within requested timelines.

VFX TOOLKIT

Visual effects are an enormously broad field. At times the scale feels overwhelming. There is just not enough time to learn all that is required to handle any situation. The secret is that it cannot be done. Do not worry about it. Visual effects cannot be learned in one semester. Nor can they be learned from a coach or watching from lectures and tutorials. The only way to master visual effects is to jump into them. Get your hands dirty and understand them from the inside-out. They are a representation of your entire human experience … and then some. Anything and everything you know or understand will find its way, at least allegorically, into your visual effects. It is surprising how the art of pizza making finds its way into the creation of particle systems or the movement of ants in their colony finds its way into crowd simulations. One artist confided that his experience with watercolors made him a better proceduralist because he didn't quite know the exact details but when he applied the rules, he could predict the general outcome.

Knowing everything is not required for creating beautiful, effective visual effects. Being resourceful of all of your experiences is very useful. Students starting on their visual effects journey may be less overwhelmed when adopting this strategy. Learn one effect and apply it toward the next situation in a robust manner. Make suitable modifications. After that effect, learn another. Whether the artist wants to or not, the lessons learned from the prior two experiences support and bolster the third and subsequent effects. In addition to borrowing from older effects, students should call upon anything and everything she has ever learned. When analyzed and applied, processes for creating anything are useful inspiration. The same strategy for distributing pepperoni on pizza has also been used for providing initial positions for particle insects on floors. The key takeaway from this rule is to always be learning. Learn from old visual effects and learn from the experiences of life. With a bit of creative imagination, they integrate wonderfully.

VISUAL EFFECTS LAYERS

One of the most effective strategies for creating complicated visual effects is to break the effect into multiple layers of simple effects. A common dilemma many beginning artists attempt is trying to be efficient and combining all effect components into one layer. They quickly discover they are juggling more than they are able to handle.

Creating visual effects in layers has multiple benefits. When working with unique layers, the artist has infinite access and control over the components in that layer. The stack of layers is infinitely expandable. New layers can be added up until the point of final delivery. The holistic visual effect becomes more stable and less fragile. Individual layers are updated and removed without significant impact. Effect maintenance becomes easier. The artist has less concern about breaking the entire effect when manipulating one layer at a time. Ordering the precedence of components becomes easier as well. An effect lower in the presentation sequence can be brought forward with little concern of damaging the entire effect. Novice artists are often deterred by the amount of overhead required to partition the effect into layers. However, the extra control empowered by the decomposition more than outweighs the extra time to implement the system.

STUDENTS OF ANIMATION

The following rule is simple but must be obeyed. All visual effects artists must be students of animation. Visual effects flow from animation. In the early days of computer graphics production when the term "visual effects" had not been coined, all effects were referred to as "computer animation." Without outstanding animation, a visual effect is just a pretty picture. Effects need to move as natural components of their story worlds. Artists must continuously strive for story world integration and traditional animation contributes significantly. The twelve principles of animation, described by Ollie Johnston and Frank Thomas in their book *The Illusion of Life: Disney Animation*, are essential and must be present in every visual effect. The twelve principles are as follows:

1. Squash and stretch
2. Anticipation
3. Staging
4. Straight ahead action and pose to pose
5. Follow through and overlapping animation
6. Slow in and slow out
7. Arc
8. Secondary action
9. Timing
10. Exaggeration
11. Solid Drawing
12. Appeal

Some of the concepts do not translate directly into modern, three-dimensional, real-time graphics, such as "Solid Drawing." However, understanding and application of the essence of these concepts will provide life in every visual effect. Every visual effects artist should have a copy!

BE A MAGICIAN

Visual effects artists are magicians. Time after time, they make something appear from thin air, make things disappear, and otherwise make the unbelievable appear real. All participants observing visual effects are impacted by their presence, yet very few understand how they are generated.

Due to the lack of audience understanding, artists must learn to "fake it." They must present their material as if always intended, regardless of intended impact, or apparent difficulty. Let the audience judge for themselves based on their emotional responses. Implementation details are inconsequential as long as effects deliver their intentions.

Visual effects artists need to master "sleight-of-hand," the mysterious art of redirecting the audience to look someplace other than a point of interest. The location of concern is often a mistake or unwanted phenomenon, such as a misbehaving simulation. For example, mists and fogs are often placed to obscure poorly modeled environments. The skill of redirecting the audience's attention is very helpful in many situations, especially when hiding unintended information. Distractions are the basic tools of redirection. Visual contrasts grab the audience's primary attention, even for short periods of time. Similarly, regions of kinetic and frantic activity appeal to the animal instincts in our brains and force our attention to focus on those areas of interest.

With great skills of redirection and "sleight-of-hand," comes great responsibility. When overwhelmed with a multitude of visual effects, skeptical individuals search for visual incongruities. "What is being hidden?" Such skeptical individuals are rare but the artist must be aware that chronically employing effects for hiding undesirable phenomena will eventually raise suspicion.

SIMULATION

Simulations are important aspects of visual effects. An entire chapter of this book is devoted to the subject. Simulations are essential elements for making story worlds credible. They make certain visual effects possible that would be impossible to generate by hand. They are also a significant industry unto themselves that educate, model, and save lives because they reproduce reality without generating harm to life and property. Simulations are useful yet they are boring. They simulate reality. Imaginations are larger than real life and the emotional impact of our memory is more dramatic than duplicated reality. Visual effects artists should use simulation for generating emotional responses which are larger than real life, not just for imitating reality.

Simulations are crucial tools all visual effects artists must integrate with their collections of skills. Regardless of the artists' tool of choice (Houdini, Maya, Blender, in-engine, custom built, etc.), all visual effects artists need to dedicate resources to mastering their simulation packages. No two implementations are the same and each requires time and dedication to master. However, artists should not stop at mastery and continuously employ simulations as the foundation for generating larger than life emotions.

Physics plays an important role in simulation. Unlike animation, visual effects artists do not need to be students of physics. Simulation packages handle the theory and implement the math. However, familiarity with the basic principles, such as Newton's three laws, will assist the artist in creating more lifelike, satisfying simulations.

SIMULATIONS CONSUME CAREERS

The title of this rule is misleading as the implementation of simulations is essential to artists' careers. They are extraordinarily slow and expensive to develop. When the simulations are fast and inexpensive, artists compromise too much control and artistic freedom. Unless handled and developed properly, simulations could consume or destroy artists' careers. Time is money. Simulations are slow and consume great amounts of time and computational resources. The artist must fight the beast and learn how to develop simulations without them destroying their careers.

FIGURE 2.9 Original and proxy collision environments.

The most significant threats to a young visual artist's career are their impatience and their pride. To survive, artists must adopt methodical strategies, contrary to obvious approaches. They must swallow their prides and avoid striving for that mythical, one-take final. Reverting the effect to a prior version or implementing with a new strategy is often the key for moving forward. Production scenes are often computationally resource demanding, even before simulation. Artists must recognize those situations and develop their simulations in simpler scenes or proxy environments. Working within a simple scene provides proof-of-concept where the artist can iterate quickly, experiment, and make radical changes. Artists will recognize when the scene is too simple and adjust accordingly without slowing down for long simulation processing (Figure 2.9).

The urge for generating final simulations in first attempts must be resisted. Start tiny and build up. When simulating rigid bodies, animate one or two objects at first. Once these are visually adequate, double the number and adjust. Continue iterating until the desired number of objects is present. Only perform the final simulation once or twice after it has been thoroughly tested. When working with particles, start with only 1% of the desired count and build up. When generating volumetrics, start with tiny, thumbnail-sized volumes and gradually build upwards until the artist understands how to simulate the full volume only once. Crowd simulations should start with only one or two agents. Complex animations and deformations should start with low-resolution proxies. When simulations are unable to achieve their desired scale, alternative compromises or redirections may be necessary. The important factor is to not be hindered by slow simulation times and strive to generate the final simulation only once.

HYPER-REALITY

The following rule is not valid when creating visual effects for serious games or life-dependent simulations. For all other applications, visual effects need to be big. Everyone has their own perspective on what reality is. No two people match. Imaginations are emotionally driven and tend to be larger than reality. Don't disappoint the audience by delivering reality. Deliver images that satisfy their imaginations. Tell the story, not the truth. Consider the emotional impact a visual effect contributes toward the story, not to how real it is. Even when striving to duplicate reality, emotionally charge the visual effect at least just a little flare. In the movie *Titanic*, did the falling man need to hit the propeller? The extra flipping and twisting provided just enough emotional impact to make the tragedy an unforgettable experience. Start creating visual effects to duplicate reality, and then increase them to notch 11.

TEASE THE AUDIENCE!

More is not always better. Visual effects can be like sugar. Sometimes too much is distracting and competes for attention. The emotional context of the experience drives the scale of the visual effect. The emotions of suspicion, anticipation, and dread require more subtlety than those of shock and awe. Suspenseful emotions demand just a bit of information and often none. Allow the audience to fill in the gaps with their imaginations. Imaginations create greater senses of fear and dread than any visual effect can. A great example is the shark from the movie *Jaws*. Luckily, for the filmmaker Steven Spielberg, the shark model was broken for most of the film's shooting and could not be used until the end. By the time the audience sees the shark for the first time, they are filled with so much fear and anticipation, its initial presence becomes an unforgettable experience.

The audience wants to be seduced. They want to be drawn into the emotional impact of the experience. By teasing the audience and showing just a hint of the visual effect, their imaginations are sent into overdrive. Their curiosity takes over and they allow themselves to get sucked into the situation. When answers are finally given, their revelations become memorable events.

ITERATE!

An artist's value as a content producer is based purely on the number of iterations she can crank out. In simpler terms, more iterations provide better visual effects. Despite what they may project, no artist produces world-class visual effects in their first attempt. Some even believe no visual effect is ever done until all its resources are depleted.

The key to mastering this rule is to start immediately with a little bit of something. That something may be a simple stand-in object (a box, cylinder, or sphere), a proxy effect, a copied (stolen) effect, or direct tutorial results. Anything will do if the effect is represented. The artist iteratively builds on this initial foundation and grows it into a world-class effect. When estimating time for the creation of any asset (not just visual effects), always allot resources for at least five iterations: a place holder, a proxy, a first attempt, a better attempt, and a final, best attempt.

The placeholder attempt only establishes effect presence in the scene and not much else. Because this first version is exceedingly rough, the artist may wish to color it outrageously or employ an obnoxious texture map. Visualizing the first version like this informs the rest of the team the artist is aware of its crudeness and will assuredly correct its appearance before final delivery.

The proxy iteration establishes size, volume, silhouette, and initial speed. Once the general size, shape, and speed of the asset are present, the artist may proceed developing the effect. The proxy is still very rough and may look nothing like the final asset. As long as its scene presence is accounted for, it becomes a valid and live scene entity. Establishing the asset's rough memory footprint is also beneficial to the development team as it allocates the necessary resources for the final effect, assisting other developers to accommodate.

The first attempt is the initial attempt creating a final game asset. The effect should contribute to the minimal viable product of the scene and not much else. Although achieving its desired intention, the asset is still very rough in this stage and is in no way deliverable. This is a "C" level asset.

The better attempt is the first version that not only satisfies its initial requirements but also appears complete enough to release. The asset is at a "B" level or is titled as "CBB," *could be better*. The visual quality can still be improved. However, if the resources (time, money, etc.) were suddenly removed, the product is still in a shippable state. All assets should strive to get to this stage.

The final iteration is the best version the assets can be considering its allotted resources. The effect is now *world-class*. An indication of a well-produced experience is where all assets achieve this level. This is the "A" level. The final product is world-class when all of its assets are world-class.

NO ROADBLOCKS

During the development cycle for any visual effect, it is not uncommon to encounter situations where some effect component, or the entire effect, does not function as intended. This situation is called a roadblock. A visual effects artist must never allow a roadblock to stop progress. No visual effects artist can know all the solutions to all production problems. The resolution to any situation is not a knowledge-based solution but one based on discipline.

The moment a visual effects artist encounters a roadblock, a timer starts. The length of this timer is unique and must be defined by the artist, whether it be 30 minutes, an hour, or an entire day. During that time, the artist does everything within power to resolve the situation. Once the timer is complete, the artists must stop working and seek outside assistance. The source for the consultation can come from anywhere: documentation, other artists, on-line forums, the software manufacturer, web-based articles, and tutorials. When no immediate resolution is found, the artist may insert a proxy object that declares "Working Effect Goes Here!" and begin progress on a different effect. Artists have been rumored to be roadblocked for days, weeks, and even months. This is unacceptable.

Artists may wish to employ the 70% rule. Do not strive to push an effect to 100% completeness during its first attempt. Try to pull away and take a break at the 70% completion point. After the break, it is highly likely the effect will be seen from a new perspective and be completed easily. Designs change quickly in real-time production. It is entirely possible the effect will not need to be driven to 100% completion within a short period of time.

Mentally breaking away from the problem keeps the creative momentum flowing. Many times, the source for the roadblock stems from not a lack of talent and knowledge but from an awkward mental state. External consultation and focusing on different problems shift the artist's mental state. Sometimes this change of perspective results from a simple good night's sleep or a decent meal. When the artist approaches the roadblock from a different mental state, new factors and radical, invisible strategies become apparent and empower the artist to overcome the roadblock. In the unlikely event that the roadblock does halt production, the artist must collaborate with the designers and invent a new effect that skates around or avoids the problem completely. The question is not what to do if roadblocks are encountered, it is what to do when they happen. This is a guarantee. When approached with humble discipline, no roadblock will ever stand in the way of a visual effects artist's progression.

ART BEFORE TECHNOLOGY

Modern visual effects toolsets are loaded with fancy technologies. It is important to remember creating a visual effect to look pleasing and integrating it seamlessly with its environment is more important than the tools used for its generation. Young visual effects artists are often guilty of forgetting this when attempting to impress potential companies with their technical skills. Visual effects artists must be artists first. A visual effect's aesthetic carries more weight than the sophistication employed for its creation. Technology can be taught and transferred from experienced artists more rapidly than artistic skills. When judging art portfolios, experienced artists value eye pleasing, traditional effects over sophisticated, ugly effects. Artists with solid aesthetic foundations have more potential than those without.

VISUAL INTEGRITY

This last rule is far from the least. Visual consistency of the effects in a piece of media must be maintained! Inconsistency translates to incongruent story worlds. The overall impact visual effects have on the audience is measured exclusively on how consistent they are throughout the duration of the media. As projects continue to grow in complexity, this is a hard rule to obey, especially with larger teams. Smaller teams have an easier time communicating and maintaining a level of consistent quality. Larger teams are more challenged. Artists often have different expectations from their leads. A multitude of different effects is more difficult to regulate than just a few. Larger teams often run out of time and money.

Audiences only observe visual effects when they draw attention to themselves. (Of course, there are few experiences which are intentionally outrageous!) When presented effectively, visual effects complement the story as integral story world components. The audience defers asking, "Wow! How did they do that?" until after the experience. Regretfully, attention to visual effects is generated from contrast in visual quality. Without consistency, the audience asks questions. They feel taken advantage of. When an experience has mostly great visual effects and a few that are less than outstanding, the audience asks, "Why are they, (the developers), not delivering? I feel ripped off!" A single outstanding visual effect in a mediocre film demands audience attention. Audiences ask, "Why didn't they spread the VFX budget over the entire film?"

Modern audiences are sophisticated and somewhat unimpressionable. They now expect to see the unexpected. The novelty of visual effects has worn off. All that is left are consistent story world experiences. Unless studied in computer graphics or visual effects, audiences do not understand the hard work required to create them. Audiences never notice poor visual effects until there are better ones displayed in the same experience. Visual effects artists exhaust themselves to create memorable visual effects. They also need to strive just as hard to maintain consistency.

CONCLUSION

The rules in this chapter are not necessarily listed in order of precedence but flow logically. No two careers are the same and luckily, no two artists think the same. The relevancy of each rule should be examined by each artist before taken to heart. They are basic guidelines artists should consider as they embark on a very challenging yet rewarding career.

INTRODUCTION

In Chapter 2 of this book, one of the primary rules of visual effects states any visual effect MUST integrate within its environment. Shadows are a big part of proper integration and they can be achieved with clever software and a few extra character components. What is more challenging and taxes the artistic skill of the visual effects artist is the ability to perfectly match the lighting of an effect's environment and render its components such that they visually integrate within the scene. Perfectly matching the colors of the environment is a crucial first task to such integrations. To understand how to match colors, some color theory must be explored as a fundamental skill set required to assemble a proper amalgamation of color mixtures.

By traditional standards, color theory is a set of practical guidelines, which not only explains how color is represented but also how colors interact with each other. This chapter, however, dives deeper than the introduction of color wheels, primary, secondary, and tertiary colors, and explores the mathematical constraints of representing proper colors on modern display devices and explains the necessary and proper treatment of colors to combine them realistically. In other words, without an essential understanding of color theory, good looking visual effects are hard to achieve. There isn't enough post-processing power available to make poorly rendered visual effects look like they belong in their environment. Poorly rendered effects appear visually off: their colors are not as crisp as they need to be, their contrasts not as sharp, and their gradients not as smooth. The purpose of this chapter is not to chastise the visual effects community for generating poorly rendered effects but provide a set of guidelines and best practices which will help identify good visual effects artists from the great.

As in traditional Color Theory, this chapter begins with a description of what color is and how human beings perceive it. The mathematical representation of color is then discussed to expose the limitations of digitally representing color. These limitations are considered when exploring the question, "Can Photo-Realism exist?" They are also considered when explaining the proper way of handling essential color combination techniques. Properly combining colors are not only essential for rendering new and interesting layers of color but also integrating them into pre-existing scenes.

COLOR IN REALITY

We humans define our reality by our five senses. For most of us, our dominant sense is vision. Light is required for any vision to occur. Light is purely the presence of electromagnetic energy which vibrates roughly between 400 and 700 nm and a frequency range between 430 and 750 THz. It is special as it behaves as a wave and as a particle. During the daytime, this electromagnetic radiation from the sun literally fills the volume of our reality as light enters and continuously bounces off objects until the energy is depleted. During the night, when the sun's electromagnetic energy is not present, we humans are not able to visibly perceive those objects. The objects are still there, we are just unable to see them. The physical objects of reality exist with or without the presence of light. We, as humans, prefer seeing them instead of relying on just touch, smell, and possibly taste (Figure 3.1).

We cannot see light until it bounces off objects. During every collision, some of the particle aspects of light, called photons, are absorbed into the object's surface while others are reflected. As part of the light is absorbed into an object's surface, some of the visible light's energy is lost as heat. The remaining photons bounce, and we can see them. They enter through the outermost part of the human eye, called the cornea, and are bent toward the pupil which controls the amount of light that hits the lens. The lens then focuses the remaining photons on a layer of nerve cells in the back of our eye called the retina. The nerve cells of the retina are sensitive to the photons of light that hit them (Figure 3.2).

DOI: 10.1201/9781003009795-4

FIGURE 3.1 Reality with or without light.

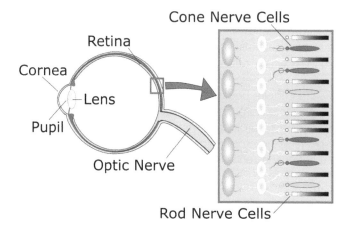

FIGURE 3.2 The human eye.

The retina has two kinds of nerve cells that react to electromagnetic radiation: rods and cones. Rods only have one photopigment in them thus are used to measure brightness. There are roughly 110 million rods in each human eye. Cones are used to measure color. There are roughly 6 million cones in each human eye, each with three photopigments. The "Short" photopigments are sensitive to wavelengths close to 420 nm or the "blue" colors. The Medium photopigments pick up wavelengths around 530 nm, and the "green" colors and the long photopigments are sensitive to the 560 nm wavelengths or the "red" colors (Figure 3.3).

These three photopigments in our retinas allow us humans to perceive approximately 10 million different colors. This number of colors may seem adequate but does not sample the entire light spectrum equally. Shorter wavelengths in the 10–400 nm range make up the ultraviolet spectrum and longer wavelengths, in the 700 nm–1 mm range, constitute the infrared. Certain animals, such as the Bluebottle Butterfly and the Mantis Shrimp, have more than three types of photopigment receptors that not only allow them to see more variation of visible light but also into the ultraviolet and infrared spectrums. While they may have more types of photoreceptors, the scarcity of these receptors prevents them from observing these alternative colors with any real fidelity.

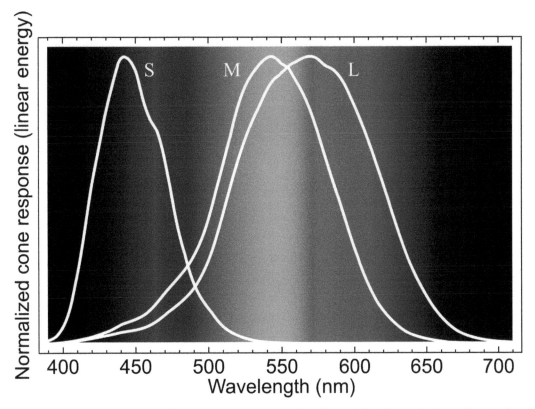

FIGURE 3.3 Photopigment wavelengths. (Modified from https://commons.wikimedia.org/wiki/File:Cone-fundamentals-with-srgb-spectrum.svg.)

REPRESENTATION OF COLOR

Pure light is called white light. White light is the summation of all reflected colors or the color of light with no colors removed. There are multiple ways of representing color depending upon the context with which we observe them.

RGB Color

Additive colors are considered as "pure" colors which sum to form white light. They are represented by amounts of blue, green, and red colors, corresponding to the short, medium, and long wavelength receptors in our eyes. Because additive colors are represented by amounts of red, green, and blue, they are called RGB colors. RGB is the color language of computer graphics since monitors and all other visual display devices are light emitting objects. All objects, represented in a visual display device must be represented in red, green, and blue values (Figure 3.4).

Typically, RGB color is represented by three 8-bit values, which is known as 24-bit RGB color or "True Color." Each color is represented by 8 bits of data or 256 values $(2^8 = 256)$. Three channels of 8-bit color, or 24 bits total, represents over 16 million colors (Figure 3.5).

24-Bit color Spectrum = $R * G * B$

$= (2^8) * (2^8) * (2^8)$

$= 256 * 256 * 256$

$= 16,777,216$

8-Bit Color Spectrum has 16,777,216 potential colors

RGB

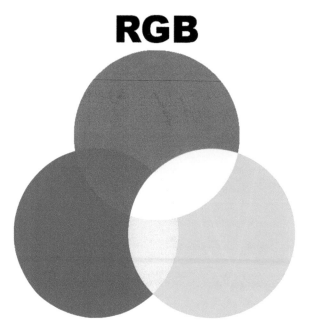

FIGURE 3.4 RGB color.

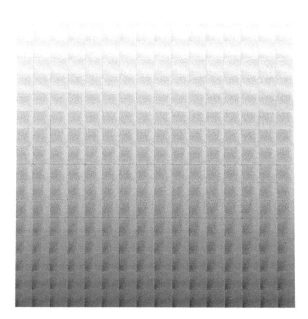

FIGURE 3.5 All 16,777,216 colors.

CMYK Color

Subtractive colors are "impure" as they represent white light after reflecting off a surface, where some of the light is absorbed while the rest is reflected. A red object looks red because its surface absorbs all white light and reflects only the red. Subtractive colors are represented by yellow, magenta, and cyan since these are the reflecting colors after white light bounces off a surface and the primary colors, blue, green, and red, respectively, have been absorbed (Figure 3.6).

CMY

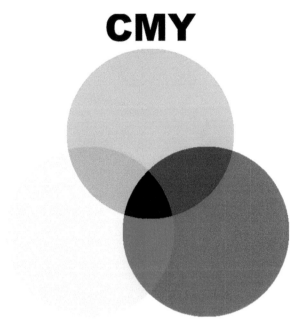

FIGURE 3.6 CMY color.

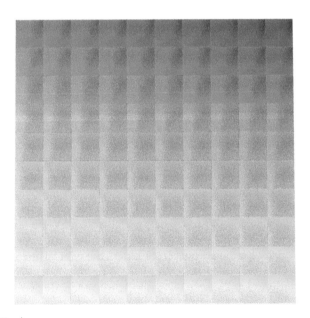

FIGURE 3.7 Appearance of CMY color.

Cyan results from the absorption of red light and the reflection of green and blue. Magenta is the result when green light is absorbed, and red and blue lights are reflected. Yellow is the result after blue is absorbed and red and green are reflected (Figure 3.7).

The color of all physical objects that do not emit light is represented by CMY values. Regretfully, the mixing of CMY colors is a bit tricky since impurities of pigments, when mixing cyan, magenta, and yellow to get black, tend to cause black colors to look brown. To avoid this phenomenon, people who create and mix colors for a living, such as printers, have a fourth color, black, which is represented by the letter, "K," which stands for "key."

TABLE 3.1 RGB and CMYK Colors

Color	Color Name	(R, G, B)	(C, M, Y, K)
⬛	Black	(0, 0, 0)	(0, 0, 0, 1)
⬜	White	(255, 255, 255)	(0, 0, 0, 0)
⬛	Red	(255, 0, 0)	(0, 1, 1, 0)
⬜	Green	(0, 255, 0)	(1, 0, 1, 0)
⬛	Blue	(0, 0, 255)	(1, 1, 0, 0)
⬜	Yellow	(255, 255, 0)	(0, 0, 1, 0)
⬛	Magenta	(255, 0, 255)	(0, 1, 0, 0)
⬜	Cyan	(0, 255, 255)	(1, 0, 0, 0)

Therefore, subtractive color is represented by four values, CMYK. Typically, each channel of CMYK color is represented as a percentage or a value between 0 and 100, or between 0 and 1 (Table 3.1).

HSV and HSL Color

HSV color and its cousin, HSL color, are alternative color representations to RGB. Designed in the 1970s, they were created to more closely model human color response. HSV stands for hue, saturation, and value. HSL stands for hue, saturation, and lightness. Instead of the traditional orthogonal axes of X, Y, and Z, both representations correspond to cylinders defined by circular angle, radius, and height. The circular angle, or Hue, starts at red primary at 0°, passes through green primary at 120°, blue primary at 240°, and then wraps back to red at 360°. The pure fully saturated primary colors of red, yellow, green, cyan, blue, and magenta are arranged along the perimeter of the cylinder. The center core of the cylinder consists of the chromatic removal of color or the neutral gray colors. The radius of the cylinder, or saturation, represents the amount of chroma ranging from 0, or pure gray, to a value of 1, or full color. The height of the cylinder center axis ranges from black, (0.0), to white, (1.0). Height is the dimension where these two models differ. In HSV, the value represents the height of the cylinder where 0.0 corresponds to black on the bottom and 1.0 corresponds to full color on top. In HSL, light also represents the height of the cylinder starting at 0.0, or black, but with full color manifesting at 0.5 lightness and pure white at lightness of 1.0. In both models, the mixing toward black, creates shades of color but does not change saturation. In HSV, the tinting of color with white affects saturation. Tinting with white does not affect saturation in HSL (Figure 3.8 and Table 3.2).

Because the values of Hue are represented in angles of a repeating circle instead of distances in a non-repeating range of colors, HSV and HSL colors are awkward to mix and blend and difficult to perform mathematical operations. However, in real-time visual effects, the cyclical behavior makes them very useful in the generation of random colors. When RGB colors are randomized, each red, green, and blue channel must be randomized independently resulting in unequal distributions of colors with respect to saturation and value (or lightness). Essentially the colors do not look integrated. By only randomizing the hue in HSV (or HSL) colors and limiting the variations in saturation and value (or lightness), the resulting colors tend to be homogeneous with smooth distributions over their full spectrum. In other words, the resulting colors appear to integrate more naturally and are easier to manipulate (Figure 3.9).

HSV   HSL

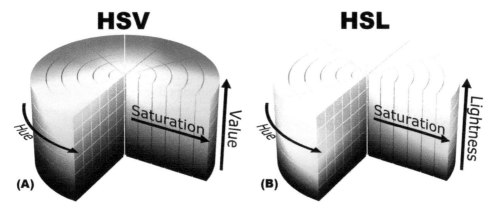

FIGURE 3.8 HSV and HSL color cylinders. ((A) Modified from Shark D [CC BY-SA 3.0 (https://creativecommons.org/licenses/by-sa/3.0)], (B) from Shark D [CC BY-SA 3.0 (https://creativecommons.org/licenses/by-sa/3.0)].)

TABLE 3.2 HSV and HSL Color

Color	Color Name	(H, S, V)	(H, S, L)
	Black	(*, *, 0)	(*, *, 0)
	White	(*, 0, 1)	(*, *, 1)
	Red	(0°, 1, 1)	(0°, 1, 0.5)
	Yellow	(60°, 1, 1)	(60°, 1, 0.5)
	Green	(120°, 1, 1)	(120°, 1, 0.5)
	Cyan	(180°, 1, 1)	(180°, 1, 0.5)
	Blue	(240°, 1, 1)	(240°, 1, 0.5)
	Magenta	(300°, 1, 1)	(300°, 1, 0.5)

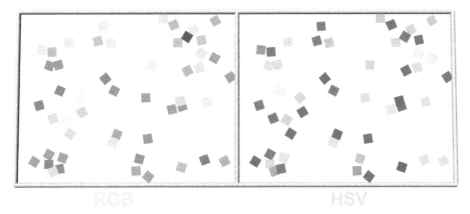

FIGURE 3.9 Random colors; HSV versus RGB.

Other Color Models

There are other color models which may have once been used for image processing but are now rare in real-time visual effects. These models are based on or are loosely like the YUV encoding system. This system was created to help integrate color information with black and white analog television signals. The YUV system was used for the European PAL composite signal. Y corresponds to the luma component or the brightness, which was already transmitted as the black and white television signal. U and V correspond to the X and Y axes, respectively, of the UV color plane where red is represented in the upper left corner, green in the lower left, blue in the lower right, and magenta in the upper right (Figures 3.10 and 3.11).

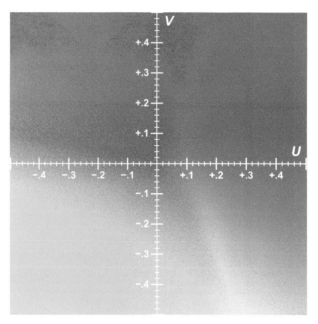

FIGURE 3.10 U–V color plane where Y=0.5 (Modified from user: Tonyle. CC BY-SA 3.0, http://creativecommons.org/licenses/by-sa/3.0/.)

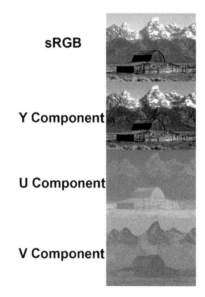

FIGURE 3.11 An RGB image with its Y, U, and V components. (Modified from User: Brianski [Public domain].)

YIQ, a derivation of the YUV system, is used for the NTSC color TV system. This format was popular for certain color image processing techniques such as increasing global contrast. When applied to RGB images the color balance integrity is altered. When applied to YIQ images, only the brightness levels of the image are adjusted. The three components of YIQ correspond to luminance, Y, and two different chrominance channels, I and Q. The I channel corresponds to the orange and blue spectrum and the Q corresponds to the purple and green. The IQ color plane is like the UV plane except rotated 33° and the red and blue channels swapped (Figures 3.12 and 3.13).

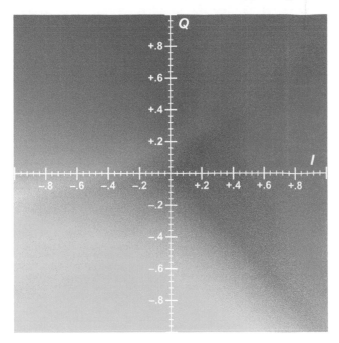

FIGURE 3.12 The YIQ color space at Y=0.5 (Modified from user: Tonyle. CC BY-SA 3.0. http://creativecommons.org/licenses/by-sa/3.0/.)

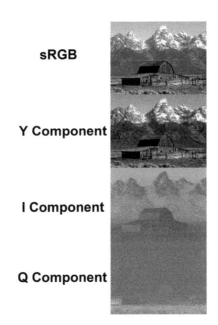

FIGURE 3.13 An RGB image with its Y, I, and Q components. (Modified from Tokachu at English Wikipedia [CC BY-SA 3.0 (http://creativecommons.org/licenses/by-sa/3.0/)].)

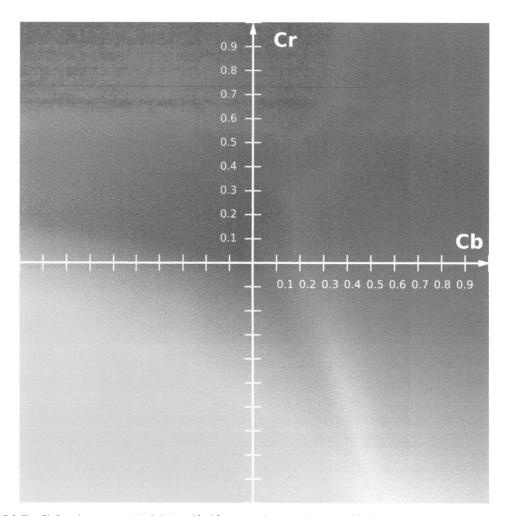

FIGURE 3.14 The CbCr color space at $Y'=0.5$. (Modified from user: Simon A. Eugster [Public domain].)

YCbCr is a system very similar to YUV but used primarily for digital encoding that is found in MPEG, JPEG, and HDMI formats. Like YUV, the Y information corresponds to luma or image brightness and Cb and Cr channels correspond to the same axes of the UV color space. While both systems sample from the same color space, the calculations for chrominance in Cr and Cr are more suited for digital representation than the UV analog system (Figures 3.14 and 3.15).

GAMUT

Not all visual display devices are created equally. In fact, it is often quite difficult to keep multiple devices of the same make and model displaying the same image at the same time (Figure 3.16).

Although it is a never-ending task, it is the job of the colorist or the color engineer to calibrate each display device in a facility to a common standard. That standard is known as a gamut. Since no current device can display the full-color extent as seen by the human eye, any device can only display a portion or subset of the full range of visible color. Gamut is the subset of colors which can be accurately represented in a specific circumstance with given color space and display device. Typically drawn against the CIE 1931 chromaticity diagram, gamut is represented as a triangular footprint covering a subset of full-color space.

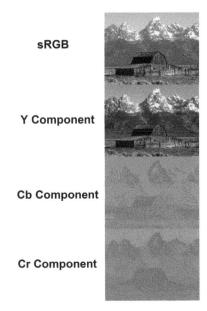

sRGB

Y Component

Cb Component

Cr Component

FIGURE 3.15 An RGB image with its Y, Cb, and Cr components. (Modified from Mike1024 [Public domain].)

FIGURE 3.16 An image displayed in both RGB and CMYK color spaces. (Modified from original Image by Pierre Blanche [Creative Commons Zero License].)

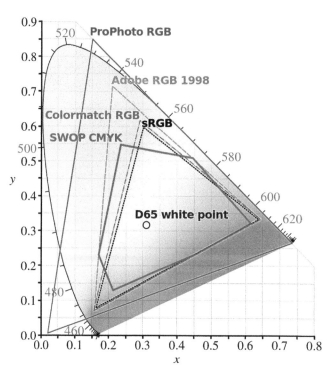

FIGURE 3.17 Adobe RGB versus sRGB gamuts within CIE 1931. (Modified from users: BenRG and cmglee - CIE1931xy blank.svg, CC BY-SA 3.0, https://commons.wikimedia.org/w/index.php?curid=32158329.)

Figure 3.17 displays the gamuts of several common color spaces including standard RGB (sRGB), drawn as a dotted black line, and SWOP CMYK, drawn as a solid magenta line. While capturing 90% of the extent of human vision, ProPhoto RGB color space has the widest gamut and is much wider than home video or sRGB. A monochrome display device is a one-dimensional curve through color space.

IS "PHOTO-REAL" ACHIEVABLE?

Since video display devices share a gamut which is narrower than photo color space, a question arises, "Can photo-real images be displayed in real-time video display devices?" To answer "yes" to this question, three other conditions must be satisfied first:

1. Does the capture of light result in a digital image whose numerical values represent the relative light levels that were present at the time of sampling?

2. Does the producer of the synthetic images, a renderer, generate images whose pixel values are proportional to what natural light would do?

3. Does the final display device accurately turn the image back into light?

The answer to condition 2 is, "Yes." Modern real-time, physically based rendering (PBR) engines with integrated ray tracing can generate pixels, which closely represent the natural behavior of light.

The answer to condition 1 is, "Maybe." While photos can capture 90% of the extent of human vision, the full spectrum cannot be fully represented. If the ProPhoto RGB color space represents the widest gamut achievable by a sampling device, then it possibly defines what is understood to be "Photo-real."

Regretfully, the answer to condition 3 is a definite, "No." Real-time rendering engines can only render to sRGB display devices. Since sRGB has a relatively narrow gamut compared to ProPhoto and the full CIE1931 color spaces, no modern display device can ever turn the rendered image back into what is defined or understood as real light.

Even though photo-realism cannot be technically achieved, does it really matter? Within the context of real-time visual effects, Photo-realism may not be relevant. Real-time display devices are convenient, portable, and relatively easy to manipulate. They are not intended to be placed in a side-by-side comparison against naked, visible reality. Whenever anything real is sampled, it must be stored in some format which is smaller than the extent of human vision. Modern, real-time renderers can produce images which replicate the physical nature of light. When the sampled photo-real imagery is displayed on the same limited display devices as the fabricated imagery, then the ability to duplicate physical reality becomes irrelevant.

LINEAR COLOR

Light Emission versus Perceptual Brightness

Figure 3.18 represents 32 bars of grayscale spanning from pure black to perfect white. The difference in the amount of emitted light between any two bars is constant. Figure 3.19 also represents 32 bars of grayscale spanning from black to white but in a smooth, linear gradation. Even though the gradation of the bars is perceived as linear, the difference in the amount of light between any two bars is anything but. The reason for this discrepancy is that the human eye does not respond to light intensity in a smooth, linear fashion. Vision, like all human sensory perception, follows a power law relationship between the magnitude of the stimulus and its perceived intensity. This relationship has a profound impact on how light is digitally stored and displayed.

Gamma versus Linear Color

As demonstrated in the Gamut section of this chapter, not all sampling and display devices are created equally. It is very difficult to get similar display devices to display similar images consistently. No current display device, or sampling device, can duplicate the full range of human vision. To make the situation a bit murkier, humans do not perceive light linearly. As demonstrated in Figure 3.18, when light is displayed nominally, in a linear manner, there appear to be large gaps in the black end of the scale and an over-emphasis of white values on the opposite end of the spectrum. To display a smooth, even spaced grayscale, the linear color space must be "bent" to fit

FIGURE 3.18 Nominal physical light intensity.

FIGURE 3.19 Perceptual brightness light intensity.

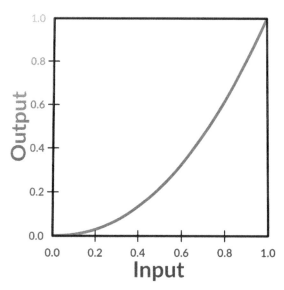

FIGURE 3.20 Graph converting linear light to smooth light.

within the same numerical range. In mathematical terms, there is a power law relationship between nominal (or linear), physical light intensity, and perceptual brightness. To fit or bend linear white light into smooth white light, a two-step process must be applied (Figure 3.20):

1. All 8-bit light input values must be converted to a range between 0.0 and 1.0. Light values between 0 and 255 will not convert properly.

2. The light values must be taken to the $\frac{1}{2.2}$ power.

Smooth Light = Linear Light$^{\frac{1}{2.2}}$

Equation 3.1 Conversion of Linear Light to Smooth Light

Visible white light is said to have a gamma value of 1.0. Once Linear Light has gone through the conversion it is said to be "Gamma Corrected," residing in what is known as "Gamma Space" and has a gamma value of 2.2.

Individual red, green, and blue components comprising white light must be converted in the same manner. Even though the human eye responds differently to each component, the conversion for each is the same. Colored light which has been Gamma corrected is labeled as sRGB color. All consumer electronic devices convert and store their color values in sRGB, Gamma corrected color space. This is done because human vision perceives linear lights as being "too dark" and "incorrect." Gamma corrected light appears "normal." Consumer devices convert white light to sRGB following a standard 2.2 gamma but with one slight deviation. The curves have a very short linear segment in the darkest end of the black spectrum to prevent a slope of infinity at a value of 0.0. Not dealing with the infinite slope makes for easier numeric calculations.

This linear segment is very small and should not be considered when converting color values by hand. Since the formula for this segment is beyond the scope of this book and electronic devices deal with the conversion automatically, a gamma conversion of 2.2 is all that is required.

The process of converting from linear space to sRGB or gamma space is called Gamma Encoding.

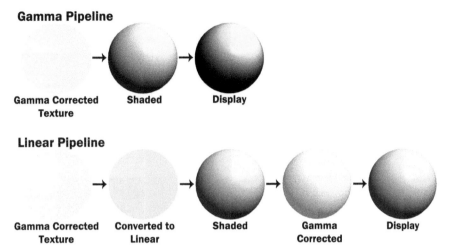

FIGURE 3.21 Linear and gamma rendering pipelines.

$$Light_{Encoded} = pow\left(Light_{linear}, \frac{1}{Gamma}\right)$$

Equation 3.2 Gamma Encoding

The process of converting from gamma space back to linear is called Gamma Decoding.

$$Light_{Linear} = pow\left(Light_{Encoded}, Gamma\right)$$

Equation 3.3 Gamma Decoding

The value of Gamma for both equations 3.2 and 3.3, is 2.2. Luckily for technical artists, the encoding and decoding of perceived colors are handled natively by the GPU and display devices.

Figure 3.21 displays the results of the actual Linear rendering pipeline and the hypothetical Gamma rendering pipeline. Both pipelines start with sRGB colors. The Gamma pipeline proceeds immediately to shading where the Linear removes the Gamma correction before. The Linear pipeline applies Gamma correction after shading. Since all display devices remove the Gamma correction, the displayed Gamma pipeline image appears too dark while the linear pipeline appears natural.

Regretfully, not converting colors before rendering or not being aware of the duality of Linear versus Gamma color presents some very tricky problems. The first problem is that the color represented in sRGB space does not manipulate as expected. The addition and multiplication of sRGB color may produce unpredictable results to an untrained artist. For example, if an art director desires an artist to create an object in a scene that appears to be 50% gray, the artist will need to give that object a white value of approximately 0.218. While 0.218 may not be a logical value for 50% gray, when the game engine renders this object, it will convert it to linear space and will appear as 50% gray.

$$50\% \, Grey = pow\left(0.218, \frac{1}{2.2}\right) = 0.50$$

Equation 3.4 50% Gray in sRGB

Suppose two game characters each have a different colored flashlight, one of medium magenta $(0.0, 0.5, 0.5)$, and one of medium yellow $(0.5, 0.5, 0.0)$. When the two characters cross their flashlight cones, the expected

FIGURE 3.22 For each image pair, the top image is interpolated in linear color space while the bottom is interpolated in sRGB.

result is supposed to be bright green. However, the result is something that looks gray, muddy, and only slightly green. The reason for this behavior is the result of the incorrect addition of sRGB colors. When the game engine converts the two flashlights, the linear magenta and yellow colors are $(0.0, 0.218, 0.218)$ and $(0.218, 0.218, 0.0)$, respectively. After the renderer adds the two colors, the sum is $(0.218, 0.436, 0.218)$. When the result is converted back to sRGB color, the color of the two crossed flashlights is $(0.5, 0.69, 0.5)$, which appears as a greenish-gray color.

Games which deal with recognizable/pantone colors, such as sports teams, must be aware of this linear color phenomenon, and intentionally convert all colors to linear color space before submitting to the rendering engine. When the colors are not converted to linear color space before rendering, the results will not match those pantone colors. Working without understanding of sRGB and linear color space will probably not ruin a final product. However, there may be just enough loss of visual fidelity to make it very difficult for an artist to understand the source of the problem and just enough for the participant to observe, "something is off with the color."

Aside from incorrect color manipulations, working improperly in sRGB color space may result in another undesirable phenomenon. Performing gradient interpolation on sRGB colors may yield unrealistic results such as appearing darker and more saturated than intended. In some situations, this may be desirable. When interpolated gradient values are used without proper linear conversion, the colors cannot be combined properly (Figure 3.22).

Similarly, in certain gamma-incorrect drawing programs, the use of soft brushes can result in strange, dark transition bands with certain vivid color combinations (Figure 3.23).

Working properly with linear and gamma correct sRGB is crucially important when dealing with Physically Based Rendering (PBR). Of the myriad of problems that can occur, there are two that occur more frequently:

1. Performing calculations correctly in linear color space and neglecting to convert them to sRGB before displaying.
2. Failing to convert sRGB textures to linear color space before performing calculations.

Any combination of these two errors will inevitably result in images with incorrect falloff, overblown highlights, and unpredictable hue and saturation shifts. Gamma incorrectness is also the culprit for many renderers outputting that, "fake, plastic, CGI look." Skin tones are almost impossible to recreate without a proper gamma-correct

FIGURE 3.23 Left drawing with correct gamma, the right without.

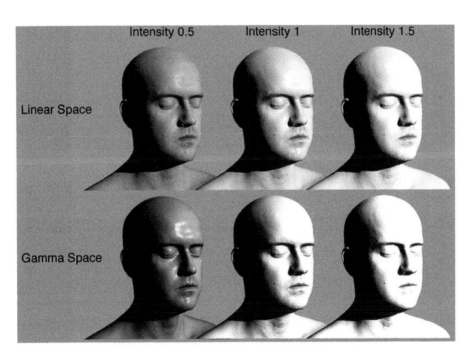

FIGURE 3.24 SkinTone reproduced with gamma-correct and incorrect textures. (Infinite 3D Head Scan by Lee Perry-Smith, licensed under a Creative Commons Attribution 3.0 Unported License (available from www.ir-ltd.net).)

workflow. Skin tones tend to appear waxy and lifeless, further widening the "Uncanny Valley" and blowing out in bright lights (Figure 3.24).

When textures and recognizable colors are input to the rendering engine and displayed on electronic devices without manipulation, the gamma encoding and decoding are imperceptible. For modern, real-time graphics production, this is an unreal possibility. To properly input recognizable colors into the rendering engine, the following three steps must be followed:

1. Each color must be decoded to linear color space by taking it to the 2.2 power. Equation 3.3.

2. The rendering engine calculates and blends colors to produce the final image.

3. The final image is re-encoded back to gamma color space by taking it to the $\frac{1}{2.2}$ power. Equation 3.2

Most display devices and GPU graphics cards perform these operations automatically. Some, but not all software, perform these conversions under certain conditions. Each rendering engine has its own peculiar behavior, and a technical artist cannot afford to assume the conversion is handled correctly by default. It is the responsibility of the technical artist to discuss with the technical director how the renderer deals with gamma-encoded colors and then must advise on suitable alterations to the graphics pipeline to deal with them properly. Thorough testing must be performed during the pre-production stage of game development to test and verify correct color handling. While the rendering pipeline cannot be assumed to handle linear color space correctly, there are two assumptions that can be made about most modern rendering engines:

1. All base colors are inputted in sRGB color space.

2. All grayscale gradients such as metal masks, roughness masks, and displacement maps, are in linear color space.

Adhering to these conventions, maintaining proper communication with the technical director and thorough testing will help ensure the rendering pipeline to be 100% gamma correct.

Calibration

Games making the conversion to gamma-correct color space in the middle of the production cycle may find themselves lost in color space where their photo-real textures reside. Different camera sampling under different lighting conditions provides an impossible task for artists to understand the accuracy of their color textures. To prevent confusion and ensure that all textures reside with a homogeneous color space, the textures must be calibrated. Proper texture calibration requires the technical artist to use a photographic color checker (called a Macbeth Chart), with every capture device and every lighting setup (Figure 2.25).

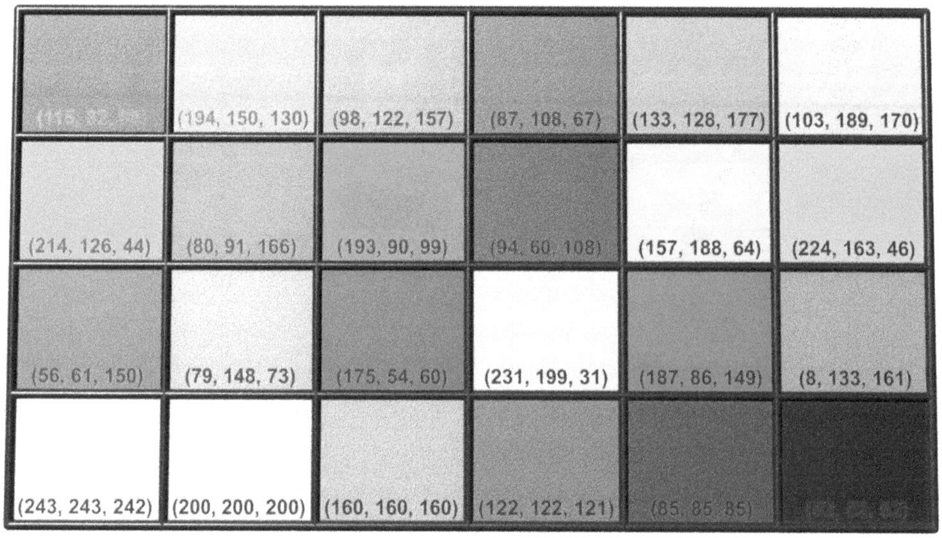

FIGURE 3.25 MacBeth chart with sRGB values.

FIGURE 3.26 Person holding a photographic color checker.

To perform a proper texture color calibration, the Technical Artist must perform the following operations for every lighting setup:

1. Capture one image sample for each lighting setup. That image must contain a photographic color checker as shown in Figure 3.26.

2. After the capture session, import the image with the color checker image into an image manipulation DCC.

3. Convert the image to linear color space.

4. Perform adjustments to the image such that each color swatch numerically matches its target value, as listed in Figure 3.25.

5. Convert the texture back to sRGB color space.

6. Apply the same corrective operations applied to the image containing the photographic color checker to all other images captured during the lighting setup.

After all images from the unique lighting setup have been conditioned with the same operations as the color checker image, all the images and textures, will reside in the proper balanced color space. The artist can then be confident that all textures have been calibrated to one homogenous color space.

BASIC COLOR BLENDING

Colors are the fundamental building blocks for all visual effects. Contrary to popular belief, there are multiple methods for blending color pairs and each technique has a dramatic and unique impact on the resulting image. Many artists claim to be able to blend colors in their head. Realistically, very few can (for example, what is Yellow plus Magenta?). Blending colors is a challenging task for anyone to do in their head and is why we use computers to do the job. Regardless of mental or computationally assisted blending, understanding how to blend colors is crucial for achieving predictable results. There are few operations that can be performed on colors. Familiarity with these techniques will empower the digital artist to produce more consistent results.

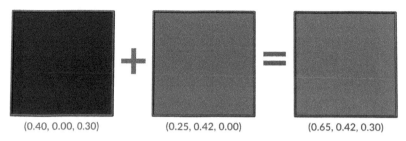

(0.40, 0.00, 0.30)   (0.25, 0.42, 0.00)   (0.65, 0.42, 0.30)

FIGURE 3.27 Color Addition.

Before performing any color blending operations, ensure the initial colors are in linear color space. In other words, before doing any operations on any colors, transform them from sRGB to linear color space. After the operations, transform them back to sRGB color space. As explained in the Linear Color section, all colors must be in linear color space to correctly perform any numerical (blending) operation.

Addition (Color Sum)

Addition is used to brighten source colors. Adding the individual components of a new image to the components of a base image will result in the lightning effect of the base image. The result of the sum of each component must be clamped at 1.0. The resulting image has no component value brighter than 1.0 (Figure 3.27).

Image C = Image A + Image B

Image C_r = Image A_r + Image B_r

Image C_g = Image A_g + Image B_g

Image C_b = Image A_b + Image B_b

Equation 3.5 Addition of Colors

The color addition operation is "Commutative" or in other words, can be performed in both directions.

Image A + Image B = Image B + Image A

Equation 3.6 Commutative Color Addition

Subtraction

Subtraction is used to darken source color. Subtracting the individual components of a new image from the components of a base image will result in the darkening effect of the base image. The result of the subtraction of each component must be clamped at 0.0. The resulting image has no color component less than 0.0 (Figure 3.28).

Image C = Image B − Image A

Image C_r = Image B_r − Image A_r

Image C_g = Image B_g − Image A_g

Image C_b = Image B_b − Image A_b

Equation 3.7 Subtraction of Colors

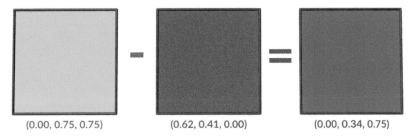

(0.00, 0.75, 0.75) (0.62, 0.41, 0.00) (0.00, 0.34, 0.75)

FIGURE 3.28 Color Subtraction.

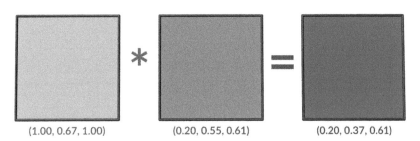

(1.00, 0.67, 1.00) (0.20, 0.55, 0.61) (0.20, 0.37, 0.61)

FIGURE 3.29 Color Multiplication.

The color subtraction operation is *not* a "Commutative" or in other words, the order of the operation has a significant impact on the result.

Image B – Image A ≠ Image A – Image B

Equation 3.8 Color Subtraction Is Not Commutative

Multiplication (Color Product)

Like subtraction, multiplication is used to darken the source image. Multiplying the individual components of a new image against the components of a base image will result in the darkening effects on the base image. The difference between multiplication and subtraction is that the multiplication result will never exceed the clamping range of 0.0 and 1.0. When an sRGB color is transformed to linear color space, the values are no longer between 0 and 255 but between 0.0 and 1.0. Since two positive values can never multiply against each other and result in a negative number, no product of two colors will ever need to be clamped. Never clamping the product of two colors results in a smoother gradation to black than color difference (Figure 3.29).

Image C = Image A * Image B

Image C_r = Image A_r * Image B_r

Image C_g = Image A_g * Image B_g

Image C_b = Image A_b * Image B_b

Equation 3.9 Multiplication of Colors

Unlike color subtraction, color multiplication is "Commutative;" the operation can be performed in both directions.

Image A * Image B = Image B * Image A

Equation 3.10 Commutativity of Color Multiplication

Division (Color Difference)

Like addition, division is used to lighten source images. While the quotient of the division will never be smaller than 0.0, it is relatively easy to compute a quotient larger than 1.0 when the new color is less bright (smaller in component value) than the base image. When the quotient of a component division exceeds 1.0, the result is clamped at 1.0.

Image C = Image B / Image A

Image C_r = Image B_r / Image A_r

Image C_g = Image B_g / Image A_g

Image C_b = Image B_b / Image A_b

Equation 3.11 Division of Colors

For example, if the base color has a value of (0.67, 0.75, 0.62) and the new color has a value (0.2, 0.2, 0.2), the resulting quotient is pure white with a value (1.0, 1.0, 1.0), since the results are clamped at 1.0. Great care must be taken when employing division to lighten an image. The new color should be a level of gray greater than the intensity, of the base color to avoid any clamping (Figure 3.30).

Like color subtraction, color division is *not* "Commutative;" the operation cannot be performed in both directions.

Image B / Image A ≠ Image A / Image B

Equation 3.12 Color Division Is Not Commutative

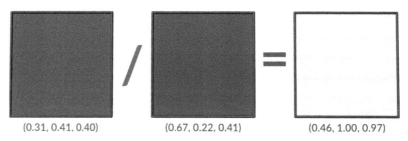

(0.31, 0.41, 0.40)   (0.67, 0.22, 0.41)   (0.46, 1.00, 0.97)

FIGURE 3.30 Color Division.

Color division is also used for removing color tint (the color of image A) from the source image (the color of image B). As the brightness of the new image approaches and surpasses the lightness of the old image, the result approaches a pure white value (Figure 3.31).

Power

Raising the power of an image will either darken or brighten the image depending on the value of the exponent. This operation does not affect the result in a linear fashion. Exponents smaller than 1.0 will brighten the source image as it pushes brighter values toward white. Similarly, values larger than 1.0 will darken the source image as it pushes darker values toward black. Not only is power used to lighten or darken an image, but it is also used to shift or enlarge the image's white or black point depending on the distance from 1.0; the further from 1.0, the larger the white or black point (Figures 3.32 and 3.33).

From equation 3.2, the power operation with an exponent of $\frac{1}{2.2}$ is used to encode visible light to sRGB color space. The resulting image is pushed toward a slower gradation from black and a faster transition to white (Figure 3.34).

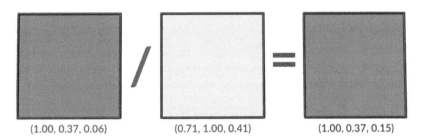

(1.00, 0.37, 0.06)   (0.71, 1.00, 0.41)   (1.00, 0.37, 0.15)

FIGURE 3.31 Removing color tint by division.

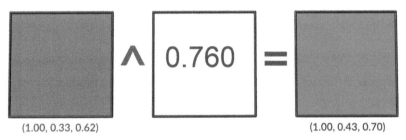

(1.00, 0.33, 0.62)   (1.00, 0.43, 0.70)

FIGURE 3.32 Effects of power with exponents less than 1.0.

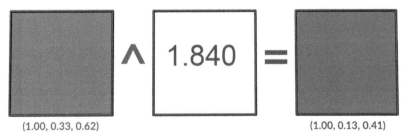

(1.00, 0.33, 0.62)   (1.00, 0.13, 0.41)

FIGURE 3.33 Effects of power with exponents greater than 1.0.

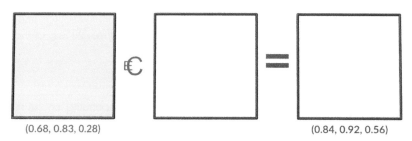

(0.68, 0.83, 0.28)   (0.84, 0.92, 0.56)

FIGURE 3.34 Color encoding.

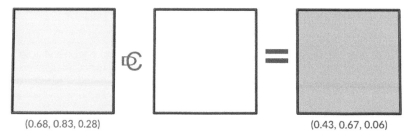

(0.68, 0.83, 0.28)   (0.43, 0.67, 0.06)

FIGURE 3.35 Color decoding.

From equation 3.3, the power exponent of 2.2 is used to decode sRGB colors to linear color space. This resulting image is pushed toward a smoother gradation to white and a faster transition from black (Figure 3.35).

Dodge

Dodging is the formal name for lightening an image. Named after the photographic process performed in the darkroom, Dodging lightens an image by burning its negative. The photographer blocks areas of an image during exposure and the areas of reduced exposure lighten the resulting image. Mathematically, the dodge operation increases the contrast of the image in areas where the result is not clamped. There are three Dodge operations that can be applied: screen, color dodge, and linear dodge:

Screen

Screen operation inverses both images, multiplies them, and then inverts the product (Figure 3.36).

$$screen = \frac{1}{\left(\frac{1}{A} \star \frac{1}{B}\right)}$$

Equation 3.13 Screen Dodge

Color Dodge

The Color Dodge operation divides the second image by the inverse of the first image (Figure 3.37).

$$Color\ Dodge = \frac{A}{\left(\frac{1}{B}\right)}$$

Equation 3.14 Color Dodge

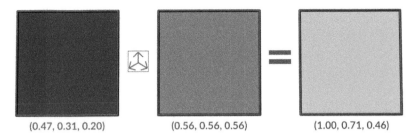

(0.47, 0.31, 0.20)   (0.56, 0.56, 0.56)   (1.00, 0.71, 0.46)

FIGURE 3.36 Screen dodge.

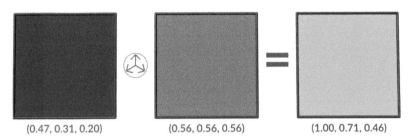

(0.47, 0.31, 0.20)   (0.56, 0.56, 0.56)   (1.00, 0.71, 0.46)

FIGURE 3.37 Color dodge.

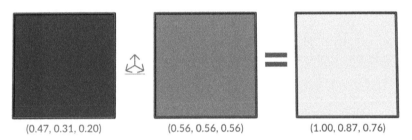

(0.47, 0.31, 0.20)   (0.56, 0.56, 0.56)   (1.00, 0.87, 0.76)

FIGURE 3.38 Linear dodge.

The base color is lightened by the new color. The brighter the new color, the more effect it has on the base color. The perceived contrast in the resulting image increases when there is no clamping. This operation may clip the highlights and is not invertible.

Linear Dodge

Linear Dodge is the exact same operation as the addition of two images, additive Blending (Figure 3.38).

Linear Dodge = $A + B$

Equation 3.15 Linear Dodge

Different from the Color Dodge operations, the resulting perceived contrast decreases when there is no clamping.

Burn

Burning is the formal name for darkening an image. Named after the photographic process performed in the darkroom, burning darkens an image by burning its positive. By placing a mask over the image and exposing light through the holes in the mask, the base image receives more light and darkens only in the holes.

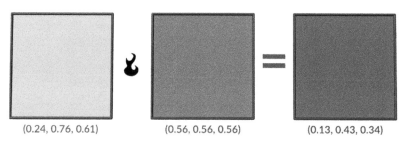

(0.24, 0.76, 0.61)   (0.56, 0.56, 0.56)   (0.13, 0.43, 0.34)

FIGURE 3.39 Multiply burn.

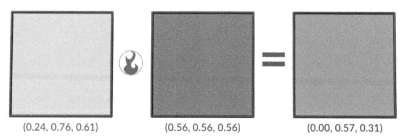

(0.24, 0.76, 0.61)   (0.56, 0.56, 0.56)   (0.00, 0.57, 0.31)

FIGURE 3.40 Color burn.

Mathematically, the Burn operation decreases the contrast of the image in areas where the result is not clamped. There are three Burn operations that can be applied: Multiply, Color Burn, and Linear Burn:

Multiply

Multiply Burn is the exact same operation as multiplying two images against each other (Figure 3.39).

Multiply Burn = $A * B$

Equation 3.16 Multiply Burn

Color Burn

The Color Burn operation takes the inverse of the second image, divides it by the first image then inverses the result (Figure 3.40).

$$\text{Color Burn} = \frac{1}{\left(\left(\frac{1}{A}\right)/B\right)}$$

Equation 3.17 Color Burn

A darker new image will have a more dramatic impact than a lighter color. The process is not invertible since there may be clipping in the dark areas of shadow.

Linear Burn

The Linear Burn operation adds the two images then subtracts 1.0 from the sum (Figure 3.41).

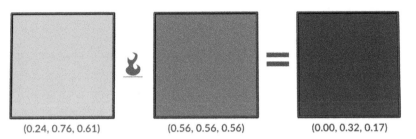

(0.24, 0.76, 0.61)   (0.56, 0.56, 0.56)   (0.00, 0.32, 0.17)

FIGURE 3.41 Linear burn.

Linear Burn = $A + B - 1.0$

Equation 3.18 Linear Burn

Performing a Linear burn has the similar effect as adding the two colors and inverting the result.

CONCLUSION

Making visual effects integrate within their contextual environments is essential when generating any visual effect. Unless the visual effect looks, feels, and behaves as if it belongs in its surrounding environment, the audience will not accept the visual effect's integrity. Matching the environment's color palette, never exceeding beyond the scene's maximum white point nor below the minimum black point, achieves this integration.

This chapter explains how lights and colors are represented and how we as humans identify color. While there are multiple ways for representing color, there are two primary techniques: RGB for additive light (all electronic displays) and CMYK for subtractive light (all physical printing and dyeing). There is no current technology that will allow for the full display of the entire visible human color spectrum. The amount or subset of the displayable color spectrum is called the gamut. Since no device can capture the full human color spectrum, true photo-realism can never be achieved. The artist has a responsibility for making a visual effect fit within the human color spectrum as close as possible.

Since no electronic display device can duplicate the full human color spectrum and humans do not perceive light linearly but in a power law relationship with real light, light is bent or "encoded" when it is recorded. The process converts linear light to Gamma 2.2 light, often called sRGB color space. Any operations upon encoded light must be first "decoded" or else unpredictable or undesirable artifacts will be generated. Once the resulting color has been calculated, it must be re-encoded else the visual integrity of the image will not be maintained. Technology has attempted to make this process transparent. Visual effects artists must be aware of its nature to create visual effects which are predictable and integrate with their contextual environments.

Colors are blended to either lighten or darken each other. To lighten an image, addition, division, or image dodging techniques are used. To darken an image subtraction, multiplication, or image burning techniques may be used. Taking the exponent, or power, will lighten or darken the image in a non-linear fashion. An image will brighten with a power less than 1.0 and will darken with a value greater than 1.0.

INTRODUCTION

Sometimes in life, the best solutions to problems require the least amount of heavy lifting. The same is true for visual effects. This perspective especially holds true when considering the primary role of visual effects contributing to the mood of the story, or gameplay, and integrating characters within their environments. Quite often the best visual effects are the simplest, requiring very little manipulation. This chapter focuses on building visual effects by simply manipulating the rendering engine, manipulating the lights, or manipulating a combination of both.

Modern real-time rendering engines are amazing! I still remember the days when it took a couple of seconds to update a wireframe display of a simple, geometric model on a Silicon Graphics workstation. The ability to observe a fully shaded cube in real-time was almost unheard of! We are now at the gateway of a new era of real-time ray tracing; an event I thought would never happen in this lifetime. Lightning-fast ray tracing and real-time photorealistic renders in VR, AR, and MR systems make this the most fascinating time to be involved in the CGI industry!

A cursory understanding of how these modern real-time engines work is essential for the modern visual effects artist. All visual effects are components of the rendering system. All visual effects, in one way or another, are rendered and integrated with the rest of the scene. Most of the time, visual effects exploit or take advantage of the behaviors and eccentricities of the rendering engine. This chapter introduces the seven stages of the modern rendering pipeline and explains how each stage may be manipulated. Transparency is a crucial component of any visual effect. The blending of pre-rendered layers is the last stage of the rendering pipeline and controls how transparency of an effect behaves. The fundamental blending techniques of this last stage are provided to give the visual effects artist full control of how their effects are layered into the scene.

All visible scene components, including visual effects, are rendered and are dependent on their relationship with the available lighting. Visual effects artists must be aware of how their effects interact with the lighting of an experience so they may manipulate the effects' appearance and maintain seamless integration with the environment. The available types of lighting are explained in this chapter and strategies and rules for adjusting the scene's lighting are explored.

Unless a visual effect is intended to be outrageous or calls attention to itself, the best visual effects are never seen. The visual effects artist's job is accomplished when the story is maintained, and the participant is invested in character or environment welfare. Often this is achieved entirely within the camera with the aid of additional post-processing operations. This chapter concludes by describing the vast array of post-processing tools available to the visual effects artist.

REAL-TIME RENDERING PIPELINE

All visual effects are rendered. In other words, everything that is seen in an experience must go through the same specific operations to be displayed. These operations are called the *Rendering Pipeline*. It does not matter if the effect is an object in the scene, a source of light which interacts with its immediate surroundings, or a possible combination of both. Every visual effect must collaborate with the rendering pipeline. Luckily, this pipeline is extraordinarily customizable. Almost every asset requires some type of pipeline customization. I label the "Art of Visual Effects" as the art of manipulating and exploiting all stages of the rendering pipeline. To understand the creation of visual effects, an artist must understand the rendering pipeline.

DOI: 10.1201/9781003009795-5

This one-to-one relationship binds the visual effect to the rendering pipeline and cannot be separated. A visual effect will only behave properly in the rendering pipeline in which it was developed. Many artists complain, "I designed this wicked visual effect in my DCC. How do I get it in my real-time rendering engine?" Regretfully they are not transferable. The DCC engine with which the original effect was developed is a unique engine; an *off-line* rendering pipeline. The real-time engine is something quite different, a *real-time* pipeline. Although they may share similar algorithms, they are quite different. The real-time engine has been optimized to create imagery at a speed of at least 90 frames per second (a standard VR requirement). The off-line engine has been designed to give the artist ultimate control of the resulting image; regardless of how long it takes to render. Like automobile engines, all rendering pipelines do essentially the same thing but in radically different ways. NASCAR and Formula One race car engines consume different fuels, behave differently, and provide output different results. Even when an effect is somehow translated from one pipeline to another, the end result does not appear the same. There are simply too many parameters required to keep them looking alike. A visual effect must be redesigned to look the same on different pipelines.

As of the time of the writing of this book, there are two primary real-time rendering pipelines; Direct 3D and OpenGL. Direct 3D is Microsoft's proprietary rendering platform initially developed to support the XBox game counsel. The language which drives this pipeline is called "HLSL." While HLSL is the official language supporting Direct 3D, other pipelines often use the language to communicate with their own pipelines. For example, the Unreal Engine, UE4, supports a custom HLSL node with which a user may write custom HLSL instructions to the UE4 engine.

OpenGL is a cross-language, cross-platform API supported by the non-profit technology consortium Khronos Group. This platform is an open standard, supported by many different engines. The language which drives this pipeline is called "GLSL." Like HLSL, GLSL is used to support many different rendering pipelines. For example, the Unity game engine supports an intermediate language which translates to HLSL or GLSL depending on the destination's platform. HLSL and GLSL are very similar. Except for a handful of different functions, data class names, texture map directionality and the location of the screen origin, the two languages are almost identical.

Apple provides its own rendering pipeline called Metal. Like Direct 3D, Metal is a proprietary license. Apple's Swift and Objective C are the languages which support the platform. Vulcan is the up and coming, next-generation OpenGL initiative. It is also a low-level, cross-platform pipeline supported by the Khronos Group. This pipeline will replace OpenGL as it continues to develop and grow in popularity. Vulcan is adaptable. It may be configured to receive input from multiple languages, including HLSL or GLSL.

The details of the HLSL and GLSL programming languages are beyond the scope of this book. Please refer to Paul Varcholik's book, *Real-time 3D Rendering with DirectX and HLSL: A Practical Guide to Graphics Programming, Lighting and Rendering for the Technical Artist*, for more thorough instruction for programming these languages.

Fluency in these languages is not necessary for manipulating real-time pipelines. Most real-time engines support interactive material editors which support the manipulation of each stage of the rendering pipeline. These material manipulations should be adequate for most visual effect applications. However, when more control is required, visual effects artists should collaborate with programmers or other technical artists familiar with these languages.

Most rendering pipelines are abstracted to the same basic seven stages: the *Input Assembler* stage, the *Vertex Shader*, the *Tessellation* stage, the *Geometry Shader*, *Rasterization*, the *Fragment* or *Pixel Shader*, and the *Color or Layer Blending* stage. The vertex buffer (also called index buffer), is a pre-pipeline memory location which feeds geometry to the Input Assembler. The frame buffer is the post-pipeline memory location where the Layer Blending stage writes its content to. The display device displays the contents from the frame buffer (Figure 4.1).

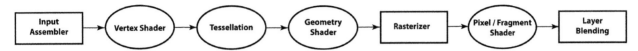

FIGURE 4.1 Real-time rendering pipeline.

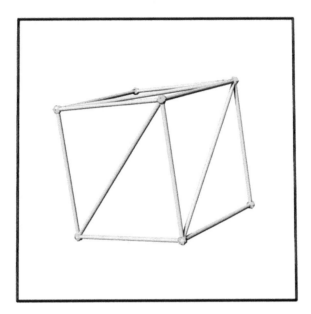

FIGURE 4.2 The input assembler stage.

Input Assembler

The Input Assembler collects the raw vertex data from the Vertex/Index buffer. It collects and organizes the vertices as triangle polygons, and keeps track of all vertex data such as position, color, texture, and normals (Figure 4.2).

A vertex index may also be employed to repeat vertex data without necessitating the duplication of the full vertex definition itself. For example, four triangles may share the exact same vertex point. Indexing references the same vertex data for each polygon, which is stored only once instead of duplicating the same vertex data four times (Figure 4.3).

While this stage is generally non-programmable, the structure of the data may be configured to conform to different templates. A visual effects artist may need to adjust the polygonal information going into the pipeline such that vertices and their tangencies are taken into consideration; an important consideration when evaluating the smoothness of a surface.

Vertex Shader

The Vertex shader is a programmable instruction set, which is run for every vertex progressing through the pipeline. While not mandatory, its typical responsibility is to transform each vertex from object model space to screen space (Figure 4.4).

As a fully programmable stage, any vertex attribute such as position, color, UV, normal, etc., may be altered. In fact, most geometric deformations and animations occur during this stage. For example, a visual effects artist may use this stage to animate a simple sine wave into the lateral movement of foliage geometry to make it

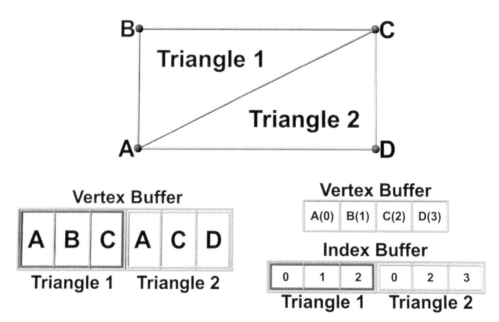

FIGURE 4.3 Vertex indexing.

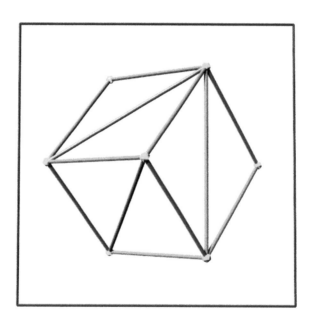

FIGURE 4.4 Vertex shader stage.

appear to be swaying in the wind. The Vertex shader is one of the most common locations for visual effects artist's manipulations.

Tessellation Stage

The Tessellation stage is a semi-programmable set of operations, which subdivides existing geometry. The amount of programmability is set by each pipeline as certain components of the Tessellation stage are programmable while others are not (Figure 4.5).

FIGURE 4.5 The tessellation stage.

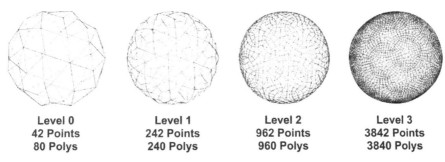

Level 0	Level 1	Level 2	Level 3
42 Points	242 Points	962 Points	3842 Points
80 Polys	240 Polys	960 Polys	3840 Polys

FIGURE 4.6 Tessellation of a sphere.

The Tessellation stage may be used to provide dynamic Levels of Detail, (LODs), to simple geometry. It also may be used to provide extra fidelity where there is limited information. For example, a high-resolution sphere can be represented as a low-resolution sphere. A visual effects artist may use the Tessellation stage to add smoothness to an otherwise coarsely defined object instance such as a bullet or similar projectile (Figure 4.6).

Geometry Shader

Like the Tessellation stage, the Geometry shader empowers the user to add, remove, or modify existing geometry but with more flexibility. Instead of executing on every point, the Geometry shader is executed on every primitive; triangle, line, or point (Figure 4.7).

A visual effects artist or programmer often uses Geometry shaders to add more "information" to existing volumes. This information may fill volumes with grass or particulate geometry such as clouds, vapor, and even hair. When additional geometry is added during the Tessellation stage, any additional procedural deformation needs to be done in the Geometry shader. Regretfully Geometry shaders are not popular with the graphics pipeline community as they are notoriously slow and beyond the scope of this text.

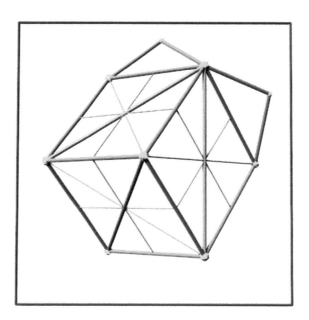

FIGURE 4.7 Geometry shader.

Rasterizer

The Rasterizer projects the 3D geometric scene onto the 2D camera plane as activated locations on the frame buffer called "pixels" or "fragments." The process of reducing 3D data to two dimensions is called *discretizing*. Aside from *discretizing* the geometry, the Rasterizer must remove or cull information that is not projected into the view frustum of the frame buffer. Culled information includes primitives which are occluded by other primitives, geometry which reaches beyond the boundaries of the frame, and other primitives which face away from the camera and are otherwise unrenderable (Figure 4.8).

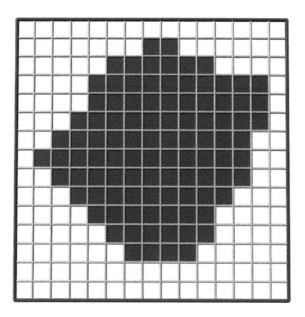

FIGURE 4.8 Rasterizer stage.

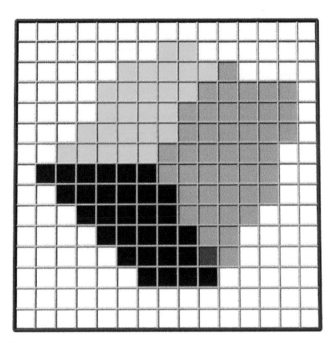

FIGURE 4.9 Pixel/fragment shader.

Each pixel inherits the vertex attributes which are projected upon it. These attributes include information such as the position (transformed to screen space), color, texture coordinates, normal values, and even relative depth information between the camera and the 3D geometry. Once the visible vertices have been activated as pixels, the pixels in between are engaged and their attributes are interpolated. The Rasterizing stage is not programmable. However, it may be configured to allow primitives facing away from the camera to be rendered.

Pixel/Fragment Shader

The Pixel/Fragment shader is executed on every rasterized fragment. The output of this shader is the pixel's final rendered color and transparency value (called *alpha*). All interpolated vertex information and all scene lighting information are required for these renderings (Figure 4.9).

Like the other shaders in the pipeline, this stage is entirely programmable. Aside from the vertex shader, the Pixel/Fragment shader receives the most amount of attention from shader authors. No other stage in the pipeline has more potential for controlling the final visual output of the geometry.

Layer Blending Stage

Each unique call to a Pixel/Fragment shader is rendered to a single layer in the framebuffer. Multiple calls to the same shader but with different input, such as textures, are considered unique. Each one of these unique layers is referred to as a *draw*. The layer blending stage, often called the output merging stage, takes the color information for each equivalent pixel position on each draw and applies blending operations to merge them into a 1-pixel value. The transparency and depth information of each pixel in a draw are taken into consideration during these blending operations (Figure 4.10).

While not programmable, this stage is configurable. The configurations available during this stage are described later in this section.

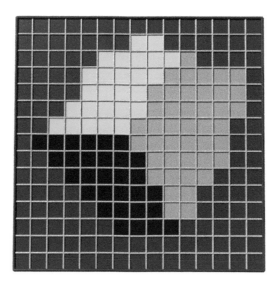

FIGURE 4.10 Layer blending stage.

REAL-TIME TRANSPARENCY AND BLENDING

The Layer Blending stage is not programmable but is highly configurable. These configurations empower the visual effects artist to combine colors in almost every method described in Chapter 3. Sophisticated techniques, called *depth and stencil tests*, order the triangles coming through the render pipeline so the furthest triangles from the camera are rendered first and placed in the frame buffer. Nearer transparent or semi-transparent triangles are blended upon all pre-blended pixels. The pre-rendered, pre-blended color is called the *destination* color and the newly rendered pixel is referred to as the *source* color (Figure 4.11).

The Layer Blending stage is ruled by a single equation: The final color is the result of a blending operation performed over the product of the source pixel color and its blending factor and the product of the destination pixel color and its blending factor.

Final color = (Source Pixel Color * Source Blending Factor) blending operation

(Destination Pixel Color * Destination Blending Factor)

Equation 4.1 Layer Blending Equation

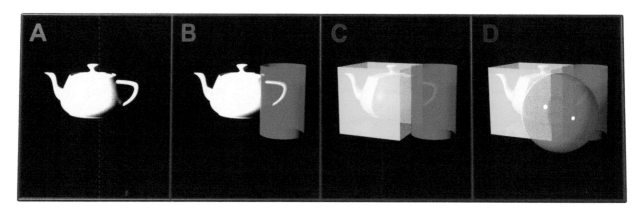

FIGURE 4.11 Blending of multiple layers.

TABLE 4.1 Available Blending Operations

Operator	Operation
+	Source Product + Destination Product
−	Source Product − Destination Product
Inverse −	Destination Product − Source Product
Minimum	min(Source Product, Destination Product)
Maximum	max(Source Product, Destination Product)

TABLE 4.2 Possible Blend Factors

Source Alpha	Destination Color	Constant Color
Inverse Source Alpha	Inverse Destination Color	Inverse Constant Color
Source Color	Zero (Black)	Constant Alpha
Inverse Source Color	One (No Change)	Inverse Constant Alpha

There are five possible blending operations. The first operation is *addition* of the source product and destination product. The second is the *difference*. The third, called *the inverse difference*, is the difference between the destination product and the source product. The fourth is the *minimum* or the darker of the two products. The final operation is the *maximum* or lighter of the two products (Table 4.1).

The transparency value of a pixel is called its *alpha* value. There are 12 possible blend factors which consider pixel color, alpha value, and/or a constant value (Table 4.2).

The five blending operations and 12 possible blend factors provide 720 possible blending configurations. The most common configurations are described below.

Alpha Blending

The most common blending configuration is *Alpha Blending*. Alpha blending is the sum of the product of the source color with its alpha value and the product of the destination color and the inverse of the source alpha.

$$\text{Final Color} = \text{Source Color} * (\text{Source Alpha}) + \text{Destination Color} * (1 - \text{Source Alpha})$$

Equation 4.2 Alpha Blending Configuration

Often called "*A over B*," alpha blending is the workhorse for color blending (Figure 4.12).

Since this configuration is used so often, most folks think the color blending stage simply adds the two layers. This is not the case. The source alpha value must be considered. This technique is also called "Keying." The name comes from the source alpha channel which removes just the correct amount of background color in order to maintain source color integrity. By multiplying the inverse of the source alpha against the background color, a hole (*keyhole*) is cut into the background, which will fit the source image perfectly (Figure 4.13).

FIGURE 4.12 Alpha blending.

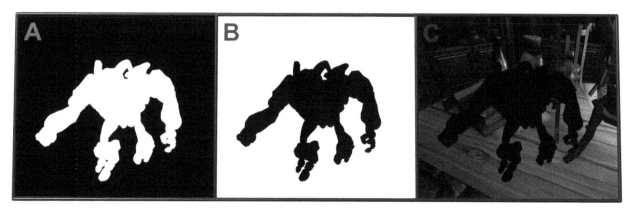

FIGURE 4.13 Alpha keying.

Additive Blending

Additive blending, which is also known as *Linear Dodge*, is the sum of the source color and the destination color. The combination is achieved by multiplying the source and the destination colors by the constant 1.0.

$$\text{Final Color} = \text{Source Color} * (1.0) + \text{Destination Color} * (1.0)$$

Equation 4.3 Additive Blending Configuration

Adding the source color to the destination color will result in the lightening effect of the source color. The result of the sum must be clamped at 1.0 thus the resulting image has no pixel value brighter than 1.0 (Figure 4.14).

Multiplicative Blending

Multiplicative blending, which is also known as *Color Product* or *Multiply Burn*, is the product of the source and destination colors. This combination is achieved by multiplying the source color by the constant 0.0 and then adding to the product of the destination and source colors.

$$\text{Final Color} = \text{Source Color} * (0.0) + \text{Destination Color} * (\text{Source Color})$$

Equation 4.4 Multiplicative Blending Configuration

FIGURE 4.14 Additive blending.

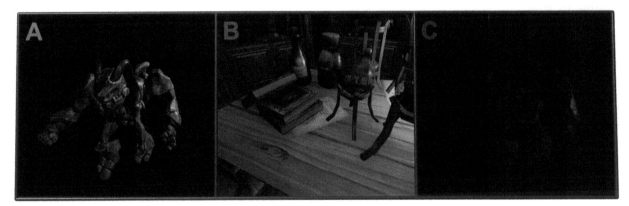

FIGURE 4.15 Multiplicative blending.

Multiplying the source color against the destination will result in darkening of the base image. Since the values of the components of the color are bound between 0.0 and 1.0, the product of the two colors will never be lower than 0.0, resulting in a smooth gradient to black (Figure 4.15).

Divisional Blending

Divisional blending, which is also known as *Color Difference*, is the product of the destination color and the inverse of the source color. Like multiplicative blending, this combination is achieved by multiplying the source color against the constant 0.0 and adding to the product of the source color and the inverse of the source color.

Final Color = Source Color * (0.0) + Destination Color * (Inverse Source Color)

Equation 4.5 Divisional Blending Configuration

Like Addition, divisional blending is used to lighten the source color. While the product of the combination will never be smaller than 0.0, it is relatively easy to compute a product larger than 1.0 when the destination color is darker (smaller in component value) than the source color. When the product exceeds 1.0, the result is clamped to 1.0 (Figure 4.16).

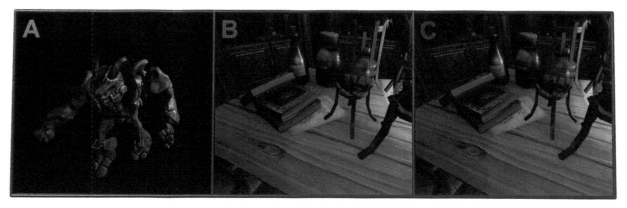

FIGURE 4.16 Divisional blending.

Alpha Testing

Before large memory computers, colors were stored with only 1 bit of or no alpha. *Alpha Testing* is used as a hard transparency technique as pixels are either completely opaque or transparent. When 1 bit of alpha information is present, the blending configuration is the same as modern alpha blending.

Final Color = Source Color * (Source Alpha) + Destination Color * (Inverse Source Alpha)

Equation 4.6 1-Bit Alpha Testing

When there is no alpha information, the source color is *tested* for a value greater than black, 0.0. When not black, the blend factor constant is set to 1.0. Otherwise, the constant is 0.0.

Final Color = Source Color * (Constant) + Destination Color * (Inverse Constant)

Equation 4.7 0-Bit Alpha Testing

The combinations are typically blocky since there are no soft edges between source and destination colors. Alpha Testing is rarely used unless a more nostalgic, vintage look is desired (Figure 4.17).

FIGURE 4.17 Alpha test.

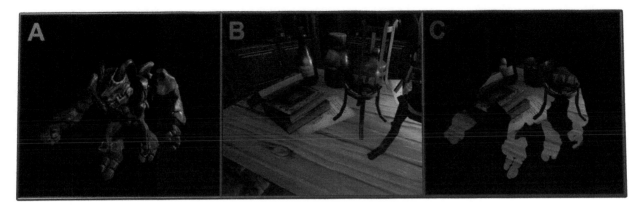

FIGURE 4.18 Inside blending.

Inside Blending

Inside blending, which is also known as *atop* blending, is a very special configuration that is used to isolate the destination color within the source color. This effect is configured by multiplying the source color by the constant 0.0 and adding to the product of the destination color and the source alpha.

Final Color = Source Color * (0.0) + Destination Color * (Source Alpha)

Equation 4.8 Inside Blending Configuration

Inside blending is a visual effects-driven configuration where the result is typically used as a source for a different destination (Figure 4.18).

Outside Blending

Outside blending is another special configuration that is used to remove only the source image from the destination. Like inside blending, the source color is multiplied against constant 0.0 and added to the product of the destination and the inverse of the source alpha.

Final Color = Source Color * (0.0) + Destination Color * (Inverse Source Alpha)

Equation 4.9 Outside Blending Configuration

The result of this combination is a *Window Frame*-like effect that is typically used as a source to frame or isolate the destination (Figure 4.19).

RAY TRACING

The most exciting technological developments in real-time rendering have been the optimization of real-time ray tracing. Companies such as NVidia have been investing heavily in this endeavor and their efforts are ready to pay off. The technology that seemed like science fiction in the 1980s and 1990s has arrived. Accurate shadows, reflections, refractions, and global illumination are now available in high-end, real-time systems.

The current, traditional real-time rendering pipeline revolves around the rasterizer projecting the 3D geometric scene onto a frame buffer within the image plane of the camera. Ray tracing is the opposite concept. Sampling rays are projected from the camera through the image plane and return only with the accumulated lighting information of the objects in the 3D scene they intersect. This paradigm flip motivates the ray tracing pipeline to

FIGURE 4.19 Outside blending.

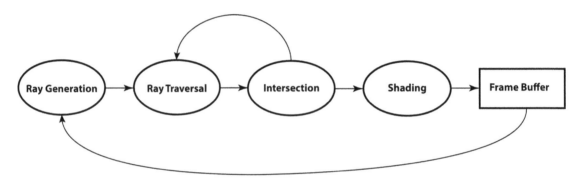

FIGURE 4.20 Real-time ray tracing pipeline.

behave differently from the traditional rasterizing pipeline. As of the time of the writing of this book, real-time ray tracing is still a relatively new technology and in many respects is still developing. Many details will inevitably change. The core components as mentioned in this text will remain consistent until the next major evolution in computer graphics (Figure 4.20).

Ray-Tracing Pipeline

Ray Generation Stage

The *Ray Generation* stage is the initial stage of the ray tracing pipeline. Rays are generated from the focal point of the camera, through a 2D camera-plane grid and projected on a vector trajectory into the 3D scene (Figure 4.21).

Ray Traversal Stage

The projected rays traverse through the scene searching for scene objects to intersect during the *Ray Traversal* stage. Bounding Volume Hierarchy and other acceleration algorithms assist the rays to traverse through the shortest path in 3D space to their first intersection. These acceleration algorithms are beyond the scope of this text.

Intersection Stage

When all possible object intersections are located during the Ray Traversal stage, the *Intersection* stage computes the intersection positions of the rays with 3D geometric scene objects. When no intersections are discovered, the rays' progress returns to the Ray Traversal stage.

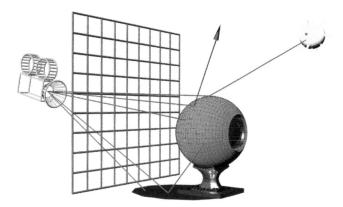

FIGURE 4.21 Ray generation stage.

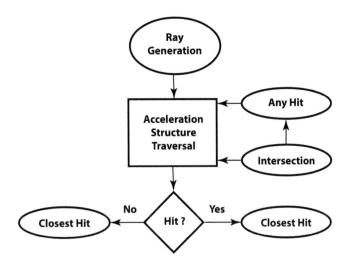

FIGURE 4.22 Ray tracing shader pipeline.

Shading Stage

The Shading stage computes the amount of light present on the discovered intersection positions. Additional rays are recursively shot back into the scene as newly generated rays to consider all illumination contributions from source lights and other reflecting objects. Upon the rays' recursive return to the Shading stage, the lighting information for the intersection is computed and returned to the frame buffer.

Ray Tracing Shader Pipeline

The ray tracing pipeline requires different programmable shaders to control the rays' behaviors and calculate the shading information of each intersection position. The new shaders include the *Raygen* shader, the *Ray Intersection* shader, and three Intersection shaders: the *Closest Hit* shader, the *Any Hit* shader, and *Miss* shader (Figure 4.22).

Raygen Shader

The Raygen shader engages the Ray Generation stage by originating rays from the camera and through the 2D display grid. Once the final shaded value for the associated pixels is calculated and returned, the Raygen shader writes the final output to the frame buffer.

Intersection Shader

The Intersection Shader calculates arbitrary ray intersections against 3D primitives. Not limited to triangles, other valid 3D primitive types include volume datasets, splines, subdivision surfaces, and points.

Closest Hit Shader

The Closest Hit shader performs the shading calculations for the intersection points. In order to perform these shading calculations, additional rays are spawned to collect shadow data and global influences from other objects in the scene. This shader most closely represents the traditional pixel/fragment shader.

Any Hit Shader

The Any Hit shader is invoked upon the intersection of a ray against any scene primitive. The shader may choose to ignore the intersection entirely, as when dealing with transparent objects, or pass on computed shading data.

Miss Shader

Miss shader is invoked when no valid ray intersection is calculated. This shader typically behaves as an environmental shader returning infinite lighting information.

LIGHTING AND LIGHTING VFX

As discussed in the previous section, the rendering pipeline provides the fundamental building blocks for all visual effects. Many of the intricate manipulations of the pipeline are complicated and out of scope of this chapter. Fortunately, many other components of the pipeline are also powerful and easy to manipulate. Of these, lights and lighting effects are some of the easiest objects to control and have the potential for the greatest impact on the emotional tone and feel of the entire CGI experience.

All off-line visual effects used in film and television must be lit and rendered to integrate with their pre-captured environments. All pre-recorded content contains the lighting established by the director and cinematographer. Off-line visual effect lighting attempts to duplicate these lights to make the added characters, props, and visual effects feel like they belong in the scene. In real-time applications, there is no difference between environment and effect lighting. The lighting affecting the mood and emotional tone for characters and environments is also the same lighting impacting visual effects and is not expected to aid with the integration of those effects. Chapter 1 delegates the primary responsibility of real-time visual effects to the contribution of mood to the interactive experience. Within the context of this responsibility, lighting becomes the most primitive, foundational, and essential of all visual effects. Real-time lighting accomplishes this role in three different ways: It moves story and gameplay; it manipulates the behavior and appearance of all shadows, and it integrates all characters and environments.

Lighting to Move Story and Gameplay

Lights are the most primitive of all visual effects. As visual effects, they manipulate story and gameplay by directing the viewer's eye, creating depth, enhancing mood, atmosphere, drama, conveying time, and revealing character personality.

By directing the viewer's eyes, lights show the viewer where to look by enhancing what in the scene is important while minimizing what isn't. Not all real-time scenes are dramatic. However, lights help the scene create a greater emotional impact on the viewer beyond the sum of the individual emotional contributions of each component. Lights can make a well-composed scene look stunning, or they may rescue a less than perfect scene composition.

All CGI is an inherent two-dimensional medium whether as a mobile device, a computer monitor, or as an AR or VR display device. Lights must generate a visual illusion to assist the viewer in observing the scene as three dimensions instead of two. Lights perform this depth generating effect using the following techniques: linear perspective, value, color, atmosphere, scale relationships, volume, and planes of light.

Enhancing mood, atmosphere, and drama through lighting is a technique passed down from traditional stage performance and modern film cinematography. Real-time lighting is the modern incarnation of this venerable art form. Through the consideration of shape, rhythm, balance and style, lighting impacts the mood and drama of every experience.

Lighting communicates the time and day of the season for every real-time scene. Lighting communicates optimistic and cheerful mornings and lonely and pessimistic nights. Lighting for winter communicates hibernation, dormancy, and even death while summer projects the feeling that it is time to get things done. Lighting expresses time more than any lengthy exposition or description.

Visual effects lighting attributes character to environments as well as their inhabitants. While environmental lighting tends to vary from level to level or scene to scene, consistent treatment of the lighting for characters and locations administers uniform instructions on how these individual components are to be perceived.

Lighting to Manipulate Shadows

Shadows are an important component of any visual effect as they add realism to the scene and anchor the character, or visual effect, to the scene. Shadow mastery is a milestone all visual effects artists should strive for.

Although shadows are essential for any three-dimensional environment, they are also very expensive to compute. Expensiveness describes the computational workload placed on the rendering engine. A cheap process demands less processing output from the engine where an expensive process requires more. The computational cost of shadow processing depends on the context of each real-time application. Great planning must be devoted to the creation of shadows. Visual effects artists must be in communication with lighters and other technical artists to ensure responsible yet effective creation of shadows. Understanding of how lights interact and generate shadows is part of that communication.

Unless a ray tracer is performing the rendering, artists will need to consider the nature of shadows and the lights generating them; are they static, dynamic, or mobile? Since static lights bake shadow information into textures, they create the easiest and cheapest shadows. Depth maps used for the calculation of shadows are generated and stored during a lighting "pre-processing" stage. The relative proximity of the lights and objects is assumed not to change. When an object's position dynamically changes then the depth maps need to be calculated once every frame for every shadow light in the scene. The pre-processing of depth maps makes shadow calculations computationally expensive. Unless accommodations are made to the rendering engine to handle such demands, an effective strategy is limiting the number of dynamic lights in a scene to one. Most rendering engines can afford at least one shadow light per scene. When a shadow light cannot fit within the engine's budget, cheating methods need to be incorporated. A popular trick is to place a "blobby" character at the base of a dynamic character. A blobby character is a dark, flat, non-descript, articulated character whose joint chain mimics the joints of the dynamic character. Since it moves the same as the dynamic character, the dark character appears to be its shadow. The angle between the character and the light source controls the orientation and length of the dark shadow object (Figure 4.23).

While this flat, "blobby," character seems like extra effort to create, within the context of the rendering engine, it is faster to compute than a traditional shadow.

FIGURE 4.23 Blobby shadow character.

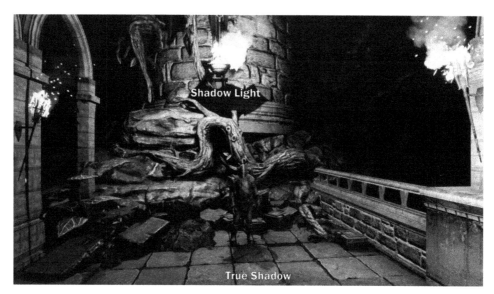

FIGURE 4.24 Overwhelming the viewing audience.

The most expensive and potentially demanding lighting scenario is a moving light source that generates dynamic shadows. Examples are a character holding a flashlight or the front headlights of a moving vehicle. There is almost no trick that can be applied to this situation. In most circumstances, the rendering team is faced with the task of optimizing all other scene components efficiently enough to handle the demands of the mobile light. Occasionally, especially with horror-based experiences, the rendering team turns off all shadow generation in the hope the audience is too preoccupied with the next jump-scare to notice the missing shadows.

Context of the shadow location must also be considered. Generating shadows indoors often requires less planning than outdoor lighting. This may seem contrary to expectations but consider the viewing audiences' expectations. Indoor environments typically have many lights, all of which can be potential shadow generators (Figure 4.24).

FIGURE 4.25 Rotated shadows.

The environment may contain so many potential shadow-generating lights, the viewers' brains are overwhelmed. The allowance of only one shadow-generating light will match viewers' expectations. Often, artists get away with omitting new shadows in the scene, saving the one shadow light for a special light emitter such as a spotlight or a roaring fireplace. This slight bit of redirection is a lighting artist's best friend when dealing with an otherwise unmanageable scene.

This same, "redirection" technique is a bit more difficult to implement outdoors. In exterior daytime scenes, there can only be one shadow generating light; the sun. (My sympathies go to a production crew dealing with more than one sun.) This one dynamic shadow light generates excellent homogeneous shadows over the entire scene.

Exterior nighttime lighting environments are problematic. In an exterior night scene, all lights are expected to be shadow generating. The rendering programmers and technical artists may be able to pool their resources and optimize the scene adequately to render multiple shadow lights. Regretfully, most situations require other tricks to satisfy the audience's expectations. An overwhelming, single moonlight may be able to wash out all other contributing shadows. Multiple blobby shadow characters may also be considered. Another trick is to render only one shadow then duplicate it and rotate it multiple times to accommodate other shadow-generating lights in the scene (Figure 4.25).

The parallax for the duplicated shadows using this technique will be incorrect. However, the development team counts on the viewing audience not being able to tell the real shadow from the fakes. The only other viable alternative is to overwhelm the audience with too many potential lights yet provide only one, true shadow generator. For example, the overwhelming moonlight may wash out all other potential shadows. In this scenario, the development team wagers the audience will not be able to observe the difference.

Lights to Interact with Characters and Environments

Just as shadows anchor effects to their environments, similar anchoring occurs when the effects emit their own light. The narrative nature of visual effects motivates characters to be light emitters. For example, a magic spell may spill light onto its environment, a missile's exhaust may illuminate the ground underneath as it passes by, and a demon's burning eyes may flood the scene with warm light. It is very important for the visual effects artist to include such light sources and create them responsibly to maintain frame rate and real-time stability.

FIGURE 4.26 Parenting a light source to a character or effect.

Creating interactive light sources associated with effects is just as important as creating them in the first place. Typically, lights are not intrinsic parts of characters or effects. Light sources need to be parented to components of the character such that they move in sync with the character (Figure 4.26).

The parent lights illuminate the character as well as its nearby environment. As the character is impacted by the light the same way the environment is, the viewer readily accepts the character belonging to the environment.

Often, these external light sources have bright intensity but fast falloff. The short falloff distance prevents the audience from inspecting the integrity of the lights and, when done properly, are never consciously seen. Due to the narrative nature of the light sources, the light colors are often non-white. My lighting students may cry "Foul!" as some part of the scene is being lit with a non-white light. However, when the lights' falloff distance is short, their impact on the environment is relatively small. The scene experiences none of the distracting artifacts associated with colored lights. When done responsibly, I encourage artists to use as many of these quick falloff-colored lights as possible to assist anchoring characters to their environment and enhancing the story.

There are two reasons why these light sources need to be external from the actual character. The first reason is because of emissive materials. For convenience purposes, an artist may create some portion of the character's surface material to have emissive properties. Although they may appear to be emitting light, emissive materials are not light sources. Naive artists waste thousands of hours trying to understand why their emissive materials have no impact on their nearby surroundings. Technically, the emissive material property is an embedded visual effect provided by the engine developer to appear as if material generates light. It does not. An external light must be provided to make the emissive material project light as it visually appears to.

The second reason why an external light must be created is also somewhat sneaky. Rendering engine developers empower their particle systems to not only generate particles but also treat those particles as light sources. These light sources are rendered as movable, shadow-generating lights. For simplification purposes, this function is often not editable. This is extraordinarily dangerous. In the previous section, this situation was identified as the most expensive of all lighting scenarios and should be avoided at all costs. Even when a particle generator emits a single, light-emitting, animated sprite, that single particle could cause the rendering frame rate to plummet. The best strategy is to parent the external light offset from the center of the particle system and hope the viewers don't notice the discrepancy. As of writing this book, certain rendering engine developers are experimenting with

FIGURE 4.27 The effects of skylights.

exposing full control over their particle systems such that artists have full control over particle attributes and lights they may emit. This is not yet standard protocol. It is the artists' responsibility to investigate the generation of any light source and verify that it does not negatively impact rendering performance.

Types of Lights

There are five types of basic lights that can be found in every rendering engine toolkit: Skylights, Directional lights, point lights, spotlights, and area lights. While some rendering engines have more, most start with these basic five.

Skylight

Skylights, sometimes called ambient lights, are intended to be reflections of the color of the surrounding sky. Technically, they are not light sources. They are offsets from black. For reasons that are mentioned later in this chapter, artists must never allow scenes to reach absolute black color, sRGB (0, 0, 0). Skylights add offsets to the entire scene and establish the base color of the darkest shadows. Sometimes they are represented as cube maps encompassing the scene (Figure 4.27).

While skylights provide what appears to be, "free" light, they should be used with caution. Since they emit no light, they generate no shadow. They need to be treated as immovable and may not be altered. When skylights become too intense, they flatten the scene. Sense of depth is lost, and objects appear to be situated in a single plane. Certain visual effects do call for the flattening of the stage. However, unless the desired mood of the environment calls for this flattening effect, skylights should be used very sparingly.

Directional Lights

Directional lights are the shadow generating workhorses for most real-time renderers. They have no position, cannot be scaled, and have no falloff. Their only measurable attribute is their orientation. They represent an infinite amount of parallel light rays originating from one giant light source such as the sun or the moon. Directional lights are ideal choices for key light sources (Figure 4.28).

Because of their infinitely parallel nature, directional lights make excellent primary shadow generators. All objects in the scene share the same shadow effect and thus appear to co-exist within the same environment. While directional lights behave ideally outdoors, they may be challenging to implement indoors. Since directional lights

FIGURE 4.28 Visual behavior of directional lights.

FIGURE 4.29 Dramatic occluded directional light.

have no location, they are typically occluded by any form of geometry. Windows, doors, and other openings can make dramatic use of this phenomenon (Figure 4.29).

Unless the rendering engine can be configured to allow indoor directional lights, the lighting artist will need to devise other techniques to simulate the effects of parallel light. To avoid this occluding structure limitation, certain rendering engines implement a "god-ray" visual effect. Occluding geometry, assisted with false volumetric fog, sculpt the light into shafts, which appear to have volume (Figure 4.30).

Since directional lights simulate the effects of very large light sources such as the sun or moon, pure white light should be rarely used. Just a hint of warmth does a good job simulating natural sunlight. A touch of cool color does a good job simulating lunar lighting.

FIGURE 4.30 God-ray generating directional light.

Point Light

Point lights provide excellent fill light opportunities. They are omnidirectional balls of light that are easily placed into exact locations. Like physical lights, their light intensity reduces roughly proportional to the inverse of the distance squared to the light.

$$\text{Point Light Intensity} = \frac{1}{\text{Distance}^2}$$

Equation 4.10 Point Light Intensity

This attenuation causes the light intensity to drop very quickly at a certain distance from the light. The *Attenuation Radius* controls the distance over which the light intensity reduces to zero (Figure 4.31).

Certain rendering engines allow point lights to have an exponential falloff. Smaller exponents create slower falloffs where larger exponents are faster (Figure 4.32).

Falloff and position make point lights very effective in providing volumes of light which bring spherical volumes of light into darkness. When used indoors, a point light with reduced intensity and greater attenuation radius, can provide similar lighting coverage as directional lighting.

Spotlights

Spotlights combine the positional control of point lights and the orientation control of directional lights. Like point lights, they may be positioned into the exact location where light is needed. Like directional lights, they may be pointed in a specific direction (Figure 4.33).

Spotlights emit a cone-shaped volume of light which only influences those objects in the scene contained within the cone. The length of spotlight cones is controlled by an attenuation radius. Most rendering engines expose two cone angles controlling the lateral falloff of the cone. The inner cone controls the outer range of maximum core intensity. The outer cone angle controls the outer edge where the light intensity reduces to zero (Figure 4.34).

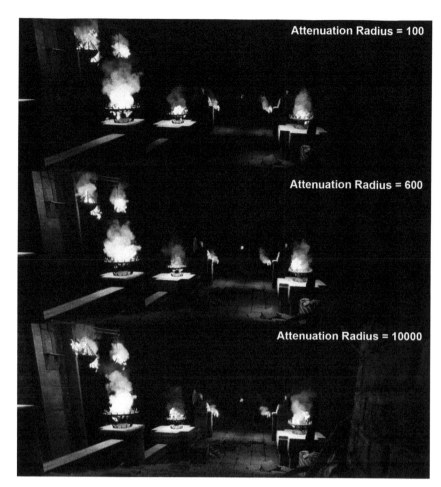

FIGURE 4.31 Point light attenuation.

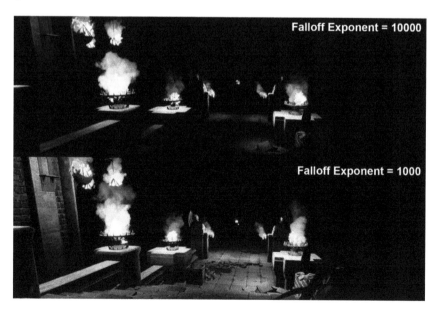

FIGURE 4.32 Inverse square versus exponential falloff.

Before Spotlight

After Spotlight

FIGURE 4.33 Spotlight behavior.

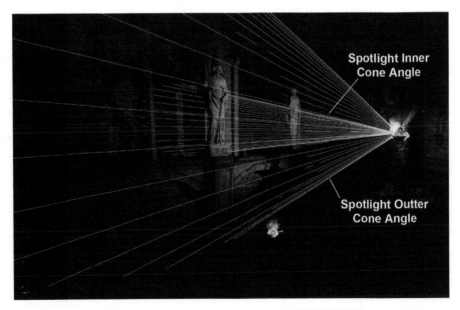

Spotlight Inner
Cone Angle

Spotlight Outter
Cone Angle

FIGURE 4.34 Spotlight control.

FIGURE 4.35 Sconce lights.

Spotlights are very effective at preventing light from spilling over into undesirable areas. For example, a sconce light projects light in an exclusively upward direction. A spotlight provides the interactive lighting behavior of the sconce with its environment (Figure 4.35).

Area Lights

Area lights, *Rectangle lights*, or *Rectangular lights* simulate the light behavior of rectangular objects such as monitors, light fixtures, or sconces. Like spotlights, area lights project light in a specific direction. Instead of the shape of a cone, the volume of light originates from a rectangle (Figure 4.36).

The light's width and height control the core area of influence in the shape of a rectangle. The barn door angels control the spread from the base of the light. Like point and spotlights, the attenuation radius controls the distance of falloff, perpendicular to the shape of the rectangle (Figure 4.37).

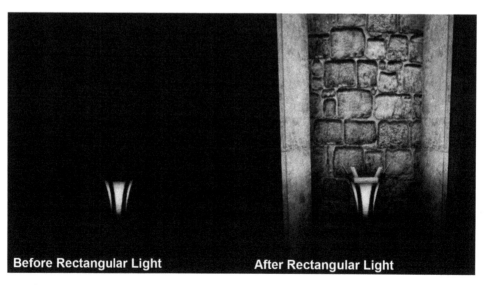

FIGURE 4.36 Area/rectangular light behavior.

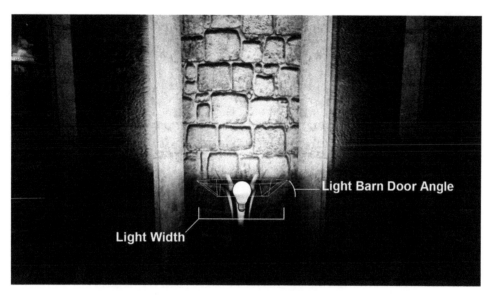

FIGURE 4.37 Area light control.

Area lights are excellent simulators of large light emitters where no light is allowed behind the light object.

Lighting Strategies

Most lighting for a visual effect or scene starts with basic three-point lighting. Three-point lighting strategy heralds from traditional cinematography and is an appropriate start for most lighting situations. The three-point lighting strategy starts with a *Key Light* and is then followed by a *Fill Light*. The role of the last light, the *Rim Light*, varies between real-time and off-line rendering and provides the greatest amount of creative artist freedom (Figure 4.38).

FIGURE 4.38 Scene with three-point lighting strategy.

Key Light

The *Key Light*, or primary light, provides most of the light in the scene or level. Its purpose is to provide most of the diffuse and specular lighting. This light brings a certain homogeneity to the visual environment. This light generates the scene's primary shadows. For most real-time situations, the rendering budget will usually allow for just one shadow light which should come from the key light. Other lights may complement the key light to provide multiple specular hits. However, the best convention employs just one shadow light (Figure 4.39).

Directional lights emit most of the visible light when the action is outdoors. When indoors, directional lights have problems with occlusion and are often replaced with spotlights. Wide spotlight cones cover as much of the environment as possible. While extra point lights provide extra specular kicks, it is still best convention to employ just one shadow light per indoor environment (Figure 4.40).

FIGURE 4.39 Before Key Light.

FIGURE 4.40 Key light contribution.

Fill Light

While the Key Light is typically just one light, the *Fill Light* may be provided by multiple lights. The primary purpose of the fill light is to bring up the darkest areas of the environment or to provide some luminance in areas of total darkness. Fill lights typically illuminate the darkest environmental shadows (Figure 4.41).

Point lights are often used for providing fill light. When configured with wide attenuation, soft intensity, and no shadows, point lights provide inexpensive service to the scene. The lighting artist must exhibit constraint when the rendering engine is equipped with some sort of *Ambient light* control. Ambient lights are not actual lights, but mathematical offsets applied before the scene is rendered. Ambient lights flatten scenes and remove depth. As an alternative to ambient, employ point lights which are inexpensive and provide the artist with enough artistic control to bring up the darkest shadows in the scene (Figure 4.42).

FIGURE 4.41 Fill light strategy.

FIGURE 4.42 Fill light contribution.

From the level design perspective, fill lights create contrast, areas of interest, and subtle directional indicators which help guide the attention of the participant. Fill lights play an important role establishing the mood and feeling of the scene.

Small kicker lights are often used to provide interactive visual effects in the scene such as candles, lamps, or fires. In these situations, point lights with short attenuations and bright intensities are used instead of spotlights. Characters approaching these interactive lights are impacted only when they are in proximity to the light's attenuation radius. Interactive lights help integrate the character into the environment and provide a holistic feeling to the scene.

Rim Light

Once used as a cinematographic special effect, the *Rim Light* provides the artist with a great amount of visual effects control. Traditionally, the rim light is a special spotlight placed behind an actor or actress to produce a rim, halo, or glint around their silhouette. The bright silhouette set against the darker background creates contrast in the scene and maintains the topology of the character it frames. Rim lights are used to set off special scene objects such as hair, teeth, and eyes.

Off-line renderers easily render rim lights since the camera's position is always understood. Rim lights may be used in real-time rendering but will not work with all camera positions. Real-time rim lights are only effective from one camera perspective unless the environment prevents the players from observing the light from multiple angles (Figure 4.43).

As visual effects, rim lights may be procedurally animated to always frame desired characters for participant cameras. Certain cell shaders use this technique to maintain consistent rim lighting, independent of the players' position. For this technique, each character rig is equipped with multiple rim lights which dynamically reposition themselves behind the character facing the player camera (Figure 4.44).

Other Lighting Strategies

As a visual effects tool, lighting provides simple yet profound methods for generating emotional tone in the level or scene. As with any powerful tool, rules must be followed to wield the power properly. While coverage of all

FIGURE 4.43 Rim light strategy.

FIGURE 4.44 Rim light contribution.

lighting rules is beyond the scope of this text, the included guidelines guarantee effective and responsible lighting.

While it is difficult to select which of the two following rules to mention first, I'll choose the one that will most probably be broken first and is the most difficult to recover from. While the temptation is very strong, resist the compulsion to use colored lights for your primary key light. Colored lights make for good fill and artistic rim lights. However, colored lights should not be used as key lights. There are three reasons for this. Initially, most artists, and even the most experienced lighters, find the math behind color blending to be challenging. Many unpredictable and uncontrollable artifacts generate from loss of control of simple color combinations. Materials do not behave as expected. Materials tuned in neutral lighting may produce strange or unexpected lighting phenomena when under the influence of unanticipated colored lights. The presence of colored lights makes forensic lighting difficult. When key lights are neutral, undesirable phenomena are debugged with simple material examination instead of juggling multiple improperly generated materials and off-colored lights. Colored lights have an unpredictable impact on post-process behavior. Like materials, all post-processes are designed with the intention of impacting neutrally lit scenes. When scenes are lit with colored lights, post-processes will misbehave. Colored lights nullify their intended behavior. This sullying behavior generates extra work for the lighting artist. When one post-process could have been used to impact the behavior of an entire level, the artist must meticulously re-adjust each colored light to generate the same desired impact.

When colored lights must be employed as key lights, manipulate the lights' temperature, also known as the kelvin parameter. Kelvins are a unit measurement for absolute temperature. Kelvin values of 6,500–8,000 K are blueish and are best suited for cloudy and overcast exterior scenes. Values between 4,500 and 6,500 K are less blue and most closely represent high noon exterior and moon lighting. Most interior fluorescent lights range from 3,100 to 4,500 K. These lights may appear less blue and warmer. While an art director may exercise artistic prerogative over a scene and choose a bluer light for interior and warmer light for the exterior, natural color temperatures are the opposite. Because of the scattering effect of the atmosphere, kelvin values between 2,000 and 3,000 K (the warmest colors) are best suited for exterior sunrise and sunset lighting. These values are also effective for most interior, incandescent lighting. Kelvin values less than 2,000 K are best reserved for candle-light and flame (Figure 4.45).

The next lighting rule may be just as important as the prior. There can be nothing in the scene, which is brighter than pure white, sRGB (1.0, 1.0, 1.0), and darker than pure black, sRGB (0.0, 0.0, 0.0). The reason for this is

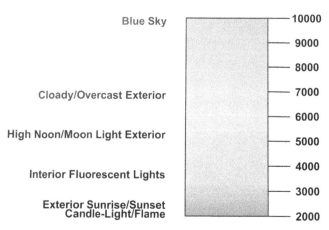

FIGURE 4.45 Kelvin temperature lighting.

mathematical. When any detail in the scene is brighter than pure white or darker than pure black, the value will be clamped. How much detail is lost is dependent on the context of the scene. The engine can only render between the values of 0.0 and 1.0. The job of the lighter is to map all possible detail between this range. When detail is greater than 0.0 and less than 1.0, values are visible. Any detail less than or equal to 0.0 or greater than or equal to 1.0 will be clamped and removed. This may seem like common sense but is a common mistake, even with experienced lighters. It is difficult to identify how much scene detail is lost due to clamping (Figure 4.46).

In figure 4.46, the regions of red color identify colors that are greater than 1.0 and the regions of green color identify colors that are darker than 0.0. In either situation, colors are being clamped and color information is lost.

This next rule may also seem like common sense but is easily broken. Scene lighting needs to be built often. The interactive viewers in modern real-time engines are programming miracles. However, unless the experience is made of pure dynamic lighting components, there is no device that will properly display what the end-user will see without building the scene's lighting. Adjust only a few lighting parameters and build the lighting to verify their impact. When too many changes are made between lighting builds, it is difficult to identify how individual adjustments impact overall lighting. This loss of lighting control makes it challenging to recover from awkward lighting situations. Returning the scene's lighting back to a desirable state is almost impossible. Consistent light rebuilding may seem long and unnecessarily slow but will save time in the long run by avoiding forensic lighting or even worse, relighting the scene.

The following section of this chapter is devoted to post-process effects. This last rule addresses the order of lighting and creating post-process effects. Post-process effects are very powerful and have a global impact on all lighting. It is important to finish all scene lighting before engaging any post-process effects. Once the effects are engaged, the scene's proper visual adjustments will be unidentifiable. Identifying future alterations to scenes' lighting or post-process effects becomes challenging. When an artist, unfamiliar with the scene's history, is tasked to make such alterations, changes to the lighting will be made to compensate for the post-process effects. This is a messy and counter-productive workflow. The best strategy is to simply avoid engaging post-process effects before the scene's lighting is complete or turning them off entirely before making any lighting adjustments.

POST-PROCESSING

Post-processing visual effects are a large subset of techniques which are extraordinarily powerful, can have a dramatic impact on the mood, tone, and emotional content of the scene, and most importantly, require no extra

FIGURE 4.46 Lighting detail lost to clamping.

geometry. Many of the techniques that impact the entire viewport thus have a sweeping impact over the entire experience. Art directors love to go wild with post-process techniques because they produce the greatest impact on the experience's final appearance and require the least amount of work. Many times, because the techniques require no extra geometry, they may be inexpensive.

This subsection of the chapter explains the technology behind the *Render Target*, the essential technology behind any post-process technique. The rest of this subsection introduces a set of image processing algorithms known as convolution operations. Convolution operations use a single mathematical operation that manipulates every screen pixel to generate the desired result. Color Grading, image blurring, as well as other in-camera phenomena such as vignetting, pixilation, distortion, and edge detection are discussed in this chapter.

To repeat the warning presented earlier in this chapter, do not engage post-processing effects until all scene lighting is complete! Otherwise, the job of lighting becomes almost impossible. The lighting and post-process effects contend for visual attention, and artists may find themselves struggling for control of the scene. Avoid wasting time! Wait until lighting is complete before engaging post-process effects.

Render Target

After rendering a pixel and blending it on top of all the other pre-shaded pixels, the rendering engine typically writes the pixel to a *Frame Buffer*, a chunk of memory that is written to the screen display. Two frame buffers are used. When one buffer is receiving new pixel information, the other is writing to the screen display. The two buffers are swapped for each new frame. When post-processes are applied, the pixels are written to a different chunk of memory called a *Render Target*. The rendering engine then renders a screen-sized quad (two triangles), to the frame buffer, using the render target as its source texture map (Figure 4.47).

Since the quad is the exact size as the display screen, there is a one-to-one correspondence between the render target and the newly rendered quad. The result of the quad rendering is written to the frame buffer, or it is written to another render target. Post-process shaders perform operations on the screen-sized quad upon rendering. Because the operations affect the entire quad uniformly, almost any camera lens or photographic process can be simulated. Post-processing is one of the most powerful yet simplest ways of manipulating the final screen image.

Eye Adaption

The most common of post-process effects is *Eye Adaption*, otherwise known as *Auto Exposure*. Eye Adaption simulates the human eye as it adapts camera light exposure, transitioning from dark light to bright or bright light to dark. Modern real-time engines typically engage this post-process by default. As a histogram-based process, a constant math function is applied to the render target to make it appear as if more light or less light is entering the scene. Lighting artists must turn this effect off before doing any lighting, shading, post-processing, or otherwise any visual effects work. Proper lighting adjustments cannot be made or verified within the context of the experience with the light exposure constantly changing. Since there is no constant base color, trying to adjust the lighting properly in an adapted scene is equivalent to throwing darts at a moving target in the dark. Once turned off, proper lighting adjustments to the scene may be made. Once the base lighting has been approved and locked, the eye adaptation may also be turned back on.

Color Filtering

Color Filtering is a simple post-process operation where every pixel in the render target is multiplied against the same, pre-generated, filter matrix. Tone mapping, color grading, and look-up tables are typical color filtering processes.

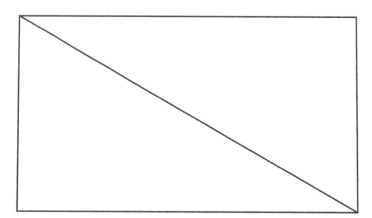

FIGURE 4.47 Screen-size render quad.

Tone Mapping

As mentioned in Chapter 3, a modern display device cannot display the fully viable range of observable colors. Tone mapping is a filter function used to map or squeeze a wide range of high dynamic range colors into a lower range the display device can handle. Hejl, Burgess-Dawson, and Hable, in a 2010 SIGGRAPH presentation, presented the following function to do this.

A = Shoulder Strength = 0.22

B = Linear Strength = 0.3

D = Toe Strength = 0.2

D = Toe Strength = 0.2

E = Toe Numerator = 0.01

F = Toe Denominator = 0.3

W = Linear White Point = 11.2

$$F(x) = \frac{x*(A*x+C*B)+D*E}{x*(A*x+B)+D*F} - \frac{E}{F}$$

$$\text{whitescale} = \frac{1.0}{f(W)}$$

$$\text{color} = f(x) * \text{whitescale}$$

$$\text{final color} = \text{pow}\left(\text{color}, \frac{1}{2.2}\right)$$

Equation 4.11 Filmic Tone Mapping; Heil, Burgess-Dawson & Hable, https://www.slideshare.net/hpduiker/ filmic-tonemapping-for-realtime-rendering-siggraph-2010-color-course

Most rendering engines provide variations of this formula with values to approximate the *Academy Color Encoding System (ACES) for television and film* as their default function. This function is known as *Filmic Tone Mapping* (Figure 4.48).

When performed as a post-process to the image, the colors get crisper and more saturated toward the bottom portion of the spectrum. Three components for the tone mapping function are exposed for the user to manipulate: the *toe*, the *linear*, and the *shoulder* portions of the curve. The toe and shoulder portions control the rate at which the curve flattens out from the bottom or top of the function. The default filmic toe increases the contrast in the darker regions. A stronger toe value increases the contrast. The shoulder has a strong influence on the total range. The larger the desired range, the more of a larger shoulder is needed. The linear portion controls the slope of the straight section in between. Black and white levels are also exposed to control the scene's blackest black or whitest white values (Figure 4.49).

FIGURE 4.48 Filmic tone mapping.

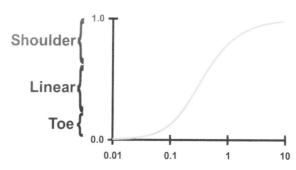

FIGURE 4.49 Tone mapping components.

Manipulating the tone mapping should be reserved for final, project-wide settings. This function creates a uniform mood or feeling over the entire project and should be constrained as one of the last adjustments made to the entire experience. Scene or time-of-day manipulations should not be achieved using tone mapping but instead using color grading techniques.

Color Grading

Like Tone Mapping, *Color Grading* is a simple and often localized offset or scalar multiplication performed on an entire scene. For example, consider an outdoor setting that is seen both during daylight and nighttime. The lighters can't use "no light" since nothing would be visible. Instead, the lighters establish a very diffusely lit, over-cast scene, and then apply a *day-for-night* color grading. A day-for-night color grading is usually a combination of desaturation, moving the midtones and highlights to a purple-blue color and neutralizing the shadows. During daylight hours, stronger, shadow-generating lights are used in conjunction with a dawn/dusk or neutral color grading. Color grading allows for very precise control to be applied for scenes employing dynamic lighting conditions (Figure 4.50).

Color Grading controls often seem overwhelmingly complex at first. In reality, they are similar controls repeated over five different regions: whites, shadows, mid-tones, highlights, and globally. Whites offset the colors of the scene so white colors can appear as truly "white." Shadows, mid-tone, and highlight sections allow the user to manipulate the saturation, contrast, gamma, gain or offset for specific shadow, mid-tone or highlight portions of the scene. Global controls empower the user to manipulate the saturation, contrast, gamma, gain, offset, and tint over the entire scene. To ensure effective color grading, base scene lighting must be as neutral or white as possible. When scene objects are neutrally lit, their behavior under the influence of biased color grading becomes predictable. Too many times I have observed inexperienced lighters lighting scenes with colored lights which turn into muddy, psychedelic fun houses when under the influence of biased color grading.

Take for example Figure 4.51. The scene was naively light with a yellowish directional light to create a strong dawn feeling. However, after the scene was color graded with a bluish color to cool things down, the colors shifted to a muddy green. The scene will need to be re-lit.

FIGURE 4.50 Day-for-night scene.

FIGURE 4.51 Incorrectly lit scene with and without color grading.

Look Up Tables (LUTS)

Before the days of high-powered color grading post-processing, the same effects were achieved by *Look Up Tables* or *LUTS*. A LUT is a texture map with single-pixel representations of the full-color spectrum (Figure 4.52).

During the influence of a look-up table, the color values of each pixel are referenced against the equivalent value in the texture map. The equivalent color value from the texture map then replaces the old color. Manipulating the scene with look-up tables produces the same effect as color grading but without the computational burden of the grading calculation.

Generating a look-up table is a six-step process

1. A high-resolution screenshot is made of the entire scene.
2. The screenshot is taken into an image manipulation software.
3. Color correction operations are applied to establish the desired look of the scene.

FIGURE 4.52 Scene color look-up table.

FIGURE 4.53 A neutral-colored look-up table texture.

4. A *Neutral Color Look Up Table* texture map is brought into the software. A neutral color look-up table is a texture without any sort of color correction or bias (Figure 4.53):.

5. The exact same operations performed on the screenshot are duplicated onto the neutral color look-up table.

6. The newly adjusted look-up table texture map is written to disc and brought into the experience to be used as a new color look-up table texture.

There are two reasons why look-up tables are rarely used. The first reason is that look-up tables are cumbersome and obsolete. Color grading can produce the same effects within the context of the experience, without the need for creating an external scene image, manipulating the image in another software, and then re-importing the new look-up texture. The second and more important reason is that scene consistency is lost on high-density range displays. All color grading, including look-up tables, are performed before the experience is tone mapped and transformed to a display's color space. Since the source image for a look-up table is captured as a screenshot on a destination display, the full display range cannot be maintained as the image is adjusted and transferred to a new look-up table texture which will be applied again by the same tone mapping. In effect, the scene is tone-mapped twice. Working with color grading speeds up the manipulation process and maintains consistency regardless of display device.

Image Blurring Techniques

Blurring convolutions are the essential components for simulating natural camera lens phenomena such as *Bloom*, *Depth of field*, and *Lens Flare*. While image blurring techniques may not be as dramatic as color grading effects, they impact the scene dramatically with just a subtle touch.

Image Blurring

There are several convolution strategies for blurring images. Three of the most common strategies are *Mean Filters*, *Weighted Average Filters*, and *Gaussian Filters*. Mean filters, otherwise known as *Box Filters*, simply average the current pixel value with a set number of its immediate neighboring pixel values. For example, a 3×3 filter averages each pixel with its 8 neighboring pixels, a 5×5 filter averages each pixel with its 24 surrounding pixels, a 7×7 filter averages its 48 pixels, etc. (Figures 4.54–4.56).

Weighted Average filters are box filters which give more weight to the current pixel than the pixel values surrounding it with the condition that the weighted sum of all the pixels must add to one. For example, when a 3×3 filter allots twice as much influence on the center pixel as its neighbors, the total sum must be divided by the total weighted contribution.

FIGURE 4.54 3×3 box filter.

FIGURE 4.55 5×5 box filter.

FIGURE 4.56 7×7 box filter.

$$\text{Final Pixel Color} = \frac{1}{10} \begin{bmatrix} 01 & 01 & 01 \\ 01 & 02 & 01 \\ 01 & 01 & 01 \end{bmatrix}$$

Equation 4.12 Weighted Average with 2 times the center pixel influence

$$\text{Final Pixel Color} = \frac{1}{18} \begin{bmatrix} 01 & 01 & 01 \\ 01 & 10 & 01 \\ 01 & 01 & 01 \end{bmatrix}$$

Equation 4.13 Weighted Average with 10 times the center pixel influence

Controlling the weight of the center pixels allows greater control of the blurring (Figures 4.57 and 4.58).

FIGURE 4.57 Weighted average of a 5×5 filter with dividing factor = 26.

FIGURE 4.58 Weighted average of a 5×5 filter with dividing factor = 36.

While box and weighted average filters are inexpensive, the most common blurring strategy is *Gaussian*. Gaussian blurring is implemented as a two-pass process: a horizontal pass and a vertical pass. In each pass, up to 32 pixels in a row or column are averaged using a standard Gaussian distribution:

$$G(x) = e^{\frac{-x^2/2\sigma}{2\pi\sigma}}$$

Equation 4.14 Gaussian Blur

The results of the horizontal first pass are written to a render target. The vertical pass is then applied to the new render target and the results are written to the frame buffer, or another render target. The value of σ controls the amount of blur. Larger values produce more blur while smaller values produce less. When computational resources are available, the smoothness of the Gaussian distribution and the control of the σ value makes Gaussian the blur strategy of choice (Figure 4.59).

FIGURE 4.59 Gaussian blur with a σ of 5.0.

FIGURE 4.60 Scene before and after bloom.

Bloom

Bloom simulates the real lens phenomena of making the brightest objects in a scene glow. In other words, the effect produces fringes of light extending beyond the borders of the brightest areas in the scene which creates the illusion of bright light overwhelming the camera (Figure 4.60).

Typically implemented in most rendering engines as a standard visual effect, Bloom is executed as a four-step process (Figures 4.61–4.63).

1. The scene is rendered to a render target.
2. The brightest elements of the render target are extracted and written to a second render target.
3. The bright elements are blurred and written to a third render target.
4. The blurred contents are blended back on top of the original render target using A over B layering and written to the frame buffer or yet another render target.

Since bloom is a four-step process, depending on the scene's complexity, it may be a very expensive effect. The artist must be responsible for real-time performance when utilizing this effect.

Depth of Field

Depth of field (DOF) simulates the real lens phenomena of blurring all elements in the scene except for those within the lens' range of sharpness. This range of sharpness is called DOF (Figure 4.64).

DOF is a cinematographic principle that extends beyond the scope of this text. While mastering DOF requires considerable dedication and practice, this section discusses the basic concepts and parameters an artist needs

FIGURE 4.61 Extracted bright elements.

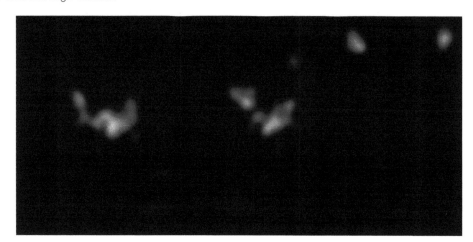

FIGURE 4.62 Blurred elements.

FIGURE 4.63 Final bloom effect.

FIGURE 4.64 Scene with depth of field.

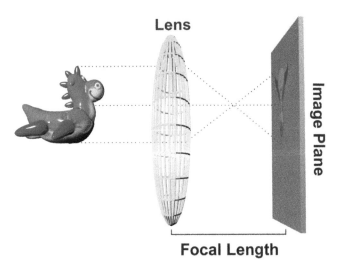

FIGURE 4.65 Camera focal length.

to consider when implementing this effect. When dealing with DOF, artists will need to consider the camera lens *Focal Length*, *F Stop*, and *Bokeh*.

The size of the DOF is controlled by the camera lens' *aperture*. A larger camera aperture produces a shallower DOF. A smaller aperture produces a deeper DOF. The aperture is a function of the camera lens' *F Stop* and *Focal Length*.

$$\text{Aperture} = \frac{\text{Focal Length}}{\text{F Stop}}$$

Equation 4.15 Camera Aperture

The camera's focal length simulates the distance between a real camera's lens and its image plane or sensor (Figure 4.65).

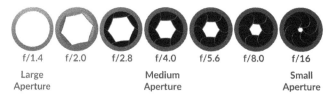

f/1.4   f/2.0   f/2.8   f/4.0   f/5.6   f/8.0   f/16

Large Aperture   Medium Aperture   Small Aperture

FIGURE 4.66 F stop/aperture comparison.

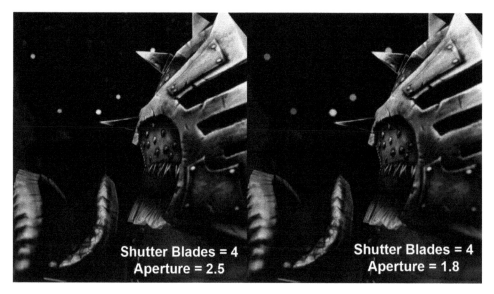

FIGURE 4.67 Rectangular and round bokeh.

As the lens' focal length increases, its field of view decreases. Increasing the lens' focal length produces a zoom-like effect making the out-of-focus areas become more pronounced.

The camera lens' F Stop simulates the size and timing of the opening of lens' diaphragm when exposing to film. The F Stop values are inversely proportional to the size of the opening. In other words, smaller F Stops simulate a larger opening. When balanced with the camera lens' focal length, a smaller F Stop results in a larger aperture which creates a shallower DOF while a larger F Stop creates a smaller aperture and deeper DOF (Figure 4.66).

Bokeh is the shape of the blur and simulates the shape of the lens' diaphragm opening. On a real camera, the number of blades forming the diaphragm controls the shape of the effect's blur. Four blades generate a rectangular blur while more blades simulate a more circular blur (Figure 4.67).

The DOF effect is simulated by breaking the scene into at least three layers: all objects between the camera and the focus distance, all objects within the focus distance range, and all objects beyond the focus distance. The algorithm blurs each layer dependent on the camera settings and the distance to the camera. Each blurred layer is written to a unique render target, and all are blended to a final frame buffer or to another render target. DOF can be an extraordinarily expensive process and should be employed with responsible consideration to real-time performance.

Lens Flare

Lens Flare simulates the real lens phenomenon of duplicating the brightest object in the scene, often seven times, and arranging the duplicates in a straight line such that the middle duplicates are the smallest with the least

FIGURE 4.68 Lens flare effect.

amount of blur and the ones on the ends are the largest with the greatest amount of blur. The angle of the line is dependent on the camera angle and the position of the light object. Lens flare effects are very good for simulating the phenomenon on such objects such as stained glass, trees and foliage, and other glass objects (Figure 4.68).

While the mathematics behind the effect is beyond the scope of this book, the results are generated in a very similar manner as a bloom effect.

1. The scene is rendered to a render target.

2. The brightest elements of the render target are extracted and written to a second render target.

3. Each of the (seven) duplicates is tinted, blurred, translated, and scaled to unique render targets.

4. All processed render targets are blended on top of the original scene render target.

Important parameters the artist needs to be aware of are the *intensity* of the lens flare, the tint of each individual flare, the *threshold* which sets the minimal brightness value of pixels contributing to the effect, and the *bokeh's* size and shape. The visual effect artist should be aware that since there are seven duplicates of the initial bright spot and seven uniquely blurred variations, the lens flare effect can be very expensive.

Emissive Materials

One of the most notorious pranksters in the computer graphics industry is the emissive material component. Emissive materials are materials with built in visual effects. They are intended to appear as if they are light sources, emitting from the material and illuminating the neighboring geometry sharing the same material. Emissive materials are very handy for creating small amounts of spillover light emanating from a tight portion of geometry, such as a demon's eyes or flashing electronics. Inexperienced artists often confuse them for being real light sources. I have had artists complain to me that although their materials have an extremely strong emissive color, they still cannot light their scene properly. Their emissive materials are visual effects, not light sources.

Emissive materials are very similar to the Bloom effect. Once rendered, the emissive materials are blurred, and their brightness is increased to accommodate any loss of illumination and the strength of the emissive color component. The result is then blended over the originally rendered content using an over or additive blend operation.

Please use emissive materials with caution. They provide very effective, small regional coverage. However, resist the urge to treat them as true light sources.

In-Camera Techniques

While color filtering and blurring constitute the most common types of post-process effects, there is an infinite number of other possible effects that may be applied to the pre-rendered scene. These effects are at least two-pass effects. In other words, all scene content is initially rendered to a render target, operations are applied and written to another render target or the frame buffer. Some of these effects include *vignetting, chromatic aberration, distortion, pixelization, dithering,* and *edge detection.*

Vignetting

Vignetting is the simulation of the natural darkening effect created by real-world camera lenses. Pixels furthest from the center of the rendering window are gradually darkened. This technique simulates dirty, old, and imperfect camera lenses (Figure 4.69).

The technique manifests itself by generating a dark ring around the viewport center. Depending on the implementation, a visual effects artist may be able to manipulate the intensity of the contrast of the darkening transition.

Chromatic Aberration

Chromatic Aberration is another lens simulation technique which color shifts the edges of a real-world camera lens. This effect is like the vignetting technique except that instead of darkening the pixels of the far edges of the viewport, their color values are shifted (Figure 4.70).

The technique's *intensity* controls how much shifting occurs at the edges. The saturation parameter controls the saturation of the shifted colors. Lower values appear more blurred while the higher values appear less.

FIGURE 4.69 Camera vignetting.

FIGURE 4.70 Chromatic aberration.

Distortion

Distortion is a simple effect which distorts one image by the values of a second image. As in all other post-process effects, the scene's image is initially rendered to a render target. The red and the green pixel values from a different, viewport-sized image are accessed. Since the red and green color values are bound between 0 and 1, the value of 0.5 is subtracted, resulting in a new value between –0.5 and 0.5. The pixels from the initial corresponding render target are then offset in position according to these new values; the red value shifts in the U or X axis and the green value in the V or Y axis. This phenomenon shifts the original image by the color values of the second image (Figure 4.71).

There is a slight error that needs to be dealt with when using this technique. Since most color channel values originate from 8-bit values between $0 \rightarrow 255$, the value of 0.5 can't possibly exist. There is no 8-bit value

FIGURE 4.71 Original image, distorting texture and final distorted image.

FIGURE 4.72 3D noise textured character.

between 127 and 128 and thus an offset value of pure 0 value cannot exist. To counteract this error, a constant value of 0.001961 is added to each offset calculation. This value is obtained by dividing 0.5 by 255.0.

$$\text{Distortion Offset Amount} = \frac{0.5}{255.0} \cong 0.001961$$

Equation 4.16 Distortion Offset Calculation

The Distortion technique was popularized for generating semi-transparent alien creatures. Instead of using pre-generated offset images, animated 3D CGI characters (rendered with a noise pattern instead of traditional shading) are used (Figure 4.72).

The noise-textured 3D characters then only distort the original image where its red and green values are non-zero. This generates a semi-transparent character running through the scene (Figure 4.73).

Pixelization

Pixelization is a simple technique for blurring a desired portion of screen space with a mosaic-like pattern. Utilized as a censoring technique, pixelization was used for blurring out faces, footage of nudity and for obscuring sensitive private information such as license plates, phone numbers, and addresses (Figure 4.74).

Pixilation is also used for simulating the limited color palette of low-resolution displays of nostalgic game systems such as the Nintendo Game Boy, Nintendo Entertainment System, the Atari 2600 game system, and early three-dimensional games such as Doom.

The effect is an inexpensive, easy, two-pass process. After the image is rendered to the render target, it is mapped to a screen quad using a special texture look-up function. Instead of mapping the render target to the screen quad pixel by pixel, this modified texture-lookup function is used:

$$\text{color}(u, v) = \text{texture}\left(\frac{\text{floor}\left(\text{screen position}(u,v) \times \text{pixelization factor}\right)}{\text{floor}\left(\text{pixelization factor}\right)}\right)$$

Equation 4.17 Pixelization Texture-Lookup

FIGURE 4.73 Distorted 3D noise textured character.

FIGURE 4.74 Censoring an image.

The modified texture-lookup function samples the image from the render target at a lower resolution which results in a chunky, semi-random appearance. The pixelization factor controls how chunky and how blurry the resulting image appears. Larger values result in an image subdivided into many smaller, more consistent looking chunks. Smaller values produce more blocky, blurry images (Figure 4.75).

Dithering

Dithering operators are great for achieving that nostalgic, Microsoft-1990s, 16-color graphics mode look. Before modern, high-end image displays, it was common to experience color-band artifacts when forcing true-color images into 256-color or 216-color "web-safe" color palettes. Banding artifacts occur as colors within certain

FIGURE 4.75 Original, high, and low pixelization factors.

ranges are converted into their nearest acceptable color. A common way of removing these artifacts is by using *dithering* or *color-quantization*. Dithering is an optical illusion which takes advantage of the eye's natural tendency to blend two colors in near proximity to each other (Figure 4.76).

Exploiting natural blending behavior also simulates transparent objects. Foreground objects are dithered against their background object to produce a transparent-like effect.

Coverage of dithering algorithms is beyond the scope of this text. However, a popular and easy implementation variation is *Ordered Dithering*. Ordered dithering uses a pre-generated "dither matrix" which acts as a threshold to control which pixels are blended. The most popular of these matrices are the Bayer matrices. Characterized by their "cross haired" patterns, Bayer matrices come in multiple sizes depending on the number of desired resulting patterns:

$$\frac{1}{4}\begin{bmatrix} 0 & 2 \\ 3 & 1 \end{bmatrix}, \frac{1}{16}\begin{bmatrix} 00 & 08 & 12 & 04 \\ 02 & 10 & 14 & 06 \\ 03 & 11 & 15 & 07 \\ 01 & 09 & 13 & 05 \end{bmatrix}, \frac{1}{64}\begin{bmatrix} 00 & 48 & 32 & 16 & 12 & 60 & 44 & 28 \\ 08 & 56 & 40 & 02 & 04 & 52 & 36 & 20 \\ 03 & 51 & 35 & 19 & 15 & 63 & 47 & 31 \\ 11 & 59 & 43 & 27 & 07 & 55 & 39 & 23 \\ 02 & 50 & 34 & 18 & 14 & 62 & 46 & 30 \\ 10 & 58 & 42 & 26 & 06 & 54 & 38 & 22 \\ 01 & 49 & 33 & 17 & 13 & 61 & 45 & 29 \\ 09 & 57 & 41 & 25 & 05 & 53 & 37 & 21 \end{bmatrix}$$

Equation 4.18 5, 17, and 65 Pattern Matrices

FIGURE 4.76 Color dithering with only two colors.

A simple approximation of the dithering effect is achieved from simple comparison of a pixel's illumination value against its corresponding value in the threshold matrix. When the value is greater, the original pixel color is not changed. When the value is less, the pixel is colored black. While this effect is not true dithering, it does produce the tell-tale, ordered dithering, cross-haired patterns (Figure 4.77).

Dithering is inexpensive and is very effective for faking transparency or generating the appearance of more colors than are present.

Edge Detection/Sobel Operator

Quite often, the outlines of objects need to be highlighted to produce a cell-shaded look. Other times, RADAR or SONAR need to be visualized by identifying the edges of objects in the scene. Edge detection strategies are used to identify these edges. Very simply, the strategies identify components in images with strong intensity contrasts, where pixels jump in intensity from one pixel to another (Figure 4.78).

While the mathematics of edge detection strategies is beyond the scope of this text, a simple filter, such as a *Sobel Operator*, is easily achieved. Sobel operators are convolution filters which take a pixel's value and add them with variations of its neighbor pixel values. The results of these convolutions identify when a pixel is on an edge or not. Sobel operators are two-pass filters which apply convolution filters horizontally and then vertically. Instead of the color intensity values, the pixel's illumination values are evaluated. Both convolutions are

FIGURE 4.77 Approximated ordered dithering.

FIGURE 4.78 Scene edge detection.

calculated, and the results are combined. When the sum reaches beyond a certain threshold, the pixel is colored black. Else, the pixel will be colored white.

$$\text{Convolution}_x = \begin{bmatrix} 01 & 00 & -1 \\ 02 & 00 & -2 \\ 01 & 00 & -1 \end{bmatrix}$$

$$\text{Convolution Value}_x \left(\text{pixel}_{22} \right) = \begin{bmatrix} 01 & 00 & -1 \\ 02 & 00 & -2 \\ 01 & 00 & -1 \end{bmatrix} \times \begin{bmatrix} \text{pixel}_{11} & \text{pixel}_{12} & \text{pixel}_{13} \\ \text{pixel}_{21} & \text{pixel}_{22} & \text{pixel}_{23} \\ \text{pixel}_{31} & \text{pixel}_{32} & \text{pixel}_{33} \end{bmatrix}$$

$$\text{Convolution Value}_x\left(\text{pixel}_{22}\right) = \text{pixel}_{11} - \text{pixel}_{13} + 2*\text{pixel}_{21} - 2*\text{pixel}_{23} + \text{pixel}_{31} - \text{pixel}_{33}$$

Equation 4.19 Calculation of the Horizontal Convolution Value

$$\text{Convolution}_y = \begin{bmatrix} -1 & -2 & -1 \\ 00 & 00 & 00 \\ +1 & +2 & +1 \end{bmatrix}$$

$$\text{Convolution Value}_y\left(\text{pixel}_{22}\right) = \begin{bmatrix} -1 & -2 & -1 \\ 00 & 00 & 00 \\ +1 & +2 & +1 \end{bmatrix} \times \begin{bmatrix} \text{pixel}_{11} & \text{pixel}_{12} & \text{pixel}_{13} \\ \text{pixel}_{21} & \text{pixel}_{22} & \text{pixel}_{23} \\ \text{pixel}_{31} & \text{pixel}_{32} & \text{pixel}_{33} \end{bmatrix}$$

$$\text{Convolution Value}_y\left(\text{pixel}_{22}\right) = \text{pixel}_{31} - \text{pixel}_{11} + 2*\text{pixel}_{32} - 2*\text{pixel}_{12} + \text{pixel}_{33} - \text{pixel}_{13}$$

Equation 4.20 Calculation of the Vertical Convolution Value

Threshold = 0.05

If $\text{Convolution Value}_x\left(\text{pixel}_{22}\right) + \text{Convolution Value}_y\left(\text{pixel}_{22}\right) >$ Threshold

$\text{Color}\left(\text{pixel}_{22}\right) = 1.0$

Else

$\text{Color}\left(\text{pixel}_{22}\right) = 0.0$

Equation 4.21 Evaluation of Convolution Values

When this strategy is applied to the illumination values of image pixels, the edges are localized and enhanced. Inexpensive to calculate, the results may be written to another render target where they may be combined with the rendered images, as they would in a cell-shader, or sent directly to the frame buffer for a RADAR effect (Figure 4.79).

FIGURE 4.79 Cell shader.

CONCLUSION

While particles and exploding objects tend to attract most of the attention in the visual effects world, most visual effects occur within the camera and don't require the contribution of other three-dimensional objects. Effects which simply and subtly manipulate the lighting, rendering, blending, and post-processing of the scene do more to influence the mood and emotional tone than any additional three-dimensional objects.

Basic understanding of the real-time rendering pipeline is all that is required to understand how all visual effects contribute to the images we see on the screen. Mastery of the programming nuances of the rendering engine is not necessary. However, the exercise of creating even a simple renderer will pay off exponentially to the pro-active, visual effects artist. At the time of this book's writing, the traditional seven stages of the rendering pipeline are the industry standard. The real-time ray tracing pipeline will change the rendering environment as machines become faster and the techniques become more stable.

The last stage of the rendering pipeline is the blending stage. This is a crucial stage for image display since it controls how all objects in the scene are blended and combined. While there is only one basic method for combining pre-rendered images, there are a multitude of sub-variations that when mastered can have a huge impact on the final visual display.

Lighting is also a vital mood and emotional tone manipulating technique. Understanding a few types of light is all that is necessary to start lighting a scene. The art of lighting is, however, a large and complicated topic. The fundamentals of lighting techniques are covered in this text. If further understanding of the art of lighting is required, the pro-active technical artist is advised to seek supplements from traditional photography, cinematography, and real-time lighting.

Once the final image is rendered, post-processing techniques provide a dramatic impact on the overall display's mood and emotional content. All post-processing techniques take advantage of a render target which stores the rendered scene to a temporary memory location to be manipulated later. Some of the most powerful and impactful tools include eye adaption, color filtering, and image blurring techniques. Other techniques which filter the render target include vignetting, chromatic aberration, distortion, pixelization, dithering, and edge detection strategies.

INTRODUCTION

As introduced in Chapter 4, all computer-generated objects must be rendered within the rendering pipeline. To satisfy all possible demands of the rendering pipeline, the real-time rendering engine must be dynamic, interoperable, and extensible. Interfacing with the engine can be a challenging endeavor. Within the real-time production environment, this interface is typically a customizable material which empowers artists, designers, and other non-technical individuals to interact with the engine without extensive understanding of its inner mechanics.

This chapter introduces the essence of materials and identifies several strategies how they may be exploited to produce extraordinary visual effects. A popular rendering strategy is *physically based rendering (PBR)*. Rules and strategies for interfacing with these modern algorithms are provided. Manipulating material behavior with simple mathematics is extraordinarily powerful. The roles of simple mathematical operations, such as addition and multiplication, are provided along with more complicated patterns such as the mighty sine wave function.

Of all possible material input methods, the most powerful is texture map animation. The fundamentals of texture mapping are explained in this chapter. Texture manipulation techniques, such as panning and rotating, are provided to demonstrate how they are some of the most effective of all visual effects tools. Examples of altering objects' surface appearances and shapes are provided.

Although stated earlier, the following concept must be reiterated. All material-based visual effects must be developed within the context of their final rendering engine. Every engine is unique and has its own thumbprint. At the time of writing this book, one effect cannot be guaranteed to look the same on two different engines. There are always subtle differences. As a rule of thumb, predictable results are achievable through pre-visualizing effects on different rendering platforms. However, the final effects must be completed within the context of their destination rendering engines.

MATERIAL PIPELINE

Rendering *shaders* and *object materials* are often confused. Within some contexts, they represent similar concepts. Shaders are, first and foremost, small computer programs which instruct rendering engines how to deform and how to *color* computer graphic objects. While the term, "*small*," is subjective, shaders may be large programs whose purpose is to complement more encompassing rendering pipelines. While there are many rendering pipelines, they all share the same essential seven stages: the input assembler, the vertex shader, the tessellation stage, the geometry shader, the rasterizer, the pixel or fragment shader, and the layer blender. Graphic programmers customize each stage to suit the needs of their current production. Pixel or fragment shaders calculate how light interacts with objects to produce the color of their corresponding pixels. Vertex shaders transform the initial geometry. Other shaders, such as tessellation and geometry shaders, define how more information is added to or removed from the resulting geometry.

While shaders can be smaller compared with the rendering pipelines they complement, they can still be large and complicated. The task of writing shaders is the domain of programmers, technical artists, and technical designers. Materials, on the other hand, are implemented to speed and simplify the shader writing process. Materials abstract the shader code process through the fine tuning of exposed shader parameters. Their input consists of constant numbers, images known as texture maps, and dynamic channel data. Instead of interacting with individual shader components, materials provide a holistic method for artists and other non-technical individuals to customize the rendering engine (Figure 5.1).

DOI: 10.1201/9781003009795-6

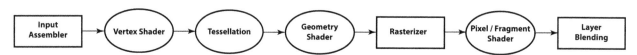

FIGURE 5.1 Material pipeline.

Materials are not passive collections of numbers and images. Most material environments provide fundamental input operations. While some engines require additional material compilation to maintain speed and efficiency, materials still provide simple and fast strategies for fine-tuning shader behavior. Simple or complex, static, or dynamic, materials constitute the aggregate of the shading pipeline and define the visual properties of three-dimensionally rendered objects.

SHADING PARADIGMS

There are two primary shading paradigms which all real-time materials must support: the old school light approximation models and the new school *PBR* techniques. The old school models approximate the behavioral characteristics of light reflecting off object surfaces. All visible light is broken into its ambient, diffuse, and specular components. The mathematical models used to generate these components are numerical approximations. PBR models attempt to accurately simulate the behavior of natural light in the real world with photorealism as an end objective.

While most modern real-time rendering engines support new school PBR techniques, there are many reasons for studying the old school paradigms. The first and foremost reason is the old school methods are still very much a part of the real-time and off-line rendering worlds. Not all real-time engines support PBR and when they do, they are implemented as optional modes. The old school models have a look that PBR techniques are unable to duplicate. They are simpler to understand and often faster to optimize. PBR algorithms are a set of strategies as opposed to a strict algorithm. Without robust investigation, they can be very difficult to implement. Many modern rendering strategies such as Ray Marching (which allows for the creation of visible geometry that exists exclusively within the shader) are dependent on the lightweight and fast nature of the old school paradigms. Use of PBR to address these circumstances is rare and challenging to implement. Photorealism is the purpose of PBR, yet these qualities are not always desired by everyone. The flexible nature of old school techniques provides for more dynamic rendering environments. Regardless of desired rendered output, materials must be robust and dynamic enough to support all visual targets.

Old School Rendering Models

The old school rendering model is traditionally referred to as the *Phong Shading* model. The Phong Shading model is the sum of three lighting components: ambient, diffuse, and specular (Figure 5.2).

Ambient Shading Component

The ambient component of light is simply an offset from black generated by the shader. This offset simulates the base color of light when in shadow. To avoid information clipping, never allow rendering pure black. Ambient components are added to the base color of the scene to prevent it from rendering black (Figure 5.3).

Care should be taken when generating the ambient component. Too much ambient light causes materials to appear self-illuminated and makes the scene lose depth and flatten.

Diffuse Shading Component

The diffuse lighting component is the foundational lighting property of a surface. This model reflects the color of an object's surface when under the influence of regular light. When someone describes a surface as having a base or *albedo* color, they are referring to the surface's diffuse component (Figure 5.4).

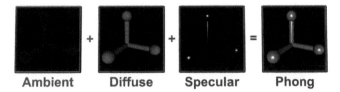

Ambient + Diffuse + Specular = Phong

FIGURE 5.2 Phong shading model.

FIGURE 5.3 Ambient component of light.

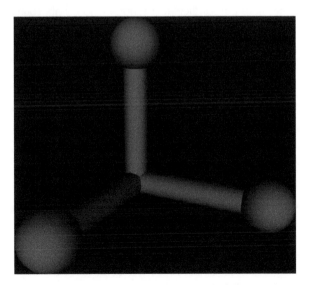

FIGURE 5.4 Diffuse lighting component.

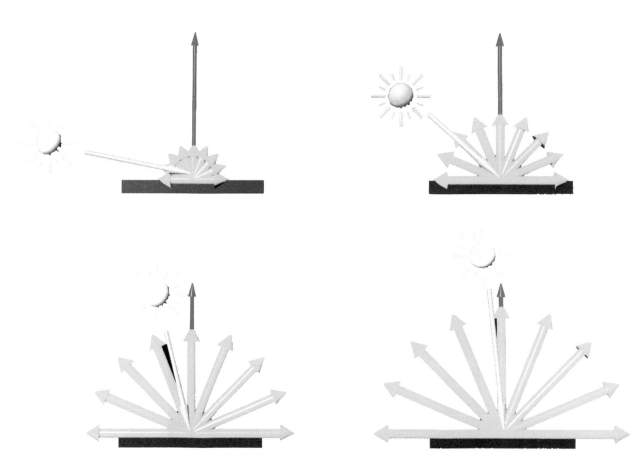

FIGURE 5.5 Lambert's cosine law.

Based on Lambert's cosine law, the diffuse component of light approximates the direct impact of light reflecting in all directions off the surface of an object. Lambert's cosine law states the amount of light reflected off the surface of an object is directly proportional to the cosine of the angle between the directions of a light source and the surface normal. In other words, the more perpendicular a surface is to a light source, the darker it will appear (Figure 5.5).

If you happen to be familiar with the cosine function, you know that the cosine value of zero angle is 1.0, $(0°) = 1.0$ and the cosine value of any angle of 90° is 0.0, $(90°) = 0.0$. When a light source is perpendicular to a surface (the angle between the light shining on the surface and the surface normal approaches 0.0), the diffuse value of the reflected light approaches a value of 1.0. When the light direction glances off the direction of the surface (the angle between the light and the surface normal approaches perpendicular or 90°), the value of the reflected light approaches a value of 0.0. When the angle of the incident light and the surface normal is greater than 90°, the cosine of the angle is less than 0.0, so we don't even consider it and leave it at 0.0. (There is no such thing as negative light!) (Figure 5.6).

The intensity formula for diffuse lighting is the cosine of the angle between the incoming light and the surface normal multiplied by a constant scalar:

Diffuse Light Intensity $(I) = k * \cos(\theta)$, where k is a constant scalar

Equation 5.1 Diffuse Lighting Model A

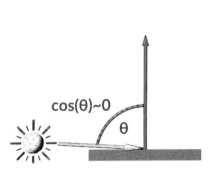
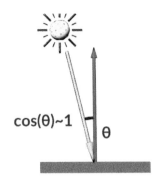

cos(θ)~0   cos(θ)~1

θ   θ

FIGURE 5.6 Cosine of the angle of the light and the surface normal.

Some folks may be aware of the Law of Cosines which states that the angle between vector *a* and vector *b* (the dot product of *a* and *b*) is the product of the length of vector *a* times the length of vector *b* times the cosine of their angle:

$$\vec{a} \cdot \vec{b} = ||a|| * ||b|| * \cos(\theta)$$

Equation 5.2 Law of Cosines

When vector *a* and vector *b* have been normalized (or their individual lengths converted to 1.0), the Law of Cosines becomes simplified:

$$\vec{a} \cdot \vec{b} = \cos(\theta)$$

Equation 5.3 Simplified Law of Cosines

When the directional vector of light, *L* and the surface normal are both normalized, the diffuse lighting model is simplified as well:

$$\text{Diffuse Light Intensity}(I) = k * \vec{L} \cdot \vec{N}$$

Equation 5.4 Diffuse Lighting Model B

Surface Normal Calculation

One important factor which is often overlooked by visual effects artists when calculating diffuse lighting is the source of the surface normal. There are three different strategies for interpolating surface normal across polygon faces: *flat* or no interpolation, *Gouraud* interpolation, and *Phong* interpolation. When employed in correct circumstances, each of these approaches may be used effectively.

Flat Interpolation

When flat or no interpolation is used, a constant surface normal is used to render across the face of the rendered polygon. This results in a faceted-looking surface which resembles a disco ball (Figure 5.7).

Gouraud Interpolation

Gouraud interpolation is an advancement on flat interpolation. Instead of using the surface normal of each polygon, the surface normals of neighboring polygons meeting at unique vertices are averaged. Full lighting is calculated at that vertex, using the averaged normal. The pixel lighting values are bi-linearly interpolated between shaded vertices. This results in a smoother surface than flat shading with only a trace of faceting. When the polygonal complexity of the object is low, this faceting becomes apparent as the lighting only appears correct at the vertices. When the complexity of the object is high, the phenomena is decreased (Figure 5.8).

FIGURE 5.7 Flat normal interpolation.

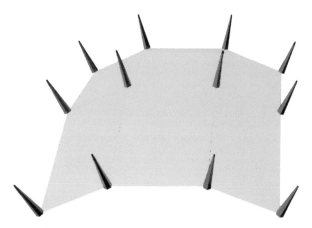

FIGURE 5.8 Gouraud interpolation.

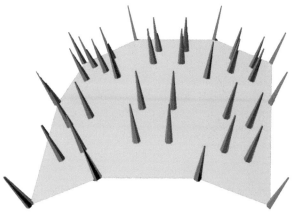

FIGURE 5.9 Phong interpolation.

Phong Interpolation

Phong Interpolation is an advancement over Gouraud interpolation. Instead of calculating the light at each vertex, Phong interpolation bi-linearly interpolates the vertex normals across the surface of each polygon and then calculates the lighting for each pixel. This results in a smoother gradient between vertices and produces almost no faceting (Figure 5.9).

Limitations of computing resources motivated early digital artists to employ the less expensive diffuse interpolating models before using Phong Interpolation. However, computational power increased dramatically, and Phong Interpolation has become the default normal interpolation technique. The use of flat and Gouraud interpolation is a stylistic choice.

Specular Shading Model

The specular lighting component is the mirror-like reflection that almost all materials emit when illuminated. To achieve believable lighting, as well as generating visual effects that integrate with their environments, the specular component, or highlight, is used to identify how irregular or smooth a surface is, how wet or dry it is, and indicate a surface's relative angle from a light source (Figure 5.10).

There are several models used to approximate the specular component. The most common model is the Phong or Blinn-Phong model. There are specialized models used for specific applications such as three-color toon-shading, hair, and fur.

All models compute specular by calculating the angle between the view and reflection vectors. The reflection vector mirrors the light vector across the surface normal. The Phong specular model is the foundation for all old school rendering models. The Phong calculation is equal to the angle between the view vector and the light reflation vector raised to some power representing the highlight spread.

In Figure 5.11, V is the incoming view direction, N is the surface normal, L is the direction from the surface to the light, and R is the direction of the reflection vector.

Phong Specular Component $= (R \cdot V)^S$

S is the size of the reflection highlight

Equation 5.5 Phong Specular Lighting Calculation

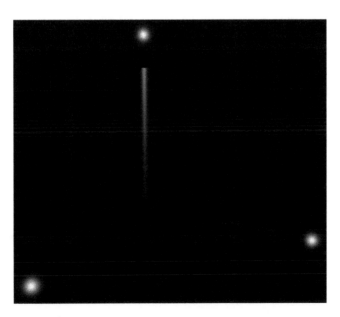

FIGURE 5.10 Specular lighting component.

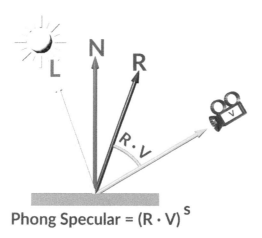

$$\text{Phong Specular} = (R \cdot V)^S$$

FIGURE 5.11 Phong specular lighting model.

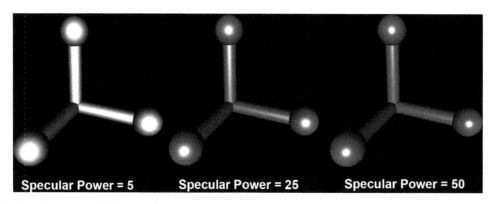

Specular Power = 5   Specular Power = 25   Specular Power = 50

FIGURE 5.12 Specular impact of different S values.

In the Phong model, S corresponds to the size of the reflection highlight. The highlight becomes tighter and sharper with larger values of S. The highlight becomes softer and more spread out with smaller values. The actual scale value of S is relative to each surface (Figure 5.12).

Since light is a predictable physical phenomenon, its reflection angle conforms with the physical law of reflection and is equal to the angle of incidence. Within the context to the direction of the surface normal, the angle of an incoming light vector, L, to a surface produces a reflecting vector, R, in the opposite direction (Figure 5.13).

This law is very easy to understand in two dimensions but gets a bit squirrely in three. The reflection vector is calculated by subtracting the light vector, L, from the product of twice the surface normal, N, with the dot product of the normal and light vectors.

Reflection Vector $= 2 * (N \cdot L) * N - L$

Equation 5.6 Reflection Vector Calculation

The explanation of this formula makes sense when viewed one piece at a time. When the light vector, L, is projected onto the surface normal, N (the vector dot product of L and N), the result is a float value, p (Figure 5.14).

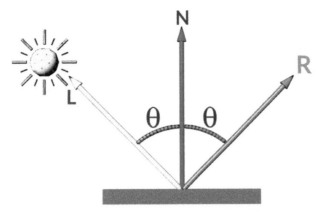

Angle of Incidence = Reflectance

FIGURE 5.13 Law of reflection.

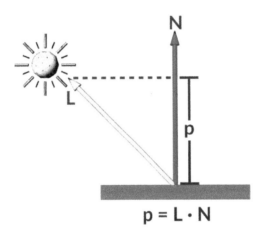

$$p = L \cdot N$$

FIGURE 5.14 The projection of light vector onto the surface normal.

When the surface normal is scaled by twice the value of p, the resulting vector, Q, is twice the relative height of the light vector, L (Figure 5.15).

The final reflection vector, R, is the result of subtracting the light vector, L, from this new vector, Q (Figure 5.16).

The generation of the reflection vector is crucial for the calculation of the specular component. This formula is commonly used in other areas of visual effects such as calculating angles of particles bouncing off surfaces and the trajectories of colliding rigid bodies.

Phong Shading Model

The old school, Phong shading model, is the combination of the ambient, diffuse, and specular lighting components (Figure 5.17).

C_A represents the ambient color of the surface, C_D represents the diffuse color of the surface, k is the diffuse scalar, C_S is the specular color of the surface, and S is the size of the specular highlight, the full Phong, old school Rendering equation is:

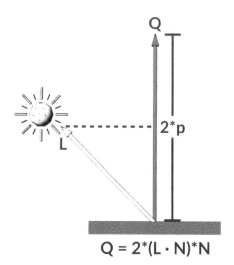

$$Q = 2*(L \cdot N)*N$$

FIGURE 5.15 Q is surface normal scaled by twice p.

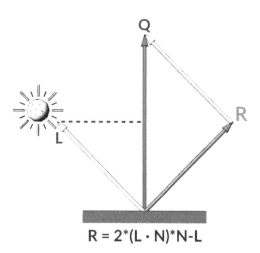

$$R = 2*(L \cdot N)*N-L$$

FIGURE 5.16 Reflection is light subtracted from Q.

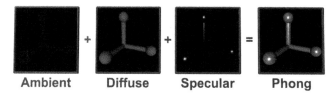

FIGURE 5.17 Old school shading model combination.

$$\text{Old School Rendering} = C_A + \left(C_D * k * N \cdot L\right) + \left(C_S * \left(\left(2*(N \cdot L)*N - L\right) \cdot V\right)^S\right)$$

Equation 5.7 Old School Rendering Formula

Unlit Shading Model

In addition to ambient, diffuse, and specular, there is often a fourth shading model associated with old school Rendering: Unlit. Unlit shading is the simplest and the fastest model to implement as it is treated as pure, constant

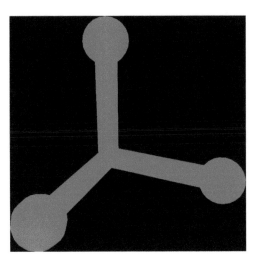

FIGURE 5.18 Unlit shading model.

color. This color may be amplified to unrealistic proportions to generate emissive characteristics. In other words, the surface appears as if it is emanating light. This makes unlit materials well suited for visual effects such as fire or self-illuminated objects. The visual effects artist must keep in mind that while the emissive nature of the material makes the surface appear to behave as a source of light, it is not. There is no light emitted from an emissive surface! The visual amplification and blurring are achieved as post-processes only and the object emits no light (Figure 5.18).

New School Rendering Models

The new school shaders and rendering models offer a paradigm shift from the old school approach. Instead of dealing with each stage of the pipeline as a separate shader and instead of breaking apart the shading calculation into individual components, the new school approach combines the entire pipeline into one uber shader. Instead of writing multiple shaders to influence specific behavior in the pipeline, artists and designers now manipulate exposed parameters impacting singular, monolithic shaders.

Part of the motivation for this paradigm shift is an attempt to depart from the lack of realism of the old school shading model. Each of the shading components of the old school model is a mathematical approximation attempting to duplicate the visible behavior of natural light. Out of context from surrounding environments, the old school lighting model appears realistic albeit somewhat "plasticky." Modern rendering approaches attempt to simulate or reproduce the physics-based, behavioral characteristics of light reflecting off real surfaces. Different types of lights behave differently with different types of surface materials. Techniques such as PBR and Global Illumination attempt to reproduce the measured, physical behavior of light on natural surfaces.

The mathematical models, formulas, and algorithms for these advanced techniques are very complicated. The Illumination model reproducing and conforming to the physical law of energy conservation is challenging to understand and almost impossible to solve. This is an over-simplistic explanation of this rendering model: the light leaving a point X on surface i (in the direction ω_o), is the sum of the light emitted by and reflected from the surface along ω_o from the small area around X (Figure 5.19).

$$L_0\left(X_i, \omega_o\right) = L_E\left(X_i, \omega_o\right) + L_R\left(X_i, \omega_i\right)$$

Equation 5.8 Rendering Formula Based on the Law of Conservation of Energy

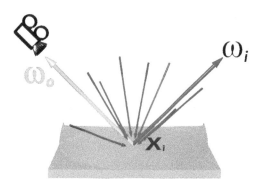

FIGURE 5.19 Visual simplification of the law of conservation of energy.

In expanded mathematical form, this formula looks like the integral:

$$L_r\left(x,\,\omega_r\right)=\int_{H^2}f_r\left(x,\omega_i\to\omega_r\right)L_i\left(x,\,\omega_{i,r}\right)\cos\theta_i'd\omega_i$$

Equation 5.9 Expanded Illumination Model

In more simplified terms, this model attempts to duplicate the energy given off at any point on the surface and is equal to the sum of all the energies of the direct and indirect sources of light (light that has been bouncing around). The intended purpose of displaying this formula is not to explain how these methods behave but to indicate their complexity.

This model is so complicated that helper functions called Bidirectional Reflectance Distribution Functions (BRDFs) are employed to describe the reflectance properties of surfaces. Even with the usage of BRDFs and other simplifications, these rendering strategies are still very delicate. Physically based lighting has often been described as not as a specific algorithm but as a collection of optimizations and limitations implemented to reproduce the physical characteristics of light reflecting from specific materials.

After the energy and time are spent implementing and optimizing PBR into a real-time engine, it does not make developmental sense to further modify or alter the code. Instead of enabling access to the inner workings of these illumination models, they are hidden from direct user access. Parameters that influence and manipulate their behavior are exposed. These parameters, within reason, are adequate to adjust the behavior of the rendering engine to generate any desired look.

While the inner workings of new school shaders are restricted from casual manipulation, there is still a direct need to understand how these complicated pieces of software behave and how they think. Hooks and anchor points are provided to inject custom code, which will not take control of the shader but will have indirect impact on shader behavior. The science of visual effects is being able to understand where these hooks and anchors are located so that their parameters may be manipulated, tweaked, and otherwise exploited to generate the desired visual phenomenon. The seven stages of the rendering pipeline are still present. However, they are now hidden within the structure of monolithic shaders. Instead of manipulating each stage directly, visual effects artists must manipulate parameters which indirectly impact multiple hidden stages of the rendering pipeline. While familiar shader inputs interface the user with the real-time engine, there is no standard for guiding their behavior.

Every engine possesses its own unique set of parameters used for manipulating its shader. Some have more than others. It is the author's intention to describe the most fundamental parameters manipulating all shaders while trying to avoid specific engine biases.

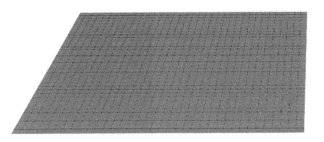
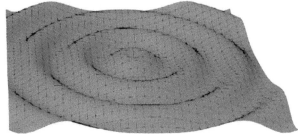

FIGURE 5.20 Normal manipulation to add detail.

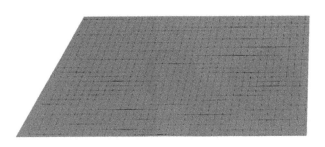
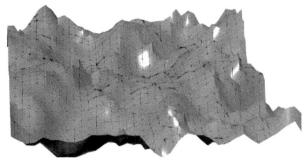

FIGURE 5.21 Offsetting vertex position to achieve a noisy structure.

Vertex Shader Parameters

While the primary duty of the vertex shader is to transform every vertex position from object model space to screen space, this is an ideal stage in the pipeline to manipulate any vertex attribute. The *normal* attribute provides access to how to deviate or offset the direction of the vertex normal. Since the diffuse and specular components are highly dependent on the normal to calculate the shading properties of the vertex, manipulating this parameter makes the object appear different going into the pixel shader. Normal manipulation alters the surface's shading behavior such as reversing the light position or making the surface appear to be inside-out or can even make the surface appear more detailed than what is presented (Figure 5.20).

The *World Space Position* attribute offsets the position of the vertex. Like manipulating the normal, the world position can be offset to create a more sophisticated topology that what was initially modelled or to receive a procedural expression, such as a sine wave or noise, which deviates the silhouette of the object (Figure 5.21).

Tessellation Parameters

The Tessellation stage adds more vertices and subdivides the initial model. A *Tessellation Factor* parameter in the material controls the number of added vertices and the amount of polygonal subdivision. Activating the tessellation in the material may also expose *Displacement* parameters to offset the positions of newly generated vertices. This is a very similar parameter to the World Space Position in the vertex shader but is only activated when the Tessellation Factor is increased beyond its default value (Figure 5.22).

Geometry Shader Parameters

As of the time of writing this book, few parameters are exposed to directly manipulate the geometry shader portion of the material. Geometry shaders are optional and non-trivial stages in the rendering pipeline. The technical demands of procedurally manipulating geometry in the shader code require a more sophisticated interface than the scope of this text.

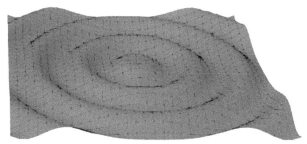

FIGURE 5.22 Tessellation displacement offsetting the position of subdivided surfaces.

FIGURE 5.23 Metallic and non-metallic surfaces.

Pixel/Fragment Shader Parameters

Shading and coloring are calculated in the pixel/fragment shader portion of the material. This component requires the greatest amount of parameter input yet provides the artist with the greatest amount of direct control over the surface's immediate appearance.

The *Base Color or Albedo input parameter* provides the fundamental diffuse value for the surface. This parameter contributes the initial bias for the diffuse, specular, and physically based shading algorithms.

The *Metallic* parameter indicates when the surface is metal or not. This parameter is rarely anything other than 0.0 or 1.0. Any value between these two extremes causes the surface to appear muddy or unworldly (Figure 5.23).

The *Specular* parameter controls the reflectiveness of non-metallic surfaces. Values range between fully reflective and non-reflective. Surfaces are very sensitive traversing from the non-reflective to the reflective. Mirror-like behavior is difficult to achieve without appearing "plastic-like." The specular parameter has no effect on metallic objects (Figure 5.24).

FIGURE 5.24 Reflective surfaces.

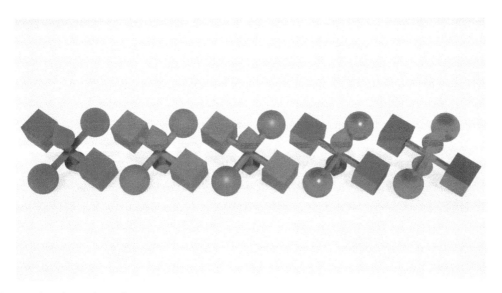

FIGURE 5.25 Rough and smooth metals.

The *Roughness* parameter controls how rough or smooth the surface is. Roughest values make metals appear to be "brushed" and non-metals appear "chalky." Smooth values make metals appear "chrome-like" (Figure 5.25).

With small specular values, non-metals are still chalky while highly specular values are almost "mirror-like" (Figure 5.26).

Just as the *Normal* parameter can be altered in the vertex shader, it plays a crucial role in almost all pixel/fragment shader calculations. Normals are manipulated at this stage of the pipeline to provide more detail to the model than is physically provided (Figure 5.27).

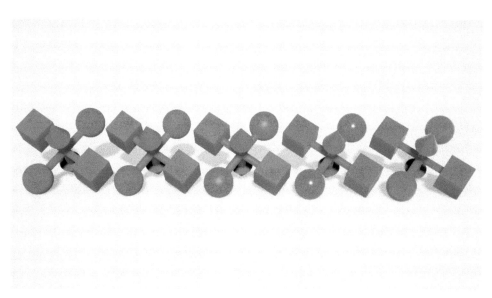

FIGURE 5.26 Rough and smooth non-metal objects.

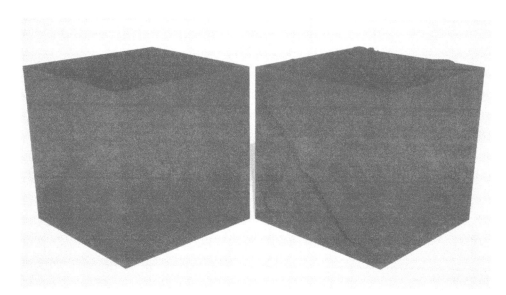

FIGURE 5.27 Manipulating normals to add more shaded detail.

For specialized shading methods, such as skin rendering, the *Subsurface Color* parameter provides a color input for light to inherit as it oscillates through the surface before being reflected out (Figure 5.28).

Most non-planar surfaces have corners, creases, nooks, and crannies which are difficult to light. Illumination models are challenged to restrict lighting and tend to over-light such areas. The *Ambient Occlusion* (AO) parameter provides extra darkening for those regions (Figure 5.29).

The *Refraction* parameter controls the amount of bend light experiences as it travels through transparent surfaces. This effect is necessary for pulling off realistic glass and water effects (Figure 5.30).

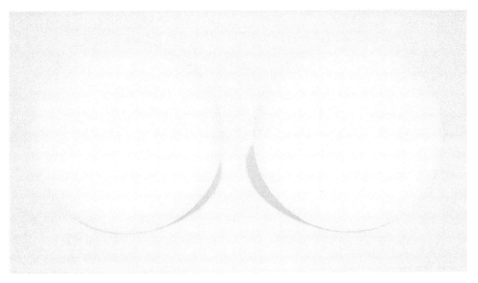

FIGURE 5.28 Surface with and without subsurface color.

Without Ambient Occlusion

With Ambient Occlusion

FIGURE 5.29 Object without and with ambient occlusion.

FIGURE 5.30 Impact of refraction on a transparent surface.

FIGURE 5.31 Pre-darkening of transparent surfaces.

The *Opacity* parameter controls how much to pre-darken the surface due to transparency. Opaque materials receive almost no brightness adjustment while transparent objects are nearly black (Figure 5.31).

Color Blending Parameters

Outside changing the blending mode of the material, *Opacity* and *Emissiveness* are the only alterable parameters, which impact how rendered surfaces are combined with pre-rendered layers. Opacity is used to darken transparent layers as they are blended with prior-rendered surfaces

Emissiveness is a post-process effect generated in the color blending stage. The *Emissive Color* parameter controls how much light the surface appears to be emitting. Since this is a post-process shading phenomenon,

FIGURE 5.32 Material without and with emissiveness.

there are no limits to what this value may be. Very bright emissive surfaces may appear to be light sources. Please be careful to understand they are not (Figure 5.32).

PBR RULES

Understanding the rules supporting PBR affords the visual effects artists a tremendous advantage when manipulating the shading pipeline to generate the desired look. PBR is a prominent member of the new school rendering paradigm. PBR is definitively biased toward realism and is a very popular shader. The best definition of PBR rendering is "A collection of rendering tools implementing concepts of global illumination to reproduce the natural behavior of physical light instead of the traditional mathematical approximations." Within the context of a real-time engine, PBR is the aggregate of rendering features, chosen by the engine developer, and manifested in one monolithic shader.

When implemented correctly, the digital artist can readily achieve realistic surfaces using PBR. Every engine implementation of PBR is different. The algorithms are highly optimized and may require the input to be very restrictive. This sensitivity makes the manipulation of PBR materials potentially dangerous. Artists should understand the inputs before diving into their manipulation.

The power of PBR lies in the usage of texture maps. Every parameter of a material can be driven by textures which allow for multiple "types" of surfaces to be represented at the same time within a single surface description. For example, PBR materials generate realistic metallic surfaces with spots of paint and rust, which are not metallic. While PBR algorithms work very hard to process the input they receive, the input may be flawed. The use of the PBR shader does not guarantee a realistic, let alone a reasonable appearance. Just as they are used to create photo-realistic looking scenes, the multi-valued texture maps can create sloppy-looking materials; surfaces that cannot exist in this world. Texture registration is also important. Corresponding texture values must align over multiple texture images, otherwise result in cheap, plastic-like surfaces (Figure 5.33).

The following section covers some of the rules necessary for achieving a realistic PBR render.

FIGURE 5.33 Good and bad PBR renders.

FIGURE 5.34 Metallic, non-metallic, and confused surfaces.

Is the Surface Metallic?

The first question that must be addressed whenever creating a PBR material is "Is the surface metallic?" This question is answered with the "Metallic" parameter. The answer is binary: "yes" or "no", black or white. There are no gray areas. Each engine is unique. For many engines, metallic elements of the surface are represented as white areas of the texture image. For other engines, it is just the opposite. While this may seem an obvious principle, it is astonishing to see how often this rule is ignored. When dealing with natural surfaces, partially metallic surfaces are extraordinarily rare (Figure 5.34).

Since metallic texture images are black and white, they should be stored in linear color space to avoid ambiguity. Metallic surfaces may be covered with paint or rust, which are non-metallic. The separation between the metal and non-metal portions of the surface must clearly identify which parts of the material are metal and which parts are not (Figure 5.35).

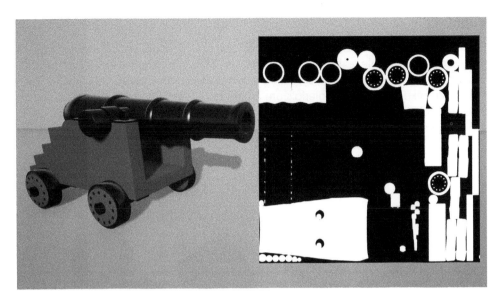

FIGURE 5.35 Metallic and non-metallic texture image.

Providing grayscale values as metallic input is not encouraged. Visual effects artists implement unworldly materials to describe alien surfaces which do not exist within our human sphere of understanding.

Normal Maps

While Normal Maps are not integral PBR rules, they are crucial for creating realistic renderings. Up-close, no surface is "perfectly smooth." All realistic surfaces have subtle bumps, undulations, and irregularities. The surface's model topology does not need to describe this fine detail. Normal texture images are excellent for holding this type of data. Normal images should always be used to store fine surface detail unless the surface's silhouette must be maintained (Figure 5.36).

FIGURE 5.36 Fine surface detail in a normal map.

Shiny or Rough?

Another question that must be answered when creating PBR surfaces is "How shiny is the surface?" The artist answers this question as a grayscale texture input to either the "Shiny" or "Roughness" material input. Unless synthetically generated, all surfaces reflect some sort of light, albeit some more than others. Very shiny surfaces are very reflective and mirror-like. Very rough materials are chalky and reflect nearly no light. Metallic objects are reflected from the surface's edge to center. Non-metallic surfaces reflect at least a small amount of light at the surface's edge and almost no light at the surface's center. This phenomenon is called the *Fresnel effect* (Figures 5.37 and 5.38).

FIGURE 5.37 Metallic versus non-metallic surface roughness.

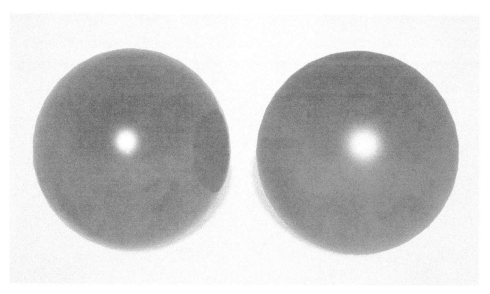

FIGURE 5.38 Fresnel effect on a non-metallic surface.

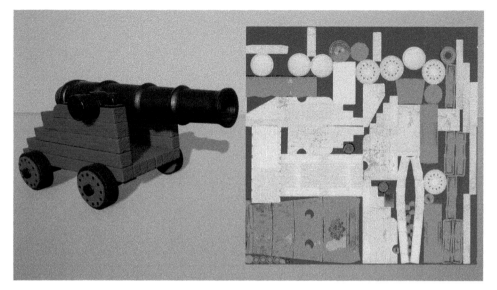

FIGURE 5.39 Shiny and rough texture.

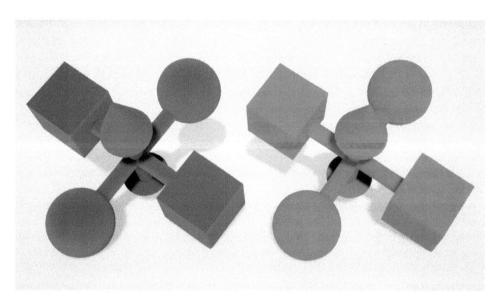

FIGURE 5.40 Extremely rough metal and non-metal surfaces.

There are no natural surfaces which reflect no light and only the smoothest, mirror-like surfaces reflect all light. Texture input may be any level of gray, depending on the material. Technically, only one channel of information is required. Texture images should be written in linear color space (Figure 5.39).

Extremely rough metal surfaces are almost indistinguishable from rough non-metal surfaces (Figure 5.40).

How Specular Is the Surface?

The specular parameter has no effect when the surface is metallic. Metal surfaces are automatically considered reflective. Instead, the parameter controls non-metal reflectivity. Unless synthetically manufactured, all surfaces exhibit at least a small percentage of specular reflectivity. All non-metallic objects should exhibit a specular

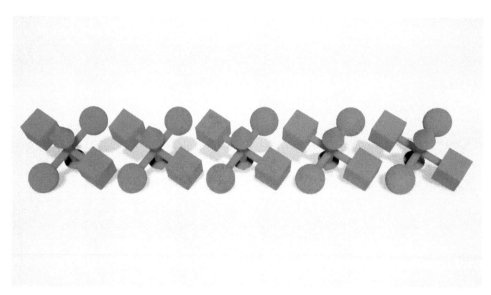

FIGURE 5.41 Low and high specular rough surface.

component from $2 \to 5\% (0.02 \to 0.05)$, all the way to 70% (0.7). Rough and non-reflective surfaces such as dirt and concrete live in the value range of $2 \to 5\%$, while smooth and reflective surfaces, such as plastic Christmas ornaments, should be no higher than 70%. To achieve a realistic rendering of non-metallic surfaces, the specular parameter must be no lower than 2% and no higher than 70%. The temptation to push the specular parameter beyond this range should be resisted. Any surface lower than 2% appears synthetic. Any surface greater than 70% is treated as metal and specularity no longer has an impact.

The contributions of the specular and roughness components of the non-metallic surface have a dramatic impact on the size and shape of the specular reflection. When the surface is rough and the specular value is small, the specular reflection is almost imperceptible. When the rough surface has a higher specular value, the specular reflection is soft and spread out (Figure 5.41).

When the non-metal surface is smooth and the specular amount is small, the specular reflection is still barely perceptible. However, with a higher specular value, the surface takes on a more polished, more reflective, mirror-like appearance (Figure 5.42).

The color of non-metal, specular reflection is dependent on the implementation of the shader. However, most implementations only allow for a white or non-colored specular reflection.

Metal surfaces do not respond to the specular component as they are considered as fully reflective. The color of the metallic specular reflection is dealt with in the following section.

What Is the Base Color?

Contrary to most artists' belief, the base color, also referred to as *albedo*, is computationally the least important component of the surface. Before the artist can define the base color, significant effort has already been made to identify when the surface is a metal or not and how rough or smooth the surface is. After these physically based rules have been established, the artist then is given the greatest amount of creative freedom. A non-metallic surface can be any color. By default, its specular reflection is almost always white (Figure 5.43).

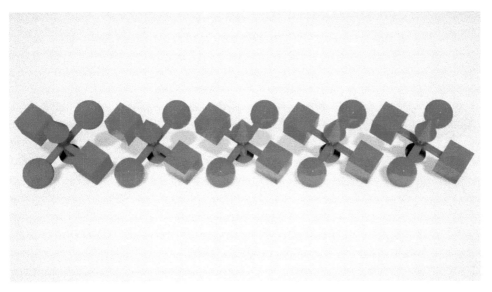

FIGURE 5.42 Low and high specular smooth surface.

FIGURE 5.43 Reflective non-metal, smooth surface.

The base color for all metals is black. All metals are considered as fully reflective thus the base color defines specular reflection. Metals' base colors define only the specular reflection, not the surface color itself (Figure 5.44).

Care must still be taken to maintain the registration of the base color images with the metallic and roughness images. Any deviation or offset will dramatically challenge the integrity of the surface (Figure 5.45).

Since this component does take advantage of the full-color spectrum, it is best practice to store these textures in sRGB color space.

FIGURE 5.44 Metal with variable specular reflectance.

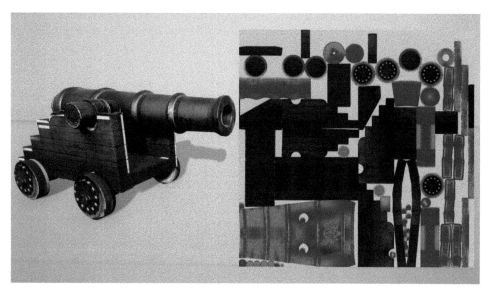

FIGURE 5.45 Poorly aligned base color.

Ambient Occlusion and Height

Ambient Occlusion (AO) and height are optional PBR parameters. Not all shaders support these factors. Not as essential as metallic, roughness, and specular, they help the surface appear more realistic.

AO defines locations on the surface where light has difficulty in reaching. These locations are typically nooks and crannies obscured in shadow. The contribution of the AO component darkens the surface and increases its contrast, making it feel crisper. The AO component pre-scales the surface's rendered color. As a single channel scalar, AO is best defined in linear color space (Figure 5.46).

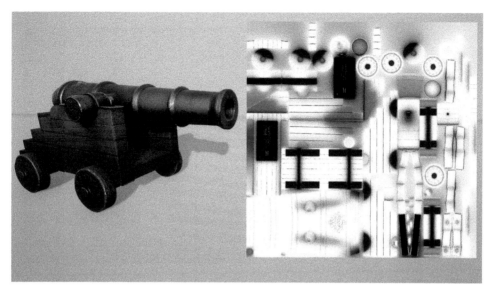

FIGURE 5.46 With ambient occlusion.

FIGURE 5.47 Height offset versus normal mapping.

Depending on the shader implementation, the *Height* components offset vertex position along the vertex normal direction. Executed in the vertex shader, it physically pushes the surface beyond what the normal map can provide. This technique alters surface silhouette while normal mapping does not (Figure 5.47).

Higher-resolution surface geometry is required to achieve smooth surface displacement. Like AO, the height value is treated as a scalar and is best represented in linear color space (Figure 5.48).

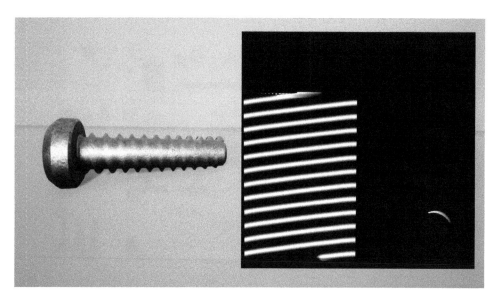

FIGURE 5.48 Height texture on surface.

BASIC MATERIAL OPERATIONS

Utilizing modern, monolithic shaders help artists and designers create outstanding work faster than old-school strategies. Unfortunately, large uber *shaders* create a false sense of security that prevents artists and designers from pushing these to their greatest potential.

Shaders' claim to transparently handle any situation does not imply a *hands*-free environment. They are effective templates, and their input data needs to be pre-processed to achieve world-class results. Many artists and designers avoid this data conditioning as a painful experience. While there is potential for mathematical ugliness, two essential strategies prevent pain: KISS and visual targets.

KISS ("Keep it simple, stupid!") is executed through two sub-steps: breaking a visual effect down to its fundamental layers and using the simplest operations to achieve them. When creating materials, folks tend to be lazy and throw operations and techniques in a random manner hoping that the "right look" magically appears. It rarely does!

Visual targets are necessary for generating painless materials! Without layered visual targets, artists may be lucky to stumble upon a look that just so happens to work. This is rarely the situation, especially during crunch periods. Blending visual targets using simple math operations almost always guarantees a successful look. These principle mathematical operations include multiplication, addition, and linear interpolation.

Multiplication

Multiplication, or burning, is the fundamental operation of multiplying a color layer against a constant, or another layer, and producing a result darker than either of the two sources. All color components are between the values of 0.1 and 1.0, and multiplying any two of them will always result in a product that is darker than both. The only exception to this principle is when one of the color components is unnaturally larger than one, resulting in a brighter product.

As the contrast between two color layers increases, so does the darkening impact of the resulting product. Multiplying a constant against an image layer is a convenient strategy for precisely reducing the intensity. Multiplying any color component by 0.0 always produces black. This technique is effective for generating masked regions, or holes, within an image. It can also be used to embed one image within another. When two images are multiplied, the brightest parts of one image manifest in the darkest portions of the other and vice versa (Figure 5.49).

Addition

Addition is used to brighten, or dodge, two color layers. It is also effective in biasing a color toward a specific direction (Figure 5.50).

When adding color values, care must be taken against inadvertently producing a sum greater than 1.0. Depending on the context, values greater than 1.0 are ignored, discounting the impact of the sum. Applying a *Clamp* operation to the result removes any artifacts created by the addition.

FIGURE 5.49 Embedding one image within another.

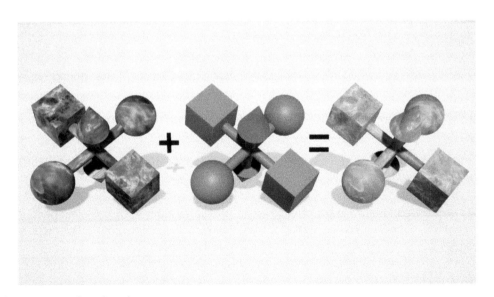

FIGURE 5.50 Biasing toward a color value.

FIGURE 5.51 Use of one minus to generate a mask.

A variation of the addition operation is in the *One Minus* operator, which subtracts the value of an input color, or constant, from 1.0, inverting the value of the original components or constant. This is a useful technique for generating garbage masks used to isolate intended areas of interest (Figure 5.51).

Linear Interpolation

Linear Interpolation, or what is fondly referred to as a *"Lerp,"* is not so much of an operation but more of a mathematical helper function. It is used for transitioning between two vectors based on some proportion between 0.0 and 1.0. This function is based on a simplification of the old slope-intercept formula you learned in middle school, $y = mx + b$. A Lerp is calculated by adding the first vector to the product of the difference between the two vectors and the proportional input. In other words, if you have two vectors, V_0 and V_1 and a proportion between them, t the lerp transition from V_0 to V_1 by the amount t is:

$$Lerp = V_0 + (V_1 - V_0) * t$$

Equation 5.10 Linear Interpolation, "Lerp," Structure

For example, when the desired transition is a little less than half of the distance, 0.45, from 69 to 84, then the lerp is:

$$Lerp = 69 + (84 - 69) * .45 = 75.75$$

$$Lerp = 75.75$$

Example 5.1 Lerping between Two Values

The lerping can be extended to any number of dimensions. Within shaders, lerping is often performed between two colors. For example, suppose the user wanted to transition 70% of the way from a sick green (.25, .9, .05) and a pastel purple (.55, .11, 1.0); then the value of the lerp is (Figure 5.52):

$$Lerp_R = .25 + (.55 - .25) * .7 = .46$$

$$Lerp_G = .9 + (.11 - .9) * .7 = .35$$

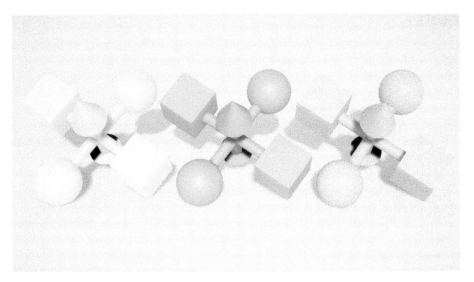

FIGURE 5.52 Lerp between sick green and pastel purple.

$$\text{Lerp}_B = .05 + (1.0 - .05) * .7 = .72$$

$$.7 \ \text{Lerp Between} (.25, .9, .05) \ \text{and} \ (.55, .11, 1.0) = (.46, .35, .72)$$

Example 5.2 Lerping between Two Colors

Material Instancing

Material Instancing, or material templating, is a service provided by the rendering engine to help the artist create rapid variations of the same material without recreating the material for every variation. Variables are used within the material definition instead of constants. The variable parameters are exposed to the material instances. Each new instance drives unique variations of the parameter values. The engine recreates the material for every variation, inserting the new parameter values for each incarnation. While the engine does the same amount of work, this process speeds up the material creation process (Figure 5.53).

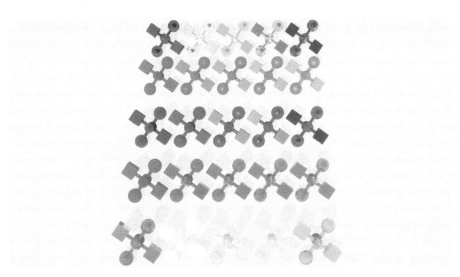

FIGURE 5.53 Multiple instances of the same material.

SHADING MODELS

Every real-time engine has its own personality. Most engines are focused on the original feature set designed by the original developers. They also contain competitively squeezed features into the configuration. All real-time engines support the following minimal set of shading modes: unlit, rasterized, ray traced, and subsurface shading.

Unlit

Unlit is a shading model that only emits a constant color. This model performs no shading. Quite often color values are inputted directly into a shader's 'Emissive' parameter which means the color value can be greater than 1.0. In this situation, the constant value goes through a blur post-process, very similar to a bloom, and blended on top of the original image. This makes the material appear as if it is glowing. This is a post-process visual effect and casts no actual light (Figure 5.54).

Rasterized

Rasterized shading models were covered earlier with the Phong and PBR techniques. Rasterization converts three-dimensional vertex information into two-dimensional bitmaps. Both shading models calculate direct and indirect lighting, shadows, reflections, and refractions.

Ray Traced

Once strictly an off-line calculation, ray tracing has recently made the transition to real time. Rasterization considers which pixels represent the objects in the scene. Ray tracing considers which objects contribute to the shading of every pixel. A scene is sampled for every pixel, from the perspective of the camera. The camera projects rays into the scene which collect and bring back the lighting contribution from all objects it collides and ricochets from. Description of the ray tracing pipeline is covered in Chapter 3 of this text. True shadows, reflections, refractions, AO, and complex opacities are calculated without the need for pre-generated texture images. Ray tracing will quickly become an essential tool for the visual effects artist's arsenal (Figure 5.55).

FIGURE 5.54 Unlit shading model.

FIGURE 5.55 Ray traced scene.

FIGURE 5.56 Subsurface shading.

Subsurface

Subsurface shading is a rasterization technique simulating the real-world phenomenon of light penetrating the surface of an object and diffusing it underneath the surface. This effect manifests itself as color underneath the object surface as observed in such materials as ice, wax, skin, and certain opaque but cloudy materials such as milk and jade. Since not all objects exhibit this phenomenon, subsurface shading is classified as its own model (Figure 5.56).

BLENDING MODES

Blending modes of a real-time engine manipulate the last stage of the rendering pipeline: mixing recently rendered objects (the source) with objects which have already been rendered (the destination). Some engines expose all possible blending options as described in Chapter 4. Some expose only a subset of default possibilities. Typically, these defaults include opaque layering, mask rendering, A over B blending, linear dodging, and multiply burning.

Opaque Layering

Opaque Layering is a blending technique allowing no light to shine through the currently rendered object. Transparency is prohibited. Source objects completely obscure destination objects. Solid materials such as plastics, metals, stone, and non-membranous organic materials such as wood are best served with this mode. Of all blending modes, opaque layering is the least computationally expensive (Figure 5.57).

Mask Rendering

One channel mask information is required for *mask rendering* mode which identifies which pixels are rendered and which ones are ignored. Object transparency is not supported. Like opaque layering, rendered source pixels occlude destination pixels. There is no difference between the two blending strategies. This technique is effective for modeling mesh grids, wire fences and other objects containing holes or gaps (Figure 5.58).

A Over B Blending

Most engine's default blending mode is A over B blending, also known as *Translucent layering*. This mode employs an opacity mask, called an alpha channel, to control how much of the source layer is blended over the destination layer:

$$\text{Translucent Layer} = \left(\text{Source} * \text{Source}_{Alpha}\right) + \left(\text{Destination} * \left(1 - \text{Source}_{Alpha}\right)\right)$$

Equation 5.11 Traditional A Over B Blending

Semi-transparent materials are best serviced by this mode (Figure 5.59).

FIGURE 5.57 Opaque layering.

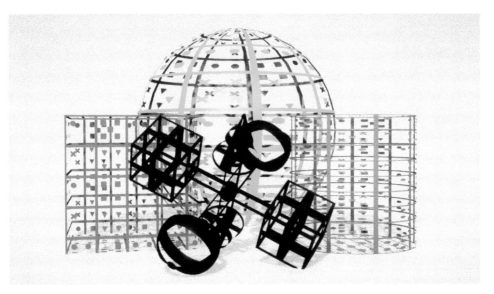

FIGURE 5.58 Mask rendering.

FIGURE 5.59 A over B blending.

Linear Dodging

Linear Dodging, *or additive blending*, produces a blend result brighter than both the source and destination layers. Both layers' pixel values are added to each other with no consideration to transparency.

Linear Dodge = Source + Destination

Equation 5.12 Linear Dodging

Since no pixel value is less than 0.0, the combined result must be brighter than either layer. Linear dodging always brightens the scene. It is most useful for blending transparent objects such as fire, pyrotechnics, and some augmented reality objects (Figure 5.60).

FIGURE 5.60 Linear dodging.

Multiply Burning

Multiply burning, *or multiplicative blending,* produces a blend result darker than both the source and destination layers. Both layers' pixel values are multiplied against each other with no consideration to transparency.

Multiply Burn = Source * Destination

Equation 5.13 Multiply Burning

Since no pixel values can be greater than 1.0, the product must be darker than either layer. Multiply burning best services semi-transparent objects which darken the scene such as sunglasses, smoke, and particle effects like ash (Figure 5.61).

FIGURE 5.61 Multiply burning.

TEXTURE MAPPING

Of all the visual effects strategies presented in this book, animated texture maps are arguably the most important. When I started my career as a Hollywood visual effects artist, I implemented more animated texture map effects than any other type. Their variety appears limitless. Artists invent new uses for them every day. Due to the magnitude of the related topic, texture mapping is broken into two sections: an explanation of the technology and how they are animated to create visual effects.

Fundamental Technology

Animating texture maps is a technique for mapping high-frequency information onto lower resolution, three-dimensional surfaces. In simpler terms, texture mapping makes complex detail appear native to geometry without increasing the surface's complexity.

Robust enough for students to get their Ph.D. in, only three concepts are required to understand how animated texture maps can be used to generate visual effects: texture images, texture coordinates, and texture space (Figure 5.62).

Texture Images

A texture image is two-dimensional information that is mapped onto three-dimensional geometry. This information may be static or dynamically animated using flipbook or procedural techniques. Static sources for these images may come from anywhere, such as photographs, paintings, drawings, or even video signals.

Two-dimensional texture images are broken into tiny individual rectangles called *texels* which are arranged into two-dimensional arrays. Each texel defines a color with red, green, blue, and sometimes transparency information. The width and height of an array are the number of texels across and up and down the image. Each texel is indexed by its relative position in the array width (*U direction*) and in the height (*V direction*) establishing the texel's U and V coordinates. The U and V indices of the array are normalized between 0.0 and 1.0 (Figure 5.63).

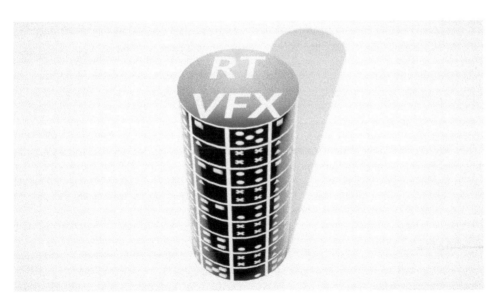

FIGURE 5.62 Multiple textures maps on the same geometry.

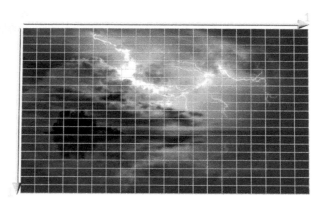

FIGURE 5.63 Texture image array.

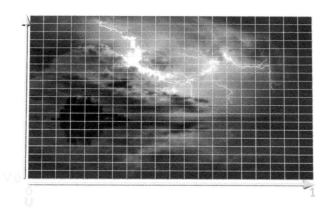

FIGURE 5.64 OpenGL texture image array.

The orientations of these U and V directions are variable and dependent on each rendering engine. For example, in Direct X engines, the coordinates of the upper-leftmost texel are [0.0, 0.0] and the lower-right are [1.0, 1.0]. In OpenGL engines, the coordinates of the lower-leftmost texel are [0.0, 0.0] and the upper-right are [1.0, 1.0]. Regardless of the direction, all interior texels are ordered predictably between the two extremes (Figure 5.64).

Texture array resolution may be any dimension. For optimization purposes, certain engines require the number of texels in an image to be a power of 2. Texture dimensions of 64, 128, 512, 1024, and 2048 are very common. When a texture image needs to cover a display device, such as monitor or window, its dimensions may duplicate the pixel dimension scale of the device. Texture dimensions of 720 × 480 or 1920 × 1080 are common.

Texture Coordinates

The texture image is mapped onto three-dimensional geometric surfaces by associating texels' UV array coordinates with corresponding geometry vertices. The UV coordinates are stored as vertex attributes. There are many techniques for assigning the UV attributes of an image to geometry vertices. Some are simple while others are extraordinarily complex. A simple technique is called *orthographic projection* of an image directly onto a rectangular surface (Figure 5.65).

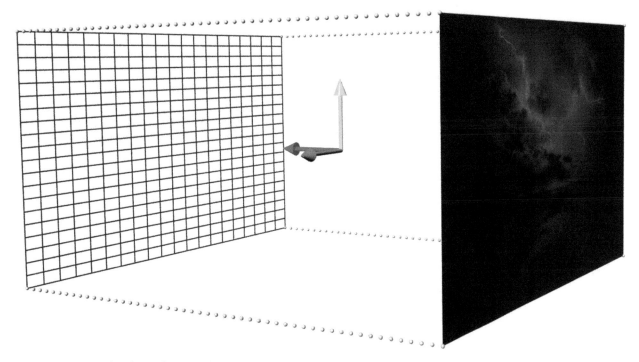

FIGURE 5.65 Simple orthographic projection.

A strong understanding of three-dimensional texturing is very helpful for a visual effects artist. Collaborating with a three-dimensional modeler can help a novice artist build an understanding of texturing techniques quickly. There are many tutorials on-line and some very good books written on this vast subject. The most important concept to keep in mind is the shape of geometry is independent of texture image size and dimension. The image may be mapped to the surface in any manner that achieves the desired look. Vertices may store multiple mappings within their attributes. Visual effects often achieve their look by cross blending multiple images.

Texture coordinates play an important role within the Rendering pipeline. Within the vertex shader, the texture coordinates may be translated, rotated, or scaled. Other vertex attributes, such as position, may also be offset or biased by mathematical functions or texture image values.

When the bitmap image is generated during the pipeline's rasterization stage, there are typically more pixels than there are object vertices. The rasterizer employs bi-linear interpolation to calculate the corresponding UV coordinates for all the pixels situated between transformed vertices. For a full description of how bi-linear interpolation works, please refer to the Rasterization section contained within *Lighting and Rendering for the Technical Artist*. The interpolation guarantees smooth attribute coverage for all pixels on the rasterized surface (Figure 5.66).

Within the pixel shader, each pixel's UV coordinates are used to identify corresponding texture image texels. Image RGBA values are transferred to corresponding pixels and used to complete shader calculations.

Texture Space

Texture space is the full mapping from three-dimensional geometry to a two-dimensional texture image. Typically, the texture space is laid out in the numerical range, [0.0, 1.0], in both the U and V directions. However, this does not have to be this way. One of the greatest powers afforded the visual effects artist is the ability to manipulate texture space of three-dimensional surfaces. By altering the surface's vertex UV coordinates, the artist has full

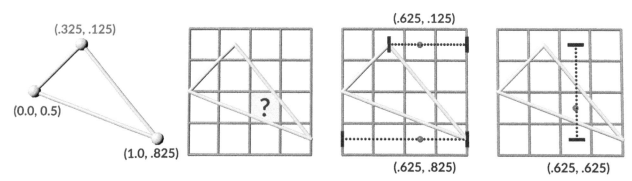

FIGURE 5.66 Bi-linear interpolation of UV coordinates.

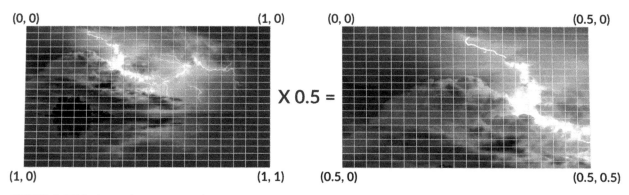

FIGURE 5.67 Reduce-scaling texture coordinates.

control over the appearance of the texture on the surface. The artist may scale, rotate, and/or offset a surface's texture space.

Scaling Texture Space
The artist may scale all a surface's texture coordinates or only a subset. The scale may be increased or decreased. When the texture space is reduced, the texture image appears larger on the surface. In other words, as the texture scale decreases, greater surface area is required to display the entire image. This has the effect of making the texture image appear to grow (Figure 5.67).

Reduce-Scaling texture space is a convenient method for limiting the exposure of texture images on a three-dimensional surface. For example, when the texture image had been broken into equal quadrants, scaling the U and V texture coordinates by 0.5 will cause only the upper left quadrant to fill the entire face (Figure 5.68).

Increase-scaling the texture space is a more complicated operation. When the vertex texture coordinates are scaled up, the texture image appears to become smaller. In other words, less surface area is required to display the entire image and the image appears to shrink. This operation creates a situation where the texture coordinates increase beyond the [0, 1] range (Figure 5.69).

When texture space exceeds this range, the artist must decide what to do with the texture information greater than 1.0. There are four address modes to handle this situation: Wrap, Mirror, Clamp, and Border. Mode selections must be made for each texture's U and V directions. They need not match each other.

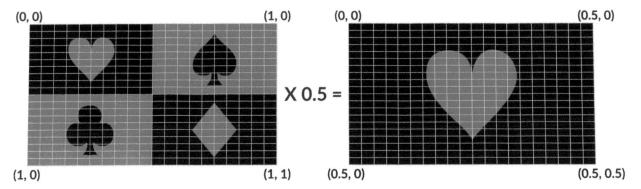

(0, 0)   (1, 0)   **X 0.5 =**   (0, 0)   (0.5, 0)

(1, 0)   (1, 1)   (0.5, 0)   (0.5, 0.5)

FIGURE 5.68 Exposing upper quadrant of texture image.

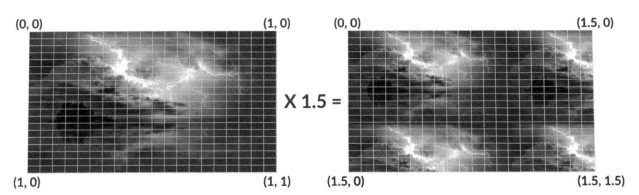

(0, 0)   (1, 0)   **X 1.5 =**   (0, 0)   (1.5, 0)

(1, 0)   (1, 1)   (1.5, 0)   (1.5, 1.5)

FIGURE 5.69 Increase-scaling texture coordinates.

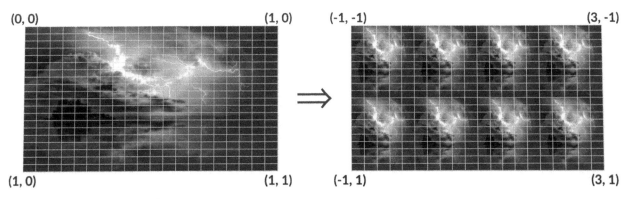

(0, 0)   (1, 0) $\Rightarrow$ (-1, -1)   (3, -1)

(1, 0)   (1, 1)   (-1, 1)   (3, 1)

FIGURE 5.70 Wrap texture mode.

Wrap Mode
Wrap mode repeats the texture image in the axis direction such that there is a continuous duplication of the image at every integer coordinate. For example, when the texture coordinates for a rectangle are (−1.0, −1.0), (3.0, −1.0), (3.0, 1.0), (−1.0, 1.0), the image is repeated four times horizontally: three in the positive direction and one in the negative (Figure 5.70).

Mirror Mode
Mirror mode flips the texture image such that vertical and horizontal symmetry is maintained between adjacent images. For example, when the texture coordinates for a rectangle are (−1.0, −1.0), (3.0, −1.0), (3.0, 1.0),

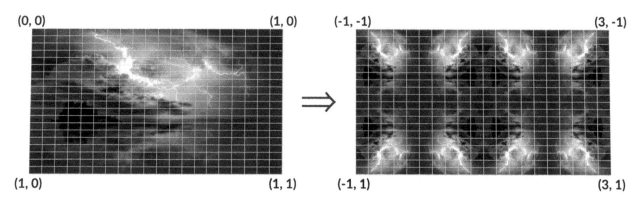

(0, 0)   (1, 0)   (-1, -1)   (3, -1)

(1, 0)   (1, 1)   (-1, 1)   (3, 1)

FIGURE 5.71 Mirror texture mode.

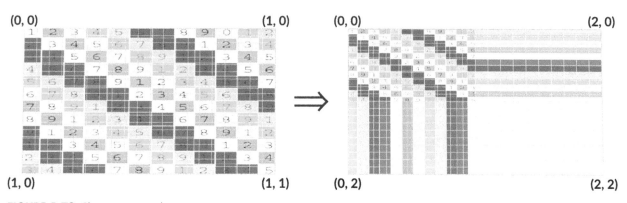

(0, 0)   (1, 0)   (0, 0)   (2, 0)

(1, 0)   (1, 1)   (0, 2)   (2, 2)

FIGURE 5.72 Clamp texture mode.

$(-1.0, 1.0)$, symmetry is maintained between all adjacent images as the image is mirrored four times horizontally (Figure 5.71).

Clamp Mode

Clamp mode smears the color of the edge pixels whose texture coordinates are above 1.0 and less than 0.0. For example, when the texture coordinates for a rectangle are $(-1.0, -1.0)$, $(2.0, -1.0)$, $(2.0, 2.0)$, $(-1.0, 2.0)$, the texture image is displayed once in the middle while the edge values greater than 1.0 and less than 0.0 are repeated to the edges (Figure 5.72).

Border Mode

Border mode returns a pre-identified color value for all texture coordinates greater than 1.0 and less than 0.0. For example, when the texture coordinates for a rectangle are $(-1.0, -1.0)$, $(2.0, -1.0)$, $(2.0, 2.0)$, $(-1.0, 2.0)$, the texture image is displayed once, in the middle of the surface, and all other returned values are the pre-identified border value (Figure 5.73).

Offsetting Texture Space

Artists may add or subtract an offset from texture coordinates. This activity causes texture images to shift horizontally or laterally. When texture coordinates exceed the $[0.0, 1.0]$ range, the textures' address mode is used to calculate the texture image value. For example, suppose a rectangular plane begins with texture coordinates at $(0.0, 0.0)$, $(1.0, 0.0)$, $(1.0, 1.0)$, $(0.0, 1.0)$ and its coordinates are shifted 0.5 in the U direction and −0.5 in the V direction. The texture image is shifted halfway toward the upper right corner of the plane while the other half of the image appears in the lower left portion of the plane (Figure 5.74).

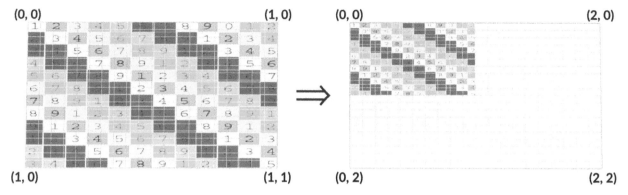

FIGURE 5.73 Border texture mode.

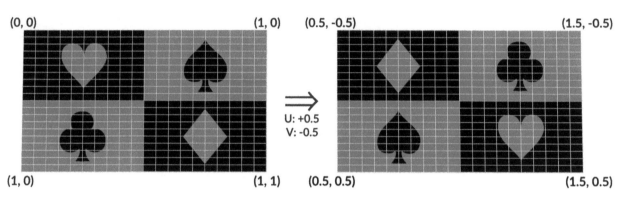

FIGURE 5.74 Shifts in the U and V texture coordinates.

Continuous offsets to texture coordinate values create a scrolling-like behavior on the surface. When the address mode is Wrap or Mirror, the texture image will repeat itself indefinitely. When the address mode is Clamp or Border, the texture image will scroll off the surface and disappear.

Scaling and Offsetting Texture Space

The artist has the greatest amount of control when the object's texture coordinates are offset and scaled. Using this technique, an artist may create multiple surfaces within just one image. Instead of replacing objects, materials, or textures, the artist scales the object's texture space and offsets the texture variation to fit the context (Figure 5.75).

A variation of this technique is called *Texture Atlasing* where all possible surface texture variations are stored on one large image. The performance gains in reduced draw calls and fewer texture swaps outweigh the extra memory costs required to store the single, larger texture. Character wardrobes or skin tones are often achieved with this technique (Figures 5.76 and 5.77).

Texture Masking

When a surface can be subdivided into four unique groups or less, a single texture image can be used for isolating those regions. Instead of providing multiple materials or textures for a common surface, a single texture image may be used to identify, or mask out, regions of information. This inexpensive yet powerful visual effects technique is called *Texture Masking*.

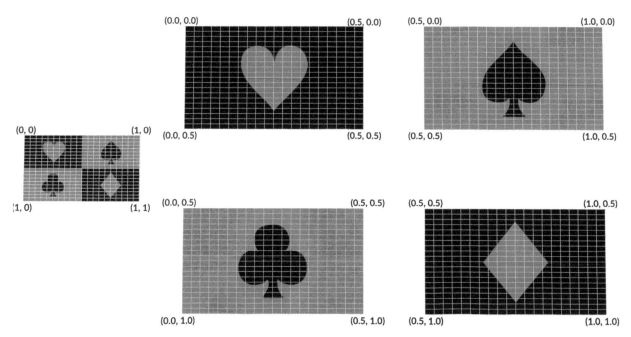

FIGURE 5.75 Multiple textures within one image.

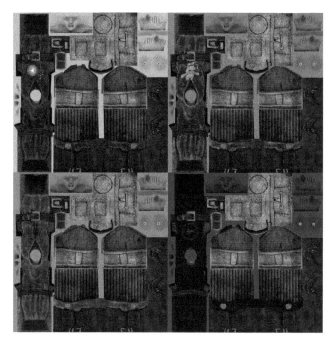

FIGURE 5.76 Texture atlasing.

Each texture image may contain up to four data channels represented as Red, Green, Blue, and Alpha. Each channel can be used to identify a unique region of geometry yet authored in context with the other channels at the same time. One texture image can identify up to four regions on the same surface, which has multiple benefits. Only one texture image needs to be authored instead of four. Managing one image instead of four eases pipeline complexity. Fewer textures also mean fewer draw calls and fewer texture swaps. Texture masking

FIGURE 5.77 Texture atlas crowd.

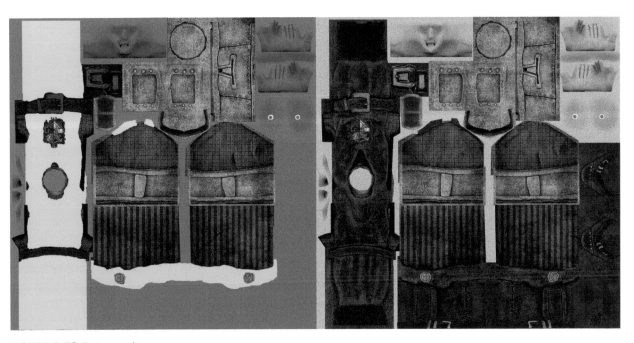

FIGURE 5.78 Texture masking.

also allows for abstracting color values. Instead of obtaining the color value from the texture image, the shader procedurally generates the color to satisfy the requirements of the situation. With this technique, virtually infinite combinations can be provided from just one texture image (Figure 5.78).

Characters within a crowd are a great example of this technique. Regardless of the variations in skin tone, shirt, pants, and shoe color, only one texture image is required.

FIGURE 5.79 Hundreds of variations of one character.

The red channel identifies skin tone. The green channel identifies shirt color. The blue channel identifies pant color. The Alpha channel identifies shoe color. During rendering, the shader randomly generates variations for each of the channels. This technique saves artists' time by authoring only one character model and one texture image. All potential skin tones and clothing variations are accommodated with relatively little work (Figure 5.79).

ANIMATED TEXTURE IMAGES

Texture space scaling and offsetting are the essential tools for animating texture images. Expanding, shrinking, offsetting, and dynamically altering vertex texture attributes contribute a significant portion of modern visual effects.

Virtual Display

Any texture mapped surface has the potential to behave as a virtual display device. During rendering, the rendering engine maps texture image arrays, or image *buffers*, onto a surface based on its texture coordinates. The content of that image buffer is irrelevant. The buffer does not need to be static. It may stay constant, or it may be updated continuously. From the engine's perspective, an image buffer with bitmap data is a usable image buffer. Within special circumstances, a streamed signal from an external source may be used to fill the image buffer, transforming the surface into a virtual, streamed display device. The practicality of this visual effect may rarely complement the context of the game's story world. However, the ability to map a dynamic stream of information to a surface has potential. Windows, portals, doors, and even wide-sweeping backgrounds may be generated outside the context of the current application, even beyond the current machine, and mapped into a scene with very little to no cost.

Flip-Booking

Like virtual displays, but somewhat more primitive, is the concept of flip-booking. Instead of accessing a dynamic image buffer, a single-texture image behaves as a static image buffer. All frames contributing toward a visual sequence are stored in one texture image as an array of smaller images. For example, a 64-frame animated sequence could be stored as a single 8×8, 4×16, 2×32 or even a 1×64 mosaic (Figure 5.80).

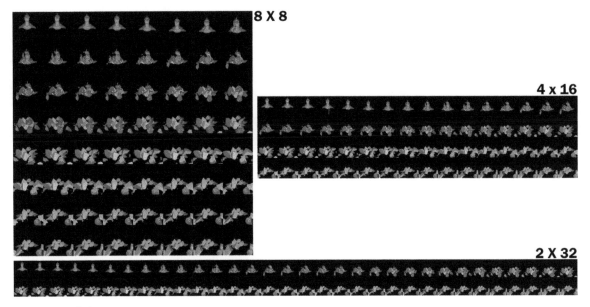

FIGURE 5.80 Multiple texture mosaics.

Before the rendering, the engine reads the entire texture image and subdivides it into a sequence of smaller images. In real-time, the images are swapped and rendered in sequential order. The sequence is recycled after the last frame is displayed.

Depending on the amount of perspective parallax in the scene, texture flip books are used to replace large amounts of complicated animated behavior with just a single texture image on a simple surface. The effectiveness of this effect is dependent on the sequence's transparency and the context of the scene being able to continuously repeat the animated sequence without drawing attention to itself.

While any dimension of mosaic may be employed, texture flip books are most easily managed when they are square in size; composed of a numerical power of two images such as 9, 16, 25, 36, 49, 64 and 81. Many rendering engines are sensitive to the size of their flip book textures. As a rule of thumb, stick with 4 × 4 and 8 × 8. Some textures, when divided unevenly could incur jittering issues, especially in slow motion. Since the individual sub-images tend to be smaller, it is best practice to render them as large in frame as possible. Any image manipulation software, such as Photoshop or Gimp, can be used to construct these flipbooks. The process for creating these mosaics can be a taxing operation. There are multiple tools available as stand-alones or as plug-ins to help facilitate this process (Figure 5.81).

Flipbooks are very popular as sprite images for particle systems. Their smaller size and ability to be played back at variable speeds makes them simple to use. Since the animated sequences can be hand drawn, flipbooks are ideal for generating stylized particle systems (Figure 5.82).

Particle effects such as explosions, debris, crumbling ground, shattering glass, and small orbiting spheres are achieved easily with flipbooks. Hand-drawn, two-dimensional animation skills are required to generate these sequences. The technique for generating these images is beyond the scope of this book. However, there are some very well-written books dedicated toward the generation of stylized natural phenomena. Some of these books include *Elemental Magic* by Joseph Gilland and *Essential Effects* by Mauro Maressa. Depending on the context of sequence usage, hand-drawn flip books may be wasteful usage of artists' time. For the duration of time the texture is visible, the extra amount of time required to duplicate and scale the sequences may not be worth the investment.

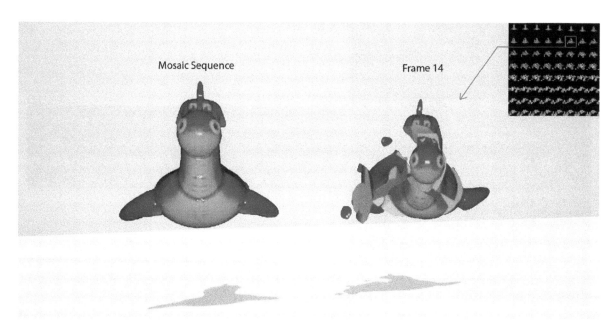

FIGURE 5.81 Texture mosaic creation process.

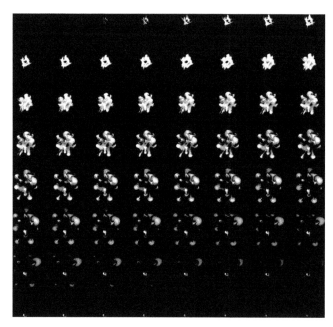

FIGURE 5.82 Stylized particle flipbook.

Panning

Panning is a solid workhorse in the visual effects world. It is a simple concept yet extraordinarily powerful. The impact of offsetting the texture coordinates of a surface was introduced earlier in this chapter. The panning operation pushes this technique and provides a continuous offset stream to surface texture coordinates. Each real-time engine implements its own variation of the strategy and manifests it as a single graph node or function, called a *panner*. Functional input consists of surface texture coordinates, a time input, and directional offsets in the *U*, *V*, or both directions (Figure 5.83).

FIGURE 5.83 Four frames of continuous texture offset.

Offsetting the texture coordinates causes the texture image *to appear* to move over its mapped surface. This is an illusion. The image does not animate, the texture coordinates on the surface change. The motion is opposite to the expected direction. For example, when a negative offset is applied, the texture appears to move to the right or in an upward direction. When the offset is positive, the image appears to move to the left or in a downward direction. The panning behavior is initially confusing. However, the understanding of coordinate offsetting instead of image shifting manifests predictable movement.

The panner function offsets texture coordinates until one of two things happens: the offset value reaches 1.0 and stops or continues indefinitely. The texture addressing mode controls this behavior. When the address mode is Wrap, the image scrolls and repeats infinitely. When the mode is Clamp or Border, the texture image scrolls off the surface. The offsets continue but the address mode repeats the border color or the colors of the edge.

The panner continuously offsets texture coordinates indefinitely during real-time execution. For example, when the texture image pans to the left (in the positive *U* direction), the texels of the leftmost portion of the image need to match the texels of the rightmost portion of the image. Lack of continuity generates a seam traveling across the surface and destroys the effect. Panning in the V direction is affected similarly. Panning introduces seams when there is no opposite edge image texel continuity.

Time increases at a constant rate and cannot be used to alter the apparent panner speed. Manipulating texture coordinate U, V scale effectively controls the offset rate. Increasing texture coordinates, scaled in the desired direction, controls the speed of the panning effect. Reducing coordinate scale slows the effect.

An interesting phenomenon happens when multiple texture images are combined at the same time. Within the images, shapes appear to swirl, interact, and play with each other. Smaller shapes and forms appear to come alive inside larger shapes. Smaller patterns may recursively "layer" indefinitely into larger patterns. Unique panner functions animate individual layers. Individual layers are often variations on the same texture coordinate set. Occasionally, layers require their own set of texture coordinates within the same shape. Layering multiple coordinate sets produces dramatic and often interesting results. The context of the material defines the animation of the individual layers.

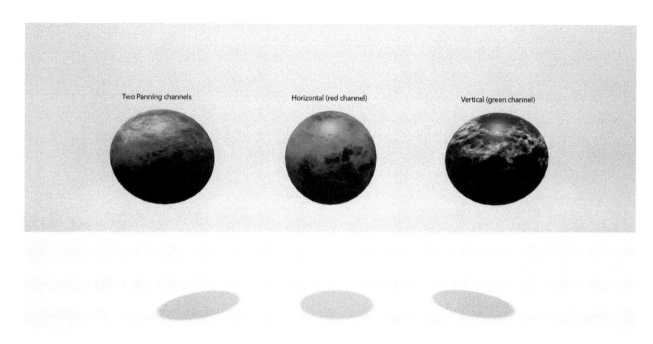

FIGURE 5.84 Adding multiple panning layers.

Three techniques may be used when combining multiple panning layers: multiplication, linear interpolation (lerping), and addition. Multiplication of layers is the easiest way to get that "texture in texture look." When two texture images multiply against each other, the bright parts of the first image appear in the dark parts of the second and the bright parts of the second appear in the dark parts of the first. Multiplying two layers against each other creates a burn effect which effectively darkens the product image. A subsequent square root of the image product offsets the darkening effect. Linear interpolating two animated texture images generates moving shadows and highlights. A third animated texture provides an interpolation factor between the prior two and is sometimes referred to as "alpha channel." An animated alpha channel may cause the resulting highlights and shadows to behave radically different from either of their source parent images. As a method for blending the colors of multiple animated texture images, addition is not extraordinarily helpful. The individual channel values sum quickly to 1.0 and are subsequently clipped. When the contributing images are bound to unique channels, addition is an excellent technique for combining multiple animated objects. For example, when a heart shape is panning in the U direction in the red channel and a diamond shape is panning in the V direction in the green channel, the two panning layers can be added without creating a clipped result (Figure 5.84).

The technique of combining panning texture images in one material is common among experienced visual effects artists. As a rule of thumb, the artist should always strive to combine at least two layers of texture images in every animated material. Multiple layers help break up the monotony of the motion and make it difficult to focus disproportionately on just one aspect of the material.

Rays, beams, non-planar projectiles, and sword swooshes are intended to be seen only once over a set period. These, and other non-repeating phenomena, are generated using non-repeating panned texture images. The texture address mode needs to be Clamp or Border. The manipulation of the panner time input controls the effect's speed (Figure 5.85).

Effects such as barber poles, tornadoes, tickers, tank treads, conveyor belts, and flowing rivers are achieved when the texture coordinates are repeated continuously (Figure 5.86).

FIGURE 5.85 Ray beams, non-linear trails, and sword swooshes.

FIGURE 5.86 Rivers, marquees, and tornadoes.

Non-Planar Trails

As a simple example of an effect intended to be seen only once, consider the *non-planar trail* effect, also known as the soul *coaster* or *magic jet trail*. This effect manifests itself as a single bolt of energy that travels along a non-planar trajectory (Figure 5.87).

The effectiveness of this effect is dependent on consistent texture coordinate placement on a non-planar mesh. The mesh starts as a simple, regularly subdivided grid with normalized texture coordinates (Figure 5.88).

FIGURE 5.87 Simple drawing of non-planar trail.

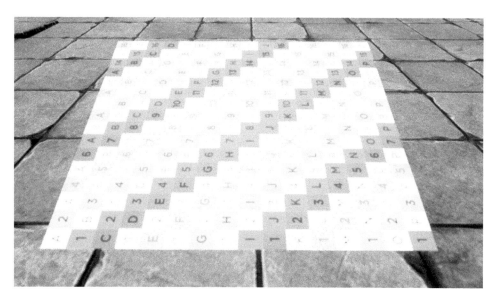

FIGURE 5.88 Initial soul coaster grid.

The mesh is then stretched, bent, and otherwise pulled into a pretzel-like shape while still maintaining the uniform placement of its subdivisions and texture coordinates. The consistent smoothness of the traveling bolt of energy is dependent on the uniform distribution of the subdivisions and the texture coordinates. It is important to maintain the normalized texture coordinate layout. While the coordinates along the traveling direction are smaller than [0, 1], the bolt of energy continues its journey. When the coordinates extend beyond the [0, 1] range, multiple bolts appear (Figure 5.89).

A texture image of the energy bolt is painted over black. It is important to maintain a sufficient black border surrounding the bolt. This border prevents clipping of the bolt image and ensures a definitive start and end for the bolt as it travels over the trail (Figure 5.90).

The mesh trail and texture image are brought into the rendering engine. It is important to maintain the texture coordinates of the trail.

FIGURE 5.89 Pretzel-like trail mesh.

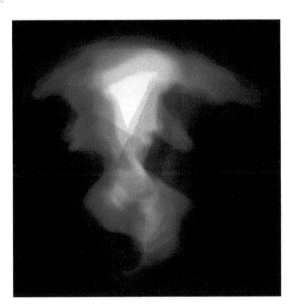

FIGURE 5.90 Energy bolt texture image.

A material for the energy bolt contains a reference to the texture image and a panner function. Depending on the context of the scene, the panner offsets the coordinates of the trail direction from 0.0 to 1.0 only once, depending on the context of the situation. The material must support an alpha channel or render black as transparent, otherwise, the bolt is boxed by the trail which destroys the effect (Figure 5.91).

When the energy bolt is rendered as a translucent-like ghost and the alpha information is unavailable, the opacity of the pixel is generated by taking the dot product of the pixel color and the vector constant, (0.299, 0.587, 0.141).

$$\text{Opacity}_{pixel} = \text{dot}\Big(\text{Color}\,(R,\,G,\,B)_{pixel}\,,\,(0.299,\,0.587,\,0.141)\Big)$$

Equation 5.14 Pixel Color Intensity

FIGURE 5.91 Missing alpha channel or opaque black.

FIGURE 5.92 Mesh trail with animated ease-in and ease-out.

This formula generates the pixel's luminance, as the human eye sees it. The calculated luminance will be used as the pixel's alpha/opacity component.

As the trail is rendered and played in real-time, the panner function offsets the surface's texture coordinates along the direction of travel which animates the energy bolt over the length of the mesh. Since the image of the energy bolt is rendered as transparent, only the bolt is visible and the trail invisible.

It is important to note that this technique animates the bolt linearly over the length of the trail. When an ease-in or ease-out animation is required, the timing input to the panner function must be adjusted. An art-directable technique, is to bias the distribution of mesh subdivisions of the original model, towards the beginning or end of the trail model. The more concentrated the distribution of subdivisions, the slower the bolt appears to travel (Figure 5.92).

Flowing Lava River

A flowing lava river is a simple example of a continuously animated effect. A lava river is a luminous river of slow-moving, incendiary sludge.

Unlike the mesh trail created in the prior example, the river mesh does not require uniform distribution of the texture coordinates over the length of the mesh. In fact, to appear more realistic, the distribution should avoid linear sections. The texture coordinates should not be consistent. The mesh's edge loops should be allowed to bunch up around corners, bends, and other obstructions found in the river. The bunching and binding duplicate the natural phenomenon of the river flowing faster in smoother, linear sections and stagnating and slowing down when forced to flow around corners and obstacles (Figure 5.93).

When the rendering engine supports multiple texture coordinate sets, at least two sets of texture coordinates should be used. The second coordinate set will create a different flow speed, providing a random shadow-like appearance in the lava.

The flowing lava river example requires three infinite texture images. The images should be infinite in the direction of lava travel since a visible seam identifying the beginning and end of the image is undesirable.

The first texture image, the *Lava*, is a sludgy, noisy surface of reds, oranges, and blacks. This image provides the overall appearance of the river. The second image, the *Shadow*, *reduces* the sludgy frequency and appears darker. This image provides shadows and irregularities that appear to float under the surface of the first image. The third image, the *Mask*, is a soft, medium-frequency noise. It interpolates between the prior two images and is represented by a grayscale (Figure 5.94).

The material for this effect requires three separate panner functions, one for each texture image. The overall speed of the river is adjusted through the panner manipulating the Lava image. The speed of the Shadow image panner may be slower or faster than the first panner, depending on the perspective of the environment. The mask panner rate is adjusted to conform to the needs of the scene. Use an alternative texture coordinate set with this panner when available.

FIGURE 5.93 Lava river wireframe mesh.

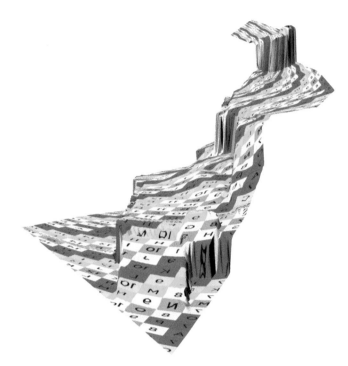

FIGURE 5.94 Lava river texture images.

A linear interpolation (lerp) between the lava and the shadow layers is fed into the base color of the material. The mask provides the interpolation amount. When available, the lerp should be fed into the emissive input. When the value is amplified greater than 1.0, the river appears to glow.

A cheaper, less art-directable variation of this effect uses only one lava texture image. A second image is fabricated by darkening a copy of the original Lava image. The two images are multiplied against each other, instead of using a lerp operation. This multiplication causes the bright portions of the second image to appear in the dark parts of the first and the dark parts of the first to appear in the bright parts of the second. The multiplication of the two images reduces the gamma of the product. Taking the square root of the product returns the image back to the original intensity level.

Rotating

Like panning, rotating the object's texture coordinates is performed by a rotator node or function. The input consists of the surface's texture coordinates and a timing variable. The center point of rotation may also be inputted to the rotator function.

For every frame, a local angle is offset by the timing variable and the texture coordinates. The rotation formula for angular offset θ is:

$$\text{Texture Coordinates}[U, V] = [U * \cos(\theta) + V * \sin(\theta), V * \cos(\theta) - U * \sin(\theta)]$$

Equation 5.15 Texture Coordinate Rotation

When the engine's trigonometric functions are calculated in radians, remember to translate the angle, θ, to radians instead of degrees (Figure 5.95).

FIGURE 5.95 Texture coordinates rotated 30°.

FIGURE 5.96 Extreme image appearing in corners.

When rotating texture coordinates, the visual effects artist must remember the object's coordinate values are rotating and not the texture itself. A strange phenomenon happens when the rotational amount is near 45°. Any part of the original image which is sufficiently close to the left, right, upper, or lower edges, will appear in the corners of the offset surface (Figure 5.96).

There are three methods to resolve this situation: the addressing mode, a modification to the rotation calculation, and a garbage mask. Setting the texture image's addressing mode to Clamp will prevent any texture coordinates from exceeding 1.0. Likewise, the numerical results of the rotational formula may also be clamped between 0.0 and 1.0. The third method involves a *garbage mask*. A garbage mask is a simple monochrome image multiplied against the rotated texture image. The desirable areas are white while the undesirable areas are black. The black areas nullify undesirable phenomena from the transformed texture image. Borrowed from film visual effects, garbage masks are an extremely convenient technique for removing unwanted image regions.

Magic Rings

The magic rings a mage throws when casting a spell are a simple example of the coordinate rotation technique. The effect may have up to four concentric uniquely colored rings from each texture image, all rotating at different rates.

The most important component of this effect is the texture image itself. The image is created such that each ring is colored as a primary color (red, green, blue, and alpha) isolated on each channel (Figure 5.97).

Within the material, there are simply four rotator nodes or functions: one for each of the channels. Each function receives its own rotational offset speed. Each color channel isolates its individual ring (Figure 5.98).

FIGURE 5.97 Magic ring texture image and alpha channel.

FIGURE 5.98 Isolated color channels.

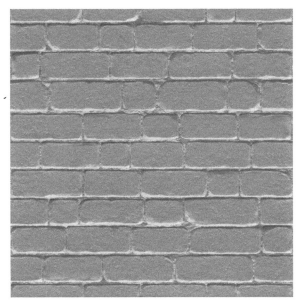

FIGURE 5.99 Normal texture image.

Each ring's channel is multiplied against a unique color, which may come from any source. The sum of the four products is inputted to the surface's base color. Opacity, driven by channel intensity, is used to generate semi-transparent rings.

Normal Mapping

Normal Mapping is a technique for biasing surface normals, making their geometry appear to have more detail than present. Texture images store the normal directions, but the values do not represent color. Instead, they represent vertex normal vectors normalized to 0.0 to 1.0 space (Figure 5.99).

During pixel shader lighting calculations, new normal vectors, read from texture maps, replace values inherited from the vertex shader. The changes in the normal vectors cause the diffuse and specular components to behave differently, altering the appearance of the surface topology. Most often this technique is used for adding surface detail to the appearance of the geometry. This is a good technique for economically adding more complexity to the surface without paying for additional geometry. The new normal vectors alter the appearance of the rendered image without changing the surface's topology (Figure 5.100).

While this technique is typically used for surface modeling, it can be used as an effective visual effect. For all purposes, the normal map is a texture image whose texture coordinates can be animated. Animated normal texture images are an ideal solution for generating the appearance of shifting, rotating, undulating, or burrowing under a rendered surface. Take, for example, a magical wart on a witch's face. Animated normal maps can move the bump y wart easily with artistic control.

PROCEDURAL TEXTURES

Procedural textures provide an alternative from referencing external images for supplemental color and transparency information. Instead of being sourced from pre-generated images, mathematical functions generate surface detail. This definition may sound sterile and devoid of creativity. However, once mastered, procedural textures can be utilized toward any creative endeavor.

FIGURE 5.100 Normal mapped surface.

Procedural textures are an extraordinarily broad topic (The reader is invited to explore *Lighting and Rendering for the Technical Artist* for a more thorough treatment of the subject). This portion of this chapter starts with identifying the most common math functions used for priming more elaborate procedural behavior. The sine wave is arguably the most dynamic and useful single function in the visual effects artist's arsenal. The final group of functions, chaos, noise, and fractals, is also essential in every visual effects artist's repertoire.

Mathematical Functions

A mere subset of all mathematical functions, the functions introduced in this portion of this chapter are the fundamental building blocks of all procedural textures. They are the foundations for more complicated procedural operations and are useful for providing initial surface color value.

ABS

ABS, or otherwise known as *absolute value*, returns the positive magnitude of its input, regardless of sign. An alternative perspective may be the inputted value's distance from zero (Figure 5.101).

$$x = -69$$

$$y = 76$$

$$abs(x) = 69$$

$$abs(y) = 76$$

Equation 5.16 Positive and Negative Absolute Value Examples

Step

The step function is used for generating hard transitions in pixel sequences. It compares two values and returns a 0.0 or a 1.0 based on which of the two initial values is larger. The following example expression paints the first third of an object's surface black and the remaining surface red (Figure 5.102).

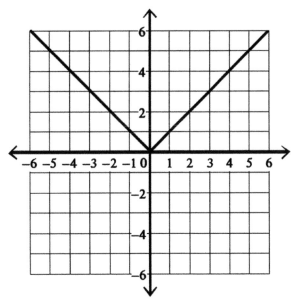

FIGURE 5.101 Graph of absolute value.

FIGURE 5.102 Example step function.

$$color_{RGB} = float3(1.0, 0.0, 0.0) * step(.333, texcoord_U)$$

Equation 5.17 Example Step Function

The hard transition between 0.0 and 1.0 makes the step function useful for creating boundaries or partitioning the surface.

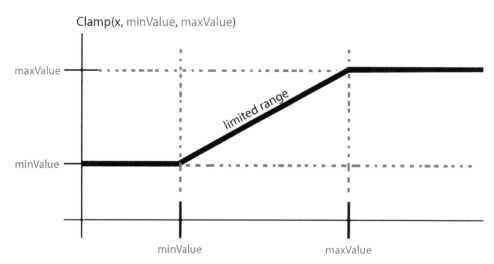

FIGURE 5.103 Example clamp function.

Clamp

The clamp function creates a numerical fence, bounding coordinate values. The function forces an input value between a specified minimum and maximum range. Values outside of the range are converted to the nearest minimum or maximum value. The following example creates a smooth vertical transition from dark to semi-bright gray (Figure 5.103).

$$color_{RGB} = clamp(texcoord_V, 0.2, 0.8)$$

Equation 5.18 Example Clamp Function

The clamp function prevents coordinate values from exceeding desired ranges.

Linear Step

The linear step function returns a linear interpolation between 0.0 and 1.0 based on the proportional distance a value, X, is from a minimal value, A, and from a maximum value, B. Linear step produces a linear transition between 0.0 and 1.0. In the following example, the linear step function generates a linear transition from black to green but only in the middle half of the surface (Figure 5.104).

$$color_{RGB} = float3(0.0, 1.0, 0.0) * linearstep(0.25, 0.75, texcoord_v)$$

Equation 5.19 Example Linear Step Function

The linear step function is generated by clamping the distance between X and A, divided by the distance between B and A:

$$linear\ step = clamp\left(\left(\frac{X-A}{B-A}\right), 0.0, 1.0\right)$$

Equation 5.20 Linear Step Formula

The linear step function is identified by its straight curve (Figure 5.105):

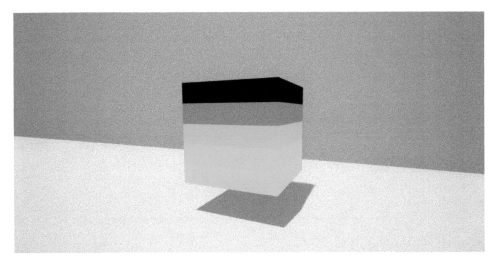

FIGURE 5.104 Example linear step function.

FIGURE 5.105 Linear step transition.

Smoothstep

The smoothstep function returns a smooth, hermite interpolation between 0.0 and 1.0 based on the proportional distance a value, X, is from a minimal value, A, and from a maximum value, B. Smoothstep generates a smooth gradation between 0.0 and 1.0. In the following example, the smoothstep function generates a smooth gradation from black to green but only in the middle half of the surface (Figure 5.106).

$$color_{RGB} = float3\,(0.0,\, 1.0,\, 0.0)\, {}^*\,smoothstep\,(0.25,\, 0.75,\, texcoord_V)$$

Equation 5.21 Example Smoothstep Function

FIGURE 5.106 Example smoothstep function.

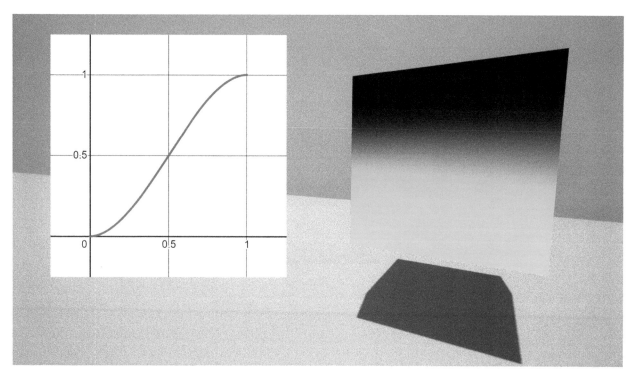

FIGURE 5.107 Smoothstep transition.

The smoothstep function simulates what is otherwise known as a *Hermite Cubic spline* which is achieved by the formula:

smoothstep = 3.0 * X * X − 2.0 * X * X * X

Equation 5.22 Hermite Cubic Spline

The transition is identified by its smooth, 'S' shaped curve (Figure 5.107):

Animators will recognize this as the traditional '*Ease*' transition.

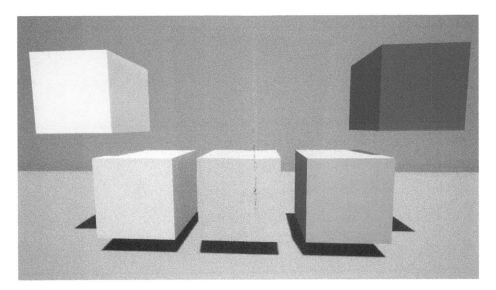

FIGURE 5.108 Example linear interpolation.

Linear Interpolation

A bit more useful than the linear step function is the *linear Interpolation* function, also known as the *lerp* or *mix* function. Unlike linear step, lerp creates a linear transition between any two states. The following example lerps between yellow and blue, midway through the surface (Figure 5.108).

$$color_{RGB} = lerp\left(float3\left(1.0,\ 1.0,\ 0.0\right),\ float3\left(0.0,\ 0.0, 1.0\right),\ X\right)$$

Equation 5.23 Example Linear Interpolation

While *A* and *B* are abstracted state values and *X* is a value between 0.0 and 1.0, linear interpolation is achieved by the traditional "Blend" formula:

$$\text{Linear Interpolation} = \left(A * X\right) + \left(B * \left(1.0 - X\right)\right)$$

Equation 5.24 Linear Interpolation Formula

Linear step is not implemented within most modern function libraries where linear interpolation is implemented. There are three reasons for this. They both produce the same linear transition over the same range so there is redundancy. Since the extreme state values of the linear interpolation are abstract and not bound between the scalar values of 0.0 and 1.0 lerping is more convenient to use than linear stepping. The third reason is linear stepping involves a division operation. On the rare occasion the two extreme values are equivalent, the linear step is undefined. The opportunity to remove a "division by zero" situation is always more desirable.

Disks

Creating circles or disks is not a typical math function but could be converted to one when needed. The technique's strategy simply considers when the current pixel position is within the radius of the disk. When it is within the radius of the disk, a new color is drawn. When the new pixel is outside the radius, a background color is used. The required input is the disk's center (d), the current pixel texture coordinate (p), and the disk's radius. The length of the current pixel texture coordinate from the disk's center is calculated using the Pythagorean Theorem. When the length is less than the radius, that position is in the disk. Otherwise, it is outside and ignored (Figure 5.109).

FIGURE 5.109 Procedural disk.

FIGURE 5.110 Procedural smooth box.

$$\text{length} = \sqrt{\left(p_x - d_x\right)^2 + \left(p_Y - d_Y\right)^2 + \left(p_Z - d_Z\right)^2}$$

if length < radius
    color = Red

else
    color = color

Equation 5.25 Disk Formula

Boxes

Two-dimensional boxes, while not as simple as disks, are an application of four-*step* functions applied to the current pixel's position *(p)* and the bottom left *(bl)* and top right *(tr)* corners of the box. During each color calculation, the pixel's position is tested against the bounding box defined by the bottom-left and upper-right corners. When pixels position is bounded by the box a value of 1.0 is returned. Otherwise 0.0 is returned (Figure 5.110).

$$val = step\left(bl_X, p_X\right)$$

$$val^* = step\left(bl_Y, p_Y\right)$$

$$val^* = 1.0 - step\left(tr_Y, p_Y\right)$$

$$val^* = 1.0 - step\left(tr_X, p_X\right)$$

Equation 5.26 Smooth Box Formula

Anti-Aliasing

When creating procedural textures, anti-aliasing is not so much of a function but more of a strategy for removing hard edges. Hard edges are removed in a two-step process. The first step employs the smoothstep function when considering when the current point is within or outside a function. Instead of returning a binary value of "0 or 1," "Yes or No," "True or False," "On or Off," the smoothstep function returns a gradient between 0.0 and 1.0. A small offset *distance* (*d*), provides the size of the gradient. The second step uses the result of the smoothstep function to linear interpolation between the new color and the background.

Consider the boundary test values of the disks or the box step operations. These values return a 1.0 or 0.0, which generate hard, jagged edges. A smoothstep operation generates a small gradient, smoothening hard edges when linear interpolated with the background. The small offset distance (*d*) scales the gradient (Figures 5.111 and 5.112).

$$d = 0.005$$

$$color_{RGB} = lerp\left(Red, color_{RGB}, smoothstep\left(radius - d, radius + d, length\right)\right)$$

Equation 5.27 Smooth Disk Formula

FIGURE 5.111 Disk after Smoothstep.

FIGURE 5.112 Box after Smoothstep.

$d = 0.005$

$value = \text{smoothstep}\left(bl_X - d, bl_X + d, \ p_X\right)$

$value^\star = \text{smoothstep}\left(bl_Y - d, bl_Y + d, \ p_Y\right)$

$value^\star = 1 - \text{smoothstep}\left(tr_Y - d, tr_Y + d, \ p_Y\right)$

$value^\star = 1 - \text{smoothstep}\left(tr_X - d, tr_X + d, \ p_X\right)$

Equation 5.28 Smooth Box Formula

Line Plotting

Line Plotting takes an abstract mathematical function, for example, $f(x) = x^3\left(6x^2 - 15x\right)$, and plots a corresponding line on the surface texture. This operation is very similar to disk computation. The texture U coordinate is first evaluated in the function. Then the difference between the evaluation and the original coordinate is calculated. When the ABS of the difference is less than the line thickness, the pixel is colored. Otherwise, it is colored the background color (Figure 5.113).

$x = \text{texcoord}_U$

$\text{Function Value} = x^3\left(6x^2 - 15x\right)$

$\text{Function Value} = abs\left(\text{Function Value} - \text{texcoord}_U\right)$

if value < line thickness

$color_{RGB} = \text{Black}$

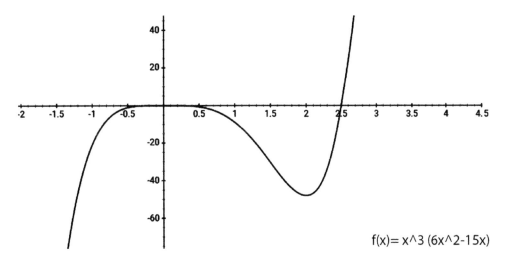

$$f(x) = x^3 (6x^2-15x)$$

FIGURE 5.113 Line plot of $f(x) = x^3 (6x^2 - 15x)$.

else

$color_{RGB} = color_{RGB}$

Equation 5.29 Line Plotting Formula

Sine Wave

Of all the functions at a visual effects artist's disposal, a favorite is the sine wave. This function is simple, versatile, and very dependable. It is simple since it only takes one input, the frequency, and produces one output, between −1.0 and 1.0. The sine wave is used as a simple math function or as a wave generator. Due to its simplicity, the sine function only produces one range of output, which is extraordinarily predictable. This predictability makes the sine function, and its brother cosine, the "go-to" functions for almost all wave-like behavior.

Functional Attributes

The sine function only requires one input, the frequency, which is a steadily increasing or decreasing offset. When the frequency is constant, the sine wave output is constant. Time is the typical frequency offset. However, any consistently increasing or decreasing value will work. Coordinate values, including all texture coordinates, make excellent inputs for the sine wave. Any parameter that can be counted provides excellent input when continuously increasing or decreasing.

The output of the sine wave continuously fluctuates between 1.0 and −1.0. A cyclical pattern, upon outputting a value of 1.0, it immediately outputs smaller numbers until reaching −1.0. Upon that point, the function increases until hitting 1.0 and starting over again (Figure 5.114).

The sine function's dependability makes it extraordinarily versatile.

The cosine function exhibits the exact same behavior as the sine wave except it is 90 degrees offset from the sine wave, meaning it is always a quarter cycle behind the sine wave. When the sine function outputs 1.0 the cosine outputs 0.0. When the sine wave outputs 0.0 the cosine wave outputs 1.0 and so on (Figure 5.115).

By themselves, the two functions are interchangeable unless the output at time = 0.0 needs to be 1.0, which requires the sine function. An output value of 0.0 requires cosine. When combined on orthogonal, *X* and *Y* axes,

Y= 2.5sin(**x**)

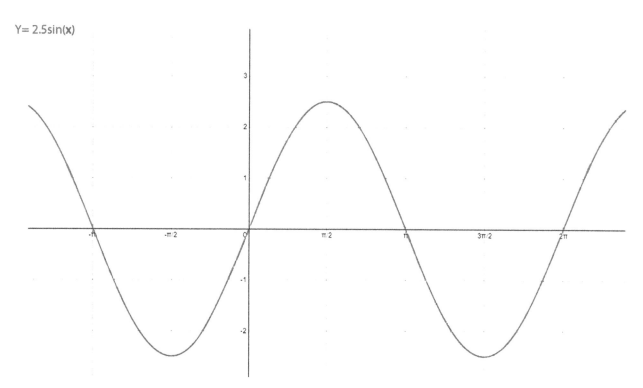

FIGURE 5.114 Sine function progression.

Y=2.5cos(x)
Y=2.5sin(x)

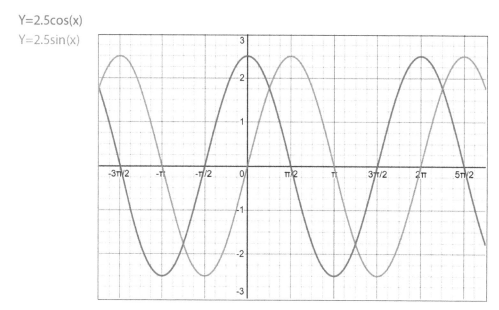

FIGURE 5.115 Sine and cosine function progression.

they represent the coordinates of a circle. For example, when angle is the input, plotting the cosine function output on the *X-axis* and the sine function output on the *Y axis* produces a perfect circle. Since the output magnitude for both functions is no greater than 1.0, the radius of the circle is 1.0. As the angle increases from 0° to 360° (or 0 to 2π in radians), the output draws a circle in a counterclockwise direction (Figure 5.116).

Angle = 200

Unit Circle - Sine

Unit Circle - Cosine

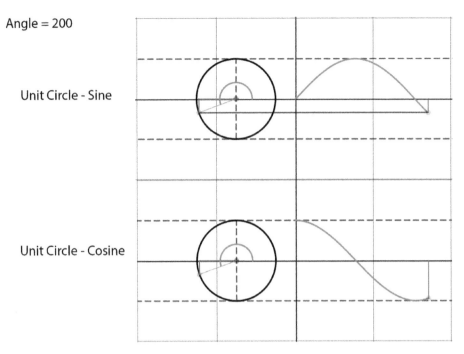

FIGURE 5.116 Circle plotting with sine and cosine.

Wave-Like Attributes

As a wave generator, sine has four primary attributes: frequency, phase, amplitude, and offset.

Wave Output = Offset + Amplitude * sin (Frequency + Phase)

Equation 5.30 Sine Wave Attribute Function

Frequency

Frequency defines the rate at which the input increases or decreases. The rate at which the sine wave oscillates between 1.0 and −1.0 is in direct proportion to the scale of the frequency. Larger frequencies generate faster oscillation. Smaller frequencies generate slower (Figure 5.117).

Frequency is often represented as a scalar multiplied against a constantly changing input, such as time.

Frequency = Scalar * Time

Equation 5.31 Wave input Frequency

Phase

Phase is used to offset frequency, biasing it in a positive or negative direction. Phase does not scale the frequency, it biases it. (Figure 5.118).

For example, the cosine wave is just a sine wave with a constant phase shift of −90°. By default, phase has 0.0 value.

Time is also a common phase shift. Iteratively offsetting the frequency creates motion in the sine wave. A changing phase variable oscillates the sine wave predictively without changing the scale of the frequency.

Low Frequency   High Frequency

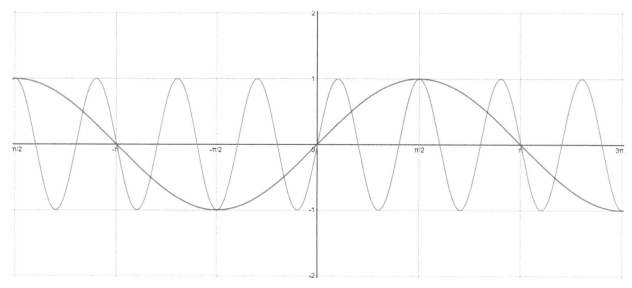

FIGURE 5.117 Small and large frequencies.

90 Degree Phase-Shift

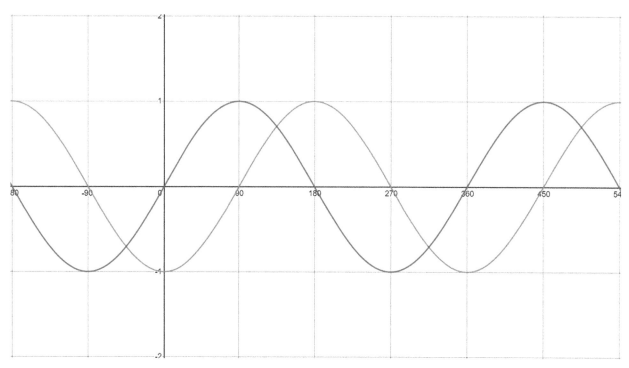

FIGURE 5.118 Sine wave with a 90° phase shift.

Like frequency, phase may also be a changing value multiplied by a scalar.

Phase = Scalar * Time

Equation 5.32 Wave Input Phase

Wave Angle

The combination of the frequency and the phase create the *Wave Angle*. The wave angle is also synonymous for sine function input.

Wave Angle = Frequency + Phase

Equation 5.33 Wave Angle

Sine Function Output = $\sin(\text{wave angle})$

Equation 5.34 Wave Angle Sine Output

Viewing the sine input as wave angle helps differentiate the roles of frequency and phase. While both are used synonymously, a good rule of thumb is to allow the frequency to be a constant value and phase to be a changing value. The frequency controls the amount of apparent detail. The phase controls animation speed. For example, consider the two functions (Figure 5.119):

wave = $\sin(\pi + \text{Time})$

wave = $\sin(10 * \pi + \text{Time})$

While the second function has more information and is bumpier than the first, they both move at the same rate (Figure 5.120).

Consider the next two functions:

wave = $\sin(\pi + \text{Time})$

wave = $\sin(\pi + 10 * \text{Time})$

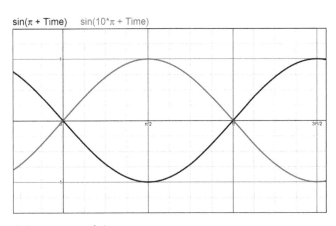

FIGURE 5.119 Two functions with the same rate of change.

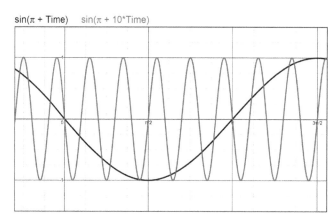

FIGURE 5.120 Function with different rate of change.

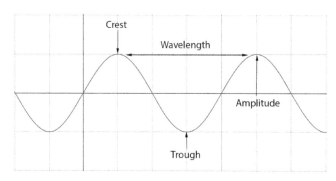

FIGURE 5.121 Amplitude of wave.

Both functions return the same amount of information and are equally bumpy, but the second function moves faster than the first.

The roles of frequency and phase are subjective. The artist is encouraged to adopt and maintain a consistent convention to avoid confusion.

Amplitude
Since the sine wave only outputs between 1.0 and −1.0, it is extraordinarily scalable. Amplitude scales the distance of the sine wave's trough and crest (Figure 5.121).

It is important to note that the sizes of the trough and crest amplitudes are always equivalent. The total distance between the wave's crest and trough, called *wave magnitude*, is two times the amplitude.

Wave Magnitude = 2.0 * Amplitude

Equation 5.35 Wave Magnitude

Offset
The offset shifts the output of the sine wave in a positive or negative direction. Offset biases the wave's output but does not impact the wave's fundamental behavior (Figure 5.122).

Through manipulation of offset and amplitude, any sine wave can be fitted to any desired range. This range is achieved by adding the average of the minimum and maximum values and the product of half the difference between the desired minimum and maximum values and the sine wave.

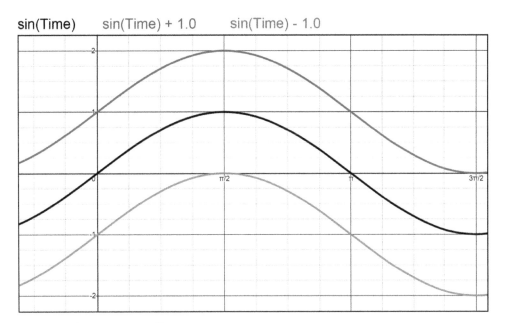

sin(Time)   sin(Time) + 1.0   sin(Time) - 1.0

FIGURE 5.122 Positive and negative wave offsets.

$$\text{Wave Range} = \left[\text{Minimum, Maximum}\right] = \left(\frac{\text{Minimum} + \text{Maximum}}{2.0}\right) + \left(\frac{\text{Maximum} - \text{Minimum}}{2.0}\right)\sin\left(\text{Wave Angle}\right)$$

Equation 5.36 Fitting Sine Wave to Desired Range

By adjusting the wave angle and fitting the output to the desired range using offset and amplitude, the sine wave oscillates between any range of two numbers.

Sine Wave Uses

When periodic behavior is desired, the sine function is a quick alternative for the panner function. Sine has other applications including a blend controller, a position oscillator, a blinker, a circle generator, and a waveform generator.

Ease-Like Interpolation

When an object has only two phases between which it needs to oscillate, and the transition needs to have an "ease-in/ease-out" like behavior, a sine function is a great solution. The sine function may be used in conjunction with a linear interpolation function.

$$\text{NonLinear Blend}\left(A \rightarrow B\right) = \text{Lerp}\left(A,\ B,\ .5 + .5 * \sin\left(\text{frequency}\right)\right)$$

Equation 5.37 Sine as a Lerp Controller

When the lerp operation needs to be avoided, it may be supplemented with another sine function.

$$\text{NonLinear Blend}\left(A \rightarrow B\right) = \left(A * \left(.5 + .5\sin\left(f\right)\right)\right) + \left(B * \left(.5 - .5\sin\left(f\right)\right)\right)$$

Equation 5.38 Sine as a Non-Linear Blender

Oscillation

When an object needs to move from position A to position B with regularity, nothing is more effective than a sine wave.

$$\text{Object Position}_{A \leftrightarrow B} = \text{Position}_A + \left(\frac{\text{distance}\left(\text{Position}_A, \ \text{Position}_B\right)}{2} \right)\left(1 + \sin\left(f\right)\right)$$

Equation 5.39 Oscillation between Two Positions

When sharper impact is needed, as with a bouncing object, then all that is needed is an ABS function.

$$\text{Object Position}_Y = abs\left(\left(0.5 * \text{Bounce Height}\right)\left(1 + \sin\left(f\right)\right)\right)$$

Equation 5.40 Object Bounce Formula

Blinking

When objects need to change states regularly, such as blinking lights, sine functions are ideal controllers.

$$\text{Intensity}_{\text{Light}} = \sin\left(\text{frequency}\right)$$

Equation 5.41 Blinking Light Formula

The prior equation assumes that the object can handle values between 0.0 and 1.0, such as a rheostat. When the object is only allotted an *on* state and an *off* state, a step function will force the results to be 0.0 or 1.0. $\text{Intensity}_{\text{Light}} = \left(\text{frequency}\right)$.

Equation 5.42 Blinking Light with only "On" or "off" States

Circles

The sine and cosine functions return the coordinates of a circle. When the output of the sine function is assigned to one axis and the output from the cosine function assigned to another orthogonal axis, the result is a circular plot. By default, the circle's radius is 1.0 and needs to be scaled appropriately (Figures 5.123 and 5.124).

$$\text{position}_X = \text{Radius} * \cos\left(\text{frequency}\right)$$

$$\text{position}_Y = \text{Radius} * \sin\left(\text{frequency}\right)$$

Equation 5.43 Circular Coordinates

Unique radii for each axis generate an ellipse-like shape.

$$\text{position}_X = \text{Radius}_X * \cos\left(\text{frequency}\right)$$

$$\text{position}_Y = \text{Radius}_Y * \sin\left(\text{frequency}\right)$$

Equation 5.44 Ellipse Coordinates

Wavy Shapes

The up and down shape of the sine wave function provides realistic, wave-like form for objects such as flags and water (Figure 5.125).

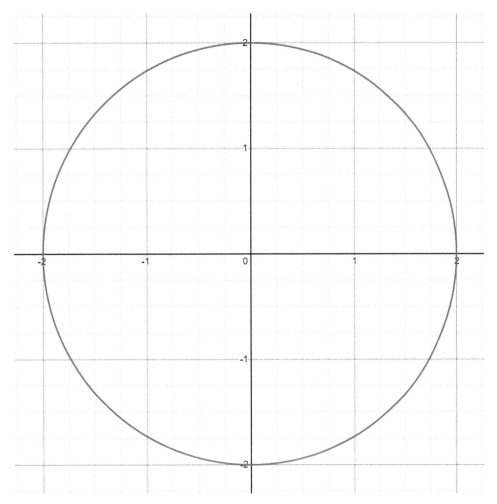

FIGURE 5.123 Plotted circle.

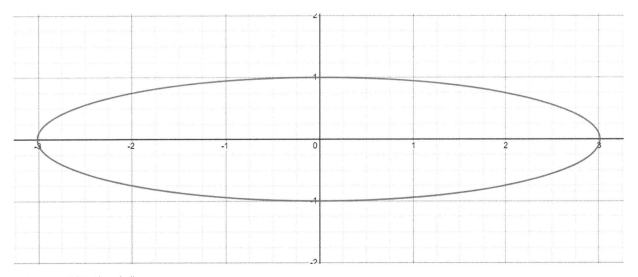

FIGURE 5.124 Plotted ellipse.

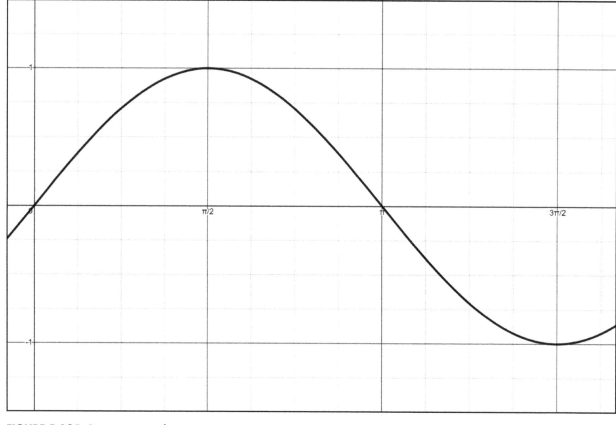

FIGURE 5.125 One generation of sine wave.

$$vertexPosition_Y = wave\ height * \sin\left(wave\ frequency * vertexPosition_X\right)$$

Equation 5.45 Basic Wave-Like Behavior

The variations to the above formula are limited only by the artist's imagination. Adding multiple sine waves generates more irregularity (Figure 5.126).

$$vertexPosition_Y = wave\ height * \sin\left(wave\ frequency * vertexPosition_X\right)$$
$$+.5 * wave\ height * \sin\left(4 * wave\ frequency * vertexPosition_X\right)$$

Equation 5.46 Two Generations of Sine Wave

Reducing the scale with each generation while increasing the frequency generates fractal-like behavior. This is explored further in the following section.

Randomness, Noise, and Fractals

Natural and organic patterns are achieved with randomness, noise, and fractals. These topics make up an entire sub-section of mathematics. In this section, instead of attempting thorough coverage of the topic, the author provides a rough explanation of the concepts which scratch at the surface of this wide field. There are many fine books that give the topic deeper explanation. For more information on fractals, please examine Math and Physics *for the Technical Artist.*

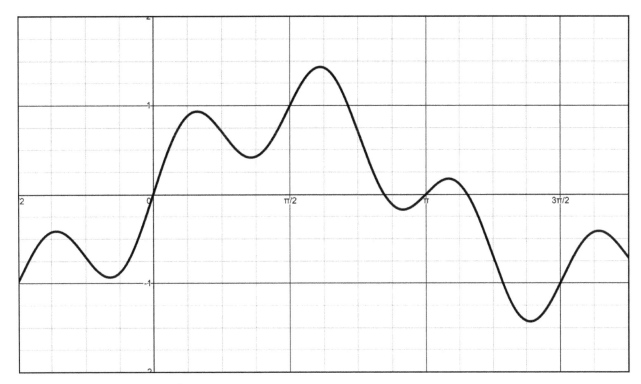

FIGURE 5.126 Two generations of sine wave.

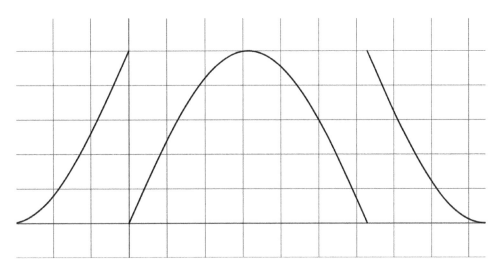

FIGURE 5.127 Fractional sine values.

Randomness

Randomness is the foundation for generating organic patterns. Ironically, visual effects artists desire random-appearing numbers but do not require true random numbers. Once a pattern is created to produce just the correct visual look, the output is expected to be repeatable provided the same input. *Pseudo-Random* generators provide deterministic, predictable output given specific input, or *seed values*. Of the many available random algorithms, one of simplest is returning the fractional value of the sine function (Figure 5.127).

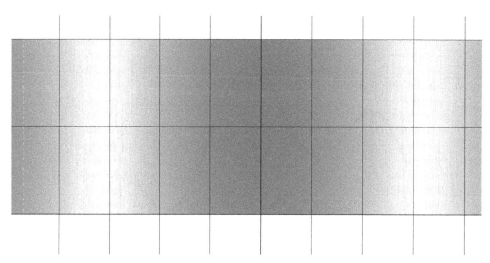

FIGURE 5.128 Pseudo-random function output.

$$\text{Random Value} = \text{frac}\left(\sin\left(x\right)\right)$$

Equation 5.47 Pseudo-Random Number Generator

While at first the output of this function does not appear to be random, when the frequency of the sine function is multiplied by 100,000, the results are different and appear to be random (Figure 5.128).

$$\text{Random Value}\left(\text{random}\right) = \text{frac}\left(\left(x\right)\right)$$

Equation 5.48 Pseudo-Random Number Generator

This technique provides the visual effects artist with a simple method for generating predictable yet random-appearing behavior.

Manipulation of the seed values also encourages the most aesthetic results from any random function. The function remains constant yet some of its output values may be more aesthetically pleasing than others. It is impossible to predict until the results from each seed are fully calculated. When build farms or multiple CPUs are available, the artist may take advantage of *step-wedges*. A step-wedge is a procedural collection of random sequences driven by constantly changing seeds. When the wedge is allowed to process for multiple hours, the artist and art director examine the calculated sequences and identify the seed values that produce the most desirable results.

Multi-Dimensional Randomness

The randomness formula presented in the previous subsection is good for one dimension. When dealing with texture images and texture coordinates, at least two dimensions must be covered and at least three when dealing with color and vertex position. The simplest approach is to isolate and process just one component at a time. For example, random position is achieved by randomizing each of the X, Y, and Z positional components independently.

$$\text{position}_X = \text{random}\left(X\right)$$

$$\text{position}_Y = \text{random}\left(Y\right)$$

$$position_Z = random(Z)$$

Equation 5.49 Component-wise Randomness

A single random value from an input given vector is generated by taking the dot product of the vector with a separate seed vector. The dot-product is calculated by adding the products of corresponding components.

$$Dot - Product(A, B) = A_X * B_X + A_Y * B_Y + A_Z * B_Z + \cdots$$

Equation 5.50 Dot-Product of Two Vectors

The result of a dot-product is always a single float value, regardless of the dimensions of the two vectors. Most math libraries implement this function as the *dot()* function. The single float result is then inputted to the random function.

$$Random2D(Vector_A) = frac(dot(Vector_A, Seed\ Vector))$$

Texture coordinates can be represented as two-dimensional vectors. The random output of input two-dimensional texture coordinates produces pixel illumination values which take on the appearance of white noise (Figure 5.129).

The pseudo-random seed vector can be of arbitrary value: for example, (12.989799, 77.450668, 23.528691). Depending on the implementation of the math library, this pseudo-random number is called the random *seed*. The consistency of the seed value guarantees reproducible results from the random function. An easily remembered seed value is a notable date, such as an artist's birthday. When more random numbers are desired, the time of day or the amount of time since gameplay started is used. When the seed value is consistent, the random results are reproduced predictably.

FIGURE 5.129 Two-dimensional randomness.

Noise

Nature rarely displays pure white noise. It manifests itself in patterns that appear random but also have a sense of flow and quasi-direction (Figure 5.130).

My favorite description of noise is the path of an inebriated person, walking home from the bar. While the person's path appears to be random, haphazard, and even doubles upon itself, at the end of the journey a single trail is generated. The noise algorithm was created in the early 1980s when Ken Perlin was commissioned to create visual effects for the movie *Tron*.

Roughly described, the noise algorithm is the smooth interpolation between sequential random points. Consider a one-dimensional sequence of random values. Accept only the integer value of the input and ignore the fractional portions between the points. The graph appears to be a sequence of randomly shaped boxes (Figure 5.131).

An alligator-tooth graph is generated when the fractional parts are used to linearly interpolate between the integer values (Figure 5.132).

FIGURE 5.130 Randomness in nature. (Courtesy of Trace Hudson from Pexels.)

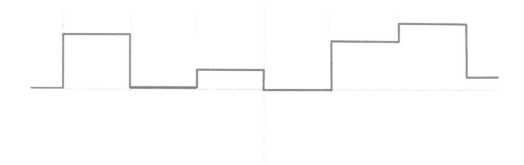

FIGURE 5.131 Y = random (floor(X)).

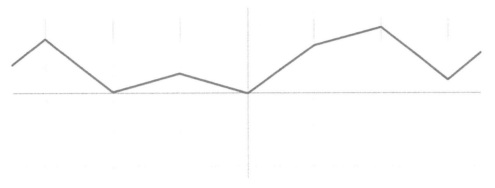

FIGURE 5.132 Linear interpolation of successive random points.

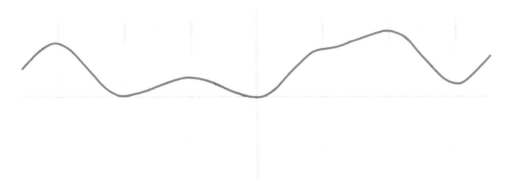

FIGURE 5.133 Smoothstep interpolation of points.

Take this a step further. Instead of doing a linear interpolation, do a smoothstep interpolation between values. This is a crude representation of noise (Figure 5.133).

The function for one-dimensional noise is the smooth interpolation of successive random integers.

$$rx = \text{randomInt}(X)$$

$$\text{Noise 1D} = \text{lerp}\left(\text{floor}(rx),\ \text{floor}(\text{rand}(rx)+1.0),\ \text{smoothstep}\left(0.0,\ 1.0,\ \text{frac}(\text{rand}(rx))\right)\right)$$

Equation 5.51 One Dimensional Noise

Instead of using the smoothstep function, many visual effects artists like creating their own interpolating functions such as cubic or quantic splines.

Two-Dimensional Noise

Extrapolating from one-dimensional noise to two-dimensional noise is not as easy as the transition from one- to two-dimensional randomness. Instead of performing a dot-product on a single two-dimensional vector, four random vectors (points), must be considered; the current point, the next point in the first dimension, the next point in the second dimension, and the next point in both dimensions (Figure 5.134).

Smoothly interpolated values between the upper two and bottom two points are calculated. A third interpolation between these two new values generates the resulting two-dimensional noise value (Figure 5.135).

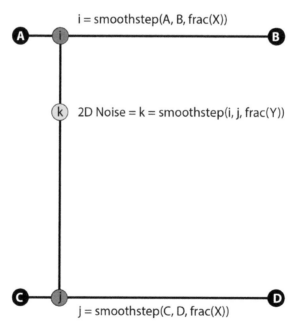

A = Random(X, Y)
B = Random(X+1, Y)
C = Random(X, Y+1)
D = Random(X+1, Y+1)

A　　　　　　　　　　　　　　　**B**

C　　　　　　　　　　　　　　　**D**

FIGURE 5.134 Two-dimensional point interpolation.

i = smoothstep(A, B, frac(X))

A—i————————————————**B**

(k) 2D Noise = k = smoothstep(i, j, frac(Y))

C—j————————————————**D**
j = smoothstep(C, D, frac(X))

FIGURE 5.135 Two-dimensional interpolation of noise.

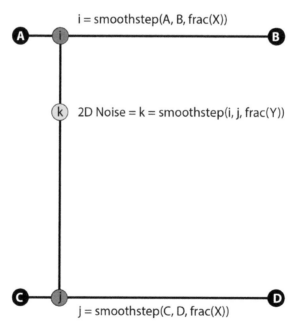

$$a = \text{random}\left(A_{X,Y}\right)$$

$$b = \text{random}\left(A_{X+1,Y}\right)$$

$$c = \text{random}\left(A_{X,Y+1}\right)$$

$$d = \text{random}\left(A_{X+1,Y+1}\right)$$

$$SS1 = \text{smoothstep}\left(0.0,\ 1.0,\ \text{frac}\left(X\right)\right)$$

$$SS2 = \text{smoothstep}\left(0.0,\ 1.0,\ \text{frac}\left(Y\right)\right)$$

$$2D\ \text{Noise}\left(A_{X,Y}\right) = \text{lerp}\left(\text{lerp}\left(a,\ b,\ SS1\right),\ \text{lerp}\left(c,\ d,\ SS1\right),\ \text{smoothstep}\left(0.0,\ 1.0,\ SS2\right)\right)$$

Equation 5.52 Two-Dimensional Noise Interpolation

The result of these interpolations is a two-dimensional, cloud-like pattern (Figure 5.136).

Fractal Noise

Fractal Brownian Motion is the sequential phase of evolution within the contexts of randomness and noise. While fractals, as a mathematical discipline, are beyond the scope of this text, the main concepts are easy to follow. Fractals are mathematical patterns, which exhibit a property called "*Self-Similarity*." A self-similar pattern duplicates itself, indefinitely, within itself.

For example, a Koch triangle starts as a simple, equilateral triangle (Figure 5.137).

When every edge of the triangle is replaced by the same triangular bump, the triangle takes on more of a star shape appearance (Figure 5.138).

FIGURE 5.136 Two-dimensional noise.

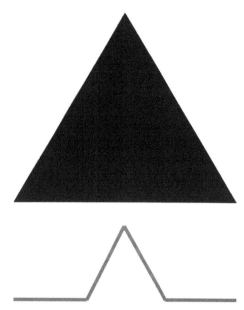

FIGURE 5.137 First Koch triangle iteration and bump.

FIGURE 5.138 Two iterations of the Koch triangle.

Within each iteration, every edge is replaced by the bump, halved in scale, and the shape takes on a more snowflake appearance. When allowed to iterate indefinitely, the snowflake becomes infinitely complex but still maintains its initial triangular shape. This is self-similar behavior (Figure 5.139).

This same, self-similar behavior can be extended to a simple sine wave. When for every subsequent iteration, the sine wave is added to itself with the frequency doubled and the amplitude halved. The sine wave remains the same but with multiple sine waves embedded within (Figures 5.140–5.144).

$$value = amplitude * \sin\left(x * frequency\right)$$

Equation 5.53 First Iteration of Sine Wave

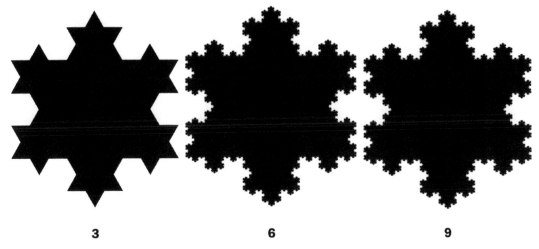

3   6   9

FIGURE 5.139 Three, six, and nine iterations of the Koch triangle.

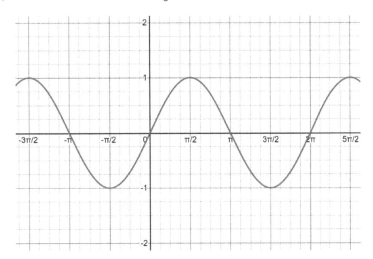

FIGURE 5.140 Sine wave.

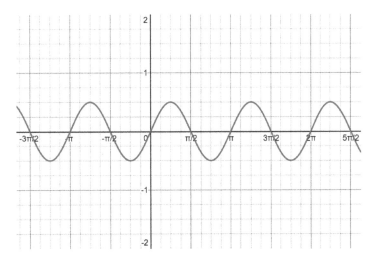

FIGURE 5.141 Sine wave half amplitude and double frequency.

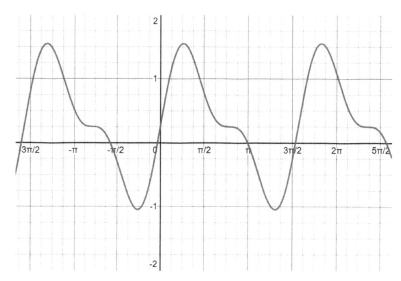

FIGURE 5.142 Two sine waves added.

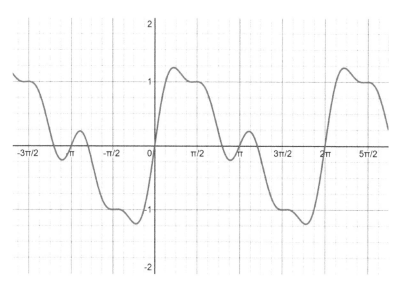

FIGURE 5.143 Three sine wave iterations.

Fractal Brownian Motion, or *fractal noise*, is the result when the sine wave of the prior example is replaced with noise. For the below example, assume the amplitude is halved and the frequency doubled with every iteration (Figures 5.145–5.147).

$$value = amplitude * noise(x * frequency)$$

Equation 5.54 First Iteration of Noise

One-dimensional noise fractal functions may be extended into multiple dimensions (Figure 5.148).

Borrowing from acoustic terminology, the number of iterations in a system is called the number of *octaves*. The change in amplitude within each octave is the *lacunarity*. The change in amplitude within each octave is the *gain*. Octaves, lacunarity and gain controls are exposed to the user in most fractal noise implementations.

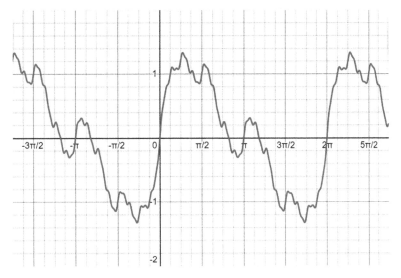

FIGURE 5.144 Six sine wave iterations.

FIGURE 5.145 One iteration of noise.

FIGURE 5.146 Three noise iterations.

FIGURE 5.147 Six noise iterations.

FIGURE 5.148 Three-dimensional noise fractal.

Since the texel scale of procedural texture images cannot get smaller than a single pixel, the number of octaves for any fractal noise is limited between six and eight. The number of octaves controls the sharpness of the noise pattern. Octave values beyond eight are rarely noticeable (Figure 5.149).

The lacunarity controls the granularity of the fractal. Values between one and two are typically very coarse. Greater values of lacunarity cause the fractal to appear more granular (Figure 5.150).

Like the number of octaves, gain controls the contrast of the fractal. Values near 1.0 create extreme contrast in the pattern. As the gain reduces, so does the fractal's contrast. As the gain nears 0.0, the fractal smoothens (Figure 5.151).

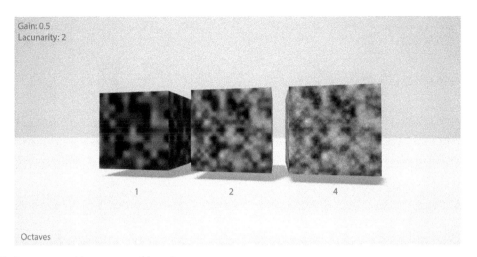

FIGURE 5.149 One, two, and four octaves of fractal noise.

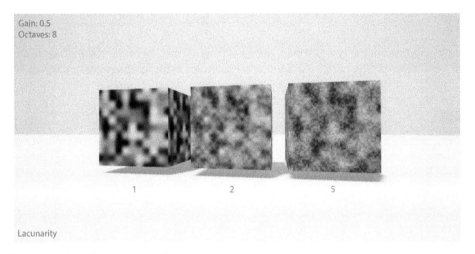

FIGURE 5.150 Lacunarity values of one, two, and four.

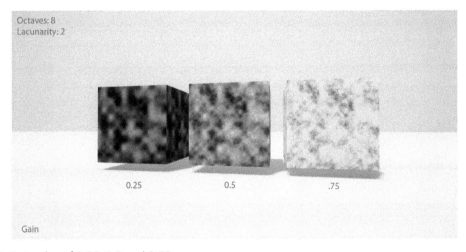

FIGURE 5.151 Gain values of 0.25, 0.5, and 0.75.

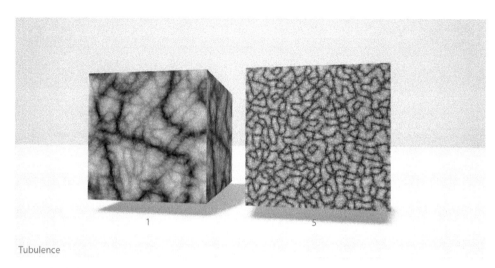

Tubulence

FIGURE 5.152 Fractal turbulence.

A common variation of fractal noise is *turbulence*. Instead of raw noise, the ABS of the noise is multiplied against the amplitude for each octave. This added ABS function generates sharp creases and valleys in the resulting pattern (Figure 5.152).

VERTEX OFFSET

Up until this section, all the effects covered in this chapter have been executed within the pixel shader. Effects executed in the vertex shader are a bit more challenging to understand but can have a significantly more profound effect on the visual appearance of a three-dimensional object.

Definition

When geometry data first flows into the rendering pipeline through the input assembler, it must first go through the vertex shader. The vertex data contains all possible information required to create the three-dimensional model. The minimal information is the vertex position. The vertex position is a four-dimensional float vector storing the X, Y, Z, and W components. The W component stores the state of the position vector. A W value of 1.0 is an indication that the vertex is a point in space. A value of 0.0 is an indication that the vector is a direction. Other vertex information may include the texture coordinates, the vertex color, vertex normal information, and joint weighting information. There may be multiple datasets for each type of information, such as multiple sets of texture coordinates.

All vertex shader data is alterable. Other than the generation and destruction of new vertices (which happens in the Tessellation and Geometry Shaders), any aspect of geometry can be altered. This gives the artist unlimited capacity for manipulating geometry. The exposition of altering any vertex attribute is powerful, yet deliberate intention is required to prevent the modification from looking like pure chaos.

Vertex Offset and Surface Silhouette

Instead of manipulating color information, the vertex shader is better suited for offsetting vertex positions. Normal mapping, as described earlier in this chapter, deviates vertex normals in the pixel shader to generate the appearance of non-existent surface detail. Within the vertex shader, the vertex position is offset, changing the silhouette of the object's surface. Normal mapping is adequate when silhouette is irrelevant to the integrity of the visual effect. Vertex offset strategies are required to maintain silhouette integrity.

Character Animation

All articulated character animation happens in the vertex shader. For every frame, for every vertex, the vertex shader considers the contributing influence of all character joints. Based on accumulated joint influences and the current joint positions, the shader calculates and applies new offsets for the vertices, maintaining relative position to their associated joints. The accumulated effect is articulated character animation.

Displacement Mapping

One of the more powerful yet simple techniques for adding extra object surface detail is displacement mapping. Displacement mapping requires vertex normal, vertex texture coordinates, a texture image, and a displacement amount. The texture image may be monochrome since the data from only one channel is required. This image should be in linear color space. For every frame, the vertex texture coordinates are used to access the corresponding texture image values. These values are between 0.0 and 1.0. Multiplying the vertex normal against the texture image value and displacement amount generates a vertex offset vector. The current vertex position is offset along this vector, deforming the surface to conform with the texture image (Figures 5.153 and 5.154).

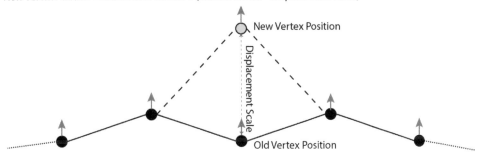

Displacement Scale = Texture Image Value * Displacement Amount
New Vertex Position = Old Vertex Position + (Vertex Normal * Displacement Scale)

FIGURE 5.153 Vertex offset by displacement amount.

FIGURE 5.154 Accumulated surface offset.

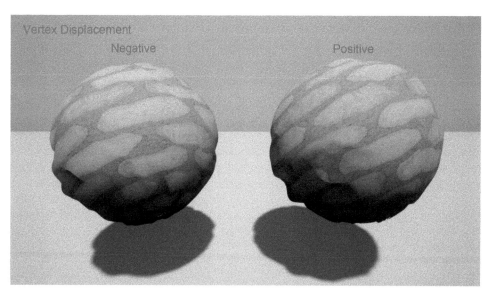

FIGURE 5.155 Positive and negative vertex offsets.

$$\text{New Position}_{\text{Vertex}} = \text{Old Position}_{\text{Vertex}} + \left(\text{Normal}_{\text{Vertex}} * \text{Value}_{\text{Texture Image}} * \text{Displacement Amount}\right)$$

Equation 5.55 Vertex Displacement Offset

The displacement amount is constant over the entire surface, scaling the overall effect. The larger the value, the further the displacement. Displacement polarity is also considered. Positive displacement displaced vertices in an outward direction. Negative values displace vertices in an inward direction (Figure 5.155).

Since the vertex offsets are calculated on a per-frame basis, animated texture images are used to animate the offsets. This powerful deformation technique is good for making a character's skin crawl, bubble, or otherwise undulate. For example, any effect where an insect or foreign entity burrows under the skin of another character is generated utilizing this technique.

The ability to add fine detail to the surface of an object does have a serious drawback. Adequate vertex information is required to maintain high-fidelity displacements. When the vertex resolution is inadequate to convey the information contained in the texture image, the detailed offset information is lost. Higher vertex resolution is required for highly detailed displacement (Figure 5.156).

At a certain point, a threshold of diminishing returns is achieved. When the vertex resolution for the desired effect reaches beyond a certain point, then an alternative method, such as *blend shapes*, should be considered. The context of the visual effects has a strong influence on the exact displacement technique used.

Since the amount of displacement is controlled by the displacement amount variable, a visual threshold in the vertex offset may be breached, manifesting itself in visual tears in the rendered surface. The pixel shader simply does not have adequate information to fill in all the pixel gaps (Figure 5.157).

When this happens, the only recourse is to reduce the displacement amount. The context of the visual effect will decide when this is a viable option. More vertex geometry may be added during the Tessellation stage and then further displaced in the geometry shader. However, when the effect requires these adjustments then the effect is no longer simply vertex shader-based.

Vertex Resolution

High   Low

FIGURE 5.156 High and low vertex resolution.

Surface Tearing

FIGURE 5.157 Surface tearing due to vertex displacement.

Procedural Deformations

Although surface deformation may be sensitive to inadequate vertex resolution, almost all procedural techniques used in the pixel shader can be used in the vertex shader. Vertex shaders may employ panners, rotators, and sine functions. There are additional techniques available to vertex shaders unavailable in pixel shaders such as world space relativity and bounding box information. Conceptually, these tools are a bit more challenging to understand. However, once mastered, they provide an extraordinary dimension to the artist's toolkit.

Panners

Like behavior in the pixel shader, panners can be used in the vertex shader to create animated deformations along the texture coordinates of a surface. The panner function offsets the texture coordinates of a surface along its U and V directions. Borrowing from the displacement mapping strategy, the values of the texture image are multiplied against the existing vertex normals, producing offset vectors which are added or subtracted from existing vertex positions. The result is a moving deformation along the object's surface. Since the vertex normal and

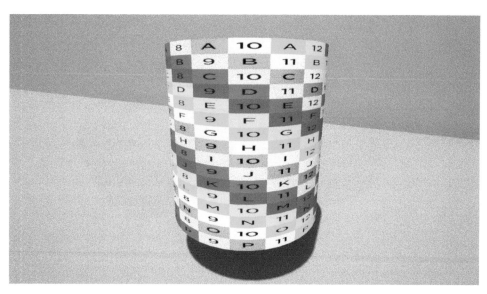

FIGURE 5.158 Tube with cylindrical texture coordinates.

the texture image values are bound between 0.0 and 1.0, an extra displacement scale variable is required to control the size of the deformation.

$$\text{New Position}_{\text{Vertex}} = \text{Old Position}_{\text{Vertex}} + (\text{Normal}_{\text{Vertex}} * \text{Value}_{\text{Texture Image}} * \text{Displacement Scale})$$

Equation 5.56 Displaced Vertex Position

Pulse Effect

Consider a tube-like surface with cylindrical texture coordinates and a texture image containing only a single radial stripe. A panner function offsets the texture coordinates to move the stripe along the length of the tube. Instead of animating the color of the tube, its vertices are offset along the position of the animated stripe. This results in a bulging ring animating along the length of the tube (Figures 5.158–5.160).

The gradient of the texture image controls the shape of the pulse. As the texture image increases in contrast, the edges of the pulse straighten (Figure 5.161).

Linear gradients produce straight edges while spline and curve-based gradients produce rounder pulses (Figure 5.162).

Using image manipulation tools, the amount of pulse displacement is subtly manipulated through the illuminance of the texture image. Gradients produced in image painting software produce texture images in linear color space. This means the displacements in the pulse appear shorter with higher contrast. Fuller, more dramatic pulses are generated when the texture images are converted to linear color space or adjusted with variable exponential power.

$$\text{Texture Image}_{\text{RGB}} = \text{power}(\text{Texture Image}_{\text{RGB}}, \text{Exponent})$$

Equation 5.57 Converting Pulse Image to Exponential Power

Exponents less than 1.0 make the pulses rounder. Exponents greater than 1.0 make the pulses appear sharper (Figure 5.163).

FIGURE 5.159 Single strip texture image.

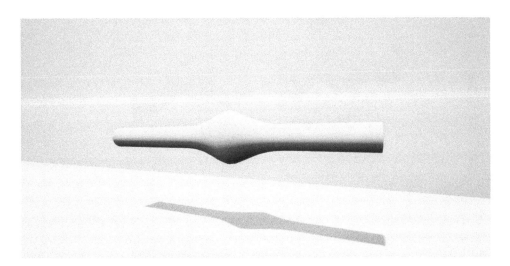

FIGURE 5.160 Bulging ring moving along tube surface.

Multiple Pulses

A single panner function may provide multiple pulses given a single texture image with only one horizontal gradient line. The Texture mode of the image needs to be set to Wrap mode for this to work. When the scale of the V texture coordinate space is increased, the vertical coverage of the texture image is crunched, allowing the texture image to be duplicated vertically. This translates into more vertical pulses on the cylinder at the same time. For example, when the scale factor for the V Texture coordinate is 4.0, there will be four pulses on the tube (Figure 5.164).

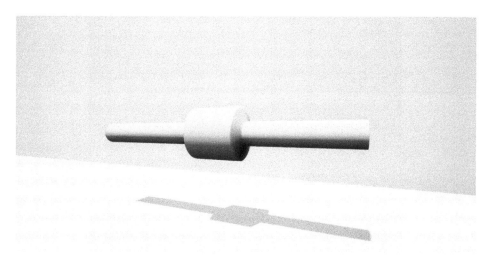

FIGURE 5.161 Square pulse texture and displacement.

FIGURE 5.162 Linear versus spline gradients.

FIGURE 5.163 Rounder and sharper pulses.

FIGURE 5.164 Four tube pulses.

FIGURE 5.165 Addition of two pulse-driven deformations.

The combination of multiple pulse deformations driven by different panners produces interesting results. When one panner offsets the texture coordinates in a positive direction and another panner offsets the texture coordinates in the opposite direction, the offsets combine to produce two pulses, one moving in one direction and the other moving in the opposite direction (Figure 5.165).

When the two pulses overlap, they combine to create larger deformations.

This effect is made more dramatic when the texture space is scaled, and more pulses are generated. The added pulses increase the frequency of the combined deformations (Figure 5.166).

Screw Pulse
Interesting phenomena occur when deformed objects have multiple sets of texture coordinates. Blending between multiple sets of coordinates produces unexpected yet predictable results such as generating a screw pulse.

FIGURE 5.166 Overlapping pulses.

FIGURE 5.167 Tube with cylindrical texture coordinates.

The first set of texture coordinates (used in the prior pulse effect example) are cylindrical. This means the V coordinate axis runs up the height of the tube and the U-axis runs along the perimeter, appearing as if an artist rolled a texture image along the outside of the tube (Figure 5.167).

The projection of a second set of coordinates, orthogonally down the Y-axis (or down the tube's length) produces an orthogonal progression spanning from one point of the tube to the other (Figure 5.168).

Linear Interpolating (lerping) between the two texture coordinates before inputting to the panner function creates a screw-like, spiral shape. For this effect to work, the U and V panning speeds need to be similar. A 50% split in the linear interpolation between the cylindrical and orthogonal coordinates creates a single pulse, which spirals up the length of the tube (Figure 5.169).

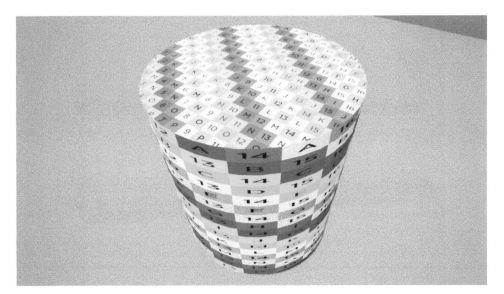

FIGURE 5.168 Tube with cylindrical and orthogonal coordinates.

FIGURE 5.169 Screw pulse.

When the linear interpolation between the two coordinates is biased toward the cylindrical coordinates, the pulse flattens. When the interpolation is biased toward the orthogonal projection, the deformation becomes more vertical (Figure 5.170).

Rotator

Just as panners can be used to animate vertex deformations on an object surface, so too can rotator functions. It is important to remember, rotator functions rotate the texture coordinates of a surface and not the actual vertices. Either a clamp texture address mode or a garbage mask is required to prevent deformations from animating outside the intended area of rotation (Figure 5.171).

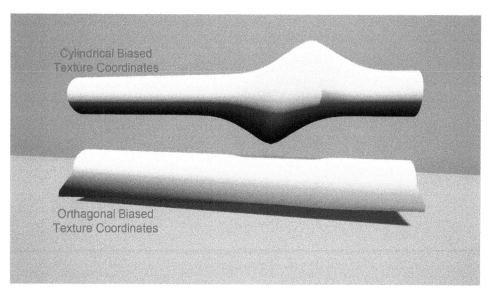

FIGURE 5.170 Biased cylindrical and orthogonal texture coordinates.

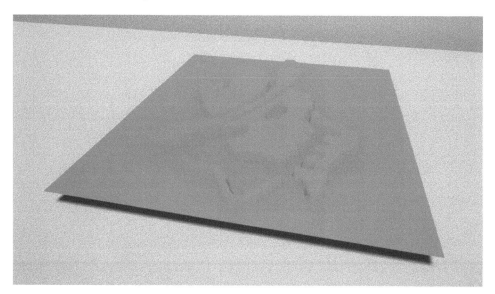

FIGURE 5.171 Rotator texture on a flat surface.

Sine Wave

Sine waves provide alternative offsetting instead of using texture images, panners, and rotators. The default sine wave output oscillates smoothly between −1.0 *and* 1.0, providing a smooth gradient positional offset. Sine wave deformation is discussed earlier in this chapter. The new vertex position is generated by adding the product of the sine wave with the original vertex position. The basic formula for offsetting in one axis direction is:

Wave Angle = $(\text{Time} + \text{Texture Coordinate}) * \text{Frequency}$

Vertex Position$_{axis}$ = Vertex Position$_{axis}$ + Amplitude $* \sin(\text{Wave Angle})$

Equation 5.58 Basic Sine Vertex Offset

FIGURE 5.172 Offset normals stay constant.

FIGURE 5.173 Small and large view angles.

An important disadvantage of using sine waves for offsetting vertices is the dependency on normal data, which provides direction for vertex displacement. The normal direction does not change to compensate for the change in surface gradient (Figure 5.172).

When the wave angle from the surface normal is small, the effect of the offset disappears. As the wave angle increases the offset becomes more apparent (Figure 5.173).

Using differential geometry, the sine function offers an approximation for updating the normal depending on the scale of the offset. For the purpose of demonstration, suppose the vertex is only being offset in the Z-axis. The generic formula for offset in the Z direction is:

$$\text{Angle} = \big(\text{Time} + \text{Texture Coordinate}\big) * \text{Frequency}$$

$$\text{Vertex Position}_Z = \text{Vertex Position}_Z + \text{Amplitude} * \sin\big(\text{Angle}\big)$$

Equation 5.59 Sine Based Z Directional Offset

While the math is beyond the scope of this book, using differential geometry and a few partial derivatives, the normal for this new vertex position can be approximated with following formula:

$$\text{Normal}_{\text{New}} = \text{normalize}\big(0.0, \ -\text{Amplitude} * \text{Frequency} * \cos\big(\text{Angle}\big), \ 1.0\big)$$

Equation 5.60 Normal Calculation

The normal direction must be adjusted for each positional offset. While these calculations increase the complexity of the material offset, they broaden the opportunity for using vertex offsets for modeling animated objects such as waving flags and water.

Waving Flag

A classic example of employing a sine function in the vertex shader is a waving flag. To demonstrate this effect, the flag geometry must be subdivided sufficiently to support the deformation, must be aligned in the positive XY plane, must have UV coordinates aligned in the XY plane, and the deformation must be allowed to happen in the Z-axis (Figure 5.174).

Since the desired deformation happens along the X-axis (U-axis), the formula for the Z deformation is:

$$\text{Angle} = \big(\text{Time} + \text{Texture Coordinate}_U\big) * \text{Frequency}$$

$$\text{Vertex Position}_Z = \text{Old Vertex Position}_Z + \text{Amplitude} * \sin\big(\text{Angle}\big)$$

Equation 5.61 Waving Flag Formula 1

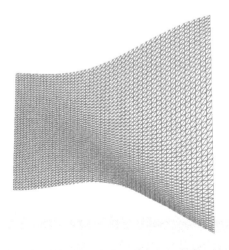
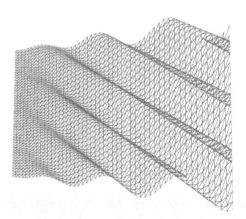

FIGURE 5.174 Waving flag setup.

While this results in an adequate waving motion, there are two problems: the flag appears to be waving toward the flagpole (aligned along the Y-Axis) and the flag is disjointed from the flagpole itself. This first problem is easily addressed by subtracting time from the texture coordinate instead of adding.

$$\text{Angle} = (\text{Texture Coordinate}_U - \text{Time}) * \text{Frequency}$$

$$\text{Vertex Position}_Z = \text{Vertex Position}_Z + \text{Amplitude} * \sin(\text{Angle})$$

Equation 5.62 Waving Flag Formula 2

Multiplying the product of the Amplitude and sine function against the U-Axis texture coordinate attaches the flag to the flagpole.

$$\text{Angle} = (\text{Texture Coordinate}_U - \text{Time}) * \text{Frequency}$$

$$\text{Vertex Position}_Z = \text{Vertex Position}_Z + \text{Texture Coordinate}_U * \text{Amplitude} * \sin(\text{Angle})$$

Equation 5.63 Waving Flag Formula 3

This multiplication minimizes the amount of deformation at the origin (the Y-Axis) and maximizes it at the end of the flag.

It is not realistic to expect a flag to deform only along its length. It also needs vertical displacement. To generate this extra displacement, add the V texture coordinate to the U texture coordinate when calculating the angle (Figure 5.175).

$$\text{Angle} = (\text{Texture Coordinate}_U + \text{Texture Coordinate}_V - \text{Time}) * \text{Frequency}$$

$$\text{Vertex Position}_Z = \text{Vertex Position}_Z + \text{Texture Coordinate}_U * \text{Amplitude} * \sin(\text{Angle})$$

Equation 5.64 Waving Flag Formula 4

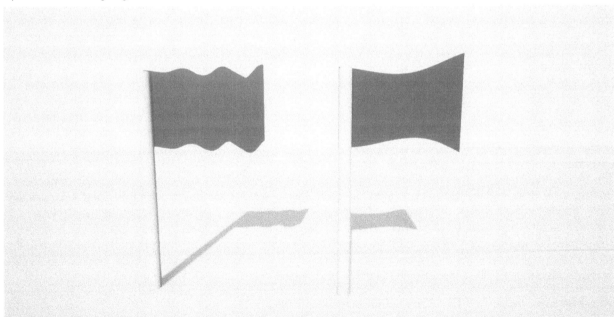

FIGURE 5.175 Waving flag.

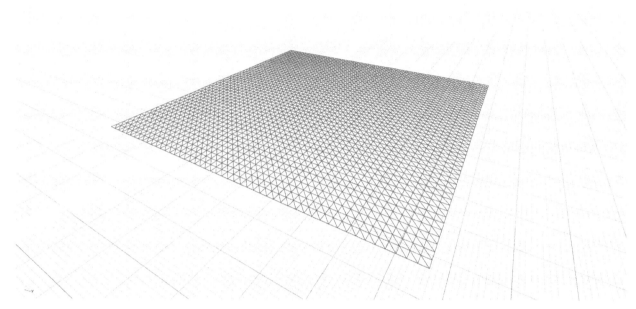

FIGURE 5.176 Water setup.

The result of this formula will produce a simple simulation of a waving flag. Rotating the flag object along the pivot axis (the Y-axis) will simulate the change of wind direction. Randomness is multiplied against the frequency and amplitude to simulate variable wind speeds. A more robust physical simulation is required for this effect to display realistic gravity.

Water

Simulating water is a very robust and complicated topic that could require a separate book to explain. When the water is not a primary visual target or is sufficiently small in frame, implementing a sine function may be adequate for generating a simple, fast, and cheap simulation. Water is visually dependent on both vertex displacement and a strong specular component. To maintain realistic specularity, the vertex normals must be re-computed every frame.

Single Wave

Like a waving flag, a highly subdivided grid geometry is needed to animate water. Unlike the flag, the water geometry needs not lay in any specific orientation since it does not need to be anchored. Modeling water takes advantage of the fractal-like technique of adding multiple iterations of the sine function, each with increased frequency and reduced amplitude. The scale of the water and the placement of the camera dictate the number of iterations (Figure 5.176).

The *Wave Angle* must be generated before calculating the sine wave. The wave angle is a function dependent on frequency, time, and the texture coordinate direction. Displacement animates through the U and V axes of the water geometry. A positive or negative U and V direction identifies when the wave is rolling away or rolling toward the camera. The speed of the wave is also a consideration. Larger, fatter waves move slowly. A speed scalar must be applied to only the time component to regulate the rolling speed. The sum of the direction and the scaled time provide the initial shape for one wave. Multiplying the frequency against this sum controls the number of waves visible across the surface, or the width of each wave.

$$\text{Wave Angle} = \text{Frequency} * \left(\text{Time} * \text{Speed} + \left(\text{Texture Coordinate}_{U \text{ or } V} \right) \right)$$

Equation 5.65 Basic Wave Angle

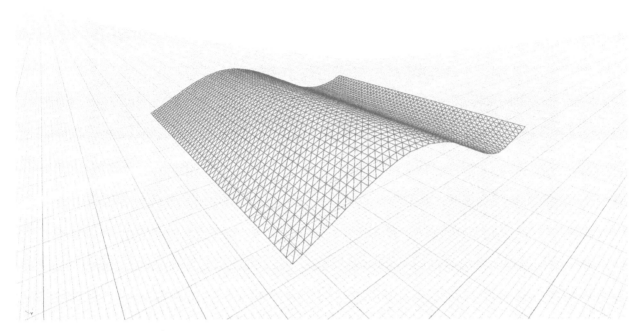

FIGURE 5.177 Basic wave surface.

Multiplying the height and the sine function generates the wave's vertical offset. The result of the wave angle, inputted to the sine function, is multiplied by the height scalar. The height scalar controls half the distance between the zenith and trough of the wave. In other words, the true height of a wave is double the visible height since the trough sits below the observed level of the water. The height scalar needs to be evaluated with respect to the wave width and frequency to remain in context with the environment. The following formula assumes the wave is offset in the positive Y direction (Figure 5.177).

$$\text{Wave Offset}_Y = \text{Height} * \sin\big(\text{Wave Angle}\big)$$

$$\text{Wave Offset} = \big(0, \text{ Wave Offset}_Y, 0\big)$$

Equation 5.66 Basic Wave Offset

Notice in the above figure, while the wireframe frame model displays animated waves, a shaded version does not. This discrepancy occurs because the vertex normals have not been adjusted to offset the specular and diffuse components of the lighting with the changes in surface gradient. New *Angular Offsets* must be applied to the vertex normals. Normal vector angular offsets are computed from the wave height, frequency, and cosine of the wave angle. The same wave angles used to calculate vertical offsets are re-used to calculate the new angular offsets.

$$\text{Normal Wave Angle} = \text{Frequency} * \big(\text{Time} * \text{Speed} + \big(\text{Texture Coordinate}_{U \text{ or } V}\big)\big)$$

Equation 5.67 Normal Wave Angle

The result of the normal wave angle inputted to a cosine function is multiplied against the negative of the height scalar (the same height scalar used in the offset formula) and the frequency scalar used to calculate the wave angle.

FIGURE 5.178 Basic shaded wave with new normals.

Angular Offset = −Height * Frequency * cos(Wave Angle)

Equation 5.68 Normal Vector Angular Offset

The angular offset is used in the component direction of deformation in the construction of the new normal vector. In the example situation, since the wave is offset in the Y-axis, the angular offset provides the normal vector Y component. The other two components are dependent on the texture coordinate axis used in the wave angle computation. Assume the U direction corresponds to the X-axis and the V direction corresponds to the Z-axis. When the wave angle is calculated using U texture coordinate, then X and Z components of the new vector are 0.0 and 1.0, respectively. When the wave angle is calculated using the V texture coordinate, the X and Z components are 1.0 and 0.0, respectively. The resulting vector must be normalized to be used as the new normal vector (Figure 5.178).

Raw Normal Vector = (0.0, Angular Offset, 1.0)

Normal Vector = Normalize(Raw Normal Vector)

Equation 5.69 Normal Vector When Offset Along U Direction

Raw Normal Vector = (1.0, Angular Offset, 0.0)

Normal Vector = Normalize(Raw Normal Vector)

Equation 5.70 Normal Vector When Offset Along V Direction

The single wave may only animate in the *U* or *V* direction of the source geometry.

Multiple waves
The wave produced with this technique is visually nice, but it is hardly thrilling. To start appearing like a realistic wave, multiple unique wave functions must be combined to form a single wave. The waves are combined by adding each wave's offsets and new normal vectors. The sum of the normal vectors must be normalized before

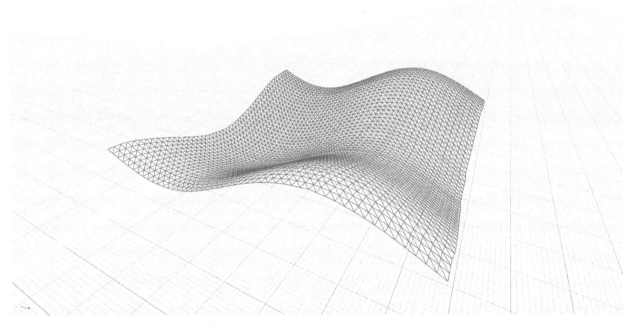

FIGURE 5.179 Combination of two wave functions.

rendering. For example, when the wave from the previous example is combined with another wave whose frequency and speed are halved and the height doubled, then the new positional offset becomes (Figure 5.179):

$$\text{Wave Angle}_1 = \text{Frequency} * \left(\text{Time} * \text{Speed} + \left(\text{Texture Coordinate}_1\right)\right)$$

$$\text{Wave Angle}_2 = 0.5 * \text{Frequency} * \left(\text{Time} * 0.5 * \text{Speed} + \left(\text{Texture Coordinate}_2\right)\right)$$

$$\text{Offset}_1 = \text{Height} * \sin\left(\text{Wave Angle}_1\right)$$

$$\text{Offset}_2 = 2 * \text{Height} * \sin\left(\text{Wave Angle}_2\right)$$

$$\text{Wave Offset} = \left(0.0, \text{Offset}_1 + \text{Offset}_2, 0.0\right)$$

Equation 5.71 Combined Wave Offset

The new normal becomes:

$$\text{Wave Angle}_1 = \text{Frequency} * \left(\text{Time} * \text{Speed} + \left(\text{Texture Coordinate}_1\right)\right)$$

$$\text{Wave Angle}_2 = 0.5 * \text{Frequency} * \left(\text{Time} * 0.5 * \text{Speed} + \left(\text{Texture Coordinate}_2\right)\right)$$

$$\text{Angular Offset}_1 = -\text{Height} * \text{Frequency} * \cos\left(\text{Wave Angle}_1\right)$$

$$\text{Angular Offset}_2 = -2.0 * \text{Height} * 0.5 * \text{Frequency} * \cos\left(\text{Wave Angle}_2\right)$$

$$\text{Raw Normal Vector}_1 = \left(\text{Component}_{x1}, \text{Angular Offset}_1, \text{Component}_{z1}\right)$$

$$\text{Raw Normal Vector}_2 = \left(\text{Component}_{X2}, \text{ Angular Offset}_2, \text{Component}_{Z2}\right)$$

$$\text{Normal Vector} = \text{Normalize}\left(\text{Raw Normal Vector}_1 + \text{Raw Normal Vector}_2\right)$$

Equation 5.72 Combined Normal Vector

Notice the wave functions do not need to use the same texture coordinates. Each function may deform along its own texture coordinate axis, in its own direction. Any number of wave functions may be combined, to suit the artists' needs. Natural looking waves are the result of the combination of a wide variety of wave functions and texture coordinates.

CIRCULAR WAVES

Circular waves, such as from water drops, use the same offset and normal formulas used for lateral and horizontal waves except with respect to texture coordinates and wave speed. Instead of using texture coordinates to fuel the sine wave calculations, the texture space distance of each vertex from some established center point is used. The distance is calculated using a modified variation of the Pythagorean Theorem:

$$\text{Distance}_{\text{Texture Space}} = \sqrt{\left(\left(\text{Tex Coord}_U - \text{Center Point}_U\right)^2 + \left(\text{Tex Coord}_V - \text{Center Point}_V\right)^2\right)}$$

Equation 5.73 Modified Pythagorean Theorem

The distance value is used as input to the sine function.

The wave speed must also be adjusted for effective circular waves. When the speed is added to the texture space distance as input to the sine function, the circular rings move inwards toward the center point, not away. The rings flow away from the center point when the speed is subtracted from the distance. The new wave offset for circular rings becomes:

$$\text{Distance}_{\text{Texture Space}} = \sqrt{\left(\left(\text{Tex Coord}_U - \text{Center Point}_U\right)^2 + \left(\text{Tex Coord}_V - \text{Center Point}_V\right)^2\right)}$$

$$\text{Wave Angle} = \text{frequency} * \left(\text{Distance}_{\text{Texture Space}} - \text{Time} * \text{Speed}\right)$$

$$\text{Wave Offset}_Y = \text{Height} * \sin\left(\text{Wave Angle}\right)$$

$$\text{Wave Offset} = \left(0, \text{ Wave Offset}_Y, 0\right)$$

Equation 5.74 Circular Wave Offsets

The normal calculations need to be adjusted using similar modifications: the wave is calculated by subtracting the wave speed from the vertex distance in texture coordinates. The rest of the normal calculations stay the same except for making the X and Z components of the normal vectors 0.0 and 1.0, respectively (Figure 5.180).

$$\text{Distance}_{\text{Texture Space}} = \sqrt{\left(\left(\text{Tex Coord}_U - \text{Center Point}_U\right)^2 + \left(\text{Tex Coord}_V - \text{Center Point}_V\right)^2\right)}$$

$$\text{Wave Angle} = \text{frequency} * \left(\text{Distance}_{\text{Texture Space}} - \text{Time} * \text{Speed}\right)$$

$$\text{Angular Offset} = -\text{Height} * \text{Frequency} * \cos\left(\text{Wave Angle}\right)$$

$$\text{Raw Normal Vector} = \left(0.0, \text{ Angular Offset}, 1.0\right)$$

FIGURE 5.180 Circular waves.

FIGURE 5.181 Combination of multiple wave types.

Normal Vector = Normalize(Raw Normal Vector)

Equation 5.75 Circular Normal Calculations

Since all waves produce wave offsets and angular offsets, circular, lateral, and horizontal waves may be combined. The formulae for combined waves are the summations of all wave and angular offsets (Figure 5.181):

$$\text{Wave Offset} = \left(0, \sum_{i=1}^{n} \text{Wave Offset}_{Y_i}, 0\right)$$

Equation 5.76 Combined Wave Offsets

$$\text{Raw Normal Vector Sum} = \sum_{i=1}^{n} \left(\text{Component}_{Xi}, \text{Angular Offset}_i, \text{Component}_{Zi} \right)$$

$$\text{Normal Vector} = \text{Normalize} \left(\text{Raw Normal Vector Sum} \right)$$

Equation 5.77 Combined Wave Normals

Shrinking and Growing

When a character is required to get very large or very small when making an entrance or exit, it can shrink or grow entirely with vertex shader adjustments. It is assumed the character can only scale from the ground-up. While not a complicated effect, there are four necessary shader functions that must be explained to achieve the effect: absolute world position, character position, object position, and bounding box position. By default, not all real-time engines support these functions. In these situations, the visual effects artist may wish to discuss their implementation with the rendering programmers.

Absolute World Position

Absolute world position is a fancy name for the vertex position in world space. When the vertex position is delivered to the vertex shader, it is in object space and needs to be transformed to absolute world space. This transformation is achieved by multiplying the vertex position against the character's world space matrix. For demonstrational purposes, the vertices' transformed, world space positions are duplicated to vertex color. Black vertices are near the world space origin. The vertices become redder as they increase along the X-axis, greener as they increase along the Y-axis, and bluer as they increase along the Z-axis (Figure 5.182).

Character Position

Character position is the position of the character's pivot point as it is animated in world space. This position is irrelevant to the shape or scale of the object. When the character position is placed in the vertex color the character appears black near the origin, red when positioned along the X-axis, green when animated along the Y-axis, and blue when animated along the Z-axis (Figure 5.183).

Object Position

The object position of a character is very similar to the character position. However, instead of the character's animated pivot position, the world space position of the centroid of the character's bounding box is returned.

FIGURE 5.182 Character in absolute world space.

FIGURE 5.183 Characters' colors based on character position.

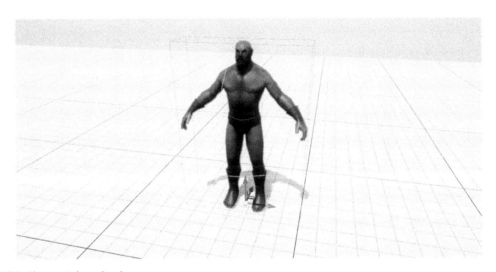

FIGURE 5.184 Character's bounding box.

Every object has a bounding box defined by its minimum and maximum X, Y, and Z coordinates (Figure 5.184).

The object position is the world space position of the character's bounding box centroid. Placing the object Position in vertex color causes the character to appear black when its center is near the origin, red when centered along the X-axis, green when centered along the Y-axis, and blue when centered along the Z-axis (Figure 5.185).

Bounding Box Position

The bounding box position returns the relative vertex position within the character's bounding box. When the bounding box position is duplicated to the vertex color channel, the aggregate color of the object is dominated by its primary axis. A tall, narrow object is "blue-ish" in color, following the Z-axis. A wider object is redder (along the X-Axis) and a deeper object is greener (along the Y-axis). A spherical object is white (Figure 5.186).

FIGURE 5.185 Character's colors based on object position.

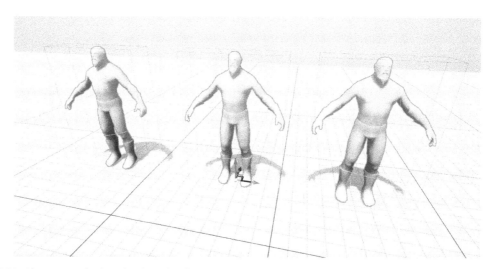

FIGURE 5.186 Character's color based on bounding box.

Object Scaling

As an initial attempt to control a character's scale, a scalar offset may be used to offset vertex world position. This translates the character back and forth along the diagonal $[1.0, 1.0, 1.0]$ and $[-1.0, -1.0, -1.0]$ vectors. The character's scale is not altered (Figure 5.187).

Vertex Position Offset = Scale Factor

Equation 5.78 Setting Vertex Offset to Scaling Factor

To scale the character, the scalar offset must be multiplied against each vertices' absolute world position before offsetting the vertices' world position. The character scales as expected but is locked to the origin. Regardless of initial character location, as the character scales, it translates toward or away from the origin (Figure 5.188).

FIGURE 5.187 Translating along diagonal vectors.

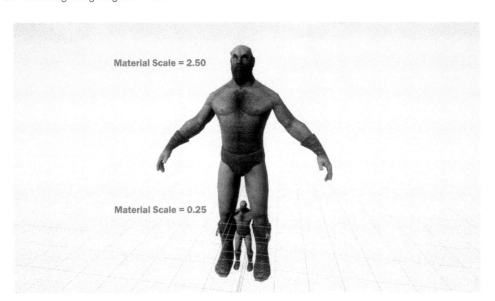

FIGURE 5.188 Scaling and translating to the origin.

Vertex position Offset = Absolute World Position * Scale Factor

Equation 5.79 Multiplying Absolute World Position by Scale Factor

Subtracting the absolute world position from the character position before multiplying against the scalar, scales the character. However, the character scales only to its pivot point, not to the ground plane. From the material context, each character's pivot is unknown thus this strategy is unpredictable (Figure 5.189).

Vertex Position Offset = (Character Position − Absolute World Position) * Scale Factor

Equation 5.80 Subtracting Absolute World Position from Character Position

FIGURE 5.189 Subtracting the world position from the character position.

FIGURE 5.190 Subtracting the world position from the object position.

A condition of this material is the object needs to scale from the ground-up, regardless of where its pivot point is located. Instead of subtracting the absolute world position from the character position, subtracting it from the object position always guarantees the object will scale to its midpoint, or the center of its bounding box (Figure 5.190).

Vertex Position Offset = (Object Position − Absolute World Position) * Scale Factor

Equation 5.81 Subtracting Absolute World Position from Object Position

To get the object to always scale from the ground up, each vertex relative position to the object's bounding box must be taken into consideration. The bounding box position provides that information, but its data must be massaged to be used properly. The only information needed is the relative height of each vertex with respect to the object's height axis. Subtracting only the vertex relative height from the Object Position properly adjusts the Object Position for each vertex. The object now scales and shrinks from the ground up, regardless of its position (Figure 5.191).

FIGURE 5.191 Subtracting vertical bounding box information.

When the vertical axis is assumed to be the Y-Axis, the formula for the vertex offset to shrink and grow from the ground up becomes:

$$\text{Vertex Position Offset} = \Big(\text{Object Position} - \big(0, \text{Height}_{\text{Bounding Box Position,}}\ 0\big) - \text{Absolute World Position}\Big) * \text{Scale Factor}$$

Equation 5.82 Final Vertex Position Offset

CONCLUSION

Of all visual effects techniques, manipulating the object material and shader provides the artist with the greatest amount of control over the final appearance of the visual effect. To take advantage of this potential, the artist must be aware of how all objects are rendered within their engine; including an understanding when objects are rendered using traditional Phong or PBR techniques. When working with materials, the artist may not have direct access to the rendering shader algorithms but will have control how objects are to be rendered and how they are to be blended. Understanding the controls for rendering and blending gives the artist an enormous amount of leverage manipulating the final effect appearance.

After mastery of how materials are implemented in the engine, understanding an effect's demand on the pixel shader, vertex shader, or both is required. Pixel shader manipulations control the visual appearance or color of the object. The vertex shader manipulates the object's deformation within the context of the material. While both shaders produce radically different results, they are adjusted using similar strategies. The most important of these strategies is the manipulation of the object's texture coordinates. Manipulating texture coordinates using tools such as panners, rotators, flipbooks, and good old math functions, empower the artist to animate the appearance of an object in any desirable direction.

INTRODUCTION

Within the context of real-time visual effects, simulations are a complex component that should be considered near the beginning of a project and not toward the end as an afterthought. Their complexity derives from their multiple direct and indirect contributions to the real-time immersive experience. Often seen but not directly noticed, simulations play a large role in the storytelling process. This role directly influences how motion is represented within the contextual story world. Since the motion may be visible or invisible, simulations are a departure from previously introduced visual effects as they may, or may not, collaborate with the rendering pipeline. Since they are not direct components of the rendering pipeline, within the context of the holistic real-time experience, they are expensive. Careful consideration must be devoted to their level of inclusion to the final product.

Storytelling Components

Simulations are important storytelling components. They provide realism to immersive experiences; they do heavy visual lifting that would be exceedingly difficult for an artist or designer to accomplish, and they provide a certain amount of eye candy.

Participants in any immersive experience or game come with large amounts of preconceived expectations of what they know or feel the story universe should behave like. Simulations provide the glue or cement to root and ground the participant into the story world. When done believably, without drawing attention to itself, the simulation maintains the sense of immersion and sustains the *suspension of disbelief* games and immersive experiences strive to maintain.

Simulations support the storytelling process. When the story evolves from the mundane to the epic, simulations step in to raise the visual quality of the experience to meet obligatory sensory demands. For example, a collapsing bridge or an avalanche is a visual phenomenon which may only happen once in a lifetime. The sensory experience must be memorable. However, simulations do not necessarily have to be epic in scale. Visual events we take for granted such as rain or snow or even a dropped teacup are labor intensive. Simulations make them possible. In the golden age of hand-drawn animation, production companies hired armies of special effects animators to hand draw each puff of smoke, each raindrop, and each snowflake. Audiences grew to expect these components. The return on investment for visualizing such phenomena no longer justifies the budgets for such armies. Simulations must carry on the responsibility inexpensively and timely.

Since simulations deal with large quantities of data rather than numerous cells of hand-drawn animation, they offer audiences perspectives unobtainable from traditional techniques. Time becomes an animatable component as events happening within milliseconds (such as the chain reaction of combustible gasses propelling a bullet) are visualized in the same context as those happening over millions of years such as the sinking and emerging of continents on Earth. Similarly, space also is animatable as an extraordinarily small event (the battle of white blood cells fighting off an invading virus) is displayed in the same scene as an epically huge event (the collision of two galaxies). The limitations of any natural, or unnatural, phenomenon supporting story world themes are limited to the time and skill of the visual effects artist and not by the visual size or complexity of the experience.

Duplicating Physics

When classifying the different types, simulations duplicate the motion physics of the story world. Considering simulations visually attempt to replicate the effects on a body when interacting with a force, the number of types explodes. Further explanations of what constitutes effects, bodies, and forces are required.

DOI: 10.1201/9781003009795-7

Effects are the strategies required to visualize the nature of a phenomenon. There are only two strategies available: keyframed and computer-generated. Keyframed effects herald back to the old, hand-drawn days of animation where each grain of sand and each piece of flying shrapnel was drawn by hand. These techniques are still used depending on the context or behavior they are simulating. When effects needs to be art-directed, because of visual style or because of strange exceptions to the physical rules of the story world, it they need to be keyframed. Similarly, some items which could be simulated, such as bouncing pigtails or flowing skirts, sometimes look better as animated keyframes.

There are two approaches to computer-generated simulations: automated and procedural. Automated simulations are driven exclusively by the rules and formulas set forth by the technical artist. This is a dual-edged sword. While this strategy is extremely repeatable and fast to generate, the final visual results may not deliver 100% of the desired impact. A simulation that produces 95% of the desired effect may appear *statistically* acceptable. However, the incorrect 5% (objects inter-penetrating each other or not colliding as expected) may disrupt the suspension of disbelief and interrupt the sense of immersion. Procedural approaches offer a compromise. Instead of replacing the artist's input when generating a phenomenon, procedural techniques leverage the artists' skills and abilities to create content that is unachievable by hand. By juxtaposing automated functionality with art-driven input, virtually any intentional phenomenon can be generated. As an example, consider a river of lava. A purely automated simulation may draw the river following a data-accurate path. However, compositionally, the river may be needed to bend right instead of left at a certain spot. The automated technique fails. A procedural approach empowers the artist or designer to hand-draw a path where the river should flow. The procedural algorithms dynamically alter the topology of the environment for the automated simulation to behave as intended. While procedural techniques provide the best of both worlds, they are also often the most difficult and time intensive to implement. Consideration for usage and return on investment must be evaluated before employing procedural approaches.

All simulations are duplications or approximations of the natural physics of the contextual story world. The photoreal world is governed by what is commonly known as Newtonian physics, classical mechanics, or kinematics. While heavily influenced by Newtonian rules, depending on the story world, not all physics follow them. Regardless of the contexts of the world, the rigidness of simulated bodies is broken into two primary types: rigid bodies and soft bodies.

Rigid body simulations, also known as rigid body dynamics (RBDs), attempt to apply the laws of physics on bodies which do not deform, creating stylistic and unrealistic simulations. Calculated with a fundamental set of formulae, they are also the easiest, fastest, and computationally cheapest. Simulations are expensive and often the performance budget allows for only rigid body simulations. Stylistically, and in a primitive sort of way, they can also be a lot of fun. Rigid bodies are simply bodies which do not deform when forces are applied to them. Often objects such as rocks, vehicles, buildings, certain props, and other environmental components are treated as rigid bodies. Although dealt with in Chapter 7, all rigid bodies are treated as particles unless constructed into a constrained lattice. All collisions performed on rigid bodies are referred to as *inelastic collisions*.

Soft bodies deform or change shape when forces are applied to them. While there are entire branches of physics devoted to the variations of such state changes, most simulations in computer graphics are governed by spring behavior or Hooke's law. Fast approximations such as Verlet integrations are employed over large surfaces. Collisions involving at least one soft surface are considered elastic collisions. Soft bodies are any objects which change shape. Examples are squishy bodies, hair, cloth, interlocked structures such as chains, and simplifications of fluids and gasses. As of the time of writing this text, tools required to simulate true volumetric bodies are unavailable as off-the-shelf products.

Articulated characters, manipulated by Ragdoll physics, are hybrid simulations. While the individual body components have little to no skeletal stiffness, the joints connecting them are spring simulated. Compromises such as Ragdoll physics help provide more realistic yet relatively computationally inexpensive simulations.

Just as there are soft and rigid bodies, there are two primary types of forces acting upon them: active and passive. Active forces include impact forces (from other objects during a collision), wind, turbulence, and any other force pushing or pulling the object. Passive forces act on the body constantly and cannot be removed without changing the state of the object. Passive examples include upward forces by any supporting surfaces, gravity, friction, drag, and lift. The computational costs associated with the number and types of forces are marginal compared to the costs associated with body type.

Departure from Other VFX

Simulations depart from other visual effects presented in this text as they may not directly alter the rendering pipeline. While many types of simulations manipulate the vertex positions within the vertex shader, not all simulations do so. The simplest, most economical of RBDs animate objects in world space and do not impede the rendering pipeline. Certain precise and complicated vertex deformations, such as fluid and fabric simulations, are calculated outside of the rendering pipeline, utilizing their own deformation sub-systems. Systems such as these are complicated and require greater development time than what is allocated to most visual effects. Ironically, every studio seems to have at least one "specialist" who is sequestered to a quiet location in the basement and allowed to return only after solving the world's most difficult simulations. Regretfully, most visual effects simulations cannot be solved by such custom fabricated tools and must be generated from off-the-shelf resources.

Some simulations are performed within the rendering pipeline. Any simulation demonstrating visual state change such as heat transfer (cold and hot), material rigidity (soft and hard), or smoothness (smooth and rough) takes place in the pixel shader. Similarly, any simulation requiring advanced rendering techniques such as ray marching volumetric representations of clouds, vapors, and fire demands implementation in the pixel shader. Production resources dictate the generation of clouds and vapors to be driven by art or generated by precise physical calculations.

Computationally Expensive

All simulations are computationally expensive. Unless the artist works with parallel physics libraries executing on the GPU, almost all simulations are calculated on the CPU. In addition to the tasks of loading and unloading data, gameplay, and interface, the computer must squeeze in a few extra cycles every frame to calculate that sine function or solve that cube root power. Scale bears heavily upon the CPU, even when dealing with simple tasks such as solving character forward kinematics. For example, without special optimizations, most game engines have trouble driving more than 100 fully articulated characters. While every real-time engine has its own efficiencies, computational resources are typically allocated to gameplay and rendering before simulations.

The physical rules governing a real-time universe must be clearly understood before CPU optimization can happen. Once established, engine performance dictates which physical phenomena must be seen, which should be seen, and which are nice but unessential.

The interactivity of a simulation is an important factor. Within this context, interactivity applies to dynamic demands of the simulation input. How much information does the simulation need to reflect the current state of the experience? As a rule of thumb, the more interactive, or dynamic the simulation is, the more expensive it will be. The most mathematically correct models are the most expensive. Can a procedural approximation be used instead? For example, when a character walks through water, must the ripples and splashes be numerically correct, or can rough functions suffice? Will the audience notice and appreciate the simulation? Will this feature sell more copies? If the simulation does not need to interact with the gameplay, how much of the simulation can be pre-generated? Depending on the complexity of the character, keyframe animation clips provide inexpensive and artistically controllable simulations. Can other techniques be applied, such as vertex caching, when articulated characters become too expensive? Pre-generated, vertex cache simulations are predictable and can be art directed. Their drawback is they are difficult to dynamically alter.

Personal Comment on Simulations

Simulations attempt to duplicate the physics of a story world. They are intended to be honest visualizations of natural phenomena. Many visualizations in the modeling, simulation, and training industries are required to have the utmost visual integrity. Lives are dependent on this visual honesty. There are no stories in these situations, just visual reenactments. They are intended to be the center of visual focus. They do not employ redirection, sleight-of-hand, or visual trickery. Outside of the context of being created for training purposes, simulation presentations are often mundane to the extent of debating if "pure" simulations are visual effects at all.

Our human brains have certain expectations. We define our realities by retelling stories founded in our sensory experiences. It is difficult to retell these stories without the influence of our emotional states at the time of the experience. Physical phenomena happen on a "large scale" during intense, emotional states of excitement, fear, or anger. Events become bigger, bolder, and larger than life. During calm emotional states, the same phenomena are tranquil and straightforward. Simulations generated out of context of emotion state, however visually epic in scale, do not have the same impact on our emotions. Within modeling and training contexts, visually epic simulations fade into the background.

If you are reading this text, then you are probably coming from an "entertainment" perspective, desiring to generate dramatic emotional impact from every experiential component. If this is true, then you are urged to not "settle" for pure simulation. They produce lackluster emotional impact and are visually boring. To achieve the desired emotional impact, artists are suggested to increase the scale of their simulations, almost to the point of being "unbelievable." Only when the simulation has achieved a sense of "hyper-Reality" will it have the desired impact on emotional state. Of course, judgment must be used to not push the effect so far that it becomes unbelievable or ludicrous. Simulations are expensive. Make sure they deliver the emotional impact they were intended for.

Chapter Layout

Surface topology is the primary object characteristic for considering types of simulation. Topology defines the geometric components comprising an object's surface representation and their order. There are four types of simulation presented in this chapter: rigid bodies, soft bodies, fluids, and volumetrics. RBDs deal with objects interacting with gravity, colliding with each other, falling apart, and blowing up. Rigid body topologies do not change. When large objects are subdivided into smaller sub-objects, the sub-objects maintain shape and do not deform. Soft bodies, on the other hand, when exposed to the same forces, deform, and do not maintain shape. They do, however, maintain topology. Fluids can be simulated as rigid bodies, soft bodies, or volumetrics. Unlike rigid or soft bodies, they can change their topology. Volumetric effects include fog, clouds, smoke, fire, and other semitransparent phenomena. Some of their implementations can be approximated with similar techniques used by rigid bodies, soft bodies, and fluids. True volumetric simulations require full, three-dimensional solutions unbound by surface topology.

RIGID BODIES

The self-assumed tagline for a certain visual effects artist is, "I blow stuff up!" This role caters to *RBDs*. RBDs are defined as simulations of basic Newtonian physics exacted upon non-deforming bodies. In other words, RBDs simulate objects that are colliding, falling apart, blowing up, or otherwise dynamically interacting with each other or gravity.

While there is a significant amount of math associated with RBD simulations, mastery is not essential to create life-like dynamic simulations. In the early days of computer graphics production, understanding Newtonian physics, mastery of vectors, matrices, and differential calculus were necessary to create the simulations. Coded by hand, RBD simulations were the domain of the most elite visual effects artists. Integration of RBD libraries with commercial, off-line DCCs removed this exclusivity. RBDs became expected features of commercially available

3D animation systems. Now, equipped only with only a rudimentary understanding of vectors, visual effects artists add life-like simulations to their visual output.

While RBDs are readily available in off-line DCCs, their computational demands on the CPU impede their inclusion into real-time engines. The millions of calculations computing the position and orientation of thousands of chunks of an exploding bridge work fine when allowed to compute overnight. The same calculations slow real-time engines to a crawl. Algorithmic optimizations and multi-threaded GPUs make real-time simulations a reality. However, this integration is still in its infancy. At the time of writing this book, real-time engines are only starting to release their fully realized RBD packages. GPUs are still dedicated to the rendering pipeline leaving simulations to compete for CPU cycles. Some enthusiasts use extra GPUs dedicated solely toward simulation. Time will only tell if this trend becomes standard practice.

Like the problem of being unable to share visual content between different rendering pipelines, simulation cannot be shared between engines. Even with the utilization of GPU resources, each engine's RBD implementation is unique and cannot be readily transferred. However, like the rendering pipeline scenario, all RBD implementations share the same concepts and should be replicable in all packages.

Non-Deforming Bodies

From the theoretical physics perspective, a rigid body is any solid which does not deform or change shape. Such objects do not exist in the real world. Even the hardest, most rigid materials start to degrade, wear down, or fall apart when forces are applied to them. However, when deformations are removed from the equation, mechanical simulations become relatively simple and easy to implement. As of the time of writing this text, most real-time applications do not demand visually accurate rigid body integrity. Technically not numerically correct, RBDs are more than adequate for most real-time simulations.

When an object is treated as a rigid body, it is treated as a particle. Particle systems, which are covered in Chapter 7, are in fact, simplified RBD implementations. Like a particle, only three crucial parameters of a rigid body are considered: the position, the orientation, and the radius (or rigid body shape). Velocity and acceleration are calculated based on the object's position over time. The objects' spin and rotation are calculated based on their orientation over time. The radius, or rigid body shape, is complicated since most rigid objects are rarely spheroidal. Calculating the objects' collision boundaries is expensive. Rotations happen about the object's center of mass which are rarely located at the object's local space origin. Particle systems are simplified RBD systems. What makes them different are the ways RBDs treat the objects' shapes and how they interact.

Newtonian Mechanics

In 1687, Isaac Newton provided three universal laws of motion which helped usher in many of the technological advancements of the Industrial Revolution. These three laws are the foundation upon which RBDs is built upon and share the same restrictions: The objects in consideration are solid and non-deforming and the objects need to be treated like particles. The laws are listed below but will not be discussed in detail. For further detail, please see their explanation in *Math and Physics for the Technical Artist*.

The first law is the law of inertia. The law states that, unless acted upon by a force, a body at rest remains at rest and a body in motion stays in motion. For simplicity, assume a force is a vector defined by direction and a magnitude. A force needs to act on a resting body to make it move. Similarly, a moving object is going to continue moving unless a force causes it to slow down and enter a non-moving state.

The second law establishes the relationship of force, mass, and acceleration. When a force causes an object to move, that force is equal to the mass of the object multiplied by its acceleration: the rate of change of its velocity.

Force = Mass * Acceleration

Equation 6.1 Newton's Second Law

The third law is the law of action and reaction. The law states, "For every action there is an equal and opposite reaction." In other words, whenever a body exerts force on another, the second body exerts a force of the same magnitude and opposite direction as the first.

Physics Engines

There are an unlimited number of implementations of physics engines. All follow the same five-step loop: Forces are applied, object's states are updated, collisions are detected, constraints are resolved, and the results are displayed (Figure 6.1).

The technical implementation of this loop is beyond the scope of this text. Understanding each of the steps will aid the visual effects artist to adjust and configure the parameters of a simulation and make it behave as intended. Understanding the fundamental RBD cycle will assist the artist in debugging simulations when results are less than desirable.

Apply Forces

The first step of the physics engine loop is to account for all the active forces within the simulation. The aggregate of all the forces acting on an object is called the net force. The net force is used for calculating the object's velocity and acceleration used during the next step of the simulation loop. The forces an object encounters are contextual, dependent on the environment in which the object itself is placed. In other words, the forces influencing a submarine beneath the water's surface are different from the forces acting on a jet fighter in aerial combat. As a simple example, consider the forces of a man pushing a sled up a snow-covered hill. The hill is pitched at a 30° incline. The sled has a mass of 5 kg. The man pushes the sled with a 100_n force at a 20° angle (Figure 6.2).

The man, sled, and hill apply forces upon each other, contributing to the net force of the system.

Forces

Forces are vectors having direction and magnitude (Figure 6.3).

According to Newton's second law, the magnitude of any force is equivalent to the object's mass multiplied against its acceleration.

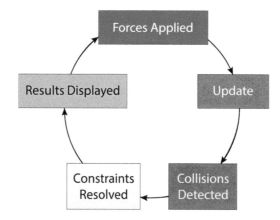

FIGURE 6.1 Physics engine loop.

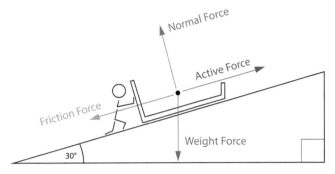

FIGURE 6.2 Man pushing a sled.

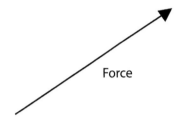

Force

FIGURE 6.3 Force vector.

F = Mass * Acceleration.

Equation 6.2 Newton's Second Law

Force is measured in units called *newtons*. One newton is equivalent to moving one kilogram one meter per one second squared.

$$1\,\text{Newton} = 1\,\frac{\text{kg m}}{s^2}$$

Equation 6.3 One Newton

One newton is equivalent to 0.2248 pounds.

$1\,\text{Newton} = 0.2248\,\text{lbs}$

Equation 6.4 Newtons in Pounds

Furthermore, the force's direction must be taken into consideration with the simulation's dimensionality. A one-dimensional simulation is simple as the direction component is either *positive* or *negative*. Most simulations occur in two-dimensional planes or in three-dimensional space. The directional components are distributed into corresponding axes (Figure 6.4).

For example, consider a two-dimensional force vector $[12.3_N,\ 10.8_N]$:

The force's magnitude is calculated by computing the magnitude, or length of the force vector. The direction is calculated by dividing the length (magnitude) into the vector's components.

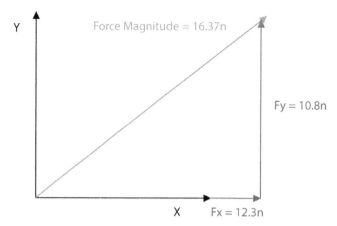

FIGURE 6.4 Two-dimensional vector.

$$2D \text{ Force} = \left[12.3_N, \ 10.8_N\right]$$

$$\text{Force Magnitude} = \sqrt{12.3^2 + 10.8^2} = 16.37_N$$

$$\text{Force Direction} = \left[\frac{12.3_N}{16.37_N}, \frac{10.8_N}{16.37_N}\right] = \left[0.75, \ 0.7\right]$$

Force has a magnitude of 16.37_N in a $\left[0.75, \ 0.7\right]$ direction

Example 6.1 Magnitude and Direction of A Force

The same rules apply for a force in three dimensions. Consider a force with a magnitude of 15.25_n with a direction of $\left[-0.57, 0.51, -0.65\right]$. To calculate the force, the magnitude is simply multiplied against each of the directional components:

$$\text{Force Magnitude} = 15.25_N$$

$$\text{Force Direction} = \left[-0.57, \ 0.51, \ -0.65\right]$$

$$3D \text{ Force} = 15.25_N * \left[-0.57, 0.51, -0.65\right] = \left[-8.69_N, \ 7.76_N, \ -9.84_N\right]$$

Example 6.2 Three-Dimensional Force Vector

There are multiple types of force and each needs to be treated according to its own specifications. The polarity of the force (if it is treated positive or negative) is based on the position of the force relative to the object's center of mass and if the force aids or opposes the acceleration of the object.

Within any environment, there are two kinds of forces impacting an object: passive and active. Passive forces are the forces induced by the environment where the object resides. These forces act on an object, regardless of intention. Certain forces are a result of object substance parameters. Gravity impacts an object since it has mass. Lift happens when the shape of one object inhibits its progress through another. For example, air creates lift for aircraft and water generates lift for aquatic vessels.

Passive forces act on objects because of their substance, not because of their direct interaction with other objects. Active forces, on the other hand, are all the other forces acting on an object not due to its environmental interactions. Active forces may aid or oppose the acceleration of an object. A horse pulling a cart is an example of an active force.

There are many potential forces to consider when analyzing the contributing forces of a simulation, each with its own contextual set of influences. For our simple example of a man pushing a sled up an icy hill, we are only considering four types of forces: the one active force (the man), and three passive forces (weight, normal, and friction).

Weight

Weight is the force the center of the earth pulls at the object. This is called gravitational force (Figure 6.5).

Since force is mass multiplied by acceleration, weight force is calculated by mass multiplied against acceleration due to gravity.

$$Weight = Mass * Acceleration_{gravity} = M * G$$

Equation 6.5 Weight Force

Active Forces

Active forces are the direct forces, which are acted upon an object by another object. These forces manifest as either a *push* action or a *pull* action. When objects collide, they exert push forces on each other. A bodybuilder pressing a heavyweight or a lever moving a large barrier are examples of push actions. Push forces are applied behind an object, relative to the direction of object acceleration. Pull forces are applied in front. A horse drawing a carriage or a truck towing a heavy load are examples of pull forces (Figure 6.6).

Normal Force

Normal force is the force of a surface pushing against an object to prevent it from falling due to weight. The gravitational force of larger objects pulls smaller objects into them. The normal force is perpendicular to the direction of the object's acceleration, in the opposite direction to the weight force (Figure 6.7).

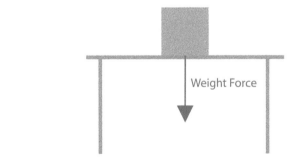

FIGURE 6.5 Force of weight.

FIGURE 6.6 Push and pull active forces.

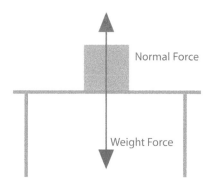

FIGURE 6.7 Normal force.

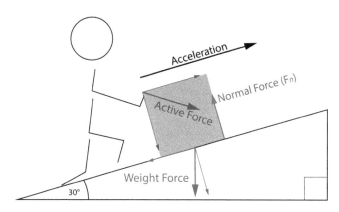

FIGURE 6.8 Vertical normal component of an active force.

The vertical components of all active forces pushing or pulling the object must be considered because their contributions may increase or decrease the normal force countering the weight force (Figure 6.8).

Normal force is the opposite of the sum of the weight and vertical components of all other active forces perpendicular to the direction of acceleration.

Normal Force $(F_N) = -\sum (\text{Weight} + \text{Active Forces})$

Equation 6.6 Normal Force

Friction

Friction is the resisting force impeding the relative motion of two objects in contact with each other. The force of friction is always opposite to the direction of acceleration (Figure 6.9).

There are two types of friction: static and kinetic. Static friction is the force that prevents an object from moving when in contact with another object. Static friction is calculated by the negative product of the coefficient of static friction and the normal force perpendicular to the direction of acceleration.

$F_s = -\mu_s * F_N$

Equation 6.7 Static Friction

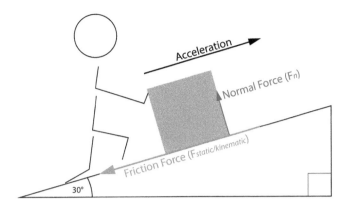

FIGURE 6.9 Friction.

The coefficient of static friction is a dimensionless scalar amount describing the friction ratios between two bodies when they are in contact. This ratio needs to be measured experimentally and cannot be calculated. Rule of thumb states two rough surfaces will have a greater static coefficient of friction than two smooth surfaces. The coefficients of static friction for any two materials are readily found on tables located on the internet. State variations of the contact, such as wet, dry, clean, dirty, or lubricated, are often taken into consideration.

Kinetic friction is the force that slows an object after movement has started. Kinetic friction is computed by taking the negative product of the coefficient of kinetic friction and the normal force perpendicular to the direction of acceleration.

$$F_k = -\mu_k * F_N$$

Equation 6.8 Kinetic Friction

Coefficients of kinetic friction are usually found in the same tables under the same conditions as the coefficients of static friction. In general, the coefficients of static friction are larger than those of kinetic friction.

Update State

The second step of the physics engine loop is to update the states of objects in motion. In other words, the objects' positions and orientations are adjusted. Newton's first law states that a body in motion stays in motion unless acted upon by a force.

Newton's second law states force equals mass times acceleration. The acceleration of an object is the division of the net of all the forces by the object's mass.

$$\text{Acceleration}_{object} = \frac{\text{Force}_{net}}{\text{Mass}_{object}} = \frac{F}{M} = A$$

Equation 6.9 Acceleration of the Object

The net of the forces acting on the object is the difference between all forces opposing the acceleration and all the forces aiding acceleration (Figure 6.10).

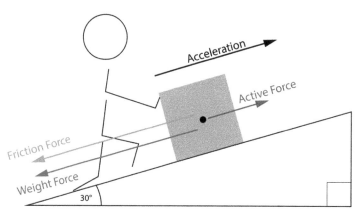

FIGURE 6.10 Net forces affecting object acceleration.

$$\text{Acceleration}_{\text{object}} = \frac{\text{Force}_{\text{net}}}{\text{Mass}_{\text{object}}} = \frac{F_{\text{aid}} - F_{\text{oppose}}}{\text{Mass}_{\text{object}}}$$

Equation 6.10 Object Acceleration Considering Net Force

This stage of the physics engine loop considers all forces acting on an object, revaluates the object's acceleration, and computes the new position and orientation based on the amount of time which has transpired since the last evaluation.

Object acceleration is the aggregate of translational acceleration and rotational acceleration. The orientation of an object does not necessarily correspond to its direction of translational acceleration. There may be rotational forces acting on the object. However, the positional accelerations are not the same as the rotational accelerations. Thus, the object may be moving in a different direction than the object is rotating.

Detect Collisions

The third step of the physics engine loop, the collision detection process, is one of the most important steps yet one of the most complicated. Computationally, it is expensive testing when objects touch other objects. To compound this complexity, every object in the simulation must be tested against every other object. In computer science, the speed of this stage is $O(n^2)$, which is a speed that makes all game developers cringe. Great attention and focus are required to optimize this performance. An entire chapter (or even a book), could be devoted just to this process. Regardless of the complexity, the purpose of this stage is to answer the question, "Do these objects collide? And if so, where is the point of collision?"

An immediate optimization of this stage is to broadly identify all objects which could potentially collide. Upon completion of this broad phase, a narrow, more expensive strategy is employed to identify all points of collision. To facilitate these phases, all real-time objects have two components: a bounding box and a collision volume. The bounding boxes are used for the broad phase and collision volumes are used for the narrow.

Bounding Boxes
Bounding boxes are the most simplistic geometric representations of the object. Due to their simplicity, artists are not typically responsible for their generation. In general, bounding boxes can be one of three types: bounding spheres, axis-extreme bounding boxes, and oriented bounding boxes.

Bounding spheres are the smallest radius required to encapsulate an object (Figure 6.11).

FIGURE 6.11 Bounding sphere of 3D object.

When considering potential collisions between any two objects, the distance between the two objects is calculated. If that distance is smaller than the sum of the two bounding sphere radiuses, there is a potential collision.

$$\text{If Distance}\left(\text{Object}_1, \text{Object}_2\right) \leq \left(\text{Radius}_1 + \text{Radius}_2\right) \rightarrow \text{Potential Collision}$$

Equation 6.11 Bounding Sphere Potential Collision

While the bounding sphere technique is fast, it is often too broad and allows too many potential collisions to proceed to the narrow phase which is significantly more expensive.

Axis-extreme bounding boxes are also simple to compute. Instead of keeping track of one distance, there are six. These six values are computed by considering every vertex of the object and recording the minimum and maximum coordinate position values in the X, Y, and Z axes. A box which conforms to the overall shape of the object is the result (Figure 6.12).

Collision detection of axis-extreme bounding boxes is more expensive than bounding spheres. However, depending on the context of the simulation, they improve the rate of detection by removing more potential collisions. The effective coverage of axis-extreme bounding boxes, combined with their ease of creation, makes them a favorite tool for game developers.

Objects which are not aligned with one of the axes in their local space could potentially be inefficient (Figure 6.13).

Rare situations such as these may warrant the need for oriented bounding boxes. Oriented bounding boxes appear like axis-extreme boxes but are oriented in such a way as to minimize the coverage of the bounding box, independent of the axis (Figure 6.14).

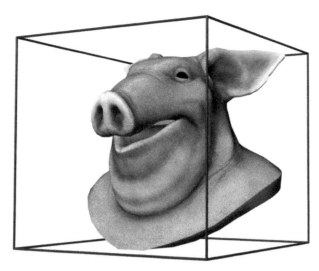

FIGURE 6.12 Axis-extreme bounding box.

FIGURE 6.13 Non-axis-aligned bounding box.

Many simulation engines perform these bounding box generations procedurally. Others expect the user to provide the information. Certain engines do both and allow art-directed customized volumes.

Collision Volumes

After the broad phase isolates only the objects that are in potential collision, collision volumes solve for all points of collision, if there are any. All objects have collision volumes which may be one of four types: bounding box, collision primitives, convex hull, or convex decomposition.

Bounding boxes are easily calculated and are relatively inexpensive when calculating the point of collision. Fidelity of collisions is compromised as bounding boxes will often produce collision points which are significantly out of the volumes of the two objects or interpenetrate too deeply. Bounding boxes may produce untrue collision points.

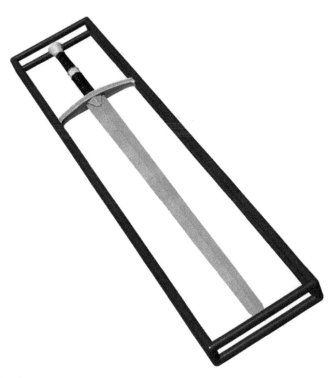

FIGURE 6.14 Oriented bounding box.

Instead of bounding boxes, collision volumes are composed of collision primitives. Collision primitives are typically boxes, tubes, and spheres. The primitives are combined to create a simple yet effective representation of the object's topology (Figure 6.15).

FIGURE 6.15 Collision primitives.

Due to their relative inexpensiveness and ability to be procedurally created, articulated characters are often composed of collision primitives. Individual primitives are parented to joints which animate them correspondingly to the character's deformed mesh (Figure 6.16).

When more collision fidelity is required, convex hulls are employed. A convex hull is the smallest two-dimensional or three-dimensional shape encapsulating an input set of points. A rubber band enclosing a set of planar points creates the shape of a two-dimensional convex hull. Shrink-wrapping around a cloud of points generates a three-dimensional convex-hull shape (Figure 6.17).

Concave elements are the indentions, valleys, and gaps the convex hull generates as it encloses the input set of points. Concave elements of a convex hull may produce untrue collisions (Figure 6.18).

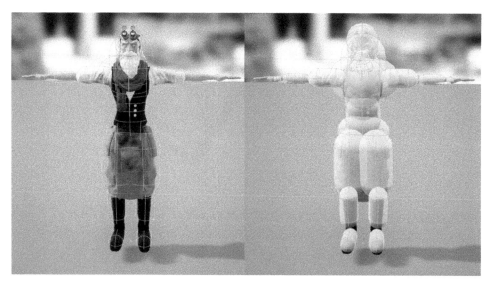

FIGURE 6.16 Character collision primitives.

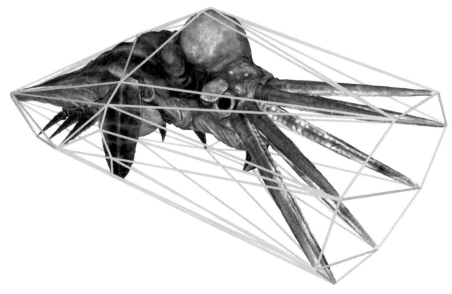

FIGURE 6.17 Three-dimensional convex hulls.

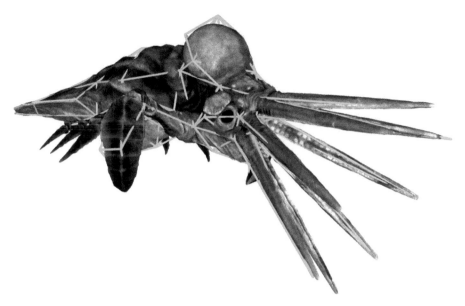

FIGURE 6.18 Concave elements in a convex hull.

Convex hulls do a good job representing convex objects since the false collisions tend to be unnoticeable. Convex hulls can be conveniently generated procedurally during pre-game processing.

When concave elements are crucial for simulation, a convenient technique called convex decomposition is employed. Generated either by hand or procedurally, the shape is broken into a set of convex shapes which are processed as a unit (Figure 6.19).

All convex shapes are available for decomposing a concave object into convex elements and are not limited to spheres, tubes, and boxes. Procedural decompositions are often very heavy as they are composed of as many small primitives providing ample coverage (Figure 6.20).

Algorithms, beyond the scope of this text, calculate the points of collision. The points of collision are then sent to the constraint stage of the simulation loop.

Solve Constraints

Once the active and passive forces of the simulation have been computed and the points of intersection have been discovered, they must be integrated during the fourth step of the physics engine loop when calculating the constraint forces. All constraint forces must be computed before the objects' final positions and orientations can be resolved. Constraints are any forces that apply restrictions to the simulation. Within any simulation, there are six degrees of freedom: three translational and three rotational. A constraint force removes, or at least inhibits, at least one of these axes of movement. The math required to calculate these forces is beyond the scope of this text. However, it is useful to understand the fundamental strategies used to calculate these forces.

Part of the reason why the math required to solve for constraints is so complicated is because each constraint cannot be calculated in isolation. All constraints acting on an object, directly or indirectly, impact the behavior of the other constraints in the system. All constraints must be solved at the same time while taking into consideration the impact of all the other constraints. Complex systems of linear equations must be established to solve for the constraints on a whole.

FIGURE 6.19 Convex decomposition.

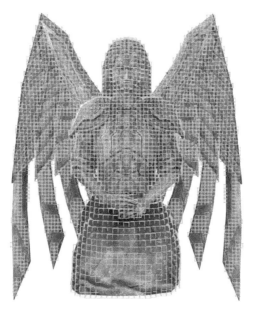

FIGURE 6.20 Complex procedural decomposition.

While there are multiple types of constraints and multiple strategies for solving them, there are two primary types of constraints to consider: joints and non-penetration constraints. A joint is a relationship between two objects that directly controls or limits the degrees of freedom on one of the objects. A hinge joint or gear link is an example of a constraint which eliminates all translational freedom and all rotational freedom except for one axis (Figure 6.21).

A ball joint is another type of constraint which promotes up to all three axes of rotation but limits all three axes of translation (Figure 6.22).

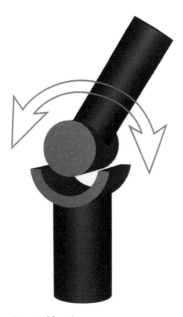

FIGURE 6.21 Hinge joint promoting one rotational axis of freedom.

FIGURE 6.22 Ball joint.

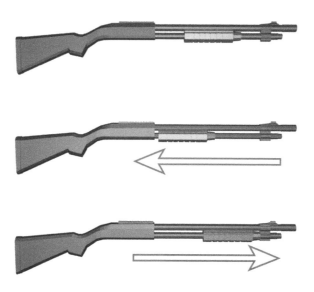

FIGURE 6.23 Slider joint.

A slider joint is a simple constraint that promotes one degree of translational freedom and removes all others (Figure 6.23).

Non-penetration constraints are used for solving collisions. They calculate the forces required to prevent two objects from inter-penetrating or rebounding from each other in unrealistic ways. While difficult to calculate, non-penetration constraints are the most common constraints forces within a simulation.

Display Results

After all forces are accounted for, all accelerations are resolved, and all positions and orientations are updated, the objects are re-drawn to the viewport during the fifth step of the physics engine loop. The simulation has completed one cycle and is done for the moment in time. Time is incremented and the simulation loop starts again from the beginning.

Material Force Attributes

For simplicity, in the prior description of the physics engine loop, only one constant active force and three passive forces (weight, normal, and friction) were considered. While the task describing all potential forces is prohibitive, the following list contains the most common forces an effects artist must contend with.

Mass

Mass is a physical property of the object that regulates its relationship with acceleration. According to Newton's second law, force equals an object's mass times its acceleration. An object of greater mass has a greater amount of associated force under the same acceleration as one of lesser mass. This is visually evident when an object is stricken by two different objects both traveling with the same acceleration. The force the object receives from the object with greater mass will be greater than the force received from the object with lesser mass (Figure 6.24).

Gravity

Gravity is the natural acceleration all objects feel when being drawn toward the centers of other objects. Within the context of physics engines, gravity is assumed to be the default acceleration all objects feel when being pulled toward the center of the Earth at $9.8 \frac{m}{sec^2}$ or $32.17 \frac{feet}{sec^2}$ (Figure 6.25).

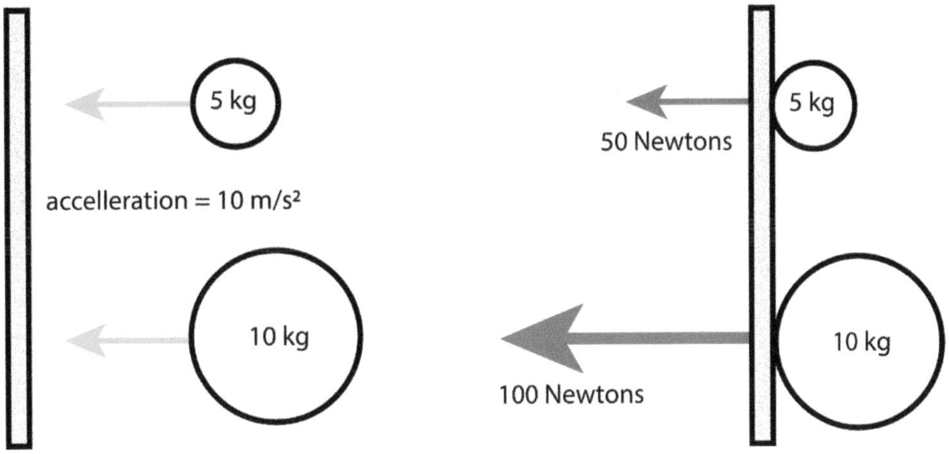

FIGURE 6.24 Impact forces of objects of lesser and greater mass.

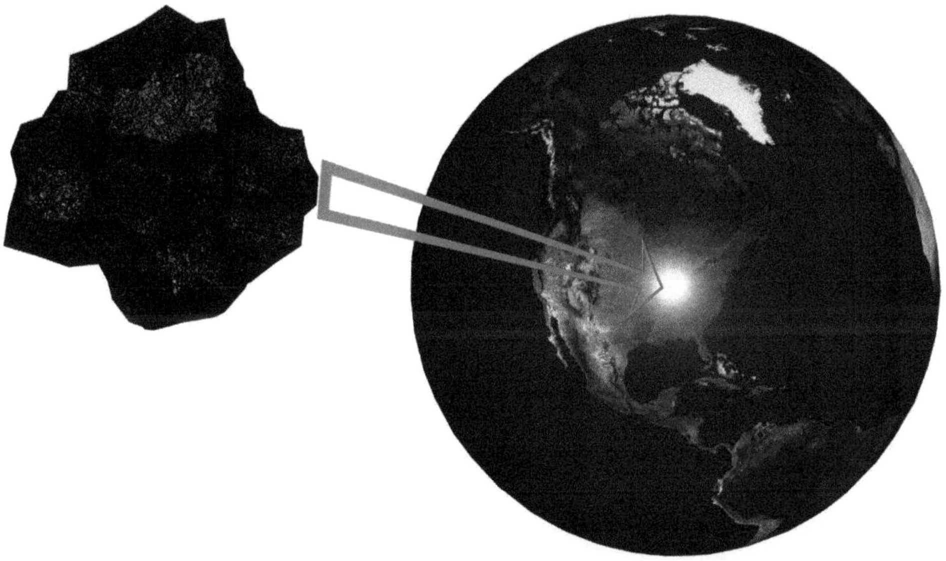

FIGURE 6.25 Gravity pulling an object.

The gravity constant is "artificially" increased to make objects fall faster or come to rest more rapidly after falling against a ground object. Subsequently, when a "floatier" effect is required, reducing gravity will do the job. While gravity is an adjustable parameter in most physics engines, unless justified by story or gameplay, its value should not be altered once it has been set in order to maintain story world integrity.

Friction

Friction is the resisting force that impedes the relative motion of two objects in contact with each other. The concept of friction is explored earlier in this chapter, in the application of the forces phase of the physics engine cycle. Friction exists in two forms: static and kinetic. Static friction is the force which prevents an object from moving when in contact with another object. Kinetic friction is the force which impedes a moving object when in contact with another object (Figure 6.26).

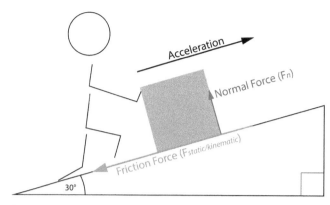

FIGURE 6.26 Static and kinetic friction.

Increasing static friction hinders or prevents motion from happening. Increasing kinetic friction causes objects, when in contact, to slow and stop more rapidly.

Drag

Like friction, drag is the force in the opposite direction of motion of an object when moving through a surrounding air or fluid. While common in hydrodynamic or aerodynamic situations, drag plays a significant role in the motion of all moving objects. For example, drag is the force which prevents falling objects from exceeding terminal velocity when in free fall. Without drag, falling objects continue accelerating indefinitely (Figure 6.27).

Compared with friction, drag is a more complicated force to calculate. The shape of the object is considered as well as the friction of the skin of the object against the surrounding air or fluid. Like friction, increasing drag will cause an object to slow over time. An object's response to drag will appear slower than the impact of friction.

Resilience and Restitution

Although massively over-simplified, the forces of resilience and restitution are labeled the "bounce" factors. Newton's third law states, "For every action there is an equal and opposite reaction." Whenever two objects collide, the forces of the two objects entering the collision are equivalent to the forces pushing them apart after

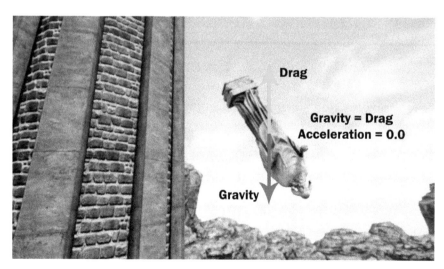

FIGURE 6.27 Drag enforcing terminal velocity.

the collision. In a perfect simulation dealing with rigid bodies, the sums of both forces entering a collision are equivalent to the forces leaving (Figure 6.28).

The resilient or restitution (bounce) factors change this redistribution of forces. An object with a bounce factor less than 1.0 absorbs some of the forces and appears to lose energy after the collision. An object with a bounce factor greater than 1.0 and appears to gain force after the collision (Figure 6.29).

Depending on the implementation of the physics engine, the bounce factors are scalars multiplying the resulting forces after a collision, approximating natural elastic behavior. Bounce factors can potentially contribute to the creation of unrealistic simulations. Scalar multiplications are approximations, not true simulations. To accurately model, thorough fluid, elastic and plastic simulations must be performed.

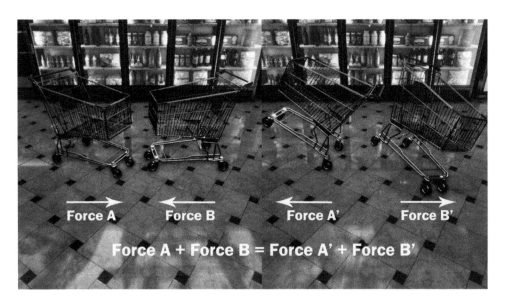

FIGURE 6.28 Forces before and after a collision.

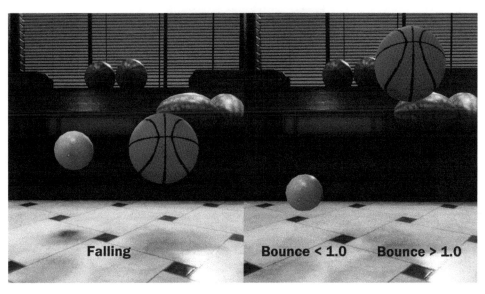

FIGURE 6.29 Bounce factors less than and greater than 1.0.

Spring (Hooke's Law)

Spring constraints are the non-rigid forces binding two objects to each other. Once a spring force has been loaded and allowed to simulate, the relative proximity between two objects oscillates until the spring force is spent and the system achieves equilibrium. Contrary to resilience and restitution, some physics systems use spring behavior to simulate non-rigid object behavior. This behavior is called Hooke's Law which states that the force required to extend or compress a spring (a non-rigid body), by some distance, scales linearly with respect to the distance (Figure 6.30).

x is extension or compression distance

k is the stiffness of the object

Spring Force = $F_s = kx$

Equation 6.12 Hooke's law

When the forces and deformations are relatively small, and the extension or compression distances are relatively small, Hooke's Law provides accurate approximations for most solid bodies. When the forces and distances exceed certain thresholds, the simulations fail.

Simple spring simulations can be found in most physics engines to simulate dynamic constraint relationships between objects, such as a character body jiggle or a spring-loaded door. Other more complicated dynamics, such as clothing simulations, require dedicated physics engines or off-line solutions.

Damping

Related to springs, wave dynamics and other oscillating systems, damping reduces, restricts, and prevents the effects of oscillation over time before equilibrium is achieved. Damping is a ratio reflecting the decay of the

FIGURE 6.30 Hooke's law.

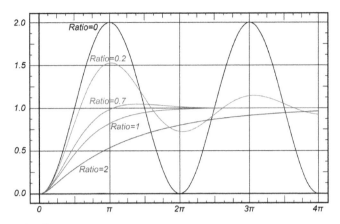

FIGURE 6.31 Various damping ratio effects.

oscillations in a system after the system has been set into action and before it equalizes. A ratio value of 0.0 means that the system is *undamped* or the oscillations do not decay over time. In other words, the system never stops oscillating. When the ratio is greater than 1.0 the system is *overdamped*. When a system is overdamped, it transitions from its active state to a state of equilibrium in a more linear manner. The greater the damping ratio, the faster the transition becomes. A ratio value of 1.0 is said to be *critically damped* or when the system achieves equilibrium with no oscillation and without being overdamped. A critically damped system achieves equilibrium in a minimal amount of time (Figure 6.31).

Impulse

Invisible to the physics engine user, impulse is the change of linear momentum over time. In mathematical terms, it is the integral of force applied to the system. While impulse is an essential component of a physics engine when dealing with forces that change over time, it is not typically an adjustable factor. Since a force may change rapidly, impulse is most often used to refer to fast acting forces or impacts. An impact is best described as an instantaneous, short-lived force acting on a system. Examples of an impact are a golf club hitting a ball, a bat hitting a baseball, or an explosion hitting an object. Impulse adds force to a system at a specific moment in time and stops.

Object Destruction

Exploding buildings, collapsing bridges, crumbling statues, and imploding structures are examples of object destruction. These effects are easy to set up, easy to instance, and almost always dramatic. Instead of relying on pure simulation, most destruction sequences possess a small component of sleight of hand and redirection. Almost all destruction sequences follow this formula.

1. Setup

2. Trigger

3. Simulation

4. Resolution

Setup

The object being destroyed is not just one object, it is at least two: a beauty object and a pre-fractured object. The beauty object is the pretty, inexpensive version of the object being destroyed. The pre-fractured object is a version of the beauty object, pre-broken into many sub-objects. Objects composed of smaller sub-objects are expensive since they resemble the beauty geometry externally and are subdivided by dense, smaller geometry internally. These fractured objects geometries do not need to be solid volumes. They do need to be three-dimensional and have separate internal material and texture. Object material is important. Broken and twisted metal needs to look like distressed metal, shattered wood needs to look like splintered wood and crumbling stone needs to look like broken rock. Initially, the dense pre-fractured objects have the same position and orientation as their original "simple" objects but are invisible.

Trigger/Distraction

Depending on the context of the visual effect, the simulation requires a trigger event to initiate. This event may be anything from a character intersecting a volume to a projectile striking an object. The character may trip, fall, or share a sullen moment of realization when encountering the trigger volume. A projectile must be visually interesting. This distraction is a decoy to prevent the audience from observing the object swap from the beauty version of the object to the pre-fractured, subdivided version, which may not match the original version with 100% integrity. The distraction also may introduce a force into the system which instigates and justifies the simulation.

Simulation

With the distracting forces already pre-estimated, the physics engine engages on the pre-fractured object and animates the simulation. The development team relinquishes control of the experience to the physics engine.

Resolution

When the simulation achieves a stable state, one of two events happens: the physics engine disengages and pre-fractured objects remain static or the engine enters a polling state. In the case of the first event, the development team must prevent characters and other forces from interacting with the fractured objects to prevent initiation of new simulations. In the case of the second event, characters interact with the fractured objects and the engine simulates the new collision activities.

Voronoi Decomposition

During the setup phase of this operation, the "beauty" object is fractured into multiple fragments which 'fit' together and when assembled, form a duplicate of the original object. Modeling the broken fragments is challenging. The task is accomplished by hand or with a "pre-simulation algorithm" which breaks the object into fragments which conform to object material properties. A common fracturing strategy is Voronoi decomposition.

Voronoi decomposition is a computational geometric algorithm used for breaking an object into smaller "cells" based on a set of input points. This fracturing can be achieved in two or three dimensions (Figures 6.32 and 6.33).

Two-dimensionally, the result is a fragmentation of a plane into "cells" surrounding each of the input points. The edges of the cells are exactly half the distance between adjacent input points or the boundary edges of the plane (Figure 6.34).

The Voronoi algorithm can be extended into three dimensions. Voronoi decomposition breaks a three-dimensional shape into multiple segments, fitting together to form perfect puzzles (Figure 6.35).

While Voronoi decomposition effectively segments an object into smaller fragments, the "Voronoi" pattern is recognizable and may distract the audience. To avoid this, artists may seek to do the fragmentation by hand or employ more complicated, off-line solutions including the use of Boolean functions to assist with the object breakup.

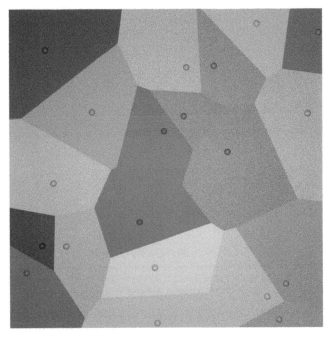

FIGURE 6.32 2D Voronoi plane and input points.

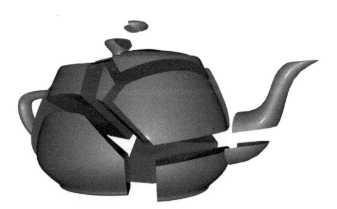

FIGURE 6.33 3D Voronoi fractured object.

Off-Line Simulation

Developing simulations within the context of real-time engines is convenient. The data stays within one package, the creation pipeline becomes simplistic, and the results are traceable. Optimized engine code provides the broadest utility. However, there are many situations when the real-time engine RBDs are inadequate. While achieving broad functionality, the required compromises limit simulation scope and capability. When the art director requests a specific look, the default engine coverage may be insufficient. Similarly, if there are specific situations within the simulation requiring art direction, the default engine may be unable to expose the necessary control. Of course, the scope and scale of the simulation may be too large for the physics engine to handle in real time. When the sheer numbers of calculations cause severe performance issues, the thematic or emotional impact of the effect may not justify the performance costs.

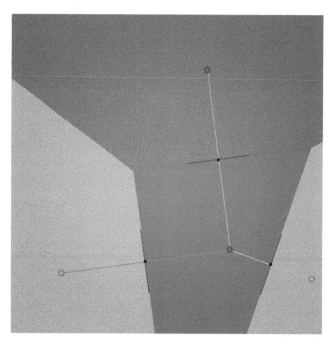

FIGURE 6.34 2D Voronoi decomposition result.

FIGURE 6.35 3D Voronoi fragmented 3D object.

Interactivity is another important consideration of the simulation. When interactivity does not reflect the interactions between the participant and the environment, the scope of the narrative is jeopardized. The visual effects artist must consider multiple questions. How unique does the simulation need to be? Are there multiple variations of the simulation? Do they behave in the same manner in every instance? Do the actions of the participant or story world agents motivate different simulated behavior? Is there a visual need for an immediate cause and effect relationship? How variable must the simulation be? How often are similar simulations observed from the same camera perspective? For example, the source for an avalanche or an exploding boat may be visually challenging to identify. Unless observed multiple times from the same perspective, simulation variations are tricky to notice. A collapsing bridge may be observed from three different perspectives: the right side, the left side, or the center. However, will there ever be a need for different perspectives?

In most scenarios, when the rigid body simulation results are inadequate or the simulation creates an undesirable computational performance drain, an alternative solution must be found. When the simulation can be observed from multiple perspectives and does not require interactivity, a pre-generated, off-line simulation can be employed. The performance costs for a pre-generated simulation are delegated to an off-line calculation and are limited by the quantity and complexity of the moving objects of the scene. Removing computational expense from the simulation opens opportunity for further situational manipulation and specific art direction. Aside from the risk of repeated exposure, the usage of pre-generated, off-line simulations is attractive. The challenge of this strategy derives from integrating the simulations into the engine and triggering their playbacks. There are three rigid body strategies: simple animation, complex animation with octopus rigs, and vertex cache animation. When off-line and real-time solutions fail to generate adequate solutions, the effects may need to go back to design and re-thought.

Simple Animation

When the number of interacting objects in a scene is small and the objects do not fragment before, during, or after collision, simple animation may provide a solution for off-line, rigid body simulation. The simulations are not confined to collisions. Falling or flying objects and projectiles take on new levels of realism, driven by pre-generated, animated clips.

All articulated characters in the engine are driven by animated clips. The position and orientation of each joint are recorded to channel data and upon triggering, the engine plays the animation data through joint channels. All objects in the real-time scene are considered as actors. Any object that collides, falls, or flies can be driven by an animation clip.

Certain real-time engines may not allow static actors to be directly driven by animation data. This limitation can be circumnavigated by creating the actor with one joint: a root joint. This root joint may be in the actor's centroid or at the base of actor contact with the ground plane. All the character's skinned weights must be devoted to this single root joint. By tricking the engine into thinking an actor is an articulated character, it will allow animation clips to play through this single root joint.

Engine restrictions on the number of animated, articulated actors may trigger a threshold of diminishing returns when a real-time simulation may be more efficient. This is a subjective call. The advantages of simple animations are multiple. They are directable. They behave exactly how they are needed. Outside of the extra time of weighting the objects' root joints, these simulations are quick to set up and easy to control.

Octopus Skeletons

Handling object destruction with simple animation is advanced through the utilization of octopus skeletons. An octopus skeleton is a control structure with one root joint parented to multiple single joint children, and a single object fragmented into multiple sub-objects. Each sub-object is weighted to a single unique joint child. Parenting multiple joints to a root joint enables the system to behave as a single unit. Destructible objects are transformed to strange, octopus-like, articulated characters with one root and multiple child joints: one for each object fragment (Figure 6.36).

The skeleton for this destructible object is created in the opposite order as a traditionally articulated character. The destruction of a pre-fractured object is simulated using an off-line simulation package. The skeleton for the destructible object is created after the simulation has been calculated and recorded. At frame zero, or at a non-simulated frame, a root joint is placed at the object's pivot point and unique child joints are positioned at the centroid of each pre-fractured segment. All vertices of each segment are fully weighted to their corresponding joint. For each frame of the simulation, the position and orientation data of the centroid of each fragment are baked into the animation curve of the corresponding joint. The pre-fractured object and its skeleton are imported

FIGURE 6.36 Octopus rig for destructible object.

FIGURE 6.37 Animating destructible octopus skeleton object.

into the engine as a skeletal mesh with joint animation curves. Removed from the off-line simulation, the pre-fractured object is static. However, as soon as the animation channels are played through the skeletal joints, the fractured object breaks apart and animates just as it did in the off-line simulation software (Figure 6.37).

Vertex Cache

When an octopus skeleton does not translate the fidelity of the simulation sufficiently, Vertex Cache Animation may be a possible alternative. Vertex cache techniques are a group of strategies which manipulate an object's vertex positions within the vertex shader of the pipeline instead of deforming the object through joints. There are multiple vertex cache variations and the strategy used to implement rigid body destruction is the simplest, manipulating only vertex positions and orientations. Intermediate to high-level shader programming skills is required to implement vertex caching. Multiple commercial implementations are available. Understanding vertex cache principles and the math supporting those principles will aid adopting any implementation.

Vertex Cache animation works by taking record of the state of every object vertex for every frame. Usually, this state information is vertex position and orientation but occasionally, the vertex normal and color are recorded. Instead of recording the full vertex parameters for every frame, only the values of vertex parameter change, or *deltas*, are recorded. These deltas represent only the changes in each vertex parameter from one frame to the next. Recording the full vertex parameter value for every frame is redundant. Capturing the deltas allows for precise changes to be recorded. The vertex deltas are written to external files for integration with the real-time engine. External data formats such as JSON are convenient and easy to implement. However, they may tend to be large and slow. Another vertex cache media format is texture maps.

Texture maps are native real-time engine components and provide effective data transportation. A small amount of math is required to translate the vertex parameter deltas to texture values. Every vertex parameter (position, orientation, normal, etc.) is broken into its x, y, and z components which map directly to the red, green, and blue texture color channels. Parameter values may range from negative to positive infinity. Texture channel values range only between 0.0 and 1.0. To convert the parameter value to texture channel value, the minimum and maximum parameter values must be recorded. The texture channel value for a vertex parameter for a specific frame is recorded as the ratio between the difference of the current value and the minimum value and the difference between the maximum and minimum values.

$$\text{Channel Parameter Value} = \frac{\left(\text{Current Value} - \text{Minimum Value}\right)}{\left(\text{Maximum Value} - \text{Minimum Value}\right)}$$

Equation 6.13 Translation from Vertex Parameter Value to Texture Channel Value

The X, Y, and Z components of a vertex parameter are stored in the red, green, and blue components of one texture image texel. Each column of texels is dedicated to an individual vertex. Rows correspond to parameter values for subsequent frames (Figure 6.38).

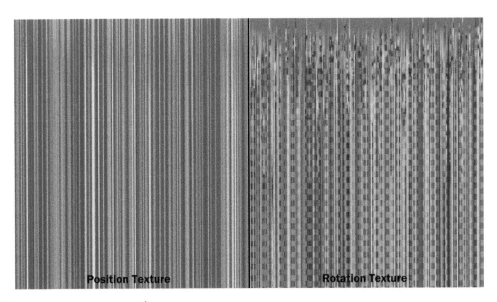

FIGURE 6.38 Vertex animation texture map layout.

Since the textures store numerical data instead of image data, they tend to have irregular dimensions. When the engine has difficulty with irregular texture sizes, the data may be padded with zeros. Each texture file corresponds to a particular vertex component. For example, since simple object destruction only requires position and orientation information, the system only produces corresponding position and rotation texture images.

Once inside the engine, the texture images are converted back to vertex parameter data within the vertex shader of the rendering pipeline. Storing the data within texture maps makes them convenient to work with. Every texel of the input texture corresponds to an equivalent vertex for a specific frame. For example, the first column of pixels is dedicated to the first vertex. The 2nd texel column holds the values for the 2nd vertex. Each row stores the vertex attribute data for a specific frame.

To compute the vertex parameter data, a channel is translated by multiplying the difference between the maximum and the minimum values by the current texture channel value and adding the product to the minimum value.

Vertex Parameter Value = Minimum Value + Channel Value * (Maximum Value − Minimum Value)

Equation 6.14 Translation from Channel Value to vertex Parameter Value

Beyond the minimum and maximum vertex parameter values, the length of the clip is the only information required by the shader. While every sequential frame of the texture is represented in one row, the shader requires reference when and where to stop, to offset timing data or scale time to speed or slow the animation.

Texture images corresponding to each vertex parameter faithfully store the necessary information required to reproduce the off-line simulation. This technique is limited by restrictions on texture size. Simulations of thousands of objects, pieces, and fragments are recreated but diminishing returns are achieved when textures grow too large. When this happens, simulation length is trimmed. When the simulation is within a cinematic, the camera cuts away before the full completion of the simulation. The parameters of the simulation are modified to terminate when the simulation terminates. Other situations require simpler objects with fewer vertices. As in any simulation, the dynamic object is swapped during initiation. Once the object breakup or destruction starts, it is difficult to track the object's visual integrity.

SOFT BODIES

Soft bodies are simulations with deformable objects. RBDs assume that the objects colliding behave as particles and do not change shape. It is assumed the simulation objects are inelastic. Soft bodies are the opposite and assume all objects are elastic. Rigid bodies and soft bodies are rarely observed together for two primary reasons. The first reason is the screen-spaces bounding entire simulations are too large to observe soft body deformations in the same context. The second reason is that unless the soft bodies are the primary focus of the simulation, their added computational expense is hard to justify.

Soft bodies maintain surface topology when deforming. Topology is the mesh layout of the surface's geometry. It is maintained when the number of vertices is constant and the relative proximity of the vertices with their neighbors remain constant. When the object breaks apart, combines, or dissolves, topology is disrupted.

Examples

Soft bodies are essential for effective visual effects animation and can be found practically anywhere. Their dynamic behavior is essential for "squash and stretch," possibly the most important principle of animation. Without soft body dynamics, follow-through, overlapping, and secondary actions, such as mouse tails or hat feathers, would be unachievable. Soft bodies are also used to exaggerate and provide a heavy motion accent. When subtle, they may not be consciously appreciated. However, without elastic behavior, many physical performances appear dead and flat.

Cloth

Animating cloth is perhaps the most common usage of soft body dynamics. From the overlapping motion of dresses and coats to the secondary movements of loose t-shirts and basketball player shorts, soft bodies are essential for establishing realistic character movement (Figure 6.39).

They bring life to environments through waving banners and flags. Different fabrics possess physical characteristics which influence how cloth moves. For example, leather moves differently from lace (Figure 6.40).

The impact of animated cloth is significant, and many real-time engines devote specialized solvers for generating optimized cloth deformations.

FIGURE 6.39 Dynamic dresses and shorts.

FIGURE 6.40 Leather versus laces animation.

Curves

Bendable objects conforming with their environments are achieved with curve simulations. Clothes, trains, animals such as snakes and lizards, and facial animations are achievable with curve dynamics (Figure 6.41).

Curves simplify the deformation process. They simulate collisions without incurring the computational costs of generating a true collision deformation. Curves provide the visual effects artist the freedom to create realistic and computationally inexpensive simulations.

Soft Containers

Soft containers are objects that can flatten, deflate, and lose volume very quickly. These are extreme squash and stretch simulations. Soft containers are objects which change volume rapidly such as balloons that lose air, sacks that bulge to the point of tearing, or pillows that deflate or compress to conform with their environment (Figure 6.42).

FIGURE 6.41 Curve dynamics.

FIGURE 6.42 Soft container.

Organic

Although organic objects squash and stretch like soft containers, they maintain volume. Marshmallows and balloons are soft yet are considered organic since their volumes are repositioned when bulging and stretching occurs (Figure 6.43).

Physical body parts such as muscles, certain facial deformations, jiggling breasts, fat deposits, and certain hair simulations fall into this category. Maintaining volume is a crucial challenge. Humans are attuned to what is considered as *natural* in the human body and are sensitive to what may be considered as *unrealistic deformation*. Careful attention must be applied toward these simulations to integrate them effectively in respective story worlds (Figure 6.44).

FIGURE 6.43 Compressed marshmallow.

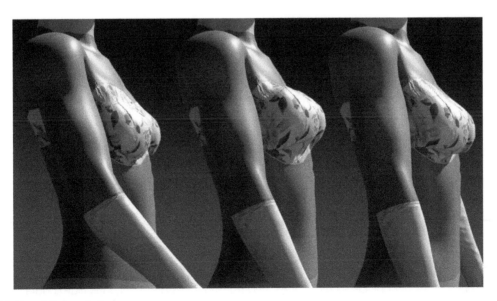

FIGURE 6.44 Unrealistic breast giggle.

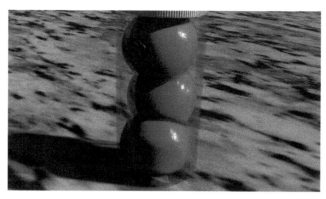

FIGURE 6.45 Organic fruits and vegetables.

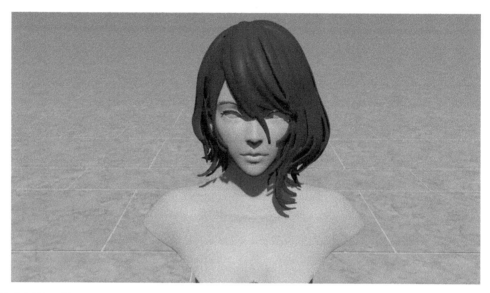

FIGURE 6.46 Solid Hair Object.

Within some circumstances, many foods, fruits, and vegetables are treated as organic objects when subtly animated to appear soft and flexible. This subtle, extra detail moves the simulation from good to best in class. Without some deformation, foods appear solid, as if made of rock or wood (Figure 6.45).

Hair is also often treated as an organic object. When the hair appears as a soft and flexible hat, treating it as an organic simulation may be a cost-effective alternative to animating every strand. Large volumes of hair that animate as a single unit make effective organic simulations (Figure 6.46).

Viscous bodily fluids which do not split into smaller droplets are also treated as organic simulations. Organic oozes, slimes, and jellies constitute members of this class. Blood has been simulated using this technique more than once. Like other organic simulations, fluid particles are bound with their neighbors with a small spring force. This force allows for extreme stretch and yet does not self-interpenetrate or collide with other objects (Figure 6.47).

Highly Articulated Objects

Long, thin, and highly flexible objects such as ropes, chains, and wires are highly articulated objects (Figure 6.48).

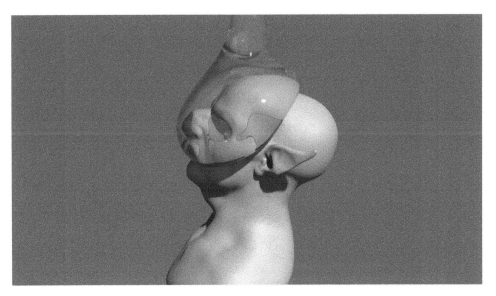

FIGURE 6.47 Slime simulation.

FIGURE 6.48 Ropes, chains and wires.

Such objects are deformed with long chains of relatively short joints (Figure 6.49).

Constrained by one or two points of contact, forces such as gravity and wind act upon the simulation. Not all points of contact are treated as articulated joints. When the forces at the point of connection are adequate to hold the shape rigid, the object is considered a static extender, contributing to the simulation but is not deformed by it (Figure 6.50).

Some real-time engines are equipped with dedicated hair simulation systems. Within these simulations, each hair follicle is treated as a wire, with its own strength, tensile, and spring properties. In such systems, the follicles are deformed parametrically and not from a joint chain. While rooted to a character's head, each follicle must

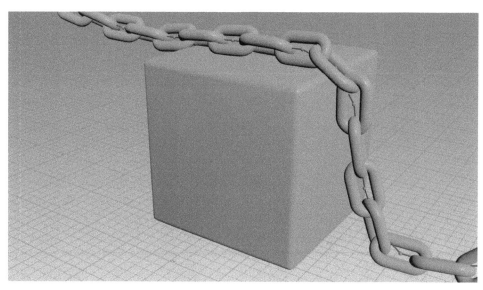

FIGURE 6.49 Highly articulated joints.

FIGURE 6.50 Chain as a static extender.

compute its movements based on the character's action and must consider the collisions with the character and other hair follicles (Figure 6.51).

The calculations for thousands of hair follicles are expensive and cheaper alternatives for animating hair are often considered.

Paper

While paper objects have similar properties to cloth, they require their own simulation systems. Unlike cloth, paper can fold and crease, necessitating stronger spring constraints within those regions. When the paper is animated without folding or creasing, it is animated as a cloth (Figure 6.52).

FIGURE 6.51 Hair as articulated object.

FIGURE 6.52 Creased paper simulation.

Ragdoll

While not realistic, Ragdoll physics is used for simulating dying or dead articulated characters, which animate to gravity as lifeless bodies, flailing around the environment, bouncing off other characters, environmental objects, and even themselves (Figure 6.53).

Articulated characters are composed of two components: the visual body mesh and the underlying skeleton made of joints simulating real bones such as elbows, knees, hips, wrists, and ankles. Unlike other visual effects which perform simulations on object meshes, Ragdoll characters simulate on the skeleton joints. The physics engine treats the skeletal joints as rigid body objects connected by static length bone constraints. The simulations animate the skeletal joints with respect to gravity and collide with other environmental objects and characters.

FIGURE 6.53 Ragdoll character.

Articulated characters simulated with ragdoll physics fall and collide with other objects in a whirlwind of flailing arms and legs. Early real-time attempts at ragdoll simulations were not convincing yet did provide new layers of realism absent from prior real-time experiences. Further refinements to the algorithms generate more reasonable simulations.

Techniques

There are four real-time strategies for simulating soft bodies: real-time simulations, skeleton-driven animations, in-material approximations, and off-line simulations. Of the four techniques, the pure real-time simulations are the most computationally expensive. The other strategies are more economical approximations of simulated behavior.

Real-Time Simulations

Real-time soft bodies, or physically based simulations, attempt to model dynamic, soft deforming behavior as a collection of particles in real time. While other dynamic surface techniques treat deforming bodies as solid objects altered by limited behavior, joint movement, or vertex offset, real-time simulations are based on physically accurate properties of deforming materials such as spring tension, damping behavior, collisions, and points of interaction. Cloth, soft containers, organic objects, paper, and ragdoll dynamics are simulated using these techniques.

Real-time simulations transform the objects into lattices of particles held together through matrices of constraints. External forces are then applied to the system. All particles have position, velocity, force, and mass attributes. On a per frame basis, all attributes are considered when recalculating each particle's position. Integration is the mathematically complicated process for solving particle positions. Integration is performed on either the CPU or GPU, depending on the visual demands for the simulations and the contexts of the simulations. Integration techniques differentiate the types and qualities of the simulations.

Springs
Real-time soft bodies are treated as lattices made of particles, each with its own mass. The particles are constrained to each other through a matrix of springs. The spring and damping behaviors of these constraints define the type of material being simulated. There are three types of springs used to model resistive properties of soft materials: structural, shearing, and bending (Figure 6.54).

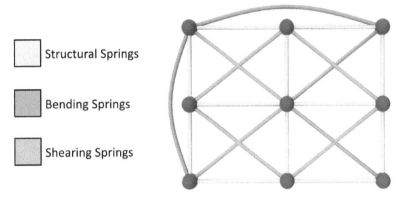

FIGURE 6.54 Structural, shearing and bending springs.

Structural springs arrange the particles into rows and columns. They maintain the topology of the surface and prevent tearing when the surface is stretched or collapsing when compressed.

Shearing springs connect particles with their diagonal neighbors. They prevent the simulation from shearing to one side, like a rhombus or a parallelogram being pushed over (Figure 6.55).

Bending springs connect each particle with its second neighbors, vertically and horizontally. In other words, each particle has four additional springs connected to neighbors of immediate neighbors (Figure 6.56).

These springs prevent simulations from creasing or folding in on themselves. They are effectively preventing surfaces from folding along edges when colliding with other objects (Figure 6.57).

Integration

The complicated process of calculating particle positions while considering their springs and external forces is called integration. The first step of integration calculates each particle's acceleration using Newton's Second Law.

$$acceleration_{particle} = \frac{1}{mass_{particle}} * force$$

Equation 6.15 Newton's Second Law

New velocities and positions are derived from the particles' acceleration. The particles' positions are updated, the forces are zeroed, and the process starts again. There are two strategies for executing this calculus-based integration: Euler and Verlet.

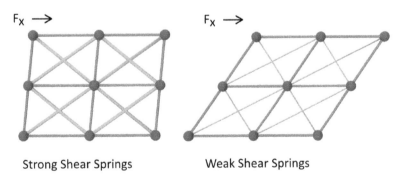

Strong Shear Springs   Weak Shear Springs

FIGURE 6.55 Shearing springs prevent surfaces from falling to one side.

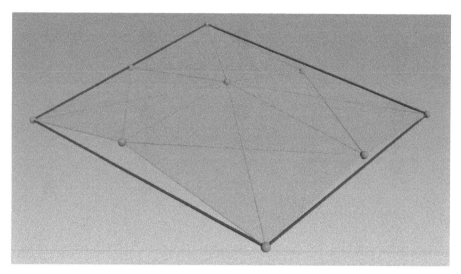

FIGURE 6.56 Bending springs connections.

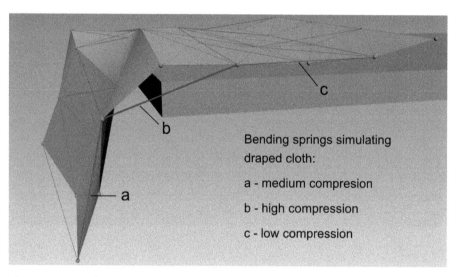

FIGURE 6.57 Bending springs around corner.

The simpler and more direct technique is Euler's Method. Euler's Method solves for the new velocity by adding the current velocity and the product of the acceleration to the change in time. The new particle position is the sum of the old particle position and the product of the new velocity and change of time.

$velocity_{new} = velocity_{old} + acceleration * \Delta time$

$position_{new} = position_{old} + velocity_{new} * \Delta time$

$\Delta time$ = Amount of time between each frame

Equation 6.16 Euler's Integration Method

While this technique is relatively easy to implement, the system generates large amounts of positive feedback and causes the variables to expand quickly and explode. This explosion can be limited by applying extreme damping forces to the springs and taking exceedingly small time increments between integrations. Even with these precautionary measures in place, the simulations still tend to be unwieldy.

Verlet integration is an alternative strategy which removes velocity from the calculations. The velocity is approximated using the difference between the particle's current and prior positions.

$$velocity\ approximation = position_{current} - position_{prior}$$

Equation 6.17 Verlet Velocity Approximation

With the velocity taken out of consideration, the new particle positions become a result of the approximated velocity and the prior particle position.

$$position_{new} = 2 * position_{current} - position_{prior} + acceleration * \Delta time^2$$

Equation 6.18 Verlet New Position Calculation

This alternative method of integrating the particles' new position is more accurate than the Euler technique. It is easy to implement and most importantly, it is more stable. There may be some concern about the approximation of the velocity jeopardizing the integrity of the simulation. Within generating visual effects, believability, performance, and stability are always more important than accuracy.

The visual results of Verlet integration should be good enough to integrate within the theme world and simulate with *relative* stability. The word, "relative," needs to be emphasized. Although Verlet integration is more stable than Euler, it is still not bomb-proof. Simulations may still explode at unexpected times or incorrectly deal with certain object collisions.

Usage

Most visual effects artists are not responsible for coding real-time simulations. Once the hard part of integration has been completed, the application is a relatively simple five-step process.

1. The artist identifies the desired simulation regions on the mesh.
2. She applies spring and damping constants to duplicate the simulated material.
3. The simulation is tested
4. Tweaks are made to the constants
5. Steps 3 and 4 are repeated iteratively until a desired behavior is achieved.

Care must be taken when using these techniques to not push them too hard. They are easy to apply but are fragile and could represent the greatest threat for breaking presence within the experience. Since even the most stable strategies are unpredictable, they are not art directable. These techniques are outstanding for creating ambient motion or activities independent of specific behavior. Visually precise effects require more controllable techniques such as skeleton-driven simulation.

Skeleton Simulations

Skeletal simulations are the brute force technique for cheaply simulating realistic soft body objects. While they do have their drawbacks, they can provide very cost-effective and visually appealing simulated solutions. Soft bodies are treated as pre-rigged characters with articulated skeletons. The skeletal joints are placed at advantageous locations which most realistically deform their corresponding meshes. The simulations are hand keyed by

FIGURE 6.58 Articulated character with extra simulation joints.

animators using memory or real media references. Some situations require motion capture data. Hair, bouncing objects and extreme organic giggle can be motion captured. Subtle muscle deformation and the flow of viscous fluids are difficult to capture (Figure 6.58).

Upon completion of the animation, the data is baked into the skeletal joints and exported to the engine as real-time animation clips. The clips are then played at selected opportunities during the real-time experience.

While the animated clips provide very art-directed motion and potentially very realistic simulations, they do have their drawbacks. Since the simulations are treated as animated characters, they can only be played at specific triggered moments. Unless the simulated motion is discrete or confusingly complex, the clip can only be displayed once to the audience. Randomly selected clips of similar nature may provide extended utility to help combat repetition. Because the clips are played at pretentious moments in the experience, they cannot react interactively with the immediate forces of the environment. Unless triggered during careful moments of confusing or imprecise stimuli, the simulation may appear out of place.

In-Material Simulations

While not as robust as full-blown simulations, in-material simulations are extremely powerful techniques for generating inexpensive and relatively high-quality visual effects. Object vertex resolution is a limiting factor. Because the calculations for the simulation are done in the rendering pipeline, excessive object complexity will cause the rendering to slow. Like artificial or "fake" simulations, their visual inaccuracy should not discount their effectiveness. Objects are deformed in the shader sufficiently to make the simulation "seem" real. When there is no direct visual interaction between simulated objects, many in-material effects can be good enough to maintain the visual standards of the theme world and provide the observer with just enough integrity to satisfy their need for visual consistency. This dynamic behavior echoes the original objective of all visual effects in not necessarily duplicating reality but providing enough substantial movement to satisfy the imaginary requirements viewers have of the current scene.

In-material simulations are not limited by the pixel shader. Beyond dynamic normal texture maps, there is not enough superficial detail on the object surface to carry the entire visual effect. Most of the heavy lifting occurs in the vertex shader. Just as the vertex shader is responsible for all articulated character movement, the vertex shader is used for simulating dynamic objects. In general, any low-amplitude deformation can be applied to an object's surface. Sensitive to object vertex resolution, the amplitude needs to be kept to a reasonable amount less tearing or the formation of undesirable surface artifacts (Figure 6.59).

Many visual effects perform well with in-material simulations. Cloth, when animated with small amplitudes of shader noise, feels alive, as if the body underneath has subtle but invisible ambient motion. A simple sine wave passing through portions of the cloth will give the cloth a feeling of being connected to the world around it. While true simulations are challenging to perform effectively in the vertex shader, when exposed to character movement, limited amounts of spring-like behavior can be simulated (Figure 6.60).

FIGURE 6.59 Surface artifacts due to high-amplitutde displacement.

FIGURE 6.60 Cloth simulated in-material.

Curve simulations are also effectively achieved within the vertex shader. When the per-frame movements of individual vertices do not exceed extreme amplitude, their animation appears smooth. Curve data is passed easily into the shader thus the object is easily deformed to match the contours of the curve. A method of mapping the deformed surface to the corresponding curve element is essential for making the effect work. A quick strategy is to map the U or V texture coordinates of the soft body object to the length of the curve (Figure 6.61).

Organic objects respond effectively to in-material simulations. To maintain scale and integrity of the organic object, the deformation amplitude must be relatively small. When direct interaction with another object during the simulation is not essential, simple noise or a sine wave passing through the object appear realistic. Limited information concerning the object's world position and gravity can be exposed to the shader to produce true, simplistic simulations. Some of the best in-material simulations can be seen with hair effects. Since the simulation happens in the shader, hair implementation is unlimited. Hair is represented as solid objects, hair helmets, cards, or individual strands (Figure 6.62).

FIGURE 6.61 Curve dynamics in-material.

FIGURE 6.62 Hair simulated in-material.

FIGURE 6.63 Foliage simulated in-material.

Grass and foliage are iconic demonstrations of in-material simulations. There is almost no scene containing grass or foliage that is not animated in the vertex shader. The scene appears dead without this now expected ambient motion. It is difficult for the audience to visualize the shape of the deforming winds. World space noise simulates the ebbing and flowing of large and small gusts of wind very effectively (Figure 6.63).

In-material simulations are essential components of any visual effects artist's tool kit. When the artist has these techniques readily available, she can bring abundant life to any dead scene.

Off-Line

There are times when true, real-time simulations may be impractical because of the scale of the simulation or simply because of the level of fine control required by the context of the experience within the theme world. In these situations, a hybrid approach is required which requires pre-generating the simulation, utilizing an external software solution, and then integrating the resulting data back into the real-time engine. These simulations have the benefit of dramatically increasing the scale of the simulation, being art-directable when needed, performing with 100% predictability within the context of the real-time engine, and depending on the implementation, being many times more efficient than a true real-time simulation.

The big challenge with off-line simulations is integrating the data back into the engine. As of the time of writing this text, there is no way to directly transfer an off-line simulation to a real-time engine. This is where the creativity and resourcefulness of the technical artist are required. While the solutions for transferring dynamic surface simulations are limited by the creativity of the technical artist, there are three primary techniques: octopus skeletal animation, vertex cache animations stored within texture maps, and vertex cache animations stored within external files.

Octopus Skeleton

Like the off-line simulation technique described in the Rigid Bodies section of this chapter, octopus animation clips are used to transfer soft body animation from a simulation software to a real-time engine. The difference in this strategy is the order the animations are placed on to the joints. Before the simulation is started, a lattice of joints is dispersed from an arbitrary anchor point and constrained to the surface at regular intervals. Consistent joint spacing is required for effective surface topology coverage (Figure 6.64).

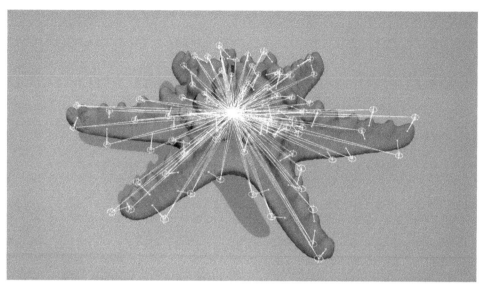

FIGURE 6.64 Joints constrained equally on a surface.

Surface points drive joint positions since they are constrained to the surface. The soft body simulation is applied to the surface. It is important to remember to temporarily disengage the joint weighting on the points on the surface which will prevent the surface from animating. Upon completion of the simulation, the joint animation is re-baked back onto the joints.

When surface weighting to the joints is reactivated, the surface is driven by the joints. The skeleton and the surface mesh are exported to the real-time engine and played as a standard skeletal mesh.

Vertex Cache
The octopus animation technique is limited by the number of joints that can be efficiently imported into and animated in the engine. When more points of contact are required, a similar vertex cache technique described in the Rigid Bodies section of this chapter can be implemented. Very few alterations need to be made to this technique when adjusting for dynamic, soft bodies. In addition to the vertex positions and orientations, the vertex normals must be written to texture. Without dynamic normals, the surface vertices will still be displaced but the surfaces will only appear to change from the perpendicular or silhouette perspectives. The vertex normals must be updated to match their positional offsets or the changes in shape will be difficult to observe. Vertex caching is a fantastic technique for capturing and displaying soft body deformations. It is relatively inexpensive and little information is needed to achieve dynamic surface motion. Vertex caching with texture maps also benefits from not dealing with the extra overhead associated with external serialization.

External Serialization
When the scale of the soft body simulation is too large for octopus skeleton or vertex caching, the last alternative is external serialization. External serialization exports vertex offsets, orientations, and normal changes to external files instead of texture maps. Often the data is stored in JSON format. Custom formats are required when the data needs to be compressed for speed and efficiency. When stored in JSON or other custom formats, the scale of the simulation data is virtually unlimited.

Importing external data into the engine and exposing it to the vertex shader requires programming overhead out of reach for many visual effects artists. Data representing changes to finely detailed soft bodies can be large and special memory handling is required. Memory management is a complicated developer's responsibility.

The visual effects artist needs to discuss with the game's technical director the following questions: How is the data handled when not being utilized? Must the unused data consume valuable storage space? Will the real-time engine divert extra resources for loading the external data before display?

Usage
Off-line solutions for implementing dynamic soft body simulations are fantastic alternatives over real-time techniques. The techniques are relatively inexpensive, and the computational costs of vertex shader deformation are marginal. As these off-line simulations are pre-generated and can be used only during pretentious situations, the technical artist needs to consider the following factors before implementing a real-time solution. When the simulation is used more than once, precautions need to be taken to prevent the participants from identifying repeating patterns. When multiple variations of the same simulations are implemented, is the system able to keep track and store the extra data?

FLUIDS

Due to their implementation challenges, fluid simulations may be the most subjective of all real-time visual effects as they have inspired countless creative strategies. Entire papers and books have been written dedicated to the mathematics and physics behind fluid simulations. Visual effects artists are skilled in their ability to redirect audience attention and divert focus when necessary. Fluid simulations almost always require some sort of redirection to prevent the audience from focusing on the effect.

Visual effects complement their story world. They support and amplify the projected mood. Crashing waves spray water and bind characters to their environments. Unless created to be the visual centerpiece of the scene, visual effects drawing too much attention distract the audience from the gameplay or intended story.

Fluid simulations are no exception from this "Be pretty but don't show off" rule. Fluid simulations draw more resources than most others. Visual effects artists need to discuss this demand with the creative and technical leads. Questions to be considered are:

- "Is the effect's impact on emotion worth the cost in resources?"
- "Will the effect deliver the greatest return on investment?"
- "Are there easier, less expensive implementations of the effect?"
- "Will the added expense of improving the quality of the effect increase sales; directly or indirectly?"
- "Is this a hero shot which demands the audience's full attention?"

The answer to these questions will have a strong impact on implementation strategies. As of the time of this book's writing, there are no pure tools to duplicate fluid behavior in real time. All fluids are simulated by strategies introduced earlier in this chapter: in-material effects, spring-based simulations, and vertex cache deformations. Ray marching is a new addition to this list and is introduced in the Volumetrics section in this chapter. Utilizing these techniques, the following types of fluid effects are considered: static fluid bodies, flowing fluids, splashes, and crashing waves.

Static Fluid Bodies

Bodies of fluid are relatively stable and do not translate overall. They are simulated only on the visible surfaces of large, simplistic geometries, such as parallelograms or flat grids. The shapes are translated vertically to manifest the appearance of tidal shifts or changing volumes due to fluid gain or removal. Modeling fluid geometry to conform with confining boundaries is a challenging task. A simple strategy of allowing the fluid topology to intersect with the surrounding environment works effectively (Figure 6.65).

FIGURE 6.65 Fluid grid intersection of pond geometry.

FIGURE 6.66 Fluid body above and below surface.

When the camera resides beneath the surface of the fluid, the geometric ceiling is simulated instead of the floor. The ceiling moves and displaces as when observed in Figure 6.66. Without light betraying relative camera placement, it is difficult for the audience to identify when simulation is above or beneath the fluid surface.

Non-simulation visual effects are used when the fluid surface is not visible. A post-process may be used to give the world a milky, hue-biased perspective. Clouds of sediment and other particulate matter float randomly, driven by noise functions. Under-water currents are simulated with flow-maps (described later in this chapter), and influence the direction and behavior of particle flow. Light hitting the irregular rippling surfaces creates focusing effects, called "caustics," on opposite surfaces. Like shadows, caustics are generated in the renderer and projected on opposing surfaces. No additional geometry is generated. The irregular appearance of caustics is

FIGURE 6.67 Undersurface caustics.

almost never simulated but approximated with noise functions. Their lack of reference makes them too expensive to truly simulate (Figure 6.67).

In-Material

When given the opportunity, visual effects artists defer to in-material solutions when animating water surfaces. The effects are generated in the vertex shader where vertices are offset, and normal values are re-approximated. The lack of actual deformed geometry makes true normal calculation challenging. Calculus-based techniques, based on surface gradient, help approximate their new values.

Depending on the needs of the simulation, complex geometry is not required. When the fluid is a background element, simple topology is acceptable.

Complex vertex deviation functions are not required either. They may be as simple as a sine wave or as sophisticated as a noise-based simulation. There are countless papers, articles, and books written about realistic fluid materials. When art styles and budgets allow for more sophisticated surface algorithms they should be explored (Figure 6.68).

When audience attention is focused elsewhere, simple and inexpensive fluid surfaces support the look, emotional tone, and feel demanded by the environment. When more attention is drawn to the fluid surface, additional resources and sophisticated algorithms simulate contextual demands.

The significant drawback of using in-material fluid simulations is they do not interact with characters or other objects. Limited amounts of external character data can be channeled to the vertex shader. However, the data's effectiveness is marginal. Depending on the requirements of the situation, the visual effects artist may choose to employ a more interactive type of simulation only in the desired areas of interaction. The surrounding areas may be animated using less interactive techniques. Other in-material effects can be added at the interaction point, on top of the existing surface. For example, when a raindrop hits a fluid surface, it causes a ripple. That ripple can be generated by an in-material function on a separate geometry, such as a sprite, and placed on top of the existing surface. The opacity of the new surface is modulated by its height (Figure 6.69).

FIGURE 6.68 Simple sine and complex noise surface functions.

FIGURE 6.69 Raindrop on fluid surface.

Standing Ripples

The top surfaces of fluid bodies are rarely smooth. Small moving bumps and irregularities break up the continuity and provide high-frequency detail to the surface. A panner-driven, highly detailed normal map is all that is needed to simulate this effect. Textures with high-frequency information work well. The higher frequency of detail exposes controls to the artist to dial in exactly the amount of desired surface irregularity.

A panner function drives the offset of the surface's texture coordinates. Instead, the surface's UV coordinates, absolute world positions (AWPs) of the vertices are used. This allows a single texture to stretch smoothly and move over the entire surface of the fluid. Note that only the horizontal planar coordinates of the surface (X and Y, or X and Z, depending on the vertical axis), are panned. A two-dimensional vector modulates the panner function speed. This vector controls the apparent direction of the movement of the ripples. The panner output is scaled to provide the artist enough freedom to dial in just the right amount of surface detail.

Water ripples appear best when traveling in more than one direction at slightly different speeds. Multiple normal texture samples are combined to provide more natural chaos. As a simple rule of thumb, two samples panning in relatively opposite directions (positive and negative directions), are combined with a third, larger, less detailed sample. The third sample provides the overall ripple direction.

Care must be taken when combining normal map values. The horizontal color channels are summed to provide the direction of the resulting normal. The vertical color channel cannot be combined with this method. Instead, the resulting vertical channel value must be derived from the tangent space provided by the horizontal channels. Many rendering engines provide functions to derive the normal vertical channel from the two horizontal channels. However, when the engine does not provide this function, it can be calculated by taking the square root of one minus the sum of the two squared horizontal channels.

$$\text{Vertical} = \sqrt{1.0 - \left(\text{Horizontal}_1 * \text{Horizontal}_1 + \text{Horizontal}_2 * \text{Horizontal}_2\right)}$$

Equation 6.19 Derivation of the Vertical Channel from the Two Horizontal Channels

Gurstner Waves

Gurstner waves do a great job simulating periodic surface waves. They capture the essence of rolling waves, especially in deep bodies of water, by considering the wave offset and the wave's crest. The full explanation behind this principle is beyond the scope of this text but a simplistic variation of Ben Cloward's technique is provided. Since the vertices of the surface are offset in the vertex shader, the surface may need to be tessellated to provide the required fidelity to pull off a decent-looking wave.

The first component that must be calculated is the inputted normalized wave direction (NWD). Wave directions must be normalized because magnitudes greater than 1.0 produce improper results when multiplied against other components.

$$\text{Normalized Wave Direction (NWD)} = \frac{\left(\text{Direction}_X, \text{Direction}_Y, \text{Direction}_Z\right)}{\sqrt{\left(\text{Direction}_X^2 + \text{Direction}_Y^2 + \text{Direction}_Z^2\right)}}$$

Equation 6.20 Normalized Wave Direction

The adjusted length of the wave is calculated by dividing 2π by the input wavelength.

$$\text{Adjusted Wavelength} = \frac{2\pi}{\text{Wavelength Input}}$$

Equation 6.21 Adjusted Wavelength

The vertex wave angle (VWA), or the angle of the wave against each vertex, is calculated by taking the dot product of the AWP of the vertex and the inputted NWD scaled by the adjusted wavelength (AWL).

$$\text{Vertex Wave Angle} = \text{dot Product}\left(\text{AWP}, \left(\text{NWD}*\text{AWL}\right)\right)$$

Equation 6.22 Vertex Wave Angle

The VWA is adjusted by subtracting the product of time and the square root of the AWL scaled by gravity, 9.8.

Adjusted Wave Angle$(AWA) = VWA - \left(Time * \sqrt{AWL * 9.8}\right)$

Equation 6.23 Adjusted Wave Angle

The vertical offset of the wave is calculated by the cosine of the adjusted wave angle (AWA) and scaled by the desired wave height (WH).

Vertical Wave Offset $(VWO) = (WH) * \cos(AWA)$

Equation 6.24 Vertical Wave Offset

The Gurstner algorithm takes into consideration the crest of the wave. A steepness ratio (SR) is calculated by dividing the inputted steepness by the AWL.

Steepness Ratio $(SR) = \dfrac{Steepness}{AWL}$

Equation 6.25 Steepness Ratio

The steepness value (SV) of the crest is calculated by scaling the sine function of the AWA by the SR and NWD.

Steepness Value $(SV) = SR * NWD * \sin(AWA)$

Equation 6.26 Steepness Value

The final vertex offset is the difference between vertical wave offset (VWO) and the SV.

Final Vertex Offset $= VWO - SV$

Equation 6.27 Final Vertex Offset

The vertices of the Gurstner wave now move as if being pushed by wave forces. However, the look is not yet complete as the vertex normals have not been adjusted. Without adjusting the normals, the offset vertices move but the surface still appears flat. The normals are adjusted in two stages: one for the horizontal offset channels and one for the vertical offsets channel.

The horizontal normal components are taken from the product of the sine function of the AWA, the adjusted wave height (AWH), and the NWD. Only the resulting horizontal components of this product are used.

Horizontal Component$_1 = \sin(AWA) * AWH * NWD_1$

Horizontal Component$_2 = \sin(AWA) * AWH * NWD_2$

Equation 6.28 Gurstner Wave Normal Horizontal Components

Similarly, the vertical normal components are computed from the difference of the product of the cosine function of the AWA and the wave steepness subtracted from 1.0.

Vertical Component = (AWA) * Wave Steepness

Equation 6.29 Gurstner Wave Normal Vertical Component

The vertical component is concatenated with the horizontal components to create a three-dimensional vector normal input.

Ray Marching

The most sophisticated in-material fluid simulation is done using a technique known as "Ray Marching." This technique can only be employed when the fluid is bound by a relatively small, transparent, container, or rigidly bound by the surface's extremes. In this scenario, the fluid is no longer treated as a fluid but a volume. The movements of the volume within the container are controlled by a volumetric simulation in the ray marching algorithm (Figure 6.70).

Ray Marching is introduced in the volumetrics portion of this chapter and explained in detail in *Lighting and Rendering for the Technical Artist*.

Spring Simulations

When the fluid simulation requires more control and interactivity than provided by in-material techniques, spring simulations make good alternatives. Spring simulations are described more thoroughly in real time in the Soft Bodies section of this chapter. Contrary to cloth, ragdoll or other real-time simulation techniques, fluid simulations are relatively stable and less likely to get out of hand.

Limited only by resources controlling available geometry, spring simulations are implemented on large grids. Diagonal edges between adjacent vertices prevent non-planar polygons from occurring during simulation (Figure 6.71).

Because the fluid surface deformation happens in the geometry, the resolution of the grid controls the fidelity of the simulation. When the fluid simulation is a non-dramatic background effect, drawing little to no attention to

FIGURE 6.70 Ray marched fluid simulations.

FIGURE 6.71 Fluid simulation grid layout.

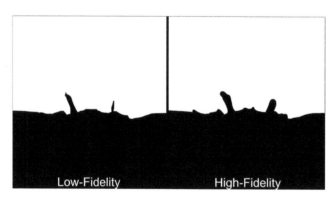

FIGURE 6.72 Low and high-fidelity fluid simulations (silhouettes).

itself, a lower resolution grid may be employed with relatively low performance costs. When the fluid is turgid and consumes large amounts of screen real estate, a higher fidelity grid is required. This is an important factor when considering the fluid's silhouette. The lower resolution fluid will create a jaggier silhouette than a higher fidelity surface (Figure 6.72).

Spring simulations are advantageous when interactivity or fine art direction is required. Specific events are treated as additional forces impacting the state of the spring environment. When external objects hit the surface, they provide extra stimuli to the simulation and are absorbed by the system by treating the events as extra impulse generators.

Vertex Caching

Vertex caching techniques are not useful when dealing with animating large bodies of fluids. The resource limitations of storing the needed vertex and normal information as well as the lengths of their animation clip data make this technique impractical. In-material and spring simulations make for better ambient environments.

Flowing Fluids

Flowing fluids are extensions of the same techniques utilized when working with static fluid bodies. Attempts to simulate the ambient movement of fluids are presented in previous sections: In-Material and Spring Simulations. These presented techniques bring flowing fluid bodies to life. Very rarely are fluids glassy smooth. The techniques in this section push them in specific directions. In-material strategies provide effective simulations with the most amount of artistic control. Spring and particle solutions provide effective flowing simulation especially with stylized fluids.

In-Material

The most effective way to create flowing rivers of fluids is to take a single piece of river geometry and pass texture maps along its surface using panner functions. Regardless of the irregularity of the shape of the river object, it must be textured as if it was a rectangular grid (Figure 6.73).

There are two ways of accomplishing this texture layout. The first technique is to model the river object as a flat rectangular surface. After the texture coordinates have been projected orthogonally onto the surface, the model is pushed and pulled into shape (Figure 6.74).

The second technique is semi-procedural. The fluid surface is shaped into the form of the river but maintains a constant topology of M rows and N columns. A second grid, of M×N dimension, is created with orthogonally projected texture coordinates. Either through a script or editor functionality, the texture coordinates of the second grid are copied to the corresponding vertices on the river object (Figure 6.75).

As input to the flowing fluid material, the artist may choose to place the panner functions on the albedo, normal, or vertex position offset inputs, or any combination of the three. When the ripples are desired to move only along

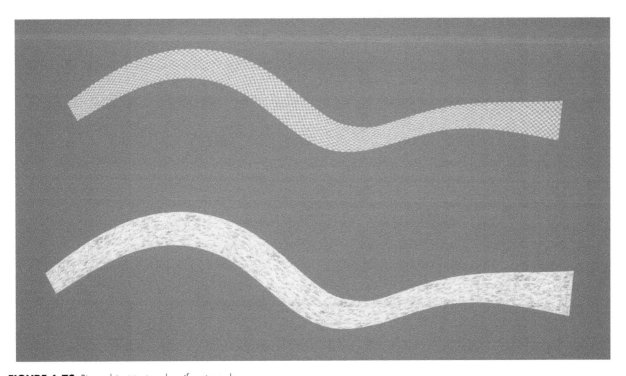

FIGURE 6.73 River object textured as if rectangular.

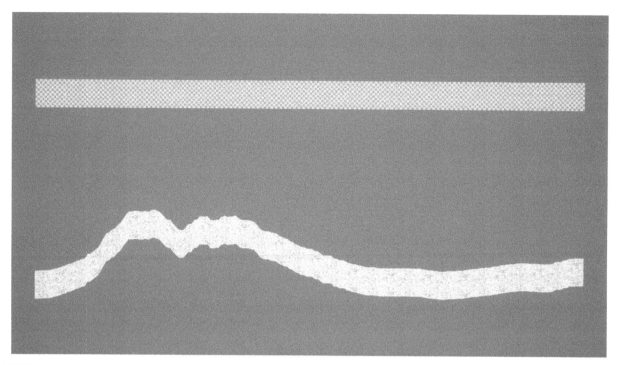

FIGURE 6.74 Rectangular surface deformed to river shape.

FIGURE 6.75 Texture coordinates copied from and M by N grid to a corresponding fluid object.

the stream, animating the normal map coordinates will suffice. When foam, sediment, or any type of cloudy nose texture is desired, animating the albedo map coordinates will deliver the desired results. Gurstner waves appear to move the surface in a vertical direction but do not appear to push the water itself. Use the panner function on the vertex offset to prevent the waves from appearing static.

To add an extra layer of realism to the flowing fluids, blend, or linear interpolate multiple panning textures. Each texture layer should pan in the same major axis direction but at different speeds. Panning along the minor axis in different and often opposite directions delivers a radical contrast in the flowing layers (Figure 6.76).

When linear interpolating, a 50/50 blend will combine two different panned textures evenly. To minimize the apparent difference in the layers, utilize a separate noise texture to modulate the interpolation.

Flow Maps/Vector Flow Fields

The usage of *Flow Maps*, or *Vector Flow Fields*, creates in-material fluids, which flow around static objects such as rocks, pillars, or other obstructions. As texture maps, they are used for deforming the base or emissive material inputs. Numerous techniques are used for generating flow maps. They are procedurally generated from simulation DCCs, such as Houdini, or hand painted using commercial DCCs, such as Substance Painter, or free programs such as *Flow Map Painter*, from TeckArtist (http://teckartist.com/?page_id=107), or *Flow Map Editor*, from Jokerminator Ink. (https://jokerminator.joomla.com/index.php/wiki/2d/flow-map-editor). Bound to two dimensions, flow maps, are displayed as red and green textures and are best visualized with flow lines instead of colors (Figure 6.77).

Since flow maps only adjust the fluid flow in a plane, only two texture channels are used, typically the red and green channels. It is important to flip the direction of the red channel to prevent the fluid from appearing to flow in the opposite direction. Flipping is achieved either in the flow map generator or in the material by subtracting the red channel value from constant value one.

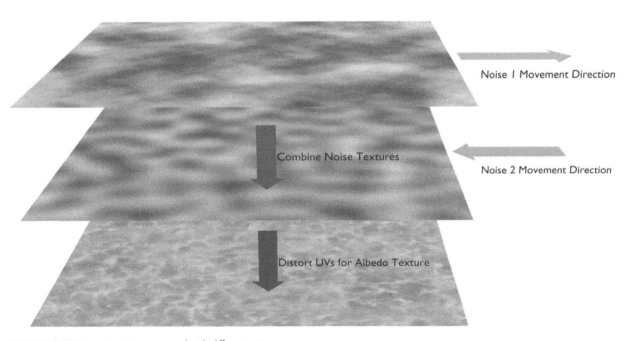

FIGURE 6.76 Layering textures panned with different rates.

FIGURE 6.77 Flow maps visualizes flow lines.

Special consideration must be made when importing the flow map into the engine. When the image is brought in as a normal map, the values will be adjusted automatically between $-1.0 \rightarrow 1.0$ space, minimizing texture compression. Texture compression causes the flows to look staggered and tiered. When not imported as a normal map, the compression should be removed. To remap the image values from $0.0 \rightarrow 1.0$ space to $-1.0 \rightarrow 1.0$ space, both channels are subtracted from constant value one and doubled.

Adjusted Red Channel$(R) = 2 * (1.0 - R)$

Adjusted Green Channel$(G) = 2 * (1.0 - G)$

Equation 6.30 Adjusted Red and Green Flow Map Channels

Once mapped to the correct numerical space, the red and green channels are added to the surface's texture coordinates. The adjusted texture coordinates sample from a noise-based texture map inputted into the material's base or emissive colors. When played, the texture map appears warped, but there is no movement (Figure 6.78).

Engine time is accessed when animating. By default, the time variable is a float value representing engine time in seconds. When time is an integer value, it needs to be converted to a float and divided at least by 100.0. Only the time's fractional amount is desired. The fractional amount starts at 0.0 and increases until hitting 1.0, upon where it resets back to 0.0. It is multiplied against adjusted flow map value before adding to the texture coordinate. The animated fractional time value increases the intensity of the flow map, which gradually warps the sampled noise texture (Figure 6.79).

The animated time value increases the flow map texture offset until its full value of 1.0 is achieved. The fractional time value and the warp amount are reset to 0.0. Resetting the warped texture is visually distracting. When graphed, the amount of flow map distortion looks like a saw-tooth pattern (Figure 6.80).

To remove this visual resetting, the distorted texture map must be linear-interpolated with another distorted texture map, which is 180° out of phase from the first. In other words, 0.5 seconds are added to the second distorted texture value. The second fractional value must be mathematically *Floor*ed to bound the result between $0.0 \rightarrow 1.0$

FIGURE 6.78 Noise-based texture sample.

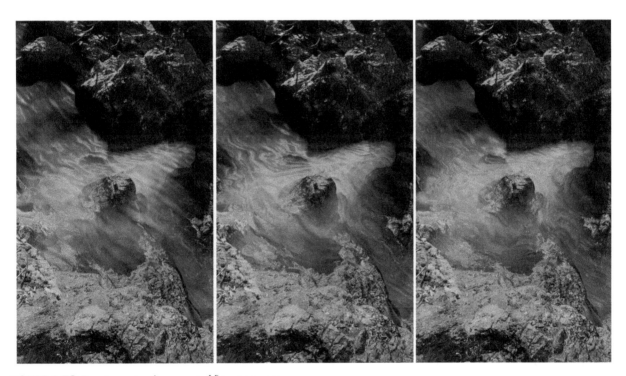

FIGURE 6.79 Time increasing the amount of flow map warp.

instead of 0.5 → 1.5. When the sawtooth pattern of the second distortion is linear interpolated with the first, the amount of distortion is never 0.0 (Figure 6.81).

The linear interpolation of the two out-of-phase noise textures lessens the amount of pulsing but still needs to be improved by modulating the interpolation. A scalar value of 0.5 is subtracted from the fractional value from either of the two phases and scaled by 2.0. This operation on the fractional value shifts it from

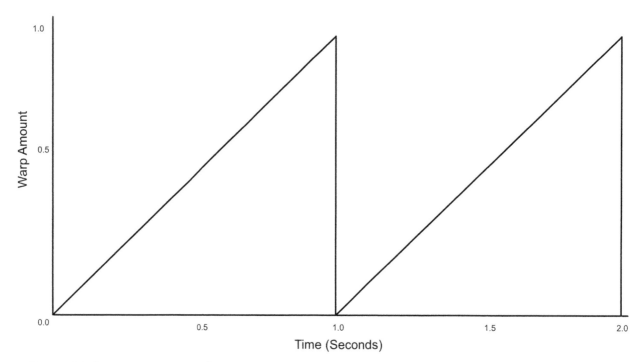

FIGURE 6.80 Flow map amount (saw-tooth pattern).

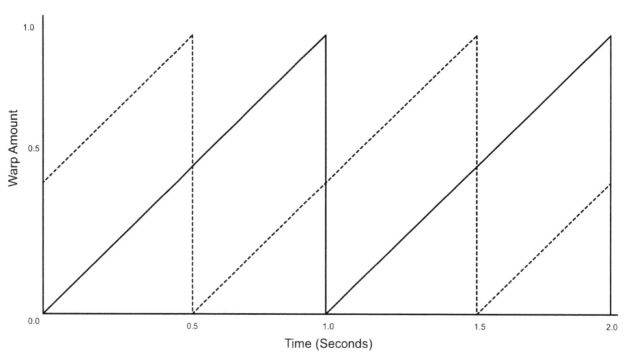

FIGURE 6.81 Combination of two phases of time (two saw-tooth patterns).

$0.0 \rightarrow 1.0$ to $-1.0 \rightarrow 1.0$. Taking the absolute value of this result doubles the rate at which the interpolation happens.

$$\text{Phase 1 Flow} = \text{Noise Texture Sample}\left(\text{Flow Map} * \text{frac}\left(\text{time}\right) + \text{Texture Coordinates}\right)$$

$$\text{Phase 2 Flow} = \text{Noise Texture Sample}\left(\text{Flow Map} * \text{frac}\left(\text{time} + 0.5\right) + \text{Texture Coordinates}\right)$$

$$\text{Interpolated Flow} = \text{lerp}\left(\text{Phase 1, Phase 2, abs}\left(2 * \left(\text{frac}\left(\text{time}\right) - 0.1\right)\right)\right)$$

Equation 6.31 Linear Interpolation of Two Flow Phases

When the pattern still pulses after performing this linear interpolation, noise is added to the time values to further modulate the interpolation. The final interpolated values are integrated with the material's base or emissive colors.

Spring

Spring simulations do not provide decent looking flowing fluid bodies. Because the vertices of the surface geometry are animated by spring behavior, they must eventually be pulled backwards toward their original positions, opposing the intended flowing effect. When the surface geometry is transformed in a rotating loop, like an escalator or a tractor tread, the effect can be pulled off. However, the return on the overhead setup may not justify its expense.

Particles

While particles are effective when animating small objects, they are poor for visualizing flowing fluids. Unless the flowing river is made of sand-like granules, particles just cannot provide the consistent topological coverage afforded by meshes and animated surface materials.

Conversely, inconsistent, irregular particle topologies provide effective cascading fluids and waterfalls. To be more precise, particles are good for modeling the falling components of a waterfall, which transition between upper and lower bodies of fluid. Waterfalls are best when broken into five visual effect components: the upper flowing surface, the falling water, the lower, agitated surface, optional mist or spray, and the lower flowing surface (Figure 6.82).

The upper, flowing body of fluid does not need to transition into the falling fluid. They are separate objects. A particle emitter, placed on the edge of the upper body, emits particles with the same initial velocity as the apparent flow speed of the upper body. The combination of the initial horizontal velocity and gravity realistically animates the particles. Irregular birthing particles prevent inconsistencies from interrupting the visual integrity between the upper surface object and the cascading waterfall.

Upon colliding with the lower body surface, the particles are killed off or made invisible. An animated piece of geometry represents the agitated water. This geometry is driven with noise-driven vertex displacements or another particle emitter. The purpose of this component is to create a visual distraction, preventing the audience from noticing the particles disappearing into the lower surface. As the amount of agitation from the surface matches the volume of falling particles, the audience will be unable to make the visual connection.

Depending on the context and size of the waterfall on screen, the artist may wish to add mist or spray particle components. These extra layers integrate the cascading fluid with the agitated surface. Since the mists and sprays are semi-transparent, they also integrate the waterfall system with the background.

FIGURE 6.82 Components of a waterfall.

The last component of the waterfall is the lower, flowing fluid layer. This layer is slightly below the agitation component and may appear as a continuation of the upper flowing body. This component does not need to have any direct interaction with its adjacent components. The noises and irregularities prevent the audience from making visual connections between animated components.

Some visual effects artists may label this five-step strategy, "cheating" since none of the adjacent components directly drives others. Audiences are challenged identifying the difference between integrated and composite systems. The amount of work required to integrate the components into one working system takes significantly longer to implement and fine tune. When broken into components, each is art-directed to achieve its visual expectation.

Splashes and Splats

Splash and splat visual effects are challenging to implement in real time. They must be animated as viscous, soft bodies, and as particle systems. Unlike cascading fluid simulations, splashes and splats do not have extra layers to distract viewers from noticing visual discontinuities between animated components. There are three techniques for accomplishing this visual effect. The first two strategies, simulation flip-booking and vertex caching, require pre-processing with off-line simulation packages. The third strategy, treating the splat as a simulated volume, is covered in the *Volumetrics* section of this chapter.

Flip-Booking

The easiest strategy for implementing splats and splashes is to treat them as animated flipbooks. While this technique is the simplest, it still requires many steps. As flipbooks, they must be generated in two phases: the off-line simulation phase and the real-time phase. Within the real-time phase, they are broken into three sub-stages: the projectile phase, the particle sprite, and decal phases.

The first step in the off-line phase is to generate a three-dimensional splat using a simulation package. The package may treat the simulation as a particle system or as a volumetric fluid. The look of the final visual effect will dictate how it is created. Implementing a neutral white or grayscale material for the fluid will provide the artist with the greatest freedom to manipulate the final appearance during the real-time stage. The simulation is

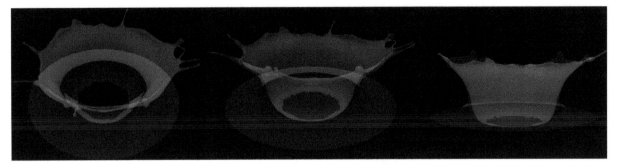

FIGURE 6.83 Higher, lower and orthogonal perspectives.

then rendered with a standard focal length lens camera. The term "standard" is subjective and is meant to include any focal length lens between 35 and 70 mm. When the lens is wider (shorter than 35 mm), the image will start to distort and appear as if in a sphere. When the lens is longer than 70 mm, the image perspective flattens and appears planar. Standard lenses are useful because their DOF is variable. The camera view angle should also approximate the most "common" visual angle. When the effect happens above the audience, the camera should be placed in a lower perspective. When lower than the audience, the perspective should be higher. When the perspective is unknown, the camera angle should be as orthogonal as possible (Figure 6.83).

Neutral white lighting should be used when illuminating and rendering over a black background. The black color will be transparent in the final effect.

Once the simulation is rendered as a sequence of images, they must be composited into a single texture mosaic. For ease of use, the mosaic should be generated from a square number (16, 36, 64, etc.) of images. Please refer to the texture mosaic portion in Chapter 5 of this text for proper texture mosaic creation (Figure 6.84).

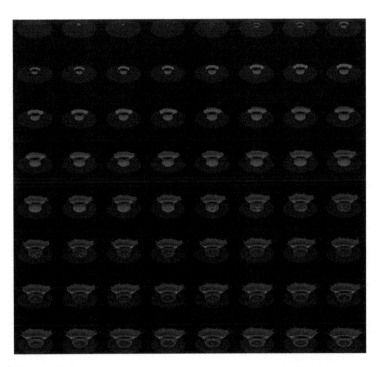

FIGURE 6.84 Splash simulation mosaic.

There are three sub-stages in the real-time phase of the slash and splat visual effect: the projectile, the particle sprite, and the decal phases. Most splashes and splats start as projectiles. Whether they start as a spherical ball of paint, a raindrop or as a tear, a simple static shape is used to represent the effect travelling from its source to the point of collision (Figure 6.85).

Upon colliding with another surface, the projectile object is replaced with at least one particle sprite. Within each sprite, the full texture flipbook is displayed. One is usually all that is required but more may be added to provide subtle amounts of depth. The artist must be careful not to generate too many sprites. The audiences' eyes are sensitive to motion and will quickly identify repeated patterns. The sprites require narrow dispersion and should remain stationary to animate without disruption (Figure 6.86).

FIGURE 6.85 Static splash projectiles.

FIGURE 6.86 Sprite-based splat.

Since the simulations are rendered over a black background, the particle sprites appear transparent except in rendered areas. During this display, the artist has influence over the final presentation of the splash. The particle material adjusts the splashes' final color and tint. Care must be taken to not tax the rendering engine when employing particle sprites. Particle sprites are notorious for driving down frame rate as multiple levels of transparency weigh down performance.

A flat, splat-like decal is used to replace the particle sprite upon completion of its flipbook. Since the perspective of the effect may not be conducive for the decal stage, it is optional. While the splat decal can be hand painted, the best source for the splat is from the original simulation. A texture derived from the last frame of the simulation is used to create the decal. This last frame may need to be re-rendered at a higher resolution or need to be touched-up to function as an effective decal. Within the context of the real-time experience, the decal should fade quickly to prevent perspective inconsistencies from damaging the integrity of the effect.

Vertex Caching

When the perspective demands of the splash effect are more demanding than what a flipbook sprite can provide, vertex caching will be required. The viscous splash vertex cache technique is like the rigid body and soft body techniques presented earlier in this chapter. The relative vertex proximity of the prior techniques remains constant through the entire simulation. The new technique departs from that strategy to allow "clumps" of simulation to stick together, animate, and break apart.

A volumetric simulation to approximate a fluid splash originates in an off-line DCC. Upon calculation of the simulation, the volume is transformed to an animated, polygonal mesh manifold encompassing the defining boundaries of the volume. This polygonal mesh must be triangulated to work properly. The mesh is exported to file as a triangle list, not as a polygonal stream. Exporting the geometry as triangles empowers each to behave as a unique entity. Like other vertex cache techniques, the positions and orientations of the center point of each triangle are written to texture for each frame of the simulation.

The triangulated geometry is imported into the engine as a single collection of small objects. A custom material integrates the texture images storing the polygonal positions and orientations. For each frame of the simulation, the vertex shader reads the position and orientation information for each triangle from the textures. It transforms the texture data from color space to vector space and offsets each triangle according to the imported position and orientation values. Each triangle is animated independently for every frame of the simulation. Groups of triangles animate as units or individual triangles break off on their own tangents. This autonomous/group duality allows the fluid body to behave in a viscous manner: sometimes as a united body and sometimes as individual particles.

Vertex Caching and Splashes

Vertex cache fluid simulations make for great splash and splat visual effects such as paintball splats, water splashes, splashing blood, and other viscous fluids. Three components are needed to achieve these effects: a projectile object, a vertex cache splash simulation, and a splash/splat decal. The three components are displayed sequentially depending on the context of the effect. Because of the rapid execution, component swapping is rarely noticeable.

The visual effect starts in a DCC as a volumetric fluid/splash simulation. An animated, triangle mesh manifold encasing the simulation volume is generated. The triangle mesh is exported as a triangle list and the positions and orientations of the mid-points of each triangle are written out to texture maps for every frame. The triangle list is imported into the engine as a unique object and the textures containing the triangular positions and orientations are integrated within the custom material vertex shader.

The projectile is generated in the engine. Projectile shapes vary from sphere to raindrop. Upon projectile collision with a surface, the transition from projectile to vertex cache simulation happens within a single frame.

FIGURE 6.87 Vertex cache splash simulation.

The transition is not questioned when the material and splash animation match the context of the projectile object. For example, a red paint ball may yield a green splash. When the splash animates and renders like thick, globular paint, few will question the green paint originating from the red ball (Figure 6.87).

Vertex cache simulations animate rapidly. When more splash volume is required, multiple splash objects can be birthed instead of just one. Each instanced object should be offset and oriented slightly by one or two frames. The purpose of the splash object is to distract attention away from the transition of the projectile geometry to the splash decal.

The splash decals are generated from multiple sources. They may be hand-painted in an image painting software. The decal may be generated by rendering the splash simulation directly from the simulation DCC using an orthographic camera: a camera perpendicular to the collision surface of the simulation. Rendering the decal during the last frame of the splash simulation is an extra touch to provide just a bit more visual integrity to the visual effect. The rendered image is manipulated within a digital painting DCC.

The decal texture is projected onto the collision surface upon completion of the vertex cache animation and dissolves over time depending on the context of the game play. Thematically, the decal is the end of the splash simulation and the material color of the simulation, and the decal should be similar. When the contrast between the simulation and the decal is too dramatic, the visual effect loses credibility.

VOLUMETRICS

Volumetrics are the visual effects handling mists, gases, clouds, flames, and vapors. Volumetric effects are the final frontier of visual effects. These effects are the last type to be mastered technologically. In many ways, real-time volumetrics is still in its infancy. The best solutions have yet to be developed. Most existing strategies are approximations already covered in this text. Off-line renderings demonstrate what these effects may look like and provide inspiring real-time targets. The real-time approximations are computationally less expensive but less effective than their true volumetric cousins. However, technology is in the middle of a generational shift in real-time computer graphics. Changes happen daily. Because of advancements in hardware technology and rendering techniques, soon all three-dimensional objects may be treated as volumes.

The Challenge

Computationally, the processing power to calculate volumetric effects is demanding. Instead of computing thousands of pixels, volumetric effects represent the movement and flow of millions of voxels. A voxel is a three-dimensional volume of arbitrary size. A volume composed of a few large voxels will appear coarse and unrefined. The same volume composed of millions of smaller voxels will appear highly detailed and intricate. The simulation algorithms driving the transformations of these voxels is rocket science, once only found on supercomputers. Demand and industry interest have driven these algorithms to become efficient enough to be processed off-line on personal computers. The computational resources driving volumetric simulations are still out of reach of real-time applications.

As most volumes are semi-transparent, the rendering demands of volumetric effects multiply their computational requirements. While any geometry may be decomposed into voxels, opaque objects maintain their manifold geometries and are simulated as rigid and soft bodies. Rendering transparent bodies is expensive. Every visible layer in the scene requires at least one pass through the traditional, rasterizing pipeline. For every semi-transparent object in the foreground, extra passes are required to render objects in the background. Each foreground pass is blended over background passes to achieve the transparent look. Volumetrics cannot be rendered with just a few passes through the pipeline. Hundreds or thousands of passes are required; all of which need to be blended according to their relative distance from the camera. When volumetric simulations are required in a real-time scenario, the development team must be aware of the computational demands. There will be a significant computational performance hit.

As a disclaimer, credit must be given to the mad-genius technical artists, currently in the industry, who are successfully generating interactive, real-time volumetric simulations. What they are achieving is mind-blowing! Effective real-time solutions and strategies do exist. However, these innovations are on the fringe of technology and are still in white-paper phases. These mad-genius technical artists are few and far between. Their strategies are achieved through extremely customized solutions, which have yet to find their way into consumer-friendly tools. Until demand drives engine development teams to integrate such strategies, most visual effects artists must resort to other volumetric approximations described earlier in this chapter.

Strategies

When considering the types of strategies used to simulate volumetric phenomena, the critical question to consider is, "How interactable does the simulation need to be?" Many of the techniques described in this book are achievable in real time when pre-processed off-line. Removing the computational demands of animating the simulation in real time makes most effects achievable. However, when pre-processed off-line, there is little to no opportunity for interaction. When interactivity is a "must-have" for the development team, certain volumetric effects may be unachievable. As of the time of writing this text, the opportunities for real-time, interactable volumetric simulations are limited. In the future, there will be advancements in hardware and tool technology and these effects will become more available.

Particles, Sprites, and Shaded Spheres

When interactivity, art direction, and customization are essential above all else, simple particle behavior is hard to beat. Fires, explosions, smoke, clouds, pyroclastic flow, mists, and sprays are suitable particle applications. Parameters such as quantity, direction, speed, scale, transparency, and age are readily exposed to the artist to be manipulated in real time or animated to react to gameplay stimuli. Under the right circumstances, the visual quality of these effects is very compelling. Be warned, this freedom does come at a price (Figure 6.88).

The volume starts as a simple, in-engine, particle system animated as a fountain, a lumbering mass, or a rolling wave. Once animated, the particles are instanced and rendered as either shaded spheres or sprites. Transparency is controlled during rendering. Depending on the context of the situation, most real-time simulations

FIGURE 6.88 In-engine example of particle volume.

kill their particles at the end-of-life expectancy. Ironically, off-line applications are more sensitive to chronology and do not kill their particles but drop their transparencies to zero. Particle age is used for debugging and tracking visual inconsistencies. Real-time applications do not have this luxury. Allocated memory must be recycled to maintain the consistent flow of particles.

Particles may be instanced as spheres rendered with a simple material composed of a simple material base color and transparency. Both of which are driven by semi-transparent, simple noise-based cloud textures. Variability in the simulation's velocity, scale and age are adjusted to avoid volumetric pattern generation (Figure 6.89).

FIGURE 6.89 Sphere texture.

FIGURE 6.90 Re-projection of light through volumetric particles.

Certain real-time engines have optimized this process to render particle spheres as volumes. Special parameters are exposed to the artist to finely adjust the visual impact of the volume without increasing performance cost. When permitted, 3D volumetric textures are effective driving these particle materials. When interconnected with light objects, the scattering of visible light through the volume is re-projected as extra, interactive light sources (Figure 6.90).

Instancing shaded spheres is effective for clouds, smoke, and smoke trails. However, because of their dependency on transparency, this technique gets expensive quickly. Sprites work very well as an alternative. A sprite is a simple, four-sided polygonal mesh which always faces the camera. Sprites may use the same materials as shaded spheres. Unless special attention is made to dither edge transparency, the side of each sprite will clip its texture and produce edge lines in the volume. To avoid this "grid-like" phenomenon, texture mosaics are used instead of static images. Texture mosaics are described further in Chapter 5. A texture mosaic is a grid of smaller sub-images pre-generated to appear like the simulated phenomenon. Within the material, each sub-image is displayed in sequence over the entire surface, producing a min-flipbook effect. For example, a fire material texture may consist of an animated sequence of 64 frames of a looping fire simulation (Figure 6.91).

Mosaics are attractive since they are extremely customizable, art directable and may originate from anywhere to match the visual style of the experience. They may be hand-drawn (immensely popular in stylized, top-down games), pre-generated using simulation DCCs or captured from real video (Figure 6.92).

The mosaic sequences must be created to loop indefinitely otherwise the sprites will, "pop," upon the conclusion of their sequences. The playbacks of each mosaic must also be uniquely offset for each sprite to avoid generating patterns with adjacent neighbors. The unique movement of each particle, their unique sequence offsets, and their transparencies compound to create faux-volume and credible volumetric simulations.

Instanced sprites and spheres are interactive, make for plausible simulations, but are extremely expensive. Layers of transparencies compound to create multiple draw calls and slow rendering. While sprites reduce the number of transparency layers compared with shaded spheres, they are still expensive. The visual effects artist must be sensitive to generate somewhat, "flattish," particle simulations or use fewer combined systems. The attractive compulsion to allow particles to get "large," to assist with particle transparency, must be avoided. Otherwise, expect a visit from the Technical Director, complaining about the framerate tanking effect.

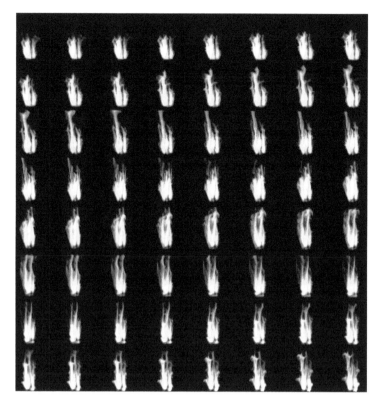

FIGURE 6.91 64 Frame fire mosaic.

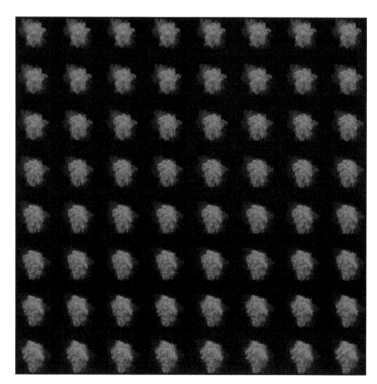

FIGURE 6.92 Stylized smoke mosaics.

Vertex Cache Simulation

When presented with incredibly challenging visual effects, vertex cache simulations are reliable go-to strategies. Volumetric simulations are no exception. In the previous section of this chapter, dealing with splashes and splats, a strategy for vertex cache simulation was introduced to visualize viscous fluid simulations. The workflow transforms a pre-generated, volumetric simulation into a triangle-mesh manifold which is exported to the engine as a triangle list. The position and orientation of each triangle is recorded to a color texture map and integrated with the object material's vertex shader to deform the triangles on a per-frame basis. This exact technique can be used to create fire, explosions, and smoke (Figure 6.93).

The big difference utilizing this strategy for volumetrics instead of viscous fluids is how the triangles are rendered. While the triangle list for viscous fluids may be mostly opaque, the triangles used for fire, gasses, and smoke must be transparent. Unlike sprites and shaded spheres, rendered detail must come from within the material and not be dependent on external textures. Low frequency and large amplitude noises are effective for linear interpolating colors. The Fresnel operator, when available, also contributes extra detail to surface rendering.

Even though this technique simulates the manifold of the simulated phenomenon and not the entire volume, the transparency still makes this effect expensive. While the layers are reduced, rendering multiple, semi-transparent layers is also expensive. Care must be taken to not compound too many of these effects within the same camera framing. Procedural noises are always more expensive than pre-generated textures when simulating turgid surface activity.

While still necessary to keep these effects in check, vertex cache simulations are relatively cheaper than particle alternatives. Being pre-generated, they can be scaled in camera frames yet cost the same as if smaller. One important detraction is that the geometry is composed of thousands of small triangles which appear "spikey." In my humble opinion, I prefer the visual quality of particle simulations compared to vertex cache. The process of generating the caches and integrating them within materials is more involved and complex than the particle materials. They are non-interactive. Visual effects artists may create long cache loops, which hide the repetitive nature of the effects. However, palettes of these effects are essential for dynamically supplying the volumetric needs for an interactive experience. Finally, even though the rendering quality of vertex cache animations has improved significantly, they have not yet achieved photorealism. Their use may be limited to stylistic applications.

FIGURE 6.93 Vertex cache generated fire.

Post-Process

Depending on the functionality of the real-time rendering engine, certain fogs, mists, and other atmospherics can be produced as post-processes. These effects are limited and can only be applied to the scene once it has been rendered. They have no opportunity for interaction. All these effects make use of the depth buffer, a cache of memory recording all pixels' relative distance to the camera. Moving cameras have a direct impact on the intensities of these effects. Using the data from the depth buffer, the post-process modulates the quantity of effect based on distance to the camera relative to a predetermined threshold. There can be no other interactions beyond the relative screen distances from the camera.

Height Fog

The height fog is a depth-based effect simulating the scattering of light through the atmosphere such that the fog effect is denser in lower altitudes of a scene and less dense in higher. The effect utilizes the depth-buffer information in conjunction with user-defined height parameters to control the density levels of the fog as well as the transition rates from dense to sparse (Figure 6.94).

Sky Atmosphere

Sky Atmosphere is a physically based simulation of the scattering effects of light passing through the gasses which surround the planet; also known as the atmosphere. The effect considers the angle of light incoming from a directional light source. The angle has a direct impact on how colors are scattered or absorbed through the particles and molecules in the atmosphere. There are two types of scattering which impact color and depth of the atmosphere: Rayleigh and Mie scattering. Rayleigh scattering takes sun angle into consideration when coloring the atmosphere. When the sun is overhead, blue light scatters more than any of the other colors. When the sun is more perpendicular to the surface, during sunrise and sunset, light travels through the atmosphere further, blue light scatters away before the other colors, leaving reds, oranges, and yellows (Figure 6.95).

Mie scattering considers the impact of dust, pollen, and air pollution, suspended in the atmosphere, upon the clarity of the sky. As particles in the atmosphere increase in density, they occlude more visible light and cause the sky to appear hazy, and generate bright halos in the atmosphere, parallel to the directional light angle. In other words, the atmospheric particles cause the sun disk, or moon disk if at night, to appear hazy depending on their density (Figure 6.96).

FIGURE 6.94 Scene with and without height fog.

FIGURE 6.95 Rayleigh mid-day and sunset scattering.

Light Shafts

Provided that scene already contains a directional light and fog/atmosphere components, light shafts are an inexpensive post-process used to simulate rays of light from the directional light source, aka god rays. Two strategies are used to create this effect. The first technique accesses the depth map information from the scene render. A mask is generated from the map and is blurred away from the light source. The blurred mask is used to occlude the fog/atmosphere layers before being blended back on top of the scene. Since this post-process only generates a mask, the effect is dependent on the visual strength of the fog/atmosphere layers (Figure 6.97).

The second strategy uses brute force to generate a bloom-like effect. The post-process accesses the final color blend, which includes any translucency or fog effects, and isolates those regions surrounding the light source. These regions are blurred and stretched radially away from the light and blended back on top of the scene, much like a light bloom. This strategy is more of a visual trick instead of a simulation, but it is art directable and is not dependent on the density of the fog layer (Figure 6.98).

FIGURE 6.96 Mie sparse and dense scattering effect.

Ray Marching

Ray marching is the most sophisticated topic in this book and one of the most versatile and important topics in the real-time visual effects world. A separate book could be dedicated to just its principles, implementations, and applications. I believe soon it will become a vital component to the fundamental rendering pipeline.

Ray marching is an in-material process. All the magic happens within the shader. There is little polygonal geometry. There are only volumes. How the volumes are rendered dictate their type of phenomenon whether they be static solids, deformable objects, fluids, or other volumetric types such as clouds, fog, mists, or combustions.

This section covers the basics of ray marching, its fundamental strategies, and concepts, followed with utilizations for generating static solids, deformable surfaces, fluids, and other volumetric phenomena. Ray marching is implemented, in most real-time engines, as a black box, transparent to the user, used for driving the most

FIGURE 6.97 Light shafts with occlusion technique.

FIGURE 6.98 Lights shafts with bloom technique.

desirable visual effects. It will take time for ray marching to be implemented within engines with enough exposure to simplify the generation of any volumetric.

Fundamental Strategy
As a disclaimer, the following explanation is an over-simplification of the ray marching process and is intended to introduce only the fundamental concepts of ray marching. Detailed implementation strategies are covered in *Lighting and Rendering for the Technical Artist*. It is, by no means, an adequate coverage of the implementations.

Ray Marching is the combination of three fundamental concepts: constructive solid geometry (CSG), signed distance fields, and the sphere tracing process.

Constructive Solid Geometry

CSG is a technique for modeling complex geometries by performing Boolean operations on simple primitives. Simple primitives are simple, abstract, geometric objects such as boxes, spheres, cylinders, or other parametric surfaces (Figure 6.99).

Simple primitives are combined to create more complex objects using Boolean operations: union, intersection, and difference. Union is the merging of two objects into one. It is equivalent to the local "OR" operation (Figure 6.100).

Intersection is the portion of the geometry common to both primitives. It is equivalent to the logical "AND" operation (Figure 6.101).

Difference is the removal of one object from another. It is equivalent to the logic expression, "A AND NOT B" (Figure 6.102).

In addition to Boolean combinations, standard transformations of translation, rotation, and scale are applied to the objects at any stage of modeling.

FIGURE 6.99 Basic abstract geometries.

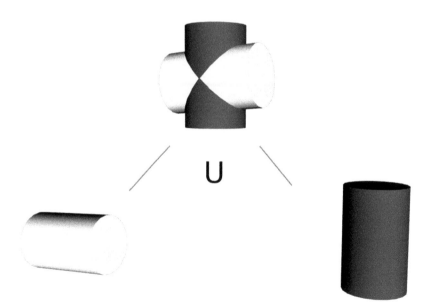

FIGURE 6.100 Union of two objects.

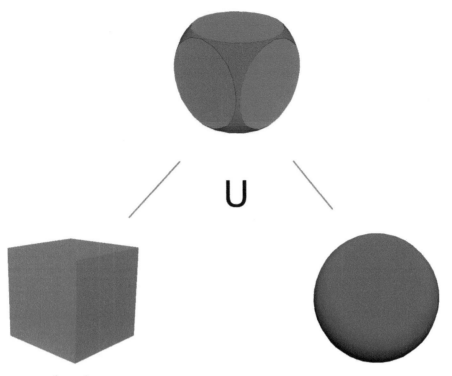

U

FIGURE 6.101 Intersection of two objects.

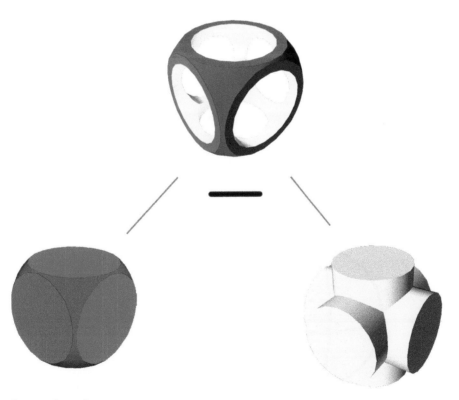

−

FIGURE 6.102 Difference of two objects.

Signed Distance Fields

A signed distance field is a function used to parametrically define a primitive object. The function simply returns the distance between a point and a volume surface. The sign of the returned value indicates if the point is in the volume (a negative value), outside the volume. (a positive value), or on the surface of the volume (value equals zero) (Figure 6.103).

For example, consider a sphere. A sphere is defined parametrically by the function:

$$f(x, y, z) = \sqrt{x^2 + y^2 + z^2} - 1$$

Equation 6.32 Function of a Sphere of Radius = 1

Mathematically, any point can exist inside, outside, or on the surface of the sphere:

Point $A : f(0.0, 0.5, 0.0) = -0.75 \rightarrow$ Inside the Sphere

Point $B : f(1.5, 0.0, 0.0) = 1.25 \rightarrow$ Outside the Sphere

Point $C : (0.0, 0.0, 1.0) = 0.0 \rightarrow$ On Surface of the Sphere

Equation 6.33 Possible Function Results

The implementation of this function is simple:

```
float sphere (float3 point, float radius)
     return length (point) - radius
```
Equation 6.34 Spherical Signed Distance Field Function

Simple Euclidean primitives can be defined by similar signed distance functions. When combined with the concepts of Constructive Solid Geometry, almost any complex geometry can be modeled.

Sphere Tracing

Ray Marching, the simplistic cousin to ray tracing, is a scene sampling technique for rendering volumes defined with signed distance fields. Like ray tracing, rays are cast from the camera, through display positions, into the scene. Unlike ray tracing, instead of stopping on the volume surface, the ray pushes through the object, always returning its signed distance field values. The ray is pushed along its path until its returned value flips from positive to negative or zero or the ray has exceeded a predetermined threshold. The distance of the point at that moment is recorded and used to render the value (Figure 6.104).

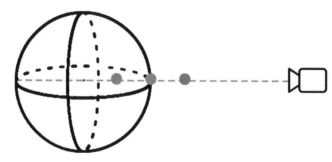

FIGURE 6.103 Possible function results.

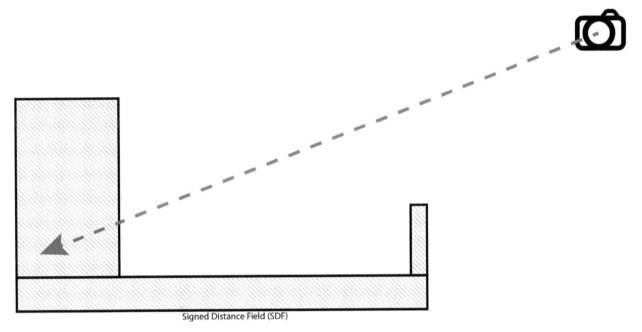

Signed Distance Field (SDF)

FIGURE 6.104 Projected ray marching through a scene.

Because the marching result does not require an exact intersection to render a point, Ray marching can be used in real-time situations unsuitable for Ray Tracing.

Pushing rays through the scene at small increments is expensive. This process is optimized with Sphere Tracing, or by pushing the ray forward at distances equivalent to the distance from the current ray position to the surface defined by the signed distance field. With this strategy, the ray intersects the volume using a few large steps instead of many small (Figure 6.105).

The rays are pushed forward while the signed distance fields return positive values. As soon as the returned value equals zero or is negative, the marching is terminated, and the object is evaluated at that distance. When the progression loop iterates more than a set number of times, the ray fails, and nothing is rendered.

The attributes of the surface influence how the pixels are rendered for each ray position. When transparent objects are encountered, the light color is evaluated at that location and the ray is pushed forward. This sampling continues until the ray intersects an opaque object or the progression meets the predetermined number of iterations. When the surface topology is precise or the volume is composed of transparent noise (such as clouds or smoke), the scene is defined with voxels: cuboid parametric shapes. The smaller, cube-like volumes, procedurally decompose any shape into abstract volumes. The fidelity of the render is determined by the resolution of the voxels. An object, viewed at far distance, can be defined by a relatively few voxels. As the camera moves closer to the object, the same volume is decomposed into a higher density of smaller voxels (Figure 6.106).

Static Solids
Static solids are the simplest ray marching utilizations. Each ray is pushed forward until intersecting the surface, as indicated by the signed distance field. The color of the surface is evaluated at that position and returned. Color attribute is stored as a surface parameter. However, the surface normal cannot be stored in the volume. To resolve this, signed distance field samples are made at exceedingly small increments along the X, Y, and Z axes and the surface gradient at the point of collision is approximated, yielding a normal used for the rendering solution.

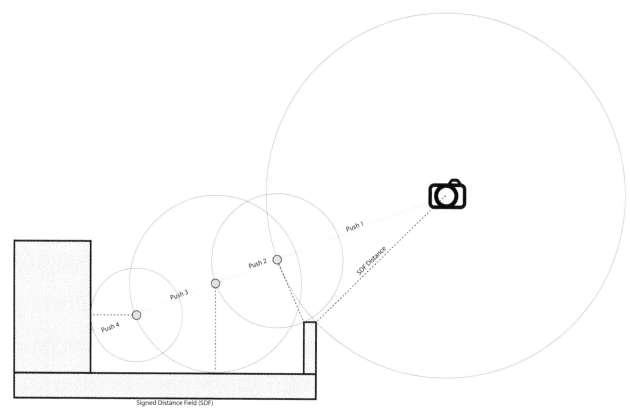

Signed Distance Field (SDF)

FIGURE 6.105 Sphere tracing sampling.

FIGURE 6.106 Object volume decomposed into voxels.

Deformable Surfaces

Deformable surfaces are ray marched as if they were static solids except their signed distance field function is updated on a per frame basis. While compensations must be made when manipulating objects as volumetric shapes instead of lattices of vertices, the simulations driving deformable volumes are the same strategies described throughout this chapter.

Liquids

Ray marching of liquids is performed like deformable surfaces except transparency is taken into consideration. When the fluid is opaque, it is treated as a deformable surface and no other technology is required beyond volumetric fluid simulation. When the object is transparent, a four-step process is required to evaluate the volume. To assist with the volumetric decomposition, fluids are composed of voxels: cube-like, mini-volumes that are stacked and piled to conform to the volumetric representation of the fluid. At the first step, a ray is marched to the surface but does not stop upon collision with the transparent surface. During the second step, the ray samples voxels as it continues its path through the volume. Often, the sampling point is between voxels and the attributes of neighboring voxels are interpolated. In the third step, the colors of each of the sampled points in the volume are calculated. In the final fourth step, starting from the rear to the front, the rendered points are blended to produce a final returned color for that ray.

Volumetric Phenomena

Volumetric Phenomena such as gasses, mists, fogs, and vapors are the most widely used applications for ray marching. At the time of writing of this text, there is no better technology for representing these phenomena, interactively: updating, changing, and conforming with dynamic characteristics in the environment. As a solution for achieving real-time, interactive gases, this technology is still in its infancy.

Like liquids, the forms of the volumes are animated through volumetric simulations. The simulations allow for interactivity with dynamic objects in the environment. When the sampled points are rendered, they are not represented as static colors, as in liquids. The points are sampled from three-dimensional noise fields. Noises are challenging to store in memory and mapping the points' location within the noise is difficult. A solution is the use of three-dimensional noise volume textures. A noise volume texture is a three-dimensional texture composed of sequential stacks of two-dimensional texture images. The two-dimensional images are stored on one, two-dimensional texture image as a texture mosaic. The texture mosaic is cycled through as an animated noise field or as multiple sampled depths of the same static noise (Figure 6.107).

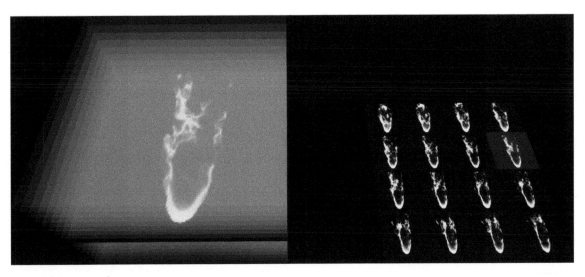

FIGURE 6.107 Noise volume texture.

Modern, real-time engines are now equipped with the ability to author these texture mosaics. Without dedicated tools, the visual effects artist must resort to old school techniques of capturing individual layers of the three-dimensional noise and assembling them into a mosaic using an image manipulation software. Care must be taken when using volume textures as they are memory intensive. For example, achieving visual integrity requires at least a 16×16 mosaic of 256×256-pixel images, translating into a $4,096 \times 4,096$-pixel resolution texture image.

Future Direction of Volumetrics

As of the time of writing this text, the real-time CGI landscape is going through tremendous change. The major game consoles and real-time engines are making generational evolutions. While the growth of hardware technology may be slowing down, the growth of software technology is in hyper-speed. The evolution of real-time ray tracing is an unprecedented event. The AI and deep learning solutions developed for de-noising ray tracing and empowering it to become real time are mind-boggling. Change is happening very rapidly. Keeping abreast of updates is a challenge.

Ray Marching provides real-time solutions for situations inappropriate for Ray Tracing, such as numerically imprecise volumetric phenomena. The combination of Ray Tracing and Ray Marching promises to be a formidable change to traditional rasterization rendering strategies. To satisfy the demands for more robust, real-time solutions, I see this evolution as unavoidable. In the future, all scene descriptions may become volumetric. The days of polygonal meshes may be numbered.

Technical artists need to keep abreast of these changes. The transition from polygonal to volumetric scene representation will have a dramatic impact on the entire art asset pipeline. The technologies for authoring assets and transitioning them to engines will change dramatically. The rendering pipeline will change from the traditional seven-stage process to the new ray-tracing pipeline. This will impact how all visual effects are generated. The best strategy for surviving such change is to understand where the technology has been, observe its current state, and try to anticipate where it is going while maintaining an open mind to the inevitable changes.

CONCLUSION

Simulations are essential components for establishing and maintaining the physical laws of the story world. They are the visual effects that interact with the physics of the world. Nothing roots characters within their physical reality more than interacting them with the natural physics of their environment. Participants feel a strong presence whenever they or their avatars interact with and conform with natural laws of their world. Of all the visual effects covered in this text, simulations are different since they do not necessarily manipulate the rendering pipeline. They may manipulate the mathematical representation of the simulated object. Departing from the rendering pipeline deviates from installed optimizations and increases their computational costs. Simulations can get expensive. There are many creative alternatives to choose from when implementing simulations, all depending on the context of the simulation. Many simulations have little impact on computational performance. The tradeoff is in real-time interactivity: the ability for the simulation to conform with environmental parameters. As a rule of thumb, the more interactive the simulation is, the more computationally expensive it will be.

Rigid body simulations are fundamental applications of Newtonian physics for non-deforming objects. Objects are treated as if they are large particles and do not deal with the added complications of deformations. Rigid body simulations are good for representing any moving object interacting with gravity, collisions, or spring behaviors. Rigid bodies are simulated in a five-stage loop called a physics engine. The physics engine loops once per frame. During each loop, the engine applies all the current relevant forces to the active objects in the scene. Each of the objects' states is updated. All collisions are then accounted for. Constraint parameters for each of the objects are then considered. The results are then displayed. Outside the real-time physics engine, off-line hybrid solutions are available. Within an off-line DCC, a rigid body simulation is pre-generated, such as an explosion or an object falling apart. The simulation is integrated back into the engine, which is played back in real time. The advantage to this technique is sophisticated simulations can be represented in real time.

Soft bodies, or objects that deform when subjected to physical forces, are more complicated than rigid bodies. Not only do the Newtonian physics apply to the objects but they become little environments themselves that move, deform, and change depending on those forces. Cloth, soft-containers, organic surfaces, highly articulated objects, paper, and ragdoll characters are examples of dynamic, deformable objects. Real-time, interactive dynamic surface deformations are handled by dedicated physics engines embedded within the GPU. When unavailable, these deformations must be handled by the CPU. When interactivity of the deformation is non-essential, there are several off-line solutions to pre-process the simulation before being displayed in the real-time environment.

Fluids are treated similarly to dynamic surfaces. Standing bodies of fluid, flowing rivers, splashes, and splats fall into this category. Simulations such as sprays and mists are handled as volumetric objects or as particles. Fluid simulations are not always interactive thus off-line, precalculated solutions are common. Unlike rigid and soft bodies, many fluids are generated in the rendering pipeline.

Volumetrics are the most challenging types of simulation. Implementation requires out-of-the-box thinking. Gases, clouds, fogs, mists, smoke, flames, and vapors fall into this category. Volumetrics represent the last visual effects frontier to tackle when implementing in real time. These simulations are still in the heavy research and development phase. When presented with a volumetric simulation, two-dimensional solutions, such as post-processing, should be considered. While not true volumetric effects, post-process simulations are still effective. There are several particle-based applications that are economical, volumetric, and potentially interactive. Particles are covered in Chapter 7. There are several hybrid solutions where volumetric simulations are pre-processed off-line and integrated back into the rendering pipeline. The most exciting yet challenging volumetric strategy is ray marching. Ray marching, like its more sophisticated cousin, ray tracing, fires rays into volumes and attempts to intersect the environmental volume and visually represent the point of collision. A key ray marching component is the signed distance field that imprecisely identifies collision points of projected rays and a surface. The imprecision of the collision calculation optimizes the process to perform in real time. The potential combination of ray marching and real-time ray tracing may alter how digital objects are represented and rendered in the digital pipeline.

INTRODUCTION

This is the last technical chapter of this book and for good reason. Of all the types of visual effects introduced in this text (lighting, in-camera, in-material, and simulations), particles can be the most involved. They are the aggregate of all the other types of effects and more. They can be light sources. They can be combined in the post-process and manipulated in-camera before display. They are geometric objects and must have material properties to be perceived. They are also simulations using mathematical and physical models for animating reality and rendering natural phenomena. Since particles are a combination of all these other effects, then "Just what are Particles?"

The answer to this question is dependent on who is being asked. The confusion surrounding particles is not found only on the academic level, it exists everywhere real-time computer graphics are found. This chronic confusion is challenging not only as an instructor but also as an employer, mentor, and businessperson. Humans are pattern making machines. We like to place things into categories; into nice, segregated boxes which help communicate and speed the thought process. These categories create confusion as they change depending on who generates them. Different companies have different wants and demands. Team leaders, mentors, and instructors come from different paths of experience and all bring their history into the classifications.

What are the differences between visual effects and particles? Whose responsibility is it to create particles? Do technical artists, visual effects artists, motion graphics artists, or motion designers create them? Don't all these different types of artists use the same tools? Yet they use them in radically different contexts with different attitudes.

The answers to these questions are not easy to define as particles exist under multiple dualities. They are simple and complex. Almost any particle system visual effect can be found as a button preset in any animation DCC. Presets do an excellent job providing at least 80% of the particle system's functionality and require little to no additional input. Yet, the achievement of the other 20% often seems to require a degree in advanced astrophysics. Modern graphical user interfaces empower any artist to deploy basic particle functionality in little to no time.

Particles in any scene are always observable. However, they are not always noticed. In many situations, particles hide in plain sight while in others they are visible, loud, and showy. Many effects require massive creativity while others mimic well understood phenomena. Artists are often expected to design entire particle systems from scratch, and other times are expected to duplicate the designs of the art director.

In all situations, particles are designed and technically intensive. Effective utilization of particles requires understanding of design, composition, layout, perspective, color theory, and animation. While all effects are intended to be seen, they must be done subtly to integrate with their story worlds. Many artists have no desire to be hindered by the technical aspects of their media, desiring to follow pre-established patterns that can be referenced like recipes from a cookbook. Dealing with the technical elements slows and hinders the creative process. From this perspective, the artist is limited only to the exposed functionality of their tool, incapable of maximizing its full potential.

Understanding of the tool's technical aspects frees the artist to maximize the full potential of the media and never be bound only to the tool's exposed functionality. As with any media, there are more applications than there are design patterns. The existing patterns must be reinvented, recirculated, and made fresh for every circumstance. This constant re-invention requires collaboration. The most effective collaborations are driven when participants share a common language, reflect and respect others' strengths and vulnerabilities.

DOI: 10.1201/9781003009795-8

This chapter is written from the technical perspective; directed toward technical artists. It is not the intention of the author to slight or dismiss the creative energies of the designer. The greatest particle artists must master both design and technical aspects. Regretfully, an entire book can be written only addressing particle design patterns. Luckily, the technical aspects of particles fit within a chapter when built upon the principles established prior in this text. This chapter strives to complement particle understanding with all that is necessary to provide a solid foundation for any artist to build particle mastery.

WHAT ARE PARTICLES?

Animatable Points in Space

Minimally, particles are abstract, animatable, points in space. The only information each particle contains is a position, an identification number, and a birth time. Technically, particles do not even need position information. A particle is located at the origin when no position is given. The identification number is an index which differentiates one particle from another. While not essential, a particle's index is an integer or a counting number. Integers consume less memory than floating-point numbers and are easier to maintain. All particles change over time. The essential component for controlling any changes is the particle's time of birth. The time of birth provides an anchor in time from which all other changes are measured. Even when the only state of change is the particle's age, its time is recorded. The number of other attributes assigned to a particle is technically unlimited. However, the minimal three attributes are position, ID, and time of birth.

All particles change. They must animate in some way or another. The particle's birth from nothing to a particle is the minimal change of state. Luckily for us, most particles do more just being birthed. Particles may be given an unlimited number of attributes and every one of the attributes is animatable.

Physics Simulation

Animated particles are nice, but they become more interesting when they are animated within the context of a physics simulation loop. Within the simulation loop, the particles are subjected to the fundamentals of Newton's three laws of motion. The first law states an object in a state of rest stays in a state of rest and an object in motion stays in motion unless acted on by an external force. In other words, a particle will continue doing whatever the particle was doing until another force is applied to it. The second law states that the force of an object is its mass multiplied by its acceleration.

$$Force_{Object} = Mass_{Object} * Acceleration_{Object}$$

Equation 7.1 Newton's Second Law

By default, particles have no mass and no change in position, thus have no acceleration. Animated, moving particles have acceleration. Combined with mass attributes, particles have force which they can apply and receive. Newton's third law states that when two objects apply forces to each other, equal and opposite forces are applied back to the objects. When particle A exerts a force, F_A, on a second particle, B, then B simultaneously exerts an equal and opposite force, F_B, on particle A. $F_A = -F_b$ (Figure 7.1).
This third law states no force can be acted upon a particle without a resulting equal and opposite force. In other words, when forces act upon each other, the net force neither increases nor decreases.

The physics simulation loop is a five-step sequence of repeating events. During the first step, forces are applied to the particles. The particles' states are updated based on Newton's three laws during the second step. All collisions are detected during the third step. In non-particle simulation engines, this can be a computationally expensive process. However, since every particle is a point in space, the computations are simple. The collisions and all other constraints are resolved during the fourth step, obeying Newton's three laws. The results are displayed during the fifth step (Figure 7.2).

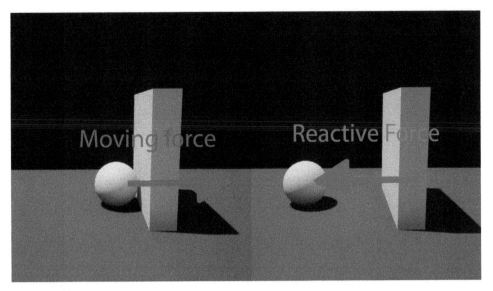

FIGURE 7.1 Newton's third law.

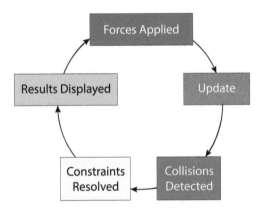

FIGURE 7.2 Particle physics loop.

The simulation loop is essential for particle behavior because it provides opportunity for forces and constraints to be applied to the particles which set them in motion. The simulation loop is similar to the more robust physics engine loop introduced in Chapter 6. Since particles are only points in space, their computational complexities are simplified which enable thousands of particles to be animated concurrently in real time.

CGI Elements

All particles are points in space. Points may have mass and scale attributes. However, points are dimensionless and are unobservable until computer graphic objects are instanced to each particle. In other words, a particle is invisible until something is attached to it. Instanced objects may be as simple as lights or triangles or as complicated as star destroyers. Until the objects are instanced to particles, they have no visual representation. With visual representation, particles become visual effects like all the other effects introduced in this book.

When lights are instanced to particles, the particles become dynamic light sources. They provide light to the environment interactively and diffusely. When a unique light source is instanced to a particle, the light's attributes

FIGURE 7.3 Particle light interacting with the environment.

are animated by the particle and interact with the environment as would the particle. Light and particle interaction integrate characters and other objects to whatever environment surrounds them (Figure 7.3).

When particles operate within a contained system, their average position may be used to instance sedentary lights that provide more consistent, diffuse light to the scene. As a component of the environment, the contributed effect of the system is treated as a stationary light source. A swarm of fireflies provides subtle, diffuse lighting to a dark forest environment (Figure 7.4).

Particles may be instanced with two-dimensional objects. Simple planar shapes such as circles, rectangles, and triangles can be instanced to particles. While these objects have no depth, they do have width, height, and position which change over time. These attributes make the particles excellent masks, mattes, and keys for post-process effects. Whenever a portion of the visible window requires isolation, particles are effective in identifying and manipulating the region of exposure. An example is a simple distortion post-process driven by the colors of particle-driven circles (Figure 7.5).

FIGURE 7.4 Particles diffusely lighting an environment.

Most often, particles are instanced with two-dimensional bitmap streams called sprites. Sprites are special objects as they have access to the pixel shader but ignore most of the rendering pipeline and are written directly to the frame buffer, which means they always face the camera. Facing the camera, regardless of position in 3D space, guarantees maximum particle visual exposure (Figure 7.6).

Particles are also instanced with three-dimensional geometry. Any form of three-dimensional object can be used. As three-dimensional objects, particles require materials and shaders. While particle materials may be constant, they have the potential to exploit the full potential of in-material visual effects. All in-material effects applied to three-dimensional geometry are applicable to instanced particles. Sophisticated particle renderers allow material attributes to be driven by the dynamic particle attributes. Particle-material interactions manifest from positionally driven particle colors all the way to particle-driven, animated characters (Figures 7.7 and 7.8).

Moments to Learn, a Lifetime to Master

Particles may be exceedingly simple, but they also may be infinitely complex. As physical simulations, they may be pre-configured to conform with a plethora of "canned" effects. The term "canned" is a metaphor for cooking. A master chef may start from scratch with every recipe, but a novice can produce similar results when using pre-combined ingredients. The process is similar when dealing with particle visual effects. The big difference with visual effects is the simple ingredients, such as color, size, and transparency, are usually configurable. With canned particle systems and preconfigured materials, a novice visual effects artist can produce excellent results in a relatively short period of time.

Particles are fully customizable. Unlimited numbers of attributes identify the particle states, all of which are animatable. Integrated within physical simulations, particles are subject to unlimited forces and constraints influencing state on a per frame basis. Instanced objects, including lights and sprites, are limited to the band-width of the rendering pipeline. As particles are aggregates of the full rendering pipeline and three-dimensional animation and simulation engines, a visual effects artist could spend an entire career devoted to the mastery of particles and particle effects.

FIGURE 7.5 Particle circles driving distortion.

FIGURE 7.6 Particles as sprites.

FIGURE 7.7 Particle position-driven color.

FIGURE 7.8 Particle-driven animated characters.

PARTICLE USAGE

Particles are tremendously versatile and can be found anywhere within the scene. Without drawing attention to themselves, particles provide life to any environment by contributing ambient motion and breaking the stillness of dead air. They can also demand attention and direct the participants' focus to either themselves or the objects they are complementing. This section lists some of the domains where particle effects are found. The included usages are not exhaustive but merely a sampling demonstrating the possible directions where particles may be used.

Atmospherics

Without drawing direct attention to themselves, particles provide significant contributions for controlling the emotional tone of a scene. Rain not only reinforces negative feelings of sadness but also provokes moments of reflection and cleansing (Figure 7.9).

FIGURE 7.9 Particle rain.

FIGURE 7.10 Particle snow.

Similarly, snow reinforces the seriousness and desperation of a situation but also reinforces moments of serenity and contemplation (Figure 7.10).

Hail is violent and serious. Nothing increases the threat of a situation more than falling, exploding chunks of ice, or steaming balls of fire (Figure 7.11).

Ambient clouds such as dust are difficult to observe consciously. Subconsciously they provide life to the scene and prevent the environment from "looking like a tomb." Computationally inexpensive, particle dust is the default visual effect for enlivening realistic-looking scenes.

FIGURE 7.11 Particle hail.

Basic Simulations

Basic simulations are essential components for any environment. They provide evidence of the natural laws of a story world yet provide familiar anchors from which all experiences draw from. Unlike atmospherics, simulations are intended to be seen and glue the audience to the physicality of the story world.

Fire is the most important, inborn simulation that represents life and safety as well as passionate destruction and waste (Figure 7.12).

Smoke is almost always present with fire. It is fire's precursor as well as its predecessor. Smoke warns of imminent danger or is the telltale evidence of destruction (Figure 7.13).

Steam is a benevolent variation of smoke. Softer and loftier, it reflects the presence of extreme heat (Figure 7.14).

FIGURE 7.12 Particle fire.

FIGURE 7.13 Particle smoke.

FIGURE 7.14 Particle steam.

The prior three simulations are essential physical components of any story world. Their direct relationship with heat requires rendering post-processing to distort the background localized directly within the realm of the simulation. Smoke, steam, and fire are transparent simulations and must be employed by the visual effects artist with care to avoid demanding too much performance from the rendering engine. By default, when investigating poor rendering performance, smoke, steam, and fire are the first culprits to be considered.

Objects falling apart and collapsing are essential components for reflecting the consequences for any decision. Object destruction is animatable by hand; however, a simple particle system interacting with simple Newtonian physics provides a better return on investment. When particle simulations are too computational resource demanding to be created in-engine, other techniques such as vertex caching, described in Chapter 6, are equally as effective (Figure 7.15).

FIGURE 7.15 Particle destruction.

FIGURE 7.16 Particle explosions.

More than just falling apart, explosions combine Newtonian forces with extreme external forces to generate the most dramatic situations. Flying chunks of debris combined with smoke and fire provide the most violent displays when the impact of an explosion needs to be pushed to the extreme (Figure 7.16).

Predictably, the most violent of explosions are also the most computationally expensive. However, since the frequency of explosions is relatively rare, most experiences should be able to withstand the sudden demand for computational resources.

Particle simulations represent extreme consequences of destruction. They can also be used to create events of order and coming together. Because all simulations can be pre-processed, their sequences of events may be displayed backward. Even when presented in reverse order, the same physics forces are still present. Instead of falling apart, objects reassemble themselves. The opportunity for these types of effects is rare. Effects artists should not forget that simulations displayed backward foster opposite emotional responses.

Trails

All particles are birthed but they are not all born at once at the same time. They are born to satisfy the contextual requirements of the effect. Trails are particle systems which birth particle streams for extended periods of time at variable locations. The result is a particle "record" of the particle birth locations and a projection of where future particles will occur.

Beams are not birthed as individual particles but as line lists: sequences of at least two particles connected sequentially by a single line. The beam's material and dynamic behavior provide the effect's narrative context. Beams are excellent for representing linear displays from ray guns to tesla coils (Figure 7.17).

Ribbons are particle breadcrumb trails which record prior particle emitter positions. Like beams, ribbons are rendered as line lists instead of individual particles. They are effective in recording where the emitter has been and give a clear indication of where the emitter is going (Figure 7.18).

FIGURE 7.17 Particle beam.

FIGURE 7.18 Particle ribbons.

FIGURE 7.19 Particle contrails.

When emitter positions are represented by individual particles instead of line lists, they are called contrails. Contrails are particles that create a feeling of being left behind the emitter instead of traveling with it (Figure 7.19).

Simple Crowd Behavior

Part of the magic of particles is that they can not only be used as placeholders for balls of fire but also for organic, three-dimensional objects. When these objects are animated with simple, looping animations, they provide animated life to story worlds, consistent to viewers' subconscious. Subtly, these particle simulations inject natural, ambient life into the world, without being too complicated.

Two-Dimensional Motion

Ground-based life often happens in a plane, or in two dimensions. Ambient herds and packs of animals, foraging across the world's surface, provide excellent background filler (Figure 7.20).

FIGURE 7.20 Particle-generated herd.

FIGURE 7.21 Particle-generated crowd.

Humans are one of the most computationally expensive CGI elements included in any scene. They require enormous amounts of processing power to model, rig, animate, and render. Non-heroic, particle-instanced crowds are an excellent alternative to the traditional character workflow of uniquely animating each character and rendering them as individual objects (Figure 7.21).

Three-Dimensional Motion

Animating ambient motion by hand in two dimensions is difficult. Without the use of particles, animating by hand in three dimensions is almost impossible. Particle work makes this a simple process. Flocking is an example application of three-dimensional particle movement. Three-dimensional flocking motion requires a little precision from a simple, "leader constraint." Detail-wise, the flocking objects tend to be simpler with little geometric complexity. Animation-wise, simple looping animation cycles are all that is needed for every instanced character. While this strategy may be too simple for anything but far-distanced crowds, there is almost no excuse for not including three-dimensional ambient motion any story world.

Birds provide life to any scene. Any establishing shot, inside any story world, appears dead without their inclusion (Figure 7.22).

Like birds, swarms of insects are essential for representing on-coming threats of imminent doom but also provide life hovering around external light sources in night scenes (Figure 7.23).

Fish travel in schools and are very rarely seen swimming on their own. Underwater worlds require schools of fish to provide ambient motion (Figure 7.24).

Other Particulates

The remaining examples are standard types of particles which don't necessarily belong to specific groups but fulfill specific responsibilities.

Fountains

Fountains are perhaps the most common and generic form of particle system. Fountains are a term for any particle system that births a steady flow of particles with initial velocities, allowing the physics of the story world to

FIGURE 7.22 Particle flock of birds.

FIGURE 7.23 Insect swarm.

FIGURE 7.24 School of fish.

FIGURE 7.25 Particle fountains.

animate their behavior. They represent anything from water spraying from a spigot, baseballs kicking out from a pitching machine, or sparks spraying from a metal grinder (Figure 7.25).

Footsteps

Whenever two objects collide, the particles birthed at the point of collision are called footsteps. Footsteps are visual cues for the audience to understand that collisions have occurred and attention should be paid to them. These can range anywhere between the dust clouds birthed when a foot collides with a surface, the kicked-up dirt when the foot leaves the surface, or the sparks given off when two metal objects strike each other (Figure 7.26).

FIGURE 7.26 Particle footsteps.

Grains

Particles take on granular behavior when they stack on top of each other and then spread to conform with the shape of a containing volume. Granular behavior can be computationally expensive and is often simulated with vertex cache techniques (Figure 7.27).

Magic

Magic particles are similar to fountains except the birthed particles' velocities may appear to originate from unseen forces and their animations are not controlled by understood physics. Magic particles are the most stylistic form of particles and provide the artist with the greatest amount of artistic liberty (Figure 7.28).

FIGURE 7.27 Particle grains.

FIGURE 7.28 Particle magic.

FIGURE 7.29 A "no particle" system.

No Particle

The last type of system, what I like to call a "No Particle" system, is where particles are birthed to instance objects that exhibit no simulated behavior. A dome emitting stars is a perfect example. Stars appear to be birthed in random locations and demonstrate no traditional particle behavior (Figure 7.29).

PARTICLE LIFE

Particle life is simple and straightforward. All particles must transition through three states: they are born, they live in a simulation, and they die.

Birth

Particle birth may be the least visually dramatic event in a particle's existence but there is much that needs to happen. Computer memory dedicated to the particle is allocated, its data is initialized and an object is instanced to it.

The time of particle birth is dependent on the context of the simulation. The particle may be born before, during, or after the real-time experience. Particles born before the start of the session are intended to be seen in action from the first visible frame, already fulfilling their original intention. Sufficient pre-simulation, or pre-roll, must happen virtually for the particle to appear natural to the world once the experience starts. "No Particle" type particles are often birthed before the experience starts. A particle's origination source is intended to be observed when the particle is born during the experience. Within this context, the particle's birth event is as visually relevant as the particle itself. Occasionally particles are born after the simulation ends. These are, of course, simulated virtually. These particles are not intended to be seen but used as data references for existing particles. Particles used as guides and as potential collisions must be pre-simulated in order for the current particle to react properly to them.

A particle is a virtual data object and is born when the computer memory for it has been allocated. As long as the memory exists for that particle, the particle is considered alive. Enough memory for the particle is required to store all of the particle's attributes. Attributes are localized variables which configure the particle's behavior and appearance. Upon its birth, all of the particle's attributes are initialized. The three attributes found in all particles are identification, time of birth, and initial position. Visibility is an optional attribute. A particle's life is independent of its visible state. Since all attributes are accounted for during a particle's birth, particles do not gain or lose attributes during their lives. If more or fewer attributes are required, the simulation is stopped, the configurations are adjusted and the simulation is started again.

Being abstract data objects, particles cannot be observed until visible objects are instanced to them. In other words, a CGI object external to the particle must be "glued" to it. That object may be a simple sprite, a two- or three-dimensional mesh, or a light. The selection of CGI object type may be deferred to after particle birth. Initially, nothing may be instanced to the particle. From the perspective of the computer, "nothing" still represents allocated memory but contains no future object's memory location.

Life in Simulation

The life of a particle is dictated by its attributes and by the physics engine driving the simulation. The attributes may be animatable with respect to the particle's life or the time of the simulation. The physics engine controls all other behavior. Just as there are multiple rendering engines, there are multiple physics engines; each with its own behaviors, quirks, and personalities. No two physics engines produce the exact same simulation data.

The most common types of particle physics engines are Newtonian, rigid body simulators. Physics engine software libraries include the Bullet Physics Library, Project Chrono, Open Source Physics, Open Dynamics Engine, PhysX, Box2D, BeamNG, Havok, and Matali Physics. Other than Newtonian RBDs, other types of physics engines include fluid dynamics, waves and acoustics, thermodynamics, electromagnetism, optics, relativity, quantum physics, astrophysics, and geophysics. Before implementing custom variations of these physics engines, the visual effects artist will save considerable time utilizing pre-created, physics API libraries.

Death

All particles must die. It is important to remember a particle's life is represented by the memory allocated for it and not by its visible state. When a particle dies, the memory allocated for the particle is returned to the computer. Whether this happens when the experience terminates or during execution, particles no longer exist when their memory becomes available for other uses, including recycling as future particles. During any simulation, there may be particles which are not in a visible state but still alive.

The particle's identification and birthdate attributes are used for calculating the particle's age as well as anchoring recorded events during the particle's life. This data is essential for refining, debugging particle behavior, and for providing reference for future particle events. The particle's identification and birthdate are essential for mapping a particle's history.

When considering future availability of relevant particle attribute data, the choice to kill a particle is a very important decision the visual effects artist will need to make. Factors such as real-time performance, resource allocation, and visual context must be considered. Can real-time experiences afford to keep old particles for reference? Does the need for displaying massive amounts of particles outweigh the need to maintain visual integrity of the system?

Here is a rule-of-thumb to follow when considering particle mortality. When the simulation is off-line, never kill particles. Their demand for resources is understood and can be balanced accordingly. When unlimited resources are available, there is no need to sacrifice potential visual integrity. However, when a particle simulation is executed in real-time, kill the particle as soon as it is no longer relevant. Memory is the most valuable resource in a real-time situation and must be conserved at all costs. The constant thirst for memory far outweighs the sacrifice of potential visual integrity.

PARTICLE SYSTEMS

The deployment of particles in a real-time experience is done through a particle system. A particle system is treated as an engine object and is composed of attributes and layers.

Engine Objects

Entire particle systems are represented as unique, real-time engine objects. All components contributing to a specific particle system must be encapsulated within a single-engine object. For example, all of the components contributing to a specific magical spell effect, or all of the components contributing to the contrails of a rocket ship, are encapsulated within single-particle system objects. Treating particle systems as engine objects promotes easy duplication, simple repurposing, and manageable maintenance. Without being contained within unique engine objects, particle systems would be unmanageable.

Like particles themselves, particle system objects are born, are functional, and must die. As with all other real-time engine objects, all particle system objects are born at the start of the experience. They remain alive throughout the existence of the experience and are terminated with the end of the application. Whether or not the system object is active or, producing particles is dependent on the context of the particle system. Its fundamental memory allocation used to be an important consideration with older generations of real-time experiences. However, advancements in technology have lessened the performance impact of dormant particle systems. The visual effects artist must be cognizant of the performance impact of multiple active systems.

Attributes

Attributes are the individual parameters used to configure each particle system. Every system is composed of hundreds of attributes. Each attribute is highly customizable and allows for an infinite number of variations and possibilities. Depending on the nature of the attribute, it may be of any data type: integer, floating-point, vector, gradient, ramp, or texture. While there are infinite ways of configuring attribute data, there are only two types of attributes: static and dynamic.

Static Attributes

Static attributes stay constant over time. They do not change. They are configured during the birth of the particle system and do not alter over the course of the entire system's existence. Constant attributes are set by the visual effects artist and are the most art directable. Since they do not change, these attributes contribute to the core look and feel of the system. Certain attributes are set randomly and allow the computer to define the constant values. Random attribute functions return values within specific ranges and must be configured to produce desirable distributions. For example, suppose the base color for a particle system needs to be random values of magenta and the random function only returns values between 0.0 and 1.0. The configuration of base color attribute could be configured with the following expression:

$$\text{Base Color} = \left(0.5 + 0.5 * \text{random}(), \; 0.1 * \text{random}(), \; 0.5 + 0.5 * \text{random}()\right)$$

Equation 7.2 Random Magenta Attribute

The interfaces for setting constant attributes are different for every engine and should always empower precise manipulation of random distribution. In addition to randomness, every engine should provide other functions to promote relative attribute distribution. Relative distributions may be configured to reflect the current state of any environment. For example, suppose the rate of particles birthed from a cone-shaped object starts small at the top of the cone and increases continuously to the bottom. Assuming the *Bounding Box* function returns values between 0.0 and 1.0, relative to the position of the base of an object, the particle birth rate attribute expression looks like:

Particle Birth Rate = Constant Birth Scale Value * Bounding Box Height (cone)

Equation 7.3 Relative Birth Rate Distribution

While constant parameters never change over the life of the particle system, random and relative functionality adds life and uncertainty to the system.

Dynamic Attributes

Dynamic attributes change over time or are animated. They may be manipulated by keyframed animation, expressions, or by code. For every frame of the particle system's existence, every dynamic attribute is evaluated even when not active. As with all computer-animated parameters, the manipulation of dynamic attributes is a collaboration of visual effects artists and the computer. All are configured by the artist and are evaluated on a per-frame basis by the computer. The results of the evaluation are set relative to the context of the visual effect. The format of the dynamic data is dependent on the interface of the engine. Attributes may be manipulated via animation curves, expressions, or ramps, based on one specific changing attribute such as system time, particle life, or any other possible parameter (Figures 7.30 and 7.31).

Many attributes are set relative to the absolute system time of the experience. For example, an erupting volcano may spit out embers and ash over the entire duration of the experience. A behavior may be set on a clock such that a tower emits fireworks on the top of every hour. An event may also be tied to a specific time according to the narrative of the environment, such as flood generating, torrential downpours, 3 hours into the experience.

Most animated attributes are set relative to the life of the particle which is crucially dependent on the particle's age. For example, suppose the base color of a particle system starts with a greenish color and fades to a reddish color over the life of the particle as the particle life attributes progress from 0.0 to 1.0. The animated attribute looks like:

Base Color = lerp $\big((0.0,\ \text{random}(),\ 0.0),\ (\text{random}(),\ 0.0,\ 0.0),\ \text{particle life}\big)$

Equation 7.4 Particle Base Color Relative to Particle Life

FIGURE 7.30 Particle size curve controlled by particle life.

FIGURE 7.31 Particle initial speed ramp dependent on distance traveled.

Other attributes are set dynamically relative to certain events happening during the execution of the experience. Event-driven attributes are similar to system time-driven attributes except the conditions are variable instead of based on the progression of the system clock. For example, a bomb may not explode until a character penetrates the bomb object's bounding box, or the particle emitter disengages 2 minutes after activation.

Layers

Particle systems contain at least one and possibly multiple layers. Particle systems are aggregates of all contributing layers. A particle system layer is a collection of all of the components required to generate one specific particle effect. For example, one of my students reverse-engineered the Ragnarok effect from the *Kingdom Hearts* game and duplicated 26 unique particle layers contributing to this total effect.

Layers contributing to a particle system do not necessarily need to be visible at all times and should be animated relative to the life of the effect. Depending on the robustness of the real-time engine, components from one layer may influence the components in another layer. Every layer is composed of three components: an emitter, particles, and forces.

Emitters

Emitters provide geometric locations from which particles are born. A particle must be birthed from an emitter. Even when an emitter only births one particle which does nothing over the duration of the experience, the emitter is still required.

Emitter Types

Point Emitter An emitter may be a point in space, a line, a polygon, a 3D mesh, a volume, a skeleton joint, another particle, or a light object. A point in space provides the three-dimensional coordinates from where particles are birthed. Single points are precise locations of particle birth when they are invisible (Figure 7.32).

Line Emitter Lines are used as emitters. The distribution over the line from which a particle is born is a configurable attribute. Particles are born at random points along the line or sequentially along its axis. Curved lines are used as emitters as well. Rain dripping from roof edges is an example of the use of line emitters (Figure 7.33).

FIGURE 7.32 Point emitter.

FIGURE 7.33 Nurbs curve emitter.

Polygon Emitter Instead of a single point or line, polygons provide a surface area from which particles are born. Like lines, birthing points are randomly distributed over the surface area or along two of the polygon's axis. Polygonal emitters are typically triangles but may be rectangles, circles, or any other type of n-gon (Figure 7.34).

Mesh Emitter Three-dimensional meshes are collections of polygons from which particles are birthed. It is important to remember particles are birthed from the skin surface of the mesh and not from within its internal volume. As with lines and polygons, mesh birthing distribution is configurable (Figure 7.35).

Volume Emitter Volume emitters are like three-dimensional mesh emitters except particles may be birthed from within the object instead of from its surface skin. The visual difference between the two is slight as the particles from the volume emitter seem slightly deeper or fuller within the three-dimensional space. The extra detail of

FIGURE 7.34 Polygonal emitter.

FIGURE 7.35 3D mesh emitter.

volumetric birthing distribution is available when the simulation can afford the extra memory required for the volume (Figure 7.36).

Single Point Variations

Joints and other particles are variations of single-point emitters. Joints are essential emitters for creating stylized streaks and trails. Other particles are used to birth more particles when collisions or similar events happen relative to the particle's life (Figure 7.37).

Lights may be used as emitters as well. They are configured as points in space, polygons, meshes, or volume emitters.

FIGURE 7.36 Volume emitter.

FIGURE 7.37 Joint emitter.

Emitter Attributes

Emitters, like particles, are configured with attributes. An emitter's position, orientation, and spawn rate are its most important attributes. The position and orientation are set during the context of the experience and through pre-animated channels. The spawn rate attribute controls the rate at which the emitter births particles. There are two types of spawn rate: stream and burst. Stream causes the emitter to birth particles at a steady, consistent rate. This value may change over the life of the emitter. Emitters are assumed to be constantly streaming over their lifetimes. Burst spawn rates only birth particles during a finite period of time. The time windows may be as short as a single frame. Unless bursts are event-driven, no further birthing is expected from the emitter. Burst start times may be offset from a specific time or event triggered. Long burst times and very slow streaming rates may appear to overlap within the context of the experience. The visual effect artist is encouraged to treat stream and burst emitters separately. Maintenance and debugging are made easier when the emitters are tagged uniquely.

Emitters are often visible objects with their own visual attributes. By default, geometric and visual attributes are passed from the parent emitter to the child particles. Particles often inherit their initial velocity and orientation from their parent emitter. As with any hierarchical system, child particles may choose to ignore or override their inherited attributes. Inheritance ensures visual consistency passing from the parent emitter to the particle children.

Particles

Within the computational core of a particle system, particles are memory chunks storing all particle attributes. Ironically, while being the hero components of a system, particles are its most passive elements. They are governed strictly by their attributes and are manipulated by the forces of the system simulation. A particle's only responsibilities are to maintain its attributes and provide a reference position for some other object to be displayed.

A particle's most important attributes are its identification, its birthtime, its position, and its object reference. A particle's identification is an index (integer) to the block of memory storing all the particles of a system. In special circumstances, they are stored as floating-point values or strings keyed to hash table memory buckets. The particle's birth time is the system time at which the particle was born. It is the basis for calculating a particle's age which is essential for interpreting the particle's state at any point along its timeline. An object reference is a link to an external object providing the visual representation for the particle. Without the reference object, the particle is not visible.

A particle's default position is the origin. When updated, position stores its location within three-dimensional world space.

Particle Attributes
Aside from identification, birthtime, object reference, and position, a particle may possess an unlimited number of other attributes. The other attributes configure the particle's behavior within the simulation and provide crucial input required to render the referenced object. The attributes listed below are the most common attributes a visual effects artist may encounter.

Render Type
Render type indicates how the particle is to be represented. This is optional since the particle does not have to be visualized. There are four types of renderable objects: sprites, meshes, ribbons, and lights. Sprites are abstract bitmap streams. Because they are written directly to the frame buffer, they must face the camera. There are two kinds of sprites: CPU and GPU sprites. CPU sprites are generated on the CPU and have the greatest amount of customizable behavior. GPU sprites are generated on the GPU and have a limited amount of customization. The maximum number of sprites birthed from the dedicated GPU may be many times greater than the number supported by the CPU. A mesh is any renderable, two- or three-dimensional object. Unlike sprites, they must maintain their own orientation. Ribbons are rendered as lines between points and are used for streaks, trails, beams, rays, and lightning. Lights are illumination generating objects. Special care must be dedicated when referencing lights onto particles. Lights can be very expensive, especially when projecting shadows. Whenever the real-time performance of the simulation decreases dramatically, light emitting particle systems are common culprits.

Lifetime
Particle Lifetime attributes are important for controlling particle life expectancy. By default, particles' lifetimes are infinite and live forever, or until the end of the simulation.

Velocity
Particle Velocity attributes direct particle magnitude and direction of travel. When establishing the direction of particle travel, the velocity attribute may or may not control the referenced object orientation (Figure 7.38).

FIGURE 7.38 Particle velocity.

Acceleration

Particle Acceleration controls the rate at which a particle's velocity increases or decreases. When force, $(F_s = -\mu_s * F_n)$, is not provided, acceleration is computed from its velocity attribute. When present, acceleration overrides and drives the velocity through the simulation.

Rotation

Rotation, like velocity, is a direction and a magnitude controlling rotational change over time. The direction of rotation is independent of the particle's velocity.

Normal

A Normal Vector attribute is often used for establishing particle orientation. This information is inherited from a particle's emitter.

Scale

The *Scale* attribute controls the instanced object's visual size. This value may be constant or animated.

Color

Color attribute influences the visual color of the instanced object. This value may be a constant value, animated, inherited from its emitter, or set during the particle render.

Texture Coordinates

Particle Texture Coordinates or UV attributes contain texture map reference information. The coordinate values may be inherited from the particle's emitter, or directly manipulated.

Visibility

The Visibility attribute dictates if a particle is visible or not. Not related to the particle's age, a particle's visibility may toggle repeatedly over its lifetime.

Opacity

Opacity controls the transparency of the particle's referenced object. Opacity plays a similar role to particle visibility.

Mass

Mass directly influences how particles interact with applied forces during simulation. This attribute is essential for evaluating Newton's second law:

$$Force_{Object} = Mass_{Object} * Acceleration_{Object}$$

Equation 7.5 Newton's Second Law

Friction

Friction attribute contributes to the particle coefficient of friction which influences the forces preventing particle motion or inhibiting particle sliding on the surface of another object. Coefficients of friction are unique for different materials and can be found on-line.

$$Friction = -Friction\ Coefficient * Normal\ Force$$

Equation 7.6 Force Due to Coefficient of Friction

Drag

Particle Drag attribute is a dimensionless number which influences the amount of force slowing particle movement when traveling through air or water.

Spring

Particle Spring manipulates the forces particles push back when linearly displaced, staying consistent with Hooke's Law.

$$Force_{Push\ Back} = -Constant_{Spring} * Vector_{Displacement}$$

Equation 7.7 Hooke's Law

Damping Ratio

Particle damping or Damping Ratio controls the rate at which particles return to their initial state when subjected to spring forces. A damping ratio of zero indicates infinite particle oscillation. A value of one indicates return to the initial state with no oscillation in the most efficient way possible. Values greater than 1 take longer to return to the initial state.

Resilience

As particles bounce, the Resilience attribute controls the amount of energy it absorbs, loses, or gains during collision, affecting subsequent particle velocity (Figure 7.39).

Affinity

Beyond the force of gravity, the particle Affinity attribute directs the attraction or repulsion of particles with other particles (Figure 7.40).

Forces

Forces are the catalysts for change within a particle simulation. They are the agitators and the equalizers. They make things happen. When particles are born, all of their attributes are inherited from their emitter parent or assigned by default during their creation. According to Newton's first law, an object at rest tends to stay at rest, or an object in motion tends to stay in motion unless acted upon by an external force. Forces interact with particles and bring them to life. Particles maintain their state until forces are acted upon them. They don't change unless interacting with forces. Forces drive the particle simulations to achieve equilibrium.

FIGURE 7.39 Negative and positive resilience.

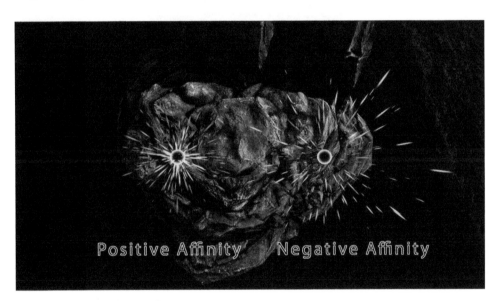

FIGURE 7.40 Positive and negative particle affinity.

Traditionally, visual effects artists are more likely to modify material attributes before employing forces to mimic natural phenomena. The artist has greater control over the particle when the physical principles over the available forces not understood. Good visual effects artists may not have degrees in college-level physics but will benefit by developing a good sense for physical motion in order to replicate natural phenomena with particles. The fundamental simulation forces are described in Chapter 6. The forces listed in this chapter are extra forces artists may inject into a particle simulation to guide and direct particle behavior to satisfy its narrative objective.

Gravity

Gravity is the force of one object with mass pulling at another object with mass. Objects with greater mass experience greater pull from gravity. Within particle systems, gravity is the force that pulls all objects toward the game

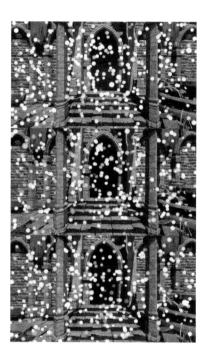

FIGURE 7.41 Pure random forces.

world's center of mass. The direction and magnitude of force of gravity change to satisfy the story world's narrative and gameplay. By default, gravity is:

$$\text{Force}_{\text{Gravity}} = 9.8\,\frac{m}{\text{seconds}^2}$$

Randomness, Noise, and Turbulence
Randomness, noise, and turbulence are irregular forces generating unpredictable behavior within a particle simulation. These forces manifest themselves as winds and other natural phenomena which are visually challenging to trace.

Random force is pure and wild. Changes in direction and amount are unpredictable. Randomness is difficult to work with as the results are too unpredictable and are difficult to art direct (Figure 7.41).

Noise and turbulence simulate the random forces that occur in nature. They are better behaved and are more art directable than randomness. They are fractal in nature and exhibit self-similarity. The direction and magnitude of noise force are in constant unpredictable change but the amount of change is related to the change of the prior frame. The changes appear to flow (Figure 7.42).

Turbulence is a type of noise force which generates deeper valleys and sharper peaks.

While challenging to achieve, the most natural looking particle simulations contain three octaves of noise. The first octave has a large magnitude and a relatively small frequency. It is populated with the second octave with a smaller magnitude and higher frequency. The third octave populates the second with the smallest magnitude and the highest frequency. A metaphor of this three-octave structure is a finely detailed world map. The first octave structure contains continental landmasses. The second octave contains the interior structure of the continents comprising mountain ranges, plains, and prairies. The third octave provides the hills and valleys of the second octave (Figure 7.43).

FIGURE 7.42 Noise forces.

FIGURE 7.43 Three octave noise.

Flow Maps and Vector Fields

Like art-directable noise, two-dimensional flow maps and three-dimensional vector fields are regions and pockets of guidable forces. They are used for providing current-flow behavior that appears somewhat random with traceable patterns. Examples include rivers and strong winds flowing around natural objects and barriers. Flow maps are defined with two-dimensional texture maps and vector fields with three-dimensional volumes. They provide art-directable, directional navigation for particles with subtle elements of randomness. Both interact with pre-existing terrain to create lines of force which curve and wrap around environmental topology. Flow maps are relatively simple and can be hand painted. Vector fields require pre-processing from sophisticated simulation tools (Figures 7.44 and 7.45).

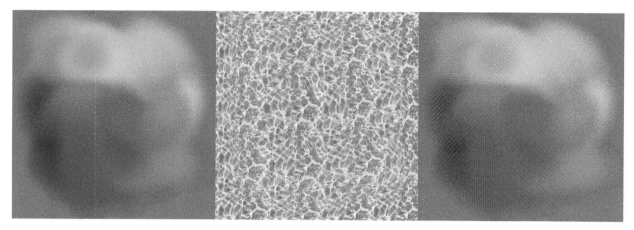

FIGURE 7.44 Two-dimensional flow map.

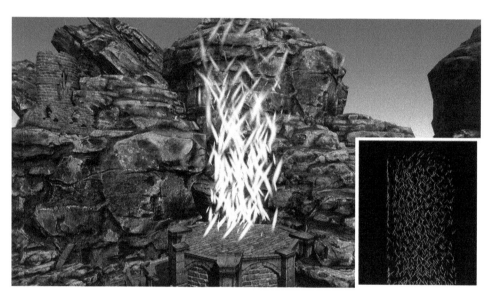

FIGURE 7.45 Three-dimensional vector fields.

Vortices

Vortices are volumetric forces which push particles along curved paths. Most forces are vector-based and have linear directions. Three-dimensional curved behavior is nearly impossible to generate without vortices. Radius and magnitude vortex attributes exert particle angular momentum (Figure 7.46).

Friction

Friction is a constant force impeding particles from moving when in contact with surfaces or slowing when actively sliding on other surfaces. Friction forces act in the opposite direction as pushing forces attempting to move particles or opposite to particles' directions of movement. Particles' coefficients of friction configure the forces required to set particles in motion or the speeds at which they come to a stop. Coefficients of friction can be found on-line and are unique for every pair of materials.

Friction Force = −Friction Coefficient * Normal Force

Equation 7.8 Friction Force

FIGURE 7.46 Particles in a vortex.

FIGURE 7.47 Force of impact and force of reflection.

Drag

Drag is the force which slows particles when traveling through liquid or air. Non-particle simulations consider object shape when calculating drag. Since particles have no shape, their drag attributes are used to calculate drag force. Drag forces generate *ease-like* behavior as they reduce particle motion to zero.

Collision

Collision forces are the resulting forces acting upon a particle after collision. According to Newton's third law, for every action there is an equal and opposite reaction. When particles collide against surfaces, they reflect along their reflection directions with the same incoming forces (Figure 7.47).

FIGURE 7.48 Particles pulled toward lead particle.

Flocking

During a crowd or flocking simulation, the flocking forces pull particles toward a leader particle. Each particle's behavior is regulated by its affinity attribute which increases or decreases the pulling force toward its leader. Minimal distance forces prevent the particles from colliding during the simulation (Figure 7.48).

VISUALIZATION

Particles are points in space. They are blocks of memory storing the particles' attributes. They occupy no volume or space. Particles are invisible.

Instanced Objects

In order to visualize or render a particle, a light emitting object, a bitmap stream or a three-dimensional object must be instanced to the particle. Once the object has been instanced to the particle, the computer renders the object and not the particle. There are three types of objects instanced to particles: sprites, geometry, and lights.

Sprites

Sprites are flat, computationally inexpensive, two-dimensional bitmap streams referenced to particles such that they always face the camera. Since they are inexpensive, many more of them can be rendered at the same time than if they were three-dimensional objects. The streams are very art-directable which make them accommodating for any situation.

In the early days of computer graphics, they were two-dimensional bitmaps (two-dimensional arrays) that were written directly to the frame buffer without layering overhead. In modern, three-dimensional real-time graphics, sprites are two-dimensional, color images which always face the camera and have transparency and alpha information. The transparency channel allows them to blend and layer with the other three-dimensional objects in the scene. They may be generated on the CPU or GPU. When created on the GPU they have no alpha information and are treated as primitive quads; billboard quads are made of two texture-mapped triangles (Figure 7.49).

While GPU sprites don't have the advantage of the alpha channel, their orientation can be changed and many more can be rendered at one time than when generated on the CPU. GPU sprites are typically used for generating small debris from explosions and do not require high-quality expensive rendering information.

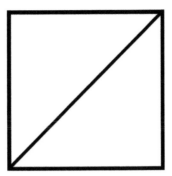

FIGURE 7.49 Billboard Quad sprite.

FIGURE 7.50 Gradient circle.

Sprite content is generated directly from the material shader as simple two-dimensional shapes such as solids, lines, or circles. A gradient circle to produces a false appearance of depth (Figure 7.50).

Static and animated texture maps are commonly used for particle sprites. Static textures are used for representing specific shapes like projectiles (Figure 7.51).

Executed as texture mosaics, animated textures are used to give the resemblance of glowing, natural phenomena such as smoke and fire (Figure 7.52).

The sprite's alpha channel not only allows them to blend with their backgrounds but also with other particle sprites. Many particle systems are a composite of multiple particles, contributing to make one effect. For example, each particle of magic fairy dust is actually a composite of three particles: a large, gradient circle to produce the glow, a smaller, brighter circle to provide the hot core, and a star made of bright lines to generate the twinkle (Figure 7.53).

FIGURE 7.51 Projectile sprite texture.

FIGURE 7.52 Particle sprite fire.

Geometry

The technology supporting particle sprites has been optimized to generate thousands of particle references with little to no cost to computational performance. Sprites are limited by their flatness. Often the referenced particle needs to have depth and be fully renderable. Full, three-dimensional geometry is required in such situations. There are three referenceable types of three-dimensional geometries available: two-dimensional geometry, three-dimensional meshes, and volumes.

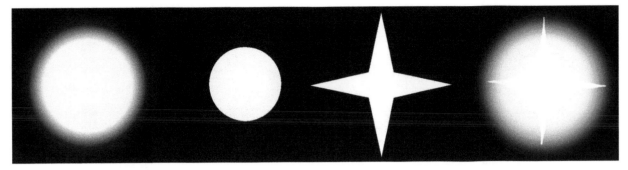

FIGURE 7.53 Fairy dust composite.

FIGURE 7.54 Particle-based fire.

Two-Dimensional Geometry

Simple geometric primitives such as lines, triangles, rectangles, and n-gons are effective particle reference objects. These objects are flat like sprites, but unlike sprites, these objects are unoptimized and fully configurable. As flat three-dimensional geometry, they are not limited to facing the camera and may have any orientation. These objects are effective for generating mattes in post-production shaders, such as displacement shaders. They are also useful for generating particle-based liquids and volumes such as fire and vapors (Figure 7.54).

Three-Dimensional Meshes

When more coherent object depth is required from a particle instance, three-dimensional mesh objects do the trick. The effects artist must configure the flatness of the instanced particle as either static or animated. Animations are generated in the vertex shader. Mesh geometry makes good particle references from large projectiles to raining frogs (Figure 7.55).

Volumes

Three-dimensional volumes may also be instanced as particles. They are material dependent and often require techniques such as volume textures or ray marching to render. This material dependency makes them computationally expensive. They should be employed with caution. Even certain small effects, such as cold breath, can damage real-time performance when the visual focus is upon characters' faces. While expensive,

FIGURE 7.55 3D particle projectiles.

FIGURE 7.56 Particle instanced fog.

volume-instanced particles are one of the only strategies for generating dynamic, interactive fogs, smokes, and vapors (Figure 7.56).

Lights

Just as particles can instance three-dimensional meshes, they also can instance lights. Depending on the engine implementation, lights are implemented as instanced objects, renderable attributes, or both. Point lights and spotlights make excellent particle instances. Lights independent of position, such as directional lights, cannot be used. Unless employed with great control, instanced lights can be extraordinarily computationally expensive. The best way to mitigate this expense is to prevent the lights from generating shadows. Not requiring shadow map generation makes instanced lights computationally achievable. Even when not generating shadows, it is a safe

FIGURE 7.57 Interactive particle lights and external light.

practice to keep the number of lighted particles to a minimum. Unless the visual effect is dependent on the individual interactivity of each particle light, such as a fountain of multi-colored sparks, it is best practice to provide an external, non-particle-based light to generate the interactivity for the entire particle system. Using this technique will minimize the computational expense and the audience will be challenged to realize the particles are not generating the interactive lights in the scene (Figure 7.57).

Materials

All particle instances require materials. The computational expense of a particle system is directly related to the performance of the particles' materials. The computational performance of a particle system can be mitigated by reducing the number of particles in the system or by using simpler materials. Please consult with Chapter 5 of this text for information on how to configure materials to satisfy the visual needs of a particle system.

Replication

Regretfully, there is no cross-package particle system compatibility. Just as no two rendering engines can reproduce the exact same output based on the same input, no two-particle engines can generate the same particle-based output. No two-particle engines are compatible with each other. Each engine provides its own interpretation of the same input.

Every particle system engine is its own unique computer program. Each handles input and memory differently. Each engine may employ custom math and physics libraries. Different implementations may produce similar results but no two systems can numerically repeat the output of each other. Even when two engines share the same math and physics libraries, they are unable to duplicate each other's output because they are two different rendering engines. Certain particle engines are performed off-line while others operate in real time. Real-time optimization creates dramatic appearance and performance differences.

From the context of a large development team, the prospect of all contributors (from concept to prototype to implementation), using the same version of the engine is impractical. There are three ways of minimizing development team differences: external off-line generation, same plug-in utilization, and doing nothing.

External, off-line generation techniques, such as vertex cache simulation, were introduced in Chapter 6. Generating source content from an external engine provides a common simulation platform from which all implementations can work from. When generated from an external source, all movement data imported into each engine is the same. The only differences are the visual idiosyncrasies associated with each rendering engine.

When distributing the same motion input is inappropriate, different particle engines can use duplicate math and physics libraries as well as particle system plug-ins. The advantage of this strategy is that no external, intermediate data is required and there is no limitation of media capacity. Regretfully, just as external data will generate similar motion, the rendered output will be different with each rendering engine.

The third and the most practical strategy is to do nothing about the visual discrepancy. Unless the particle system integrity is crucial to the visual output, as with certain types of simulation and training applications, there are very few audiences who can appreciate the differences. What the audiences do not see they will never miss. From the larger visual effects perspective, slight motion differences in particle motion are acceptable. Rendering is still a major challenge. At the time of writing this book, there is no rendering standard. While technologies such as USD, Vulcan, and MDL attempt to consolidate rendering, there is no common rendering platform. Motivating contributing parties to agree on common platforms is challenging and common platform maintenance is a daunting task.

RENDER ATTRIBUTES

All particles must be instanced by renderable sprites, geometry, or lights, each with its own requirements. Particle rendering attributes configure the rendering engine to address those needs. There are four different particle rendering attributes: sprite, mesh, ribbon, and light. Each attribute has its own benefits and drawbacks. Certain particles may contain multiple attributes. Not all render attributes are compatible with all instance objects. The compatibility of instance types and render attributes are mapped as shown in Table 7.1.

Sprite

Sprites are the default, understood render attributes for most particle engines. Sprites are two-dimensional bitmap streams referenced to a particle's on-screen position. The bitmap is written directly to the frame buffer or the render target. A bitmap is simply a two-dimensional array of color data. The bitmap stream may come from anywhere. The particles' material configures the contents of the streams. Sprite materials may only manipulate the pixel/fragment shader. Utilizing color channels and transparencies, the materials may be solid, come from two-dimensional texture images, or be created procedurally from sequences of material functions. By default, the materials are "un-lit" which means they do not go through the full rendering pipeline. Their blend modes are "additive" and brighten their underlying pixels. The un-lit, additive properties, combined with post-process blurring, provide particle materials with emissive-like quality and appear as if illuminated from internal light sources. All of these attributes, of course, are re-configurable within the material (Figure 7.58).

The bitmap streams are transformable and may be offset, rotated, or scaled relative to the particles they are referenced to. They may be stretched in the direction of the particles' velocities to produce a motion blur-like

TABLE 7.1 Particle Instance - Attribute Compatibility

	Sprite Attribute	Mesh Attribute	Ribbon Attribute	Light Attribute
Sprite	√			√
Geometry		√	√	√
Light	(Engine Dependent)			√

FIGURE 7.58 Default particle material.

effect or their orientations may be adjusted in any manner to meet the contextual demand of the particle system. Since bitmap streams are not rendered, their computational expense is limited only by the complexity of their materials. When materials are simple, systems consisting of thousands of particles are easily generated in real time with very little computational expense.

GPU Sprites

When thousands of particles are inadequate and denser, more detailed particle coverage is required, the particles may be rendered as GPU sprites. GPU sprites are spawned on the CPU but are processed and displayed directly from the GPU. The transference of sprite generation from the CPU to GPU enables a quantitatively huge increase in the number of particles (Figure 7.59).

FIGURE 7.59 Particle fountain: CPU vs. GPU.

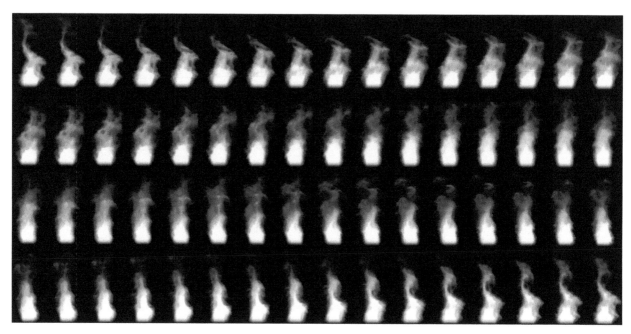

FIGURE 7.60 Animated particle sprite sheet.

The increase of particles comes at a cost. Certain attributes such as light emission, material parameter control, and other particle interactions are unavailable when processed on the GPU. However, the sheer numbers of increased particles make up for incurred loss of control. The fundamental particle attributes of location, velocity, acceleration, drag, lifetime, color, size, rotation, and sub-image index are supported.

Animated Sprites

One of the oldest applications still very popular with nostalgic games and stylized, real-time visual effects is animated sprites. Animated sprites are texture mosaic sequences of pre-generated images, called particle sprite sheets. Sub-image index is the essential attribute for displaying sprite sheets. For a detailed explanation of texture mosaic sequences, please consult Chapter 5 (Figure 7.60).

The sources for these image sequences can come from live-action footage, computer-generated renderings, or hand-drawn animations. Generating stylized, hand-drawn animation sequences are as old as animation itself and are still very popular for visual effects. Books such as *Essential Effects: Water, Fire, Wind and More* by Mauro Maressa and *Elemental Magic, The Art of Special Effects Animation* by Joseph Gilland, are excellent resources for generating hand-drawn content.

Compatible with CPU and GPU sprites, the use of animated texture mosaics is very popular for stylized explosions, impacts, projectiles, streams, and good old-fashioned magic (Figure 7.61).

Ribbon

A ribbon render is a variation of a sprite render. Particles typically have position but ribbon particles have two positions: a start and an end. When generated, the bitmap stream is stretched between the two points which produces a line. The particle's width attributes manipulate the apparent width. Depending on the engine implementation, the start and endpoint attributes may have tangent vector attributes which generate bend in the line (Figure 7.62).

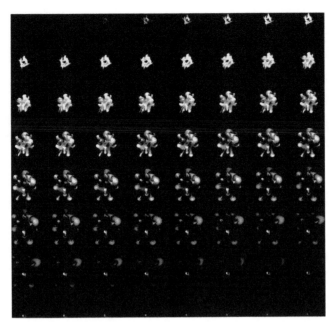

FIGURE 7.61 Stylized animated sprite visual effects.

FIGURE 7.62 Tangent vectors manipulating a ribbon particle.

Ribbon sprites are effective for generating energy beams and electrical discharges. The start and end points provide generation and termination positions for the lines. Jitter and other noise attributes generate irregularities (Figure 7.63).

When the motion of the particle is linear, ribbon sprites are useful for generating stylistic trails which may simulate motion blur or energy or exhaust discharges. The width attributes shape the lines to taper or widen at the ends. Opacity generates a fading effect. Tangent and jitter attributes create noise and irregularities (Figure 7.64).

FIGURE 7.63 Energy beam and electrical discharge particles.

FIGURE 7.64 Ribbon exhaust discharge.

Mesh

Three-dimensional mesh particle references have only been available since the development of higher-performance rendering hardware. Particles now drive the position, orientation, and scale of three-dimensional meshes instead of streamed bitmaps addressed to the display buffer. All meshes are rendered through the full rendering pipeline, even when the mesh is two-dimensional (squares, triangles, n-gons, etc.). There are two types of instanced mesh: Static Meshes and Skeletal Meshes.

Static Mesh

Static meshes are the combination of three-dimensional objects and object materials. Even when a mesh is flat, its point coordinates are still treated as three-dimensional, floating point vectors. The materials provide the artist

FIGURE 7.65 3D particle mesh instance.

full exposure to the rendering pipeline. Meshes are considered static when they do not physically deform or are not articulated. They may be transformed via the vertex shader but the core vertex positions never change. When vertex cache techniques are employed to animate meshes, they offset vertices to generate simple walk, flap, or hop clips. Static mesh objects are ideal particle instances for falling objects such as debris, ice, and hail. Scurrying flocks, herds, and swarms are effective when the sizes of the particle instances are small enough for the audience to not realize the objects are not articulated yet still have three-dimensional shapes beyond sprites (Figure 7.65).

When object movement is understood, predictable, or sourced from a pre-animated clip, static meshes are useful for generating trails. When the motion is understood, a mesh object is pre-generated to conform with the object's motion path. When combined with a material panner function, the mesh generates a particle-based trail which follows the movement of the object. For an explanation, please refer to the "Soul Coaster" effect introduced in Chapter 5 (Figure 7.66).

Skeletal Mesh

Skeletal Meshes are a more recent advancement in particle instancing. Skeletal meshes include three-dimensional mesh objects, materials, articulated skeletons and bindings which allow the skeletons to deform the meshes. While animations are always executed in the vertex shaders, the offsets are not originated in the materials but from articulated joints driving the skeletons. Character positions and orientations are still driven by particle behavior but their animations are derived from other external sources such as animation clips or procedural state-machines. Skeletal meshes are ideal for flocks, herds, and crowds where character movements are articulated and potentially dynamic. An example of such a system is a crowd of shoppers milling about a marketplace, who not only walk aimlessly in simple cycles but also stop and react to their environment. Flocks of birds who flap, turn, and swivel based on their surroundings are another example (Figure 7.67).

Light

By default, a sprite renderer provides an emissive property which appears as if the particle is glowing. In reality, the glow is a post-process rendering effect and the particle emits no light and cannot interact with or provide illumination to its surrounding environment. When particles need to interact with their environments, light render attributes are added to the particles. Light attributes manifest themselves as point lights positioned on particles which

FIGURE 7.66 Sword animated trail.

FIGURE 7.67 Skeletal mesh system.

provide illumination to their immediate surroundings. All lighting attributes such as color, intensity, and falloff are exposed to the light renderer (Figure 7.68).

Lights generated from within particle systems are extraordinarily expensive! When optimizing particle systems for poor computational performance, the presence of light attributes is often the primary culprit. Particle-based lights damage computational performance in three ways. When the rendering pipeline employs deferred lighting strategy, particle lights cannot contribute to the computational savings this technique provides. The second way is, by default, particle-generated lights are shadow generating. For every rendered frame, lightmaps must now be generated from every particle's perspective, which is computational demanding. The last way is an end-effect of the prior two factors. For every frame, every particle's illumination contribution must be evaluated for every other object in the scene. When the scene is complex, the number of lighting calculations skyrockets and the

FIGURE 7.68 Particle-driven lights.

FIGURE 7.69 Central light object in a particle system.

game performance plummets. An alternative to adding particle lights is to provide an external light, in the general center of the particle system. Since the particles are usually sprites, they are unaffected by external light. Consequently, the external light appears as if the particles are illuminating the scene. Audiences rarely notice the disconnect between individual particle movement and the illumination of the point light (Figure 7.69).

While this solution is less computationally demanding than the alternative, when producing unacceptable results, particle-based lights must be employed. When implemented responsibly, the end effect integrates the particle system with its environment effectively.

CONCLUSION

Particles are the apex of real-time visual effects as they are a combination of all other effects types: in-camera, in-material, and simulation effects. Particles are simply chunks of memory representing abstract points in space. Within that memory are attributes storing any type of data. The three minimal particle attributes are position, birth-date, and identification index. All remaining attributes are configured by the visual effects artists to maintain data necessary to fulfill the particle's contextual responsibility. Particles are animated within simple RBDs simulation systems, executing Newtonian physics on a frame-by-frame basis. Particle attributes configure the behavior of the simulation and are updated during execution. Combined with their unlimited attributes and their integration within simulations, the scope of particle possibility is infinite.

The range of particle applications is vast. "With great power comes great responsibility." Artists need to be responsible for understanding particle capabilities as well as limitations. Imagination and boundary awareness empower artists to use particles as potent visual effects problem solves. They can be used for representing any natural phenomenon such as atmospheric precipitation, fire, smoke, and fog. Within a narrative context, they are useful for informing the audience of prior locations and telescoping future directions. They can be used for representing flocks, crowds, herds, and swarms. They are also useful for representing simple simulations such as fountains, blowing sands, and even instancing randomly placed objects.

Particles are the essential components of particle systems. Within the system, they must go through a three-stage process. The first stage is when they are born. Their time of birth is configured by the visual effects artist. After birth, particles live as simulation components. Either within the simulation or at the termination of the program, particle life must terminate. Setting their birthing locations, emitters are essential system components for spawning particles. Forces must also be present in systems to shepherd particles through physical simulations. Without forces, particles do not animate. Tuples of particles, emitters, and forces combine to form layers. There may be many layers within a single particle system.

A particle is not visible until some visible object is instanced to the particle. There are three types of objects which can be instanced into particles: sprites, three-dimensional geometry, and lights. The visual properties of these objects are set by their shader materials. Practically all in-material effects are available to instanced particles. There are four types of renderings that can be applied to particle objects: sprite, ribbon, mesh, and light. A particle may be represented by more than one type of rendering, depending on the context of the simulation.

INTRODUCTION

The universe of visual effects is infinite. There are an unlimited number of techniques and an unlimited number of approaches for each of those techniques. To truly master visual effects takes a lifelong dedication to the study of visual effects as well continuous practice in art and design. This text attempts to classify most visual effects into four categories: in-camera, in-material, simulations, and particle effects. Most visual effects fall within these categories but there are some effects that do not quite fit within these labels. This chapter identifies those effects and gives them classifications of their own.

This is an unprecedented time to be part of the computer graphic imagery industry. It is evolving at a faster rate than can be kept up with and is fracturing into unlimited directions. This chapter provides a subjective compass toward the areas of most significant change and prescribes how to handle these changes.

The study of visual effects can be an overwhelming task. This chapter concludes with a few suggestions on how to deal with the copious outline of information presented in this book and the infinite journey required to fill in the information between the slots.

EXCEPTIONS

The primary objective of this book is to classify all visual effects into the four primary categories: in-camera, in-material, simulations, and particle effects. A prerequisite of this categorization is to first define what constitutes a visual effect. From the broadest production perspective, a visual effect is anything added to visual media that impacts the emotion, mood, and tone of the experience. From the more limited real-time perspective, a visual effect is any component of the art production pipeline that is not an articulately animated environment, character, or prop.

There are a few types of phenomena that do not fall within the four primary visual effects categories or within the exact realms of animation or environmental, character or prop modeling. There are three such challenging types that could be labeled under multiple categories: procedural modeling, procedural animation, and motion capture.

Procedural Modeling

Suppose the production team is tasked with generating a large medieval kingdom composed of hundreds of small buildings. Depending on the context and resources of the team, multiple departments can be approached to accomplish this task. This task could be allocated to the art department who creates a detailed painting which provides a backdrop for an infinite texture behind areas of attention. The modeling department may allocate a small army of modelers who, under the guidance of strong art direction, construct each of the buildings and attempt to assemble them into one cohesive scene. Finally, the visual effects department may be assigned this responsibility because of bandwidth issues in the other departments. The visual effects team decides to use procedural modeling to create a kingdom of medieval-looking structures.

Procedural modeling is a strategy to generate unlimited variations of well-defined templates and arrange them into coherent and organic order. In other words, procedural modeling leverages the power of the computer to create what cannot be generated by hand. Examples include large numbers of unique people, cities, forests, countries, continents, and even worlds. The visual quality of each of these components reflects the visual standard

DOI: 10.1201/9781003009795-9

expressed by the art direction. However, procedural modeling cannot be expected to generate hero, special or outrageously unique variations in the final output. These special assets must be addressed as singular, unique assets called "one-offs."

Although the visual effects department is slated for the task of modeling the kingdom, are they creating a very sophisticated model or are they creating a visual effect? This is a question many production companies deal with when scheduling extraordinarily complex models. This could be considered a task for traditional modelers, but the procedural tools and techniques are often unusual and may require more math than what is traditionally expected. The responsibility could be passed to technical artists who may not have the design experience required to generate convincing results. Some organizations punt when presented with such a situation and create a new department called "Technical Modeling." This department is usually just one or two individuals who happen to have the technical knowhow and design sensibility to accomplish the request. These departments default to other responsibilities when not generating procedural models.

Procedural Animation

All visual effects have components of animation or change. The animation comes from functional offsets in the lighting or rendering pipeline, or from simulation. Keyframe animators are responsible for articulated keyframe animation in characters, props, and environments. The differentiation between the two disciplines is fuzzy when the two overlap.

How are character based, animated effects classified? Who is responsible for character effects such as hair bounce, clothing movements, body fat and muscle jiggle, and other bouncing or swinging peripherals? This overlap of animation and visual effects extends further into crowds, armies, and flocks. The problem is more confusing when keyframe animated characters are expected to adapt interactively with terrain or react, directly or indirectly, to participant activity. Almost all real-time character animation is controlled by state-machines; animation flow-maps that blend animation clips depending on character states. Who is responsible for state-machine creation and maintenance? What if a visual effect calls for a dancing pixy composed entirely of tongues of fire? This is not just a visual effect. It requires attention from the modeling, rigging, animation, pipeline, and visual effects departments. Surely, the modelers, animators, riggers, and pipeline artists do not have the experience to pull off something like this. The responsibility then falls upon the visual effects team. This book does not cover modeling, animating, rigging, or pipeline.

To alleviate the pressure of procedural animation from visual effects departments, many companies create "Technical Animation" departments. Technical animation departments are composed of multidisciplinary artists who not only understand visual effects but also the basics of character modeling, rigging, and the animation pipeline. Procedural animation generates some of the most visually spectacular visual effects. They do, however, require an understanding of visual effects and almost all other disciplines.

Motion Capture

There are multiple perspectives on how to classify motion capture. Motion Capture is the process of capturing live, motion performances, and translating the movements into streams of animation data. When animation is not key-framed and is not sourced directly from an animator, is the motion considered a visual effect? There are some that believe that because the data does not originate from pure artistic expression, it is artificial and is therefore lumped into the procedural animation category. As procedural animation, the motion capture classification falls into visual effects limbo described in the previous section. The data requires the creation of specialized skeletons to support the motion capture models. There are data management issues requiring the transformation of motion capture information to usable animation data. The data needs to be conditioned again as it is never 100% perfect. Feet float on surfaces. Arms and legs pop due to aliasing. Characters are not oriented properly. Retargeting the data, making it work for more than one character, and conforming to character changes must be contended with.

Modern tools and artist friendly interfaces address many of these issues and empower traditional keyframe animators to work with motion capture data without additional technical assistance. With modern tools, animators easily transport the data, recondition it to satisfy the thematic needs of the experience and retarget the data to alternate characters. Most animators create keyframes sparingly when driving organic performances. Although generated from technical sources, motion capture data is still keyframe data: one data keyframe for every character animation channel for every frame. Instead of placing key frames every few frames for a few channels, motion capture data creates keyframes for every channel 30–60 times per second. The extra data is challenging to work with. Modern interfaces have made great strides improving the data manageability so any animator can condition motion captured performances to compelling animated sequences.

The question of motion capture being a visual effect is ultimately the decision of each production company. Some are confident in allowing the animators to manage the data and others delegate the responsibility to visual effects, technical, or pipeline artists.

FUTURE VFX

This is an extraordinary time to be part of the computer graphics industry. Despite machine architecture reaching the end of Moore's law, machines and technology have continued to make huge leaps in processing power. Rendering engines are now doing in real time what used to require weeks of processing time just a few decades before. Advancements in interfaces empower artists, with little to no technical know-how, with the ability to create wild, unimaginable visual effects that only the most technically sophisticated artists invented just a few years back. Rendering engines are now performing complicated simulations in real time, controlled by simple and easy to use interfaces. Real-time visual effects are becoming easier to generate, easier to manipulate, and require less technological understanding. As no visual effects are ever expected to be repeated, the cutting edge always requires sophisticated technological understanding. The three largest areas of technological advancement impacting visual effects will be rendering, artificial intelligence (AI), and virtual and augmented reality.

Rendering

Over the last 10 years, real-time time rendering has gone through radical changes. From the standardization of PBR to the arrival of real-time ray tracing, rendering has dramatically evolved and is far from complete.

Real-time ray tracing is no longer science fiction or wishful thinking. It is reality. Accurate shadows, correct reflections and refractions, and realistic global illumination are now standard real-time rendering features. Path tracing, the highly exhaustive, ground-proof generating, big brother of ray tracing, is not yet real time but will be in the near future. The utilization of ray tracing will continue to grow until it inevitably replaces rasterization as the default rendering strategy.

Ray marching, the less intelligent but remarkably fast cousin to ray tracing, is already present and is used for rendering interactive volumetrics such as liquids, vapors, and clouds. Its usage is still awkward but tools refining its interface are only months away.

Interactive volumetrics were once unachievable to real-time applications. However, with the advancements of ray marching, they have started to become common standard scene components. Combined with the extra strength of ray tracing, the elusive goal of rendering any volumetric object will soon become reality.

The evolution of volumetric rendering will continue to expand until all visible objects will be represented as volumes. This will have a dramatic impact on the entire computer graphics pipeline. Variations of specific objects are currently created to satisfy the specific needs of immediate applications. For example, the model used to represent a car 100m away is far simpler than the model used when the camera is near the surface, exposing its fine detail. When represented as a volume, only one model of the car is necessary for any circumstance as the rendering engine decides how much detail is needed based on the context of the scene. Object levels of detail (LODs) will become obsolete. The materials used to represent these new volumes will need to change. The role of texture maps will be radically altered as texture coordinates will no longer be applicable for mapping object surfaces. The removal of texture coordinates is liberating for most modelers yet threatening for visual effects artists. Animating texture coordinates is one of the most important and readily used strategies used in the visual effects toolkit. The removal of texture coordinates means the removal of visual effects' most important tools. Visual effects artists are creative and resourceful. As the evolution of rendering removes tools from artists, their creativity and ingenuity will invent newer strategies which will not only make up for the loss but will improve the entire pipeline.

Artificial Intelligence

AI technology will impact different aspects of the CGI community at different rates. Already an essential component of the rendering pipeline, it will strike hardest and most rapidly in the rigging and animation disciplines. AI and deep learning are being used to visually identify and classify organic phenomena such as voices, faces, and even biological genealogies. It is also being used to analyze biometric information for performance analysis and behavioral conditioning. AI is being taught how to model realistic human motion and generate believable, organic procedural motion. It is only a matter of time when modern animators and riggers will no longer manually manipulate animation data but guide and instruct AI-driven algorithms to generate custom yet organic performances.

The time frame for AI impacting visual effects may take longer. Visual effects are intended to complement the story and game-play of real-time experiences, impacting the emotion, mood, and tone of those experiences. How soon will it take AI to learn subtle nuances and timing of human emotion? This may be more challenging to understand than organic motion analysis. Visual effect production will be impacted when AI grasps on to these concepts. Visual effects technology will become radically less challenging and more art directable than currently available. Artists will describe intended effects and then refine the AI systems to achieve the desired emotional impact. AI visual effects systems will have access to infinite sources and techniques. The job of future visual effects artists will be to teach the AI systems which effects look good and which generate appropriate emotion. Artists will spend much of their time verifying the results of AI systems. While technical creation of visual effects will be handed to AI processes, chore technological understanding will still be required to drive advancement and innovation.

Virtual and Augmented Reality

Visual effects are no longer exclusive tools for the film and video game industries. They can be found in any real-time applications including architectural, automotive and transportation, educational, medical, communication, or location-based operations. These applications are evolving toward a multi-media heading called immersive transmedia experiences. Immersive transmedia experiences are rapidly impacting every aspect of ordinary life. They are defining what it means to be human. Today, immersive experiences are primarily executed through television, computer, mobile, and billboard display devices. Tomorrow, virtual and augmented reality equipment will dominate immersive transmedia experiences.

Storytelling is a crucial aspect of the human condition. Stories are how we communicate, learn, and entertain each other. Immersive transmedia experiences are evolving toward experiential storytelling. Philosophical opinions aside, the world that is being shaped by experiential storytelling is a market-driven economy. The market is composed primarily of choices and decisions based on emotion. Of course, facts and data have a strong impact on the decision-making process. However, in a market-driven economy, emotions tend to rule over logic. Visual effects are the most important factor in real-time experiences for impacting emotion, mood, and tone. Visual effects artists will have an incredible impact on the future of the human experience.

Visual effects play an essential role in establishing believable, alternative realities. Beyond marketing, they are crucial for making new worlds appear real, impacting all real-time experiences. Visual effects are essential components for training and education and their contributions will continue to expand. Storytelling-based communications are experiencing similar impact from visual effects. The effectiveness of journalism, medicine and the legal process is related to experiential storytelling and visual effects will continue being essential storytelling tools. At the time of writing this book, the world finds itself experiencing a shut-in cycle of interpersonal isolation. Virtual and augmented reality devices will help improve quality of life and bolster interpersonal communication. Visual effects will continue complementing and enhancing alternative reality devices.

LIFELONG PURSUIT

This book strives to introduce the primary techniques used for creating real-time visual effects. It covers the primary strategies associated with lighting and in-camera effects, in-material effects, simulations, and particle effects. Separate books could be written covering approaches and design techniques for each of these categories. Regretfully, the field cannot be mastered in a single semester nor taught by a single instructor or coach. Individuals can provide excellent feedback and constructive critique yet not provide the adequate instruction to sufficiently cover each topic. There are simply too many different real-time engines, too many different approaches, and too many styles to consider when studying in the short term. A student embarking on the study of visual effects may ponder, "If there is too much to learn, then how can I learn enough to sustain a rewarding career?" The approach to this answer is to not worry about understanding all of it. Being a functioning practitioner requires a lifelong pursuit of the study of visual effects.

Visual effects are the culmination of everything the artist has ever learned. Anything can provide motivation for either the look or the approach to a visual effect. When the artist has an intimate method for baking chocolate chip cookies, that strategy will find its way into his or her visual effects. Similarly, when the artist comes from a background in sales, marketing, or storytelling, the visual effects will subconsciously reach out and pull at the audience's heart strings. It is amazing to observe the remarkable transformation a visual effects artists' style undergoes upon simply learning the fundamental behavior of the sine wave function. Technology is constantly evolving and is difficult to stay abreast with. So too is the evolution of visual effects. Instead of trying to understand all visual effects, try taking on a more humane approach.

Every artist has his or her own style. Every artist, consciously or not, leaves their fingerprint on every effect. Artists and studios become recognizable through their work. Since no two life experiences are the same, the best learning strategy is to slowly develop individual style. Learn one effect. Understand and own it. When the original effect comes from another artist or a tutorial, embrace it. Dive into it. Reverse engineer it and understand the visual impact of every parameter change. Change the order of operations. Make that effect conform to the desired style. Make the original source unrecognizable. After completion of the first effect, celebrate and learn a second effect with the same enthusiasm offered the first. When implementing the second effect, integrate components of the first effect and anything else providing inspiration. Continue learning effects with the same strategy until the style fingerprint becomes recognizable. Patterns become evident. The time required to digest any visual effect plummets. Never stop analyzing effects, breaking them down and voraciously learning new techniques and styles. A career in visual effects is a lifelong pursuit to the study of visual effects and begins with just one effect. Good Luck!

Index

9 780367 444488